PLATO'S MORAL THEORY

Plato's Moral Theory

The Early and Middle Dialogues

TERENCE IRWIN
Cornell University

CLARENDON PRESS · OXFORD
1977

Oxford University Press, Walton Street, Oxford OX2 6DP

OXFORD LONDON GLASGOW NEW YORK
TORONTO MELBOURNE WELLINGTON CAPE TOWN
IBADAN NAIROBI DAR ES SALAAM LUSAKA ADDIS ABABA
KUALA LUMPUR SINGAPORE JAKARTA HONG KONG TOKYO
DELHI BOMBAY CALCUTTA MADRAS KARACHI

British Library Cataloguing in Publication Data
Irwin, Terence
   Plato's moral theory: the early and middle dialogues.
   Bibl. – Index.
   ISBN 0–19–824567–X
   1. Title
   170′.92′4   B398.E8
   Plato – Ethics

*Text set in 11/12pt Photon Times Roman, printed by photolithography, and bound in Great
Britain at The Pitman Press, Bath*

to

H.E.I.,   M.M.K.I.,   G.J.I.

PREFACE

This book is intended for readers who want to understand and evaluate Plato's views on ethical questions. I have assumed that they will be willing to read the Platonic dialogues closely to test my claims; but I have tried not to assume any previous knowledge of Plato, or of the questions discussed, or of the modern literature on them. Readers should be able to understand the main argument in the text without reference to the notes at the end, though, if they ignore the notes, they will miss qualifications which may complicate the position taken in the text. All Greek is transliterated, and all the Greek appearing in the main text is also translated.

Surprisingly, the large number of modern books in English on Plato includes none devoted to a systematic critical discussion of his moral theory. This does not mean that the subject has been neglected in the modern literature. Many books and papers on Plato have discussed ethical questions, and one aim of this book is to use this recent work to develop a continuous account. Some of my debts to other writers are indicated in the notes; but I have particularly benefited from the work of Crombie, Grote, Joseph, Moreau, Murphy, and Vlastos. The result is not the systematic discussion of Plato's ethics that would be desirable, but, at best, a step towards it. I have confined myself to the early and middle dialogues; and some relevant questions (e.g. Plato's views on pleasure or on the freedom of the will) are treated only briefly, or not at all. But within these limits I have tried to expound and examine what seems most interesting in Plato's central ethical doctrines; to show what questions they try to answer; to see why different answers appear in different dialogues; and to suggest some strengths and weaknesses in these answers.

Someone who tries to write a book on Plato's moral theory will soon see why such books are not so common. We cannot do justice to his ethical views without some minimal discussion of his metaphysics, epistemology, and moral psychology. And while it is hard to say something entirely original and yet plausible on these issues, it is much harder to say something uncontroversial. And so (for reasons explained in Chapter I) I have discussed these issues at some length.

My discussion, here as elsewhere, is no summary of accepted results of investigation, since I doubt if there are any of great interest; but it does not pretend to be a full-length treatment of the very complex issues which arise around the Theory of Forms.

In general, I hope I have not tried to play safe. There are fewer marks of doubt or hesitation than a more judicious writer might have included; and it would be foolish to pretend that there is no textual evidence which might seem to count against my interpretation at various points, or that no other interpretation is compatible with the evidence, or that the evidence is always clear enough to allow a final decision between competing lines of interpretation. Naturally, I hope that my account fits the evidence better than others and offers a more philosophically plausible account of Plato's views, and that anyone who takes the trouble to refute it carefully will find he has made progress in the understanding of Plato by examining what I say about him.

To prevent the book from being intolerably long and unreadable, I have rarely quoted passages from Plato in full or discussed them in detail, though I have tried to cite them fairly fully and frequently. Detailed questions of interpretation and discussion of other people's views are confined to the notes at the end. These notes are much shorter and more superficial that I would have liked if the over-all length of the book had been unimportant; but I hope they will show where doubts can fairly be raised about my account, how I try to defend it, and where opposing views can be found. The references to secondary works on Plato, and to other philosophical and classical works are selective, partly on principle, and partly, no doubt, because of my ignorance. Similarly, the bibliography (which includes a few works not mentioned in the notes) may seem long to a non-specialist; but anyone who knows a little of the literature will see that it is far from being even a fair and representative selection—less recent and non-English works are especially under-represented. But I hope to have mentioned enough to guide the reader to more detailed, and often conflicting, treatments of questions raised here.

Since much of the book concerns the treatment of central Socratic and Platonic doctrines and theses, I have often referred to them by abbreviations. Some readers have complained, with good reason, that these frequent abbreviations are inelegant and hard to remember. I could not think of any alternative without worse drawbacks; and an index of frequently used abbreviations will be found at the beginning of the book.

Chapters III—VII are descended from a doctoral dissertation, 'Theories of Virtue and Knowledge in Plato's Early and Middle Dialogues', accepted by the faculty of Princeton University in January 1973. But the revisions undertaken in 1974–5 have gone beyond simple rewriting; and I hope the delay has been worth while. A sketch of some of the material for Chapter VI, based on the dissertation, appeared in 'Recollection and Plato's Moral Theory', published in the *Review of Metaphysics*, June 1974.

In writing the dissertation and in further work on this book I have benefited from other people's advice and criticism. I have probably forgotten the source of some ideas suggested by others, and I hope these general acknowledgements will serve instead of acknowledgements on particular points. Most of all I am indebted to Gregory Vlastos, who first suggested this subject for a dissertation, guided and supervised the dissertation, and has kindly read and criticized some later material (especially in Chapter VIII). My debt to his published and unpublished writings on Plato will be obvious from my notes and bibliography. Anyone who reads his work or mine will see that he would firmly reject many of my claims; but I have disagreed with him less often than I have taken over his results and been stimulated by his questions. I have benefited even more from his teaching, his advice, his forthright and troublesome criticism, and from his characteristic generosity and helpfulness in many other ways. His qualities as a writer, teacher, and adviser set an exacting standard for anyone who knows them. Thomas Nagel read my dissertation and discussed several questions; he also criticized part of Chapter VIII at a colloquium at Princeton in December 1974. I have been stimulated and disturbed by his criticisms and his challenging views on many questions in moral philosophy. All or some parts of the dissertation in progress were read or discussed by M. F. Andic, A. J. Baxter, D. J. Furley, G. B. Kerferd, G. E. L. Owen, T. M. Penner, E. F. X. Tivnan, and P. Woodruff; I am grateful for their help. More recently M. F. Burnyeat and J. M. Cooper have kindly read later material and raised some awkward questions. J. L. Ackrill's interest and encouragement were extremely helpful in turning an unpublished manuscript into a book. Discussion of many of these questions in lectures, seminars, and tutorials with undergraduate and graduate students at Harvard has often prompted me to state some claims more clearly and abandon or modify others. Over the past few years I have often benefited from discussion of Plato with Gail Fine, from her acute criticism and encouragement, and from her own work, especially on Plato's metaphysics and epistemology, which has influenced and helped me in Chapters VI–VII. An untidy typescript was most efficiently prepared for publication by Caroline Bunton, Nanette de Maine, and Betty Lehman.

For the free time to think about these questions and write this book I am indebted to Princeton University for a graduate fellowship; to Harvard University for a Loeb Fellowship in 1971–2, for the moderate teaching load it imposes on its faculty, and for paid leave in spring 1974; and especially to the generosity of the Harvard Department of Philosophy for a Santayana Fellowship in spring 1975. For undertaking to publish this book, and for help and encouragement in preparing the final version, I am grateful to the delegates and editorial staff of the Oxford University Press.

T. H. IRWIN

Cornell University,
Ithaca, New York,
January 1976

CONTENTS

ABBREVIATIONS

I. IN THE TEXT

These are some of the more frequently used abbreviations, with the places where they are explained.

A-, B-, C-predicates:	Predicates which (A) can be explained without dispute (e.g. 'bee', 'wood'); (B) cause dispute, but with a recognized decision-procedure; (C) cause dispute with no recognized decision-procedure. VI.2.2, 7.3.
A-change:	Aspect-change; x changes from being F in one aspect to being not-F in another (e.g. from being large in relation to y to being small in relation to z). VI.8.1.
c1–c4:	The four stages of the Cave-image in the *Republic*. VII.13.1.
CA:	Craft-analogy; the analogy between virtue and craft-knowledge. III.9.1–5.
c-justice:	Common justice; the common conception of justice, referring to recognized just actions. V.4.2, VII.10.1.
D:	The deontological principle about justification. VIII.1.3.
DR:	The dialectical requirement on a definition; its constituents should be already known to the interlocutor. VI.3.1.
ED:	Elimination of disputed terms in a definition of a virtue or other moral property. III.9.5.
H:	The hedonist principle making pleasure the only measure of value. IV.2.7.
HP:	The principle of hedonistic prudence. IV.2.3.
IE:	Independent existence of Forms, independent of the existence of sensible particulars exemplifying them. VI. 9.1.
KG:	The Socratic account of each virtue as knowledge of the good. III.14.4.
KNV:	Knowledge is necessary for virtue. III.15.2.
KSV:	Knowledge is sufficient for virtue. III.11.3.
L1–L4:	The stages of the Line-image in the Republic. VII.13.1.
LC:	The *Lysis*-principle about choice; nothing chosen for the sake of something else is chosen for its own sake. III.13.4.
LG:	The *Lysis*-principle about goods; nothing contributing to another good is a good in itself. III.13.4.
M:	The single measure of value. IV.2.7.

NED: Non-elimination of disputed terms in a definition of a virtue or other moral property. III.9.5.

NR: Non-reducibility of forms to sensible properties. VI.9.1.

NTV: The non-technical conception of virtue. III.13.3.

P: The principle of prudence; choice is always guided by belief about comparative value. IV.2.7.

p-justice: Psychic justice; the conception of justice as order in the soul, corresponding to justice in the state. VII.9.3.

RV: Reciprocal implication of the virtues; each virtue requires all the others. III.14.1.

s1–s2, S1–S2:   The stages of the Sun-image in the *Republic*. VII.13.1.

S-change: Self-change; x changes in itself, from what it is at an earlier time (e.g. hot) to what it is at a later time (e.g. cold). VI.8.1.

s-justice: Socrates' conception of justice. V.4.2.

T: The teleological principle about justification. VIII.1.3.

TV: The technical conception of virtue. III.13.3.

UA: The Unity Assumption; one form for one predicate. III.2.1, 7.5.

UV: The unity of the virtues. III.14.1.

II. IN THE NOTES AND BIBLIOGRAPHY

Each work referred to in the notes is cited by the reference number assigned to it in the bibliography and by page. Articles and essays published in more than one place are cited from the source mentioned first.

Plato is cited from Burnet (136). Presocratics and Sophists are cited from DK (137).

AGP	*Archiv für Geschichte der Philosophie*
AJP	*American Journal of Philology*
APQ	*American Philosophical Quarterly*
CP	*Classical Philology*
CQ	*Classical Quarterly*
DK	H. Diels and W. Kranz, eds., *Fragmente der Vorsokratiker*, 6th edn. (1951).
JHI	*Journal of the History of Ideas*
JHP	*Journal of the History of Philosophy*
JHS	*Journal of Hellenic Studies*
JP	*Journal of Philosophy*
LSJ	H. G. Liddell and R. Scott, *Greek–English Lexicon*, 9th edn., revd. H. Stuart Jones (1940)
M	*Mind*
PAS	*Proceedings of the Aristotelian Society*
PASS	*Aristotelian Society, Supplementary Volume*
PBA	*Proceedings of the British Academy*

Phil.	*Philosophy*
Philol.	*Philologus*
Phr.	*Phronesis*
PQ	*Philosophical Quarterly*
PR	*Philosophical Review*
RM	*Review of Metaphysics*
TAPA	*Transactions of the American Philological Association*
YCS	*Yale Classical Studies*

I INTRODUCTION

1. *The questions*

The Platonic dialogues discuss central questions about morality; and both Socrates and Plato defend some controversial and puzzling answers to these questions. Both of them argue that the recognized virtues are not distinct as most people suppose, and that any virtue must be in the agent's self-interest. Socrates adds some claims refuted by Plato, that virtue is craft-knowledge and no more, and that no one can really know what is better and do what is worse. Though Plato rejects these particular paradoxes, his own position is no less paradoxical; he claims that virtue must be a good in itself, that a virtuous man will think it pays to be virtuous even if the results are disastrous and the rewards of vice are splendid; and he demands knowledge of seperated transcendent Forms of Justice, Beauty, and so on from anyone with real virtue.

It is still more surprising that Socrates and Plato profess to prove these claims by appeal to ordinary beliefs. Socrates assures his interlocutors that what they already believe commits them to acceptance of the most counter-intuitive of Socratic doctrines; and the moral doctrine in all the dialogues is meant to rest on crossexamination (*elenchos*) of interlocutors. We can fairly ask whether this method will yield any positive results at all, and whether it will yield the results Socrates and Plato claim for it.

Partly this is a historical question. Since Plato begins from ordinary beliefs of Greek interlocutors, we need to know what these ordinary beliefs are, to see if he treats them fairly, and demands reasonable concessions from someone with these beliefs. But we may also want to know whether Platonic views can be defended from other ordinary beliefs too. They may seem paradoxical to us because they depend on features of Greek moral beliefs which we reject; or they may rely on beliefs which seem equally plausible to us, so that we must decide for or against Plato for ourselves. Then we shall see how defensible Platonic views are, both for their original audience and for us.

These are the questions I shall pursue in the following chapters. First I shall briefly describe the various views of Socrates' contemporaries, to show where he begins. Then I shall discuss the main doctrines in the dialogues, and arguments for and against them which are presented or might be found. Especially I shall ask why Plato rejects some of Socrates' doctrines, and whether he changes the Socratic theory for the better.

2. Procedure

I have not discussed all the dialogues, but only those normally regarded as 'early' and 'middle'. The important discussions in dialogues later than the *Republic* deserve a seperate book to themselves; and though reference to them might cast doubt on some of my claims, I hope that in general the early and middle dialogues can be discussed by themselves without creating too many misleading impressions. I have not tried a systematic account, topic by topic, of Plato's doctrines in these dialogues, though this method would be sensible with, say, Aristotle's ethics. I have preferred to examine Plato dialogue by dialogue, though I have sometimes discussed groups of related dialogues together. This procedure has required some repetition; but I think it is the best way to discuss our initial questions.

This procedure is best if the dialogues do not all present the same theory, and if Plato rejects Socrates' doctrine on important issues for reasons of philosophical interest. To examine the development of his views, I have followed a fairly widely accepted and probable chonology of the dialogues. But I do not want primarily to argue about chronology. If we see conflicts between ethical doctrines in different dialogues, there is some reason to think Plato may have seen them too; and the conflicts may be explained in a plausible picture of Plato's development. But this reason for seeing a development in his views is not decisive by itself; philosophers do not always see conflicts in their views, and even when they do, they do not always decide what should be given up. Whatever we decide about Plato's development, the differences in the ethical doctrines of different dialogues deserve discussion in their own right.

Plato's moral theory is not always to be found in purely ethical dialogues; and if we discuss the dialogues in order, we shall not miss the development of other doctrines clearly connected with the moral theory. The early, Socratic dialogues are normally restricted to ethics; but the *Cratylus* and *Meno* discuss questions in philosophy of language and epistemology raised by Socratic ethical views; the *Phaedo* tries to connect moral doctrines with the epistemology of the Theory of Forms and the metaphysics of psychophysical dualism; the moral theory of the *Republic* is connected with all these doctrines, and equally with political doctrines. Now often Plato over-estimates the coherence of his views, and readers who wrongly take him at face value accept or reject his position as a whole; we must sometimes try to free moral doctrines from their distorting context. But Plato is not always wrong to connect his moral doctrines with his other philosophical views; here we must see whether the connection strengthens or weakens the moral doctrines. That is why I have discussed epistemology, and especially the Theory of Recollection and the Theory of Forms; a fair account of Plato's moral theory cannot ignore them.

The following chapters are meant to be an exposition of Plato's views. I cite textual evidence as fully as I can, to show that I am discussing some views he really holds. But I do not claim that the arguments for or against a particular view, or the consequences I draw from it, are always to be found in Plato, or even that he would accept them if he were asked. This way of 'reading into' the text is hard to avoid in discussing any philosopher, if we want to raise the most interesting questions about him, and to discuss him critically, instead of merely reporting what he says. With Plato it is essential. The character of a Platonic dialogue itself leaves us unsatisfied. The Socratic method, accepted by Plato in the middle dialogues too, relies on an interlocutor's acceptance of various ethical claims; if we think he is over-hasty in accepting them, and want to know how Socrates or Plato might defend them, we must look beyond the explicit argument of the dialogue. Even apart from this general feature of the dialogue form, Plato's attitude to his own views leaves us with extra work to do. Especially in the middle dialogues, he is more concerned to present and recommend his views, and especially the doctrines associated with the Theory of Forms, than to argue for them or explore their consequences in any detail. To decide what is right or wrong about his views, we must face some of the questions he avoids.

What I say about Plato will sometimes sound excessively 'charitable', in so far as I sometimes discount flaws or obscurities in his arguments, or in his defences of his claims; and in general I try to discuss those parts of his doctrine which I think are more plausible in more detail than the parts I think less plausible. Parts of Plato's theory which are extremely important to him receive brief and unsympathetic treatment from me; and the parts I discuss most are not necessarily those which matter most to him. This is the only way to find the best statement of Plato's views; when the superficial flaws are discounted, the fundamental problems are clearer.

I have attempted an exposition of Plato rather than an essay in moral theory. A critical exposition demands the judgement that this or that doctrine is more or less plausible; but I have not defended these judgements in the detail that would fairly be expected in a work on ethics. But the limited criticisms and more frequent defences are not meant as contributions to panegyric, of which Plato has more than his fair share. Instead, I hope that someone who reads the dialogues and is persuaded by my account of them will see what issues Plato raises, and what kinds of arguments are needed to decide for or against him. Much of what he says is false, and much more is confused, vague, inconclusive, and badly defended. But I hope to show that his questions and answers, right and wrong, are not of purely historical interest, and that they raise issues in ethics which justify the effort to decide for or against his views.

3. *The main issues*

I have largely ignored some of Plato's ethical doctrines, those related to his religious and political views, and the practical applications resting on more detailed claims about human nature and society. A full account of Plato's ethics should include these doctrines; I ignore them to concentrate on more general ethical questions, without claiming that my account is complete, or would survive unaltered in a complete account. The main problems are these:

1. What exactly is morality? what does it mean to say that someone is virtuous? How can he become virtuous?
2. How is morality worth while for a rational man? Or what sort of morality is worth while for a rational man?
3. How can we reach knowledge about morality? What is the right method in ethics?

These questions raise steadily more basic and more general issues. The first seeks some understanding of the recognized cases of morality; we want to know more, to teach and practice morality better. Socrates and Plato inquire into the scope of the various virtues and their relation to character and action—whether a virtue is a habit of rule-following, or a state of character irreducible to behavioural tendencies; whether it requires knowledge, or some affective condition, or both. Answers to these philosophical questions will affect our views on whether and how the virtues can be taught, and what a virtuous man should do. Unreflective, habitual right action may cause no problems in familiar situations; but if we expect a really virtuous man to cope with unfamiliar situations, and to defend his views against criticism, some better understanding of morality is needed.

The second question assumes we understand what a virtue is, and asks whether it is worth while. Plato's readers tend to assume about virtue, as we tend to assume about 'morality', that it is worth while; we are even sometimes tempted to say that a man's moral principles are simply those which define what he thinks utlimately worth while. But we also tend to think, as Plato's readers would, that morality has some fairly definite content; and then it becomes a serious question whether something with that content will really be worth while. This is the question Plato raises. It is not clear yet how we will explain 'worth while for a rational man' in the second question; but that does not stop us asking the question, any more than it stopped Socrates' contemporaries.

The third question looks more abstract and philosophical than the first two; but it is hard to avoid if we worry seriously about them. To answer the second question, we need to show that a rational man can be convinced that morality with a specific content is worth while; and to show this, we must show how a claim about morality can be justified at all. Though the third question is certainly epistemological, and leads Plato into those questions about knowledge, belief, and methods of inquiry which he discusses in the middle dialogues, it does not remove him from the moral agent's practical concerns. For Plato does not sharply distinguish the way a philosopher might argue for the truth of his theory *about* morality from the way a moral agent might decide what to do *within* morality. He has no distinction between meta-ethics and normative ethics, or between the method of philosophical argument and the method of moral deliberation.

Plato's view of moral knowledge and justification affects his view of the content of morality. He supposes that knowledge of a virtue requires an account and justification of beliefs about it, especially the belief that it is worth while; a justification must show what the point or purpose of the virtue is for the agent, that it is worth while and beneficial for him; and so the only real virtue, which we can know to be worth while, must benefit the agent. His apparently formal and abstract conditions for knowledge and justification seem to imply controversial conclusions about virtuous action. We must consider further whether Plato's conditions are fair, whether they really imply these conclusions, and what the conclusions really say. These issues are prominent in both early and middle dialogues, though Socrates and Plato offer different answers.

4. *Socrates' views*

It will be a surprise to some readers of the Socratic dialogues to be told that Socrates has a moral theory at all, or offers *answers* to our questions. A standard picture of Socrates presents him as a destructive critic of other people's views, with no positive views of his own; and the picture looks plausible if we see the apparent limitations of the elenchos, his method of cross-examination. Apparently it can expose conflicts in beliefs, but cannot resolve the conflicts one way or the other. This is a mistaken picture of the elenchos. Socrates tests an ordinary moral rule—that, say, courage is endurance—against beliefs about examples—that this or that kind of action would not be brave—and against general assumptions about virtue—that it is always admirable and worth while. He revises the rules to conform to these other beliefs, and especially to the general assumptions. The elenchos adjusts our conceptions of the virtues to our view of what is worth while over all.

These results of the elenchos may support the claim that virtue is a rational discipline worthwhile for a rational man. But the claim needs further defence; we need to know what is really worth while for a rational man. For further defence Socrates appeals to his standard model of rationality, in the procedure of productive crafts. If this craft-analogy (CA) works, a virtue will be a rational discipline. We can justify each step prescribed by a craft, by reference to its contribution to the product, and we can justify the practice of the whole craft because it produces the product we can be presumed to want. If virtue matches these conditions for being a rationally worthwhile practice, it will be justifiable in the right way; and we can claim knowledge about morality, just as a craftsman can claim knowledge of his craft, because each action can be explained and justified by reference to a previously desired and easily identified product.

Socrates' defence of the CA faces two objections.

1. We might suppose that since virtue requires an effective desire to act virtuously, and someone can know what is virtuous without wanting to do it, if he wants something else more, no craft-knowledge is sufficient for virtue. Socrates rejects these alleged cases of knowing what is virtuous and doing what is vicious; he denies the existence of incontinence altogether, and removes the threat to the CA.

2. Socrates must show that the end pursued by virtue, the final good, can be treated as the product of a craft. It must be clearly identifiable apart from disputable beliefs about the virtues; and it must

clearly be what everyone already wants most, so that knowledge of how to achieve it guarantees right action. The Socratic dialogues offer no definite account of the final good. But the *Protagoras* identifies the final good with the agent's pleasure, and makes virtue the craft of producing pleasure.

These doctrines about knowledge and action, and about the final good, support Socrates' views about the possibility of moral knowledge, and the methods of justifying virtues. They also affect his answer to our first question; for he argues that a virtue is simply craft-knowledge. Conventional views were wrong, then, to distinguish different virtues, which are really all the same craft-knowledge, and they were wrong to suppose that virtue requires any non-cognitive component. In its outlines, the over-all theory is apparently clear and coherent, and shows one way of answering the awkward questions about morality. We might reasonably decide that if Socrates' view could be accepted, it would remove some severe problems; we could explain and justify virtues by reference to a clear and intelligible account of the prudent rationality which they display.

5. *Problems in Socrates' views*

Plato's objections to Socrates begin with the *Gorgias*. First he tries to meet them with modifications which leave the major Socratic assumptions untouched. But in the *Meno* and the other middle dialogues he rejects the central Socratic doctrines.

1. These dialogues conspicuously introduce the Theory of Recollection in a discussion of how virtue can be taught, and the associated theory of separate Forms in discussions of Socrates' search for definitions. The relevance of these theories for Plato's moral doctrine is clearest if we see their effect on the CA. The CA requires definitions of the final good and the virtues without disputed terms. But Plato argues that efforts to define the virtues in undisputed terms always succumb to counter-examples, so that moral properties are irreducible to non-moral properties. This claim underlies the separation of Forms from undisputed observable properties in the middle dialogues, and indicates Plato's scepticism about the CA. For if the claim is right, moral properties cannot be objects of craft-knowledge; they can be learnt only through the elenchos, by the method of recollection.

2. The *Gorgias* and *Phaedo* suggests doubts about Socrates' denial of incontinence, which is needed to show that virtue is only craft-knowledge. These doubts are supported by anti-Socratic arguments in

Republic IV, and Plato loses this support for the CA.

3. If the CA is right, the virtuous man does not reject the non-virtuous man's choice of the ultimate end, but only his choice of instrumental means to it; the components of the final good are not chosen by rational deliberation, but are fixed for everyone. When Plato denies that the virtuous and the non-virtuous man agree on an account in undisputed terms of the good, he has to show how the virtuous man can rationally choose the components of the good. The theory of rational desire and love (*erōs*) in the *Symposium* and *Phaedrus* tries to answer this question; though the answers are sometimes vague and puzzling, Plato is right to face the question when he rejects Socrates' account of the final good.

4. If virtue is a craft, or closely enough analogous for Socrates' arguments to work, then the value of someone's being virtuous should be explained just as the value of being a craftsman should be explained. It is worth while for someone to be a craftsman because he will know and do the right actions, and will produce the right product; he has reason to value being a craftsman just in so far as he has reason to value the product expected from the craft. Socrates accepts the same account of the value of virtue; or at least the Socratic dialogues show no scepticism about this natural inference from the CA. In the middle dialogues Plato challenges this view. He argues that the virtuous man will regard his being virtuous as a good in itself for him, even apart from its results in action. If this is true, then the CA cannot fully capture the status of virtue, or the virtuous man's reasons for valuing it. The argument of the *Republic* proceeds on the assumption that Socrates is wrong, and that a satisfactory defence of justice (or any other virtue) must show how being just is worth while in itself—a condition which Socrates accepted neither explicitly nor implicitly.

5. If virtue is a craft aiming at some final good identified without appeal to moral beliefs, then it will be an open question whether the commonly recognized virtues can be recognized as virtues on these conditions. Socrates assumes that they can, and offers some arguments to support his view, for courage and temperance. But the hardest case is justice, which seems to resist identification with any craft aiming at what a rational agent will regard as the final good for him, irrespective of his moral beliefs. Socrates does not defend any account of justice which would prove what he needs. In the *Gorgias* Plato faces the issue Socrates had not faced, and tries to show how justice can be defended within Socrates' general theory. But in the

Republic he exposes the weakness of the Socratic account, and tries a new defence freed from the constraints of the CA, and therefore also without its benefits.

Socrates relies on the elenchos to discover the right account of the final good; but once that is agreed, virtue should become a craft, with its own authoritative principles like any other craft's, needing no defence from elenctic argument. In principle it should apparently be possible—though Socrates does not raise the question—to identify the final good without appeal to the elenchos; though the elenchos is a useful means of moral discovery and preliminary persuasion, it should not be necessary for moral argument or justification, once the principles of a craft have been discovered. Plato denies that the elenchos can be replaced by a craft; he allows moral knowledge only through mutual support and coherence of beliefs about the virtues and about the good, with no appeal to the external standard, identifiable without disputed moral terms, promised by the CA.

Plato's criticisms seem to threaten an awkward circle in his arguments. Socrates' demand for definitions of moral properties in non-moral terms avoids definition of one ill-understood property by reference to another which is defined in turn by reference to the first; he will not allow mention of the virtues, say, in the account of the final good. Plato's rejection of such an account of moral properties precludes justification of virtue by appeal to some external final good accepted by the non-virtuous man. Now we might agree with Plato's criticism of Socrates, and infer that morality cannot be justified by elenctic methods and by reference to the agent's good; perhaps it cannot be justified at all, or perhaps it allows some other form of justification which does not refer to the agent's good. Plato chooses neither of these options; he still requires reference to the agent's final good, and still believes that elenctic argument will yield the justification he needs.

6. *Plato's replies*

The *Republic* tries to answer Socrates' question—how virtue is good for the virtuous man—without those conditions on the final good and on desire and action which supported the CA. We can easily suppose Plato will either fail or trivially succeed. Apparently he will fail if what is 'good for' the agent or what 'contributes to his happiness (*eudaimonia*)' is clearly specified without mention of justice. Plato can hardly show that a rational pursuer of his own interest, if 'interest' is understood this way, has reason to be just. On the other hand, if justice and happiness are so vaguely specified at the outset that each can be defined by reference to the other, a solution to Plato's problem looks easy, but also trivial; for we are apparently allowed to adjust our conceptions of justice and happiness, with no external constraint, until they fit. It is never quite clear whether Plato attempts the insuperably difficult, or the self-defeatingly easy task, or some third task; the argument seems to waver between outright falsity and pointless terminological legislation.

Plato's reply proceeds in two stages. These are not always clearly recognized, and he does not recognize them himself, since he wrongly suggests that the argument is complete at the end of the first stage.

1. In Books II–IV he argues that psychic justice, the virtue which produces a structure of aims and desires analogous to the structure of a well-ordered state, is a good in itself, which a man concerned for his own good would choose for itself. Plato's defence accepts a Socratic demand, that virtue should be shown to be worth while, meaning 'worth while for, and good for, the agent', so that it can be defended as part of rational prudence. Because he rejects Socrates' denial of incontinence, Plato's conception of rational prudence includes a demand for phychic order as well as knowledge. But he still does not show why this state of character, psychic justice, requires the concern for other people's interests normally associated with justice.

2. However Plato holds views which allow him to answer this further question, though he does not use them as he should, to formulate the problem clearly and argue for his answer. To see what he *could* do, we must examine the theory of rational desire and love outlined in the *Symposium* and *Phaedrus* and suggested in the *Republic*. This theory shows how Plato might try to answer two awkward questions.

(a) We might think the psychic justice explained as 'control by rational desire' in Book IV is simply prudence in choosing means instrumental to previously desired goals. This would be quite enough for Socrates, since his view required the final good to be fixed in advance of the virtuous man's deliberation. But if Plato rejects this account of the final good, he has to explain how someone can find its constituents, and how this discovery can be a result of rational deliberation, if it does not involve only Socrates' technical deliberation.

(b) Plato must also show that someone who deliberates correctly about the components of the final good will have the just man's concern for other people's interests. He claims that the development of rational desire results in love for the Form of Justice and other moral properties, and in the desire to propagate them in other people. Since it will be in someone else's interest to become just, the just man will be concerned with other people's interests. Plato's claims clearly need careful scrutiny.

Plato's argument in the *Republic* faces a problem created by his self-imposed limitations on permissible arguments. Justice is to be chosen for itself; and so it cannot be shown to be desirable by reference to some other end to which it is instrumental. Many moralists who agree with Plato on this point infer that any attempt to justify morality on non-moral grounds must be rejected; for would these non-moral grounds not be part of the defence which is agreed to be inadmissible? More generally, if someone agrees with Plato that morality produces a desire for new ends, not simply for new instrumental means to the same ends we already desire, how can he claim that it is good for someone to accept morality? That defence seems to rest the case for morality on non-moral grounds.

Plato tries to show—though his argument is neither clear nor complete—that justice can be chosen for itself and benefit the agent. He claims that someone whose desires are rationally developed to pursue his own good will choose justice as a part of that good. To support his claim Plato in *Republic* VIII–IX contrasts the just man with other men who fulfil their desires rationally, but do not choose them rationally; anyone who pursues a plan he has rationally chosen will have reason to pursue justice for itself. Plato tries to reconcile a non-instrumental status for virtue with a justification by reference to the agent's good; despite its obscurities and dubious moves, the argument deserves attention—for it tries to reconcile two demands which can both seem plausible requirements on an ethical theory, but which seem to raise severe difficulties for each other.

7. *Criticisms of Plato*

Finally, in Chapter VIII I turn to discussion of more general questions, no longer primarily concerned with the internal coherence of Plato's argument or with the interpretation of his claims, but with his over-all conception of morality. I aim to set out the issues and remove some possible causes of misunderstanding, rather than to settle them. Two major points on which Plato has appeared to be mistaken in principle are these:

1. He is taken to be an ethical egoist, since he always insists that virtue must be good for the agent; and therefore he can apparently find no satisfactory account of what is distinctive, and hardest to justify, about morality.

2. He is a teleological moralist, since he thinks virtue is determined by reference to some overall good it promotes; and so he apparently cannot capture the distinctive features of moral obligation.

I try to show that anything plausible in the first objection collapses into the second; Plato's conception of a man's 'good' or 'happiness' need not reject the characteristic concern of morality with other people's good. It is hard to explain what kind of egoism is both clearly accepted by Plato and also clearly incompatible with the moral point of view; the critic objects to nothing in Plato which would not be equally open to objection in all teleological views of the content and justification of morality. Plato argues that morality must be part of a systematically planned life satisfying human purposes and aims as a whole, and that moral requirements should be decided by reference to this goal, which includes altruistic concerns.

The second objection, against Plato's ethical teleology, is not decisive either. Some complaints affect only certain conceptions of the over-all good; if the good includes virtue as a component, as in Plato's theory, some of the complaints are less obviously well aimed. But though Plato can be defended against these objections, his position is not immune to attack; his teleological account of concern for other people has results which conflict with central principles we are inclined to accept about the right treatment of persons. It is useful to contrast Plato's position and his opponents', though the underlying issues are too complex to allow quick solution.

I hope to separate the sound from the unsound lines of criticism, so that we do not underestimate the power, scope, and plausibility of Plato's theory, and so that we fix on the issues which really matter in deciding what is true and false in it. I do not think the theory collapses because of some simple and obviously correct knock-down objection which shows its obvious incompetence as a moral theory. The damaging objections rest on principles which themselves require further explanation and defence. If this is true, an examination of Plato's theory, its development, and its supporting arguments and assumptions, will not be a waste of time.

II THE BACKGROUND

1. *Ordinary views on morality*

1.1. *Introduction.* Like other moral philosophers, Socrates and Plato examine ordinary moral beliefs; and the problems arising in these beliefs influence their views of the important questions to be discussed. Since the ordinary beliefs they examine are not our own, it is useful to describe them in outline before we begin our discussion of Plato's arguments. A full survey of ordinary beliefs would require a detailed history of Greek moral thought; instead of trying to summarize all this history, I shall concentrate on the interlocutors in the dialogues, to find the kinds of beliefs Socrates presupposes in his audience. As well as ordinary unreflective beliefs, the dialogues present other theories of morality; these other theories set some of his questions for him. We can best identify Socrates' problems, see why they are important for him, and find the distinctive features of his questions and answers, when we have surveyed the unreflective and reflective beliefs which concern him.

Socrates inherits a vocabulary for speaking of moral questions, and this chapter is meant also to be a partial glossary for the vocabulary I shall use to represent his arguments. I speak of 'virtue', 'temperance', and so on, using common stock translations for Greek terms. But we must not at once apply all our beliefs about virtue to Plato's term '*aretē*'; I use English terms only roughly equivalent to Greek terms, attaching to them only these senses specified and suggested in this chapter.

1.2. *Socrates' questions.* In the early dialogues Socrates wants to know what courage, or temperance, or piety is. These questions are connected because each is agreed to be about a 'virtue' (*aretē*), one of quite a short list of virtues, courage, temperance, piety, justice, wisdom; with variations, the list is used several times to specify the complete virtue of a man (*La.* 199d4–e4, *Eud.* 279a4–c2, *Pr.* 329c2–d1, 329e5–330a1, *G.* 506e1–507e7, *Phd.* 69c1–2, *R.* 427d6–11.)[1] Not everyone agrees that the list is complete (*M.* 74a4–6); but it allows us some rough idea of the extension of 'virtue'. When Socrates and Plato try to prove that the virtues are all the same, or that each requires the others, they argue about this list, and suppose that if they prove these virtues are related in the appropriate way, they will have proved all they need about virtue.[2] First of all, then, we should ask what is meant by speaking of virtue and of the particular virtues.

It might seem as though we are foolishly trying to answer Socrates' questions at the outset, without attention to his arguments; for his complaint is exactly that he and his interlocutors do not know what virtue or each of the virtues is. But we are not asking the Socratic question just yet. Socrates agrees that both he and his interlocutors associate some beliefs with 'virtue', so that they agree in calling some things and not others virtues; and at the outset we want to see roughly what these beliefs are. Socrates' questions, we shall find, are far more demanding.

1.3. *Virtue and function.* Whatever is good (*agathon*) at something has a virtue or excellence (*aretē*). Plato explains virtue as excellence in a particular function or role (*ergon*) (*R.* 353b2–d1), and his explanation matches the normal use of '*aretē*'.[3] Dogs, horses, athletes can all be good or bad, possess or lack a virtue, in so far as they are good or bad at what is expected of them, in their particular role (*R.* 335b6–c2). However, Socrates is interested in one subset of virtues, those on his short list. Unlike other *aretai*, these are particularly human—not the excellences of horses or dogs or hammers—and belong to human beings apart from their other roles and functions—not to carpenters or mathematicians as such. These excellences belong to someone in his life as a whole.

1.4. *Human virtue.* Socrates accepts the standard connection between virtue and doing something well. A hammer has an excellence when it does well its characteristic activity of hammering; and Socrates infers that a good man has an excellence when he does well his characteristic activity of living (*R.* 353d3–e11). But a clearer description of this characteristic activity raises problems.

A hammer is a good one if it fulfils our legitimate expectations of a hammer and serves the purpose for which a hammer is used. But it is hard to specify the analogue for men; men are not normally used to produce some definite product, except in their roles as carpenters, doctors, and so on, who conform to the functional pattern. What are the relevant legitimate expectations about a man? It is natural to reply that since a man is not used for other people's purposes, and his function is not defined by them, the relevant expectations in this case are his own; a good man will live as his own legitimate expectations of a man require, and his virtue will be displayed in doing this well. But are there legitimate expectations which everyone will have for himself? Socrates tries to find them; he maintains that what everyone wants is some final good, a condition of 'doing well' (*eu prattein*) or 'happiness' (*eudaimonia*) (*Eud.* 278e3, 280b6). Someone who acts in the way that achieves this final good is a virtuous man. We damage dogs or horses or tools by making them less capable of performing their functions; but we 'damage' or 'harm' a man by damaging his interests, failing to do what is good for him (cf. *R.* 335b2–d13).[4]

1.5. *Virtue and other people.* However, the functional pattern for virtue can also be applied to different 'legitimate expectations'. If we think other people can have legitimate expectations of a man, these expectations will also define virtues; this is easily seen in his role as a father, a policeman, and so on. The virtue of a man in general, on this view, will be defined by what anyone else can legitimately expect of him; and here justice would be an obvious candidate for being a virtue, since other people's legitimate expectations will presumably require the virtuous man to be concerned to some extent for their interests.

These two ways of explaining the 'legitimate expectations' determining someone's virtue may produce different and even conflicting views about what a virtue is. Virtues need not all be what we would tend to call moral virtues; whether or not they include moral virtues will depend on the relevant expectations. Socrates' interlocutors face problems about the virtues partly because they assume different kinds of expectations which are sometimes hard to reconcile. In particular they derive many of their beliefs about the virtues from two different traditions of Greek moral thought, which we can call (with some oversimplification) the 'Homeric' conception and the post-Homeric 'law-conception' of virtues. It is worth while to see briefly what these two traditions say about the virtues.

2. Traditional views of virtue

2.1. *Homeric values.* The most admired Homeric man with the highest virtues (an *agathos*) displays a certain narrow range of excellences suitable for an aristocrat and a warrior; he is strong, well born, intelligent in counsel and plan, brave in battle, rich, protective of his dependents, honoured. The ideal Homeric hero, such as Odysseus, satisfies all of these conditions; but, naturally, not everyone who satisfies some satisfies them all. Achilles and Agamemnon lack wisdom, but remain *agathoi*; Paris is reproached for cowardice but remains *agathos*; the suitors behave to Penelope as no *agathos* should behave, but remain *agathoi*.[5] But poverty, or low birth, or subsequent low status, disqualify someone from being *agathos*; Odysseus, like everyone else, would have lost half his virtue if he had become a slave (*Od.* 17.320–3, 18.129–37). A man is not beyond reproach if he does only what is necessary to remain *agathos*; but these traits count heavily enough to qualify him for admiration even when he is condemned for his other failures.

2.2. *Other people's interests.* This picture of the most admired man does not make him a self-seeker, unconcerned for the good of others, primarily competitive and not co-operative. Certainly a hero wants to excel over everyone else (*Il.* 6.206–10), and especially to be recognized as excelling, to be accorded the right kinds of honour (*timē*); but to win this recognition, he is required to show concern for other people too. The Homeric hero is anxious to achieve honour for himself; but since he seeks honour from his peers, and secondarily from his inferiors, he depends on what his peers value. And what they value includes a protective attitude in the *agathos* to his inferiors (cf. *Od.* 2.230–4), co-operation with the group's projects, especially war, shown by Nestor, but not by Achilles (*Il.* 1.254–61, 9.628–42), and consideration to peers—Achilles is blamed for failing to show it to Hector's body (*Il.* 24.39–54), but commended for showing it to Priam (24.503–16). Homeric ethics does not condone unrestricted, ruthless pursuit of one's own interest.

Nevertheless, Homeric ethics differs crucially in its emphasis from later Greek ethical outlooks. Concern for others is expected of a hero; but if he falls short of what is expected here and remains rich and powerful, he remains *agathos*, and cannot be deprived of his due honour. He is expected to show concern for others to win further honour; and above all he is not honoured for being concerned for others, but for proving he has the normal traits of an *agathos*. An *agathos* who shows he can protect his dependents and be generous to strangers displays his power and wealth; he benefits dependents and strangers for this reason, not because it is in their interest. The hero is admired primarily by his peers, who naturally value some co-operative action, but primarily value the display and pursuit of honour, wealth, and power, whether or not the actions displaying them benefit the agent or other people.

2.3. *Post-Homeric ethics*. This outlook retains a widespread influence on Greek ethics, if the people who agree with Pindar are at all
numerous. Pindar does not expect the *agathos* to be shamelessly self-
seeking; he should be concerned for justice and for 'quietness'
(*hēsuchia*; *Py*. 8.1–12). But what makes him *agathos* is his birth,
status, and 'manly' characteristics—physical strength and courage;
and if he has these he cannot be refused the honour due to an *agathos*.

Though this Homeric conception of the good man remains influen-
tial, it is no longer the unchallenged ideal for Socrates' contemporaries. It suffers severe criticism from Hesiod, Solon, Xenophanes,
Aeschylus, Theognis (to some extent), and others. The most con-
venient, though over-simple, way to contrast the results of these
criticisms with Homer is to say that they produce a *law-conception* of
ethics. The central virtue is justice, prescribed by a law or some other
norm (*nomos*) concerned with all the community to which it applies,
and fixing what the good of the community requires from each of its
members. In Hesiod it is *nomos* which Zeus gives to men to stop them
preying on each other like animals (*Op*. 274–85); in Solon justice is
prescribed both by the gods and by the laws of the state (3.11–16,
30–9). Xenophanes rejects the traditional Homeric, and Pindaric, virtues, in so far as they do not benefit the state and produce life under
good laws (*eunomia*; B2).[6] The Spartans, representing all the Greeks,
are said to be subject to a ruler, law, whose prescriptions they obey
without question (Hdt. 7.104.4–5).

2.4. *Contrasts*. The conflict between the Homeric outlook and the
law-conception should not be exaggerated. We have seen that
Homeric values were not indifferent to the *agathos*'s treatment of
others. The Homeric demand that he should be a good ruler and
protector of dependents and strangers is included in the law's demand
that he should be just and law-abiding; Homeric and post-Homeric
values might well require many of the same virtues. Nor does the law-
conception necessarily reject the pursuit of honour, or the acquisition
of the goods which normally belong to the *agathos*.

But important contrasts should still be stressed:

1. The law-conception counts as *agathos* the law-abiding man,
   whether or not he is rich, powerful, and well born like the
   Homeric *agathos*.
2. Concern for others is not required of an *agathos* and justified to
   him simply as an expression of his power and resources as a
   protector, but because it benefits the community, or the part of it

which influences the content of the law.

3. Other people do not appeal exclusively to the *agathos's* desire for honour and fear of disgrace. He is also expected to obey out of respect for the law. Sometimes this respect will rest on fear of divine and human legislators, but it may also reflect men's concern for the common benefits of law.

These schematic contrasts in valuation, justification, and motivation do not imply each other; some people will accept parts of the law-conception or parts of the Homeric conception, and combinations of the two may be hard to assign definitely to either side. But these broad contrasts are the right ones to explore in Socrates' contemporaries.[7]

2.5. *Areas of conflict.* The law-conception is admirably expressed, as the view of the Athenians, in Protagoras' Great Speech (*Pr.* 320c–328d). But it is not the only view Socrates faces. The Homeric and the post-Homeric tendencies are both evident. Meno expects virtue to make someone a fairly traditional aristocrat (*M.* 71e1–5, 91a1–6), but readily admits that it requires justice and temperance (73a6–d10, 78c3–79a2)—a quite un-Homeric component of virtue which Meno finds no less natural than the traditional components.[8] These two conceptions of virtue offer clear opportunities for conflict. Neither conception explains how much a man's own aims and how much other people's expectations should count in deciding what a real virtue is; and this problem is more severe the more demanding other people's expectations become. Homeric ethics demands some concern by the *agathos* for other people's interests, but in a social order and system of values designed above all to promote the power and status of the *agathos*. A society relying on law and justice at least professes to aim at other purposes; even an aristocratic society claiming to observe law and justice prescribes concern for the interests of other people and the society, with no guarantee that they will advance the power and status of a particular *agathos*. These possibilities for conflict must soon be explored further.

3. *The recognized virtues*

3.1. *Socrates' procedure.* Socrates examines the beliefs about particular virtues and the conflicts they reveal, between the Homeric and the post-Homeric views of virtue, and between the agent's expectations and other people's. Ordinary beliefs are in the right condition for Socrates' examination, because beliefs about each virtue are derived from these different sources, and cannot easily be captured in one account which will explain them all. These opposed expectations raise problems for each virtue by itself and for the relation to each other of all the virtues supposed to belong to a good man; different virtues, and even different recognized aspects of one virtue, seem to demand incompatible actions.

3.2. *Courage*. The easiest virtue to describe seems to be courage (*andreia*). It is apparently a direct descendant of the Homeric virtue, and calling someone a 'good man' (*anēr agathos*) still tends to imply above all that he is brave.[9] And naturally the law-conception cannot dispense with courage. It seems to be an unproblematic virtue, in so far as it requires a fairly clear, limited range of actions—displays of fearlessness in battle and in other dangers to physical safety which call for prompt, daring reactions. The close association of courage with these kinds of situations and responses is reflected in Aristotle; though he allows a wider scope for courage, he still recognizes these situations as its primary area, and denies that the unexciting dangers of disease or shipwreck are part of the primary area (*EN* 1115a28–31). All these features of courage are clear in Laches' views; courage is standing firm in battle (*La*. 190e4–6), or (he later suggests) endurance (192a9–el). Though he is persuaded that there are other cases of courage too (191c7–e3), these are not the intuitive cases which fit the traditional view.[10]

For Homeric values, acting like an *agathos* is acting bravely (*Il*. 6.521–3). But the law-conception cannot endorse courage so strongly; for someone might, as Callicles advises, be fearless and resolute in ruthless pursuit of his own interest against what is lawful (*G*. 492a, *R*. 561al; Thuc. 3.82.4). And someone concerned with his own interest has equal reason to be wary of courage; for it seems to demand the kind of reckless daring and fearlessness which will seem foolish daring to a prudent man (*Pr*. 349d5–8). We can either admit these limitations in courage, and allow that it is not an unqualified virtue in the agent's interest or other people's, or revise our beliefs about what courage requires.

3.3. *Temperance*. Unlike courage, temperance (*sōphrosunē*) has no clear range or limits; the discussion in the *Charmides* is much more rambling and obscure than in the *Laches*, and it is much harder to see what kind of virtue is being discussed. In the *Laches* Socrates raises puzzles about a virtue his audience would think easy to understand—for they all 'know' roughly what kinds of actions are brave, and what character traits to expect in a brave man; Socrates tries to show that they understand courage less well than they think. Most people would more readily agree with him that temperance is hard to understand, and that the relevant actions and character traits are hard to isolate.

The term '*sōphrosunē*', and its adjective '*sōphrōn*' refer in earlier Greek to nothing more precise than 'sound mind', the condition of a person which produces sound or sensible actions.[11] Soundness may consist in sound thoughts, or sound desires, or both; earlier Greek psychological terms do not sharply distinguish cognitive and affective conditions, any more than 'sound mind' does.[12] Then *sōphrosunē* is associated with a particular kind of sound or sensible action—the action of the man who does not demand too much, and does not impetuously pursue apparent goods which will turn out to be harmful. Someone whose desires are uncontrolled will fall into this impetuous excess; and so a sound mind seems to require control of desires. *Sōphrosunē*, then, is closely attached to self-control; but it would be wrong to say that the term just means 'self-control'; besides this specialized use, it retains its broader use, referring to wisdom or good sense in general.[13] The tangled progress of the *Charmides* shows the still unspecialized character of the virtue.

3.4. *The range of temperance.* A glance at the various accounts of temperance suggested in the *Charmides* will show how its broad and heterogeneous range persists for Socrates' audience.

1. When Socrates first sees Charmides, he is excited by a desire for him which he controls only with difficulty (*Ch.* 155c–e). Here he displays the temperance associated with self-control; and though this association is examined no further in the dialogue (for reasons we must later consider) Socrates shows that it is natural enough.

2. Charmides first suggests that temperance is doing everything in an orderly and calm way (*kosmiōs kai hēsuchē(i)*, 159b2–3), including speaking and walking in the streets. He refers to the well-brought-up young aristocrat's politeness and moderation; he will be orderly because his desires are in order and do not encourage him into excessive self-assertiveness.

3. He then suggests temperance is shame or modesty (*adiōs*, 160e3–5)—suitable enough for someone who is calm and orderly, and a suitable attitude to encourage sensible, moderate action.

4. Critias' view treats temperance as 'doing one's own' (161b5–6) (*ta heautou prattein*), as opposed to 'meddling' (*polupragmosunē*; cf.

161d11). Here too a common virtue is invoked; a sound man does not meddle in other people's business, especially to promote political change. Significantly, 'non-interference' (*apragmosunē*), closely related to 'quietness' or 'calm' (*hēsuchia*) is a traditional reputed virtue of the aristocracy (cf. Thuc. 3.82.8, 2.40.2, 1.70.8–9).[14]

5. Critias then suggests that temperance is self-knowledge, associating the Delphic motto with knowledge of one's own limitations and the restraint in action that could be expected to follow (164d3–e2).

These common beliefs about temperance raise problems requiring awkward choices:

1. If temperance is associated with self-restraint, someone may wonder whether it is good for him. The aristocrat accepting Homeric or Pindaric values will limit the pursuit of his own honour and power in the interests of his peers; this aspect of temperance is heavily stressed in Pindar and other aristocratic propaganda, though not in Homer, to show critics that Homeric values do not make someone lawless and unrestrained. The law-conception needs temperance no less. These demands for moderation require frustration of a man's own desires in the interests of others, and he may ask why he should tolerate frustration if he can avoid other people's sanctions. Callicles infers that no wise man who really knows and does what is good for him will be temperate (*G.* 491d10–e2).[15]

2. Alternatively, if we insist that a temperate man has good sense and wisdom, we may change our minds about what temperance requires. We may decide we have no reason to accept the restraints imposed by customary views of temperance; instead a temperate and sensible man planning for his own good will reject conventional law-abiding morality.

Since temperance is associated both with good sense and intelligence in the agent's interest and with commonly accepted moderation, someone who rejects this moderation may or may not reject temperance too, whichever aspect of temperance he concentrates on. But at least the standard beliefs face some challenge; apparently they cannot easily show both that a temperate man acts wisely and sensibly to benefit himself and that he will observe the accepted law-abiding restraints. Traditional temperance tries to satisfy both the agent's and other people's expectations; but Callicles denies that it can satisfy both. In the *Charmides* Socrates does not discuss these challenges to recognized temperance; but the views of temperance he discusses are open to the challenges, and in the *Gorgias* he faces them.

3.5. *Piety*. Piety (*hosiotēs*) appears less often in the dialogues. But the *Euthyphro* shows the problem it raises. The dialogue reflects a traditional view of piety as part of a contract between gods and men for the exchange of goods and services; the pious man's piety is concerned with a particular area of his life, the actions and abstentions pleasing to the gods. This area need not coincide, or even overlap very much, with the areas of the other virtues; both the *Euthyphro* and *Republic* II suggest that someone can stay on good terms with the gods by performing the sacrifices and other ritual services due to them, despite his failure in the other virtues, and especially in justice. However, Greek views on piety and the gods' demands did not always divorce it from justice to other people. Hesiod, Solon, Aeschylus, all insist that the gods are concerned with justice and punish injustice in human societies. Sometimes these demands are concentrated on unjust rulers, and on such serious and polluting crimes as homicide; but these poets also suggest that injustice in a society as a whole angers the gods. Euthyphro recognizes this well-established, though not universally accepted, association of justice and piety. Though his action offends conventional views of piety which would exclude prosecution of his father, he reasonably insists that the justice of his prosecution is what matters, and that is enough to make it pious. The rest of the dialogue accepts that piety is a part of justice, but fails to show how it can be distinguished from justice as a whole.[16] The *Protagoras* is even more confident that the two virtues cannot be distinguished (*Pr.* 331a6–b8). Piety is not prominent in other dialogues; if it is no more and no less than justice, the serious problem is to give an account of justice.

3.6. *Justice*. The conflicts in ordinary beliefs about the virtues are most clearly exposed in questions about justice (*dikaiosunē*). It would not be at all natural for someone with a Homeric view of the virtues to say that justice is the whole of virtue; but for the law-conception it is an easy claim, first in an isolated passage in Theognis, and more frequently thereafter. Initially justice need not demand much more than Homeric values demand; 'helping friends and harming enemies' is quite congenial to heroic values, allowing the *agathos* to display his power and strength. But when the 'friends' include the others in a political community, and when their expectations count, the demands change. If virtue is displayed above all in actions which benefit the community, then it will be natural to associate it with law-abiding, fairness, doing one's share of what is required by the community, and in general obeying the laws and other norms (*nomoi*) which aim at the community's good. This conception of justice clearly influences Protagoras' account of human virtue in his long speech; for though other virtues are mentioned, justice is by far the most prominent.[17] Aristotle recognizes this broad scope of justice when he takes 'justice in general' to be the whole of virtue, in so far as it is required to benefit others and to do what the laws require (*EN* 1129b11–1130a5). When a man's virtue is measured by other people's expectations, justice easily expands to cover all virtue.

This view of justice emphasizes some of the more awkward problems in ordinary beliefs.

1. If justice is simply law-abiding, specified wholly by the accepted norms (*nomoi*), any law, no matter how bad or oppressive, seems to prescribe just actions. But if it is only what *just* laws prescribe, some further account of justice is needed. Though someone might argue that it is just to obey even unjust laws, he cannot identify justice with law-abiding behaviour without qualification, if he wants to distinguish just and unjust laws.

2. If someone expects his virtue to be good for him, justice seems to be a dubious virtue since both supporters and opponents agree that it benefits other people, not the agent himself (*R.* 343c1–5, 367c2–5, *EN* 1130a3–5). Radical critics denounce this conflict between recognized justice and the agent's interest, and challenge Socrates and Plato to remove the conflict.

3.7. *Wisdom*. Others besides Socrates believed that wisdom is a virtue, that a man is better off if he conducts his affairs wisely; but so far we have not said very much if we do not know the content or purpose of this wisdom (*sophia* or *phronēsis*). Someone will naturally value wisdom in the prudent pursuit of his own interests; and we have seen why a prudent man might not welcome all the recognized virtuous actions. We might infer either that those actions are not worth while, or that prudence is sometimes mistaken. Not everyone takes the first view. We might reasonably reject the prudence and forethought which makes a procrastinating, calculating Nicias, and admire the impetuous bravery of a Lamachus (Aristoph. *Ach.* 566–75, *Ran.* 1039–43, *Av.* 639–41). And we might say that if prudence conflicts with the demands of friendship or justice, so much the worse for prudence (Soph. *Phil.* 1246 f.; Thuc. 3.37.3).[18]

Either of these attitudes to wise prudence raises questions. If we readily admit a conflict between wisdom and virtue, does that mean we cannot justify being virtuous? Or if we recognize some larger kind of wisdom than merely prudential wisdom, we still must explain what that is, with no guarantee that it will justify recognized virtue either. If we are inclined to think it is somehow rational to be virtuous, one obvious form of rationality is prudential rationality, and if that clashes with virtue, we must assume the difficult task of explaining moral rationality some other way. Ordinary beliefs tend to assume that it is on the whole wise to be virtuous; but the apparent conflicts find no easy resolution in those beliefs.

4. *Theories of virtue*

4.1. *Virtue and teaching.* Others besides Socrates examine these beliefs about the virtues, and try to solve the problems they raise. Socrates' own position, and especially its distinctive features, can best be understood by comparison with these other views. Their common problem is to find what real virtues are, and especially how far the recognized virtues, as commonly understood, are real virtues. This problem is closely related to an apparently distinct problem about whether virtue can be taught. A discipline can be taught when it has some intelligible and explicable procedure; to decide what the right procedure is, we need some idea of the point or purpose of the discipline and of ways to achieve it. These conditions are satisfied by the most conspicuous example of a teachable discipline, a productive 'art' or 'craft' (*technē*) or 'science' (*epistēmē*); and if we could show that virtue is teachable as a craft, we would have shown that it is a rational discipline with some clear point.[19] For the specialized excellence of the carpenter, general, and so on, there is a craft which shows how to achieve the excellence, how to do the particular task well and reach the right product. It is natural to expect that a similar craft could be found for over-all human virtue, for living well. When we know what that craft is, we shall know how far the recognized virtues are real virtues.

At the same time, virtue does not easily conform to the pattern of a craft. A critic will reply that training in virtue is supposed to produce virtuous action, and that mere instruction in a craft does not guarantee right action; someone can act incontinently, knowing what is better and doing what is worse. Medea and Phaedra in Euripides' plays are pessimistic about the power of instruction to affect action; they know what would be better to do, for themselves and for other people, but still want to do what they believe to be worse more than they want to follow their judgement about what is better (Eur. *Med.*

1078–80, *Hipp.* 377–87).[20] If this kind of incontinence is possible, instruction in a craft need not be wholly useless in making people act virtuously; but it will not by itself produce right action. Diodotus suggests in Thucydides' Mytilenean Debate that natural tendencies in human nature are too strong for restraint by laws and other social norms (Thuc. 3.45.3). If Euripides and Diodotus are right, then mere instruction will have limited results; and since, Socrates remarks, most people agree that knowledge can be overcome by powerful desires contrary to what is believed to be best (*Pr.* 352a8–c7), a defender of virtue as a craft should show how to meet their challenge.

4.2. *Ordinary moral education.* The Homeric virtues included conditions—wealth, power, strength, and high birth—difficult or impossible to acquire by instruction. But the virtues examined by Socrates would normally be allowed to be teachable to some extent. The normal pattern of moral training is described and defended by Protagoras. A young child is told that particular actions are just or admirable or pious, and rewarded and punished for obedience and disobedience (*Pr.* 325c6–d7). Later (if he is of the right social class) he is trained in 'music' (*mousikē*); he learns to enjoy and imitate the rhythms suitable for calm and well-balanced people; and he admires and wants to imitate the right heroes of poetry (325d7–326b6); gymnastic makes his body strong enough to do what is required of a brave and enduring man (326c6–d1; *Ap.* 24d9–11). Most moral training comes, not from formal instruction in morals, but from education which produces the right physical capacities and sentiments and from the informal but ubiquitous presence of the rest of society. Everyone shares in the teaching of virtue; and a man picks it up, as he might pick up Greek, by growing up in society (327e1–328b1; *M.* 92d2–93a4; *Alc.* 110c3–111a4).

This type of education or 'culture' (*paideia*) tries to solve the problem about motivation and incontinence; for it trains someone's sentiments and emotions in the virtuous direction. But it does not show that the virtues have some clear point, or that they are systematically teachable and explicable; someone's parents and the laws and social norms prescribe all kinds of virtuous actions to him, but do not explain why they are virtuous, what their point is, how they are justified; he has no guarantee that incompatible virtues and virtuous actions are not prescribed. Someone who looks for the craft of living well cannot assume he has acquired the right actions, or some of them; his training will not have proved it to him.

4.3. *Sophistic training.* Plato mentions sophists who offer to teach virtue (*M.* 91a6–b8), the craft of living well, and to provide what traditional moral education neglects. Sometimes in modern treatments 'the sophists' are presented as critics or sceptics who undermine traditional morality and upset people's moral convictions. This is not Plato's view; and the sophists we know of share no such common aims or doctrines. The sophists Plato mentions do not criticize ordinary moral education, and do not examine the virtues it prescribes; they simply supplement it with other useful crafts—rhetoric, political techniques, natural science, all kinds of useful knowledge, in the hope that this general training will leave someone well equipped in life. Hippias is the most prominent example of such a sophist, who possesses encyclopedic knowledge and offers to transmit it to his pupils (*HMi.* 363c7–364a6, 364d3–6). In the two *Hippias* dialogues Socrates shows why he is sceptical about these kinds of claims; Hippias, for all his expertise, has nothing more than a layman's understanding of moral questions, and his encyclopedic knowledge does not help him to resolve the puzzles arising from ordinary moral beliefs.

4.4. *Protagoras.* On this issue Protagoras agrees with Socrates against sophists who follow Hippias' method of education. He rejects training in all these crafts which are useless in understanding moral and political issues; his own moral education is a refinement of ordinary moral training in the traditional virtues. He claims to be a moral teacher and to make men virtuous (*Pr.* 317b3–c1); and he agrees that he teaches men the political craft (319a3–7; cf. 322b5). But at the same time 'craft' is not quite the right word. A pupil of Protagoras will not learn expertise in some specialized craft; he will learn the general culture (*paideia*) of a good citizen (312a7–b6, 318d7–319a2). His own training, which makes people good at deliberating about their own affairs and the state's (318e5–319a2; cf. *M.* 91a1–6), supplements recognized virtue, without replacing or correcting it; in his teaching he only does better what everyone does already (327e1–328c2).

Protagoras' refusal to criticize the prescriptions of common morality or defend them against criticism is justified only if he thinks there is no basis for argument about whether it prescribes real virtue or not. His account of moral education suggests that moral beliefs are simply what is prescribed by social norm and convention; there is no way to decide that what the Athenians have taught us about justice is not about real justice, since we have no access to this supposed 'real' justice, but only to justice as taught by the Athenians. We shall be justified in accepting what the Athenians tell us as true, just as the Persians will be justified in accepting Persian norms as true (cf. *Tht.* 167c4–5).[21] This belief that virtues exist only as specified by conventions or norms (*nomoi*) does not make Protagoras a sceptic; on the contrary he uses it to refute someone who might criticize 'conventional' virtue by appeal to 'real' virtue—if we have no access to real virtue, the appeal is futile.

This general view of virtue leaves room for Protagoras' own claims; like a doctor, he knows his patients' preferences, and can prescribe what satisfies them (cf. *Tht.* 167a4–d1). And he suggests that someone's preference in life, to conduct his own and the state's affairs well, will be best served by the conventional virtues. Shared beliefs and practices prescribing justice benefit everyone (*Pr.* 327b1–4) and are necessary for a state to exist and prevent mutual aggression (322a8–c3, 324d7–e1, 326e6–327b1; cf. Anon. Iamb. 6.1; Dem. 25.15). The first qualification for a man to decide his own or the state's best interests is the justice and temperance which everyone must learn (322e2–323a4). Protagoras defends common moral beliefs against sceptical criticism, and argues that they deserve to belong to any craft for living well.

4.5. *Gorgias and rhetoric.* Gorgias does not have Protagoras' ambitions; he confines himself to teaching rhetoric.[22] He does not promise to teach virtue, but only to make men clever at speaking (*M.* 95b9–c4), and in the *Gorgias* he disclaims any expert knowledge of virtue; elsewhere, though, Plato represents him as a teacher of virtue (*Ap.* 19e1–4). These claims need not be inconsistent. If Gorgias teaches people to be good orators, and they can then be successful in private and public life, he will have taught them one kind of virtue or excellence, a capacity to obtain goods for themselves (cf. *M.* 73c6–d1, *G.* 456a7–8). He does not, however, claim to be an expert in the recognized virtues, justice, temperance, and so on; and in that sense he is not a teacher of virtue like Protagoras. He is not hostile to the recognized virtues; but he suggests, contrary to Protagoras, that they are irrelevant to the successful exercise of any specialized craft. Gorgias recognizes one important virtue—a condition which a man will regard as good for him—and identifies that with the capacity to use various capacities, his own and other people's, for his own benefit—that is the value of rhetoric. Gorgias himself approves of the recognized virtues, but does not suggest that they are necessary or sufficient for success in life; someone might use rhetoric or any other craft to achieve success by vicious methods (*G.* 456c6–457c3). Gorgias challenges Protagoras' comfortable assumption that the successful man needs the recognized virtues, though he does not challenge these virtues themselves. Polus accepts a similar attitude; though injustice may be more beneficial for the agent than justice, justice is still more admirable (*kalon*) (474c4–d2). This attitude does not by itself imply hostility to the recognized virtues, unless we believe they can be justified only by their benefits to the agent—Gorgias and Polus offer no other justification.

4.6. *Callicles.* The weaknesses in these previous views are clearly exposed in Callicles' attack on the recognized virtues. Callicles is not a sophist, but a normal cultured Athenian (*G.* 487b6–7), who none the less sees through Protagoras' defence of the standard moral education. He regards laws and social norms, and the conventional justice derived from them, as the policy of the weak and inferior majority to coerce the minority of strong and superior men against their interest (*G.* 483b6–d2). He need not dispute Protagoras' view that the existence of common principles of justice is necessary for a political community, to guarantee security and communal life. He simply denies that a superior man has any reason to respect the principles which this or that particular community imposes; he has reason to replace it, if he can, with a state which promotes his own interests more effectively. The political tone of Callicles' attack is clear; he defends oligarchic objections to democratic appeals to justice, and supports the claim of the superior men to pursue their interest without restriction by the majority.[23] But he goes beyond partisan criticism, and attacks all recognized justice and temperance because it restricts the superior man's pursuit of his own interests, and frustrates the superior man's rational self-interest to benefit others. A superior man wants to develop and increase his desires, and satisfy them, so that he fully realizes his capacity for satisfaction; only cowardice, fear of punishment from other people, or the self-punishing effects of his own 'conventional' scruples, will restrain someone from this pursuit of maximum desire-satisfaction (491e5–492b1). Callicles will remove the conflict of desires which creates the problem of incontinence by rejecting the suppression of natural urges which is required by conventional morality.

Callicles does not discredit recognized justice by showing only that it rests on convention (*nomos*), not on nature (*phusis*) (482e2–483a8).

Protagoras readily agrees that it depends on human agreement; just institutions are not found in unpolitical nature (483d2–484c3), and their prescriptions go beyond the basic desires of non-social individuals (Ant. B44, fr. A, col. 1.23–col. 2.3 = DK, pp. 346 f.; cf. col. 5.13–24 = DK, p. 350). But these points do not show that recognized justice is not desirable. It may be desirable just because it provides the security and other benefits which unsocial nature cannot provide (cf. Dem. 25.15). Callicles argues more powerfully, not that the laws and conventions are arbitrary or non-necessary, but that they conflict with the basic natural desires which (he assumes) every superior man has reason to satisfy (G. 483a8–d2; cf. Ant. B44, fr. A, col. 2.23–col. 4.8 = DK, pp. 347–9). What belongs to nature, as opposed to law, is what benefits a superior man if he need not care about anyone else's interests. Law violates his interests by forcing him to consider other people's interests, to avoid punishment (cf. Ant. B44, fr. A, col. 2.3–10 = DK, p. 347). He objects to conventional justice because it is *purely* conventional, from the superior man's point of view; he would have no reason to observe it if the majority had not agreed on it and threatened punishment for violators.

Both traditions of Greek moral thought are open to Callicles' objections. Some of his ideal certainly recalls the Homeric hero's ideal of power and success. Polus praises the tyrant's life without claiming that it is virtuous or admirable (*kalon*); Callicles' whole-hearted endorsement of vigorous and courageous (491b3, c7, 492a2) pursuit of success and power over others (491a7–b4, c6–d3) sounds more firmly Homeric. But Homeric values also demand more from a hero; he should respect his peers, co-operate with his group, and protect his dependents. Callicles denies that a superior man has any reason to observe these restraints, except in so far as they are required for the satisfaction of his desires. The attack on law-morality is still clearer. He insists that real virtues are those virtues which fulfil a man's own expectations; they may well conflict with the recognized virtues, which satisfy other people's expectations, not a superior man's. The positions of Protagoras and Gorgias were crucially vague here. Protagoras promised to teach someone how to succeed in private and public life, and assumed that such success would require the recognized virtues. Gorgias advocated rhetoric for success in life, and assumed that someone would have good reason to be just even if it did not contribute to success. Callicles argues that both these complacent assumptions are unfounded; conventional justice does not promote a superior man's interests, and therefore he has no reason to observe it.

4.7. *Thrasymachus.* Callicles' main criticism is presented, without his particular ideal, by Thrasymachus in *Republic* I. Callicles does not deny that real justice is a virtue; he believes that a right order of interpersonal relations is secured by justice and law, and simply insists that this natural justice should promote, and not restrain, the desires and interests of the superior men. Because he insists on the superior worth of the superior men, Callicles does not accept Socrates' suggestion that if the masses are collectively stronger than the superior men, their strength makes their justice real justice (*G.* 488b8–489c7). Thrasymachus accepts the suggestion rejected by Callicles; he is no revived Callicles, but a new and more damaging critic of recognized virtues. He offers no rival conception of justice to show, as Callicles showed, that it is desirable for a really virtuous man. Instead he accepts that what Callicles called 'conventional justice' is real justice, all the justice there is; justice prescribes that the weaker should do what is in the interest of the stronger, and on these terms justice is not a virtue (*R.* 338e1–339a4, 348c2–e4). In Thrasymachus' view just actions are done only by the subject: rulers are neither just nor unjust.[24] He shows that someone concerned for his own interest, whether or not he is one of Callicles' superior men, often has reason to act unustly, since his just action benefits someone else and not himself (343c1–e7).

Glaucon and Adeimantus restate Thrasymachus' position (358b7–c1), and show that it is unharmed by Protagoras' defence of justice. The security of a society observing justice is worth while for anyone who cannot always protect himself (358e3–359b5); justice benefits the collectively stronger party, the majority of men who cannot protect themselves (338e1–5; *G.* 483b4–c1, 488d5–10), and thereby benefits each member of that majority. But still each man will find it prudent sometimes to break rules of justice for his own benefit. Protagoras' defence gives a reason for wanting just institutions, not a reaon for being reliably just.

5. *Replies to the critics*

5.1. *The issues.* The attacks of critics like Callicles and Thrasymachus force a defender of conventional morality to make some awkward choices. The standard view, articulated by Protagoras, recognizes that a man has reason to pursue his own interests, and that the states and conditions good for that purpose are virtues; at the same time it expects a man to show the virtues which are good for other people's purposes. The critics argue that these two components of the standard view are incompatible; a man has reason to pursue his own interest, and no reason to do what suits other people, since it is not in his interest.

The defender has two choices. (1) He can show how it is really in my interest to be just and conventionally virtuous. (2) He can show why I have a reason to be conventionally just and virtuous even if it is not in my interest. If he tries the first reply, he can defend it in two ways. (1a) He can show that on the critic's conception of his own interest, it is in his interest to be just. (1b) He can show that the critic's conception of his own interest is wrong, and that on the right conception, it is in his interest to be conventionally just. Callicles and Thrasymachus advocate the pursuit of one's own happiness (*eudaimonia*), but do not defend their conception of happiness; for Callicles it seems to consist in the extravagant development and satisfaction of desires, for Thracymachus in more conventional goals—power, wealth, and the pleasure they produce. Both assume that a man's own good will require the satisfaction of his desires in ways which conflict with other people's interests, and that someone concerned with his own interests has no reason for concern with anyone else's interests for their own sake. Here is one suitable area for argument.[25]

5.2. *A 'conventional' reply.* Plato is the first (as far as we know) to examine and criticize in detail the position of people like Callicles and Thrasymachus; but other people consider similar kinds of criticism. The Anonymus Iamblichi defends conventional justice for its good consequences:

1. It is not mere cowardice to be law-abiding (6.1; cf. *G.* 483b6–c8); and a virtuous man need not always seek his own advantage (*pleonexia*) at other people's expense (cf. *R.* 349c4–6, *G.* 483c2, d1, 490a8); law itself is required by the necessities of nature (6.1), for the security everyone wants.

2. It is imprudent to try large-scale injustice; if justice and law are generally respected, an aspiring tyrant must be a man of steel to fight the shared interests of the many (6.2–5); only bad laws and neglect of law give a tyrant his chance (7.15–16).

3. A wise man who wants fame and status will not need to dissemble vice, but will be as virtuous as he seems (2.1–3); since laws maintain human society, other people will admire him and he will do best for himself if he is law-abiding (3.6; cf. Isoc. *Antid.* 281 f.).

This defence of virtue as the best policy does not dispose of radical criticism. Even if some law-abiding system is in everyone's interest, we might benefit by changing the system, or by breaking the rules when it is safe. Glaucon rejects the last argument; it implies that apparent justice benefits a man, and that real justice would not, if its rewards were removed. Antiphon replies reasonably that a wise man will observe the laws when there are witnesses, and not otherwise, since only the social rewards and punishments make just actions beneficial and unjust actions painful (B 44, fr. A, col. 1.12–col. 2.23 = DK, pp. 346 f.).

5.3. *Democritus*. Democritus recognizes the distinction between nature and convention exploited by the radical critics, but uses his own metaphysical theory to defend the anonymous writer's defence of conventional justice by appeal to nature. Sensible qualities exist by convention, and only atoms and void exist by nature (B 9); but the virtues exist by nature because they are conditions of the atomic structure of the soul. The best and pleasantest condition of the soul is undisturbed harmony of the atoms (B 191); harmony requires the wisdom to prevent disturbance (B 31); and wisdom requires the avoidance of the distress caused by greedy and intemperate desires, and the pursuit of recognized temperance and justice. Democritus' position is strikingly parallel to Socrates', and open to similar objections.[26] Even if he could show that stability of psychic atoms is clearly the most desirable condition, it does not follow that this stability is secured always and only by recognized justice; and we do not know from the surviving evidence that Democritus proves the connection he needs. He avoids the anonymous writer's appeals to reputation and respectability (B 264), relying on a more general metaphysical theory. But he does not refute the radical critics.

6. *Socrates' and Plato's replies*

6.1. *Restrictions on the virtues*. We should not take for granted Socrates' limitation of his inquiries to the short list of virtues which interests him. Other characteristics which benefit the agent or other people are wealth, health, strength, high birth, and so on. Homeric values readily count these as *aretai*; but Socrates ignores them. He also denies that virtues vary with sex, age, and status (*M.* 71e1–72a5), claiming that everyone needs the same virtues (73a1–c5)—though he does not imply that the same virtues will always prescribe the same actions.[27] Why does he restrict the virtues this way?

Some of these recognized *aretai* are non-voluntary; and Socrates assumes that real virtue depends on a man's own actions. He wants to know if virtue can be taught; to show that it can, he examines the apparently most teachable virtues. No one would suppose that good birth could be taught; but courage, temperance, and the rest seem to be learnt to some extent through voluntary action, though not as systematically and successfully as crafts are learnt. Socrates assumes that the virtues which count—the ones which really decide whether a man lives well—are in a man's power, and therefore that his own actions, not only external or non-voluntary conditions, influence his happiness.

These other alleged virtues are more easily dismissed if they are not real virtues at all, as Socrates believes. His comments on the failure of aristocratic parents to teach real virtue to their children show that he does not think good birth and the accepted good upbringing really produce the right results (*Pr.* 319d7–320b3, *M.* 93c6–94e2). Characters in the dialogues illustrate the problem. Lysimachus and Melesias in the *Laches* are both mediocre sons of virtuous fathers, and they want to teach their sons to be more successful than they are (*La.* 179c2–d5). In the *Charmides* Socrates emphasizes Charmides' and Critias' good family and upbringing (*Ch.* 157d9–158b5); but the dialogue suggests that these advantages do not make them really temperate.[28] The traditional virtues discounted by Socrates are natural assets which can be used well or badly, and do not deserve the title of virtues without reservations, since they will not reliably make a man good (*Eud.* 279a4–b3, 280d1–281a1), either for his own expectations or for other people's. This same argument rules out other recognized virtues which are capable of misuse, especially intelligence and skill in various crafts and techniques. Being a good orator is a good, but not an unqualified good, since the skill may sometimes be misused, and need some further virtue to use it correctly; this further virtue will be the only virtue without qualification (*Eud.* 281d2–e5, *M.* 87e5–88d3).

6.2. *Soucres of conflict.* Socrates says he is concerned with questions about 'the good' (*agathon*), 'the admirable' (*kalon*) and 'the just' (*dikaion*) (*Eu.* 7c10–d5, *Cri.* 47c9–10, *G.* 459d1–2, *R.* 493c1, 520c5; cf. Heracleitus B 102); for they seem to raise particularly intractable disputes. Justice is especially prominent because it is both the all-inclusive virtue and the hardest to reconcile with the assumption that virtue should be in the agent's interest. 'Admirable' and 'good' create their problems too. It is easy to agree that a virtue is admirable, and therefore good from some point of view; but it hardly follows that it is good for the agent.[29]

Socrates wants to know what each of the virtues is; this is a worthwhile and hard question because of the conflicting principles and demands accepted in ordinary beliefs. Different virtues raise different problems. Someone might be puzzled about which actions are temperate; should they display self-control, or good sense, and what does self-control or good sense require? He might be less puzzled about which actions are brave, but doubt whether bravery (as he understands it) is really a virtue. Though he could recognize just actions in ordinary conditions, he might be puzzled when the laws are silent or apparently wrong, and doubt whether it is always worth while to be just. These problems about the virtues may be concealed if the actions prescribed by conventional morality for normal conditions are not clearly incompatible; but the problems will emerge when someone accepts Socrates' invitation to describe the standard (*paradeigma*) for judging something virtuous, and finds that he judges by standards which produce conflicting results. And this conflict will affect someone's actions, in more difficult situations where conventional morality gives uncertain guidance; if he can rely on no definite prescription to do this or that, and tries to find the right principles to project from familiar to unfamiliar conditions, he may find conflicting principles with conflicting demands. That is why questions about the virtues cause apparently insoluble disputes.

6.3. *Socrates' questions.* Socrates looks for an answer to his 'what is it?' question which will provide clear guidance for judgements about whether something is virtuous (cf. *Eu.* 6e3–6). He is not simply seeking clarification of the common concept of bravery or temperance. Prodicus looks for this kind of clarification by distinguishing the meanings of terms likely to be confused; his clarifications are important, when they distinguish courage from mere daring (*La.* 197b6–c1, d1–5). But Socrates goes beyond Prodicus' interests.[30] He wants not merely a clear statement of the meaning of moral terms, but something much harder to achieve, an account of the virtues which will be a better guide to action than the conflicting beliefs of ordinary morality.

However, Socrates does not find the right accounts. He exposes the conflicts and inconsistencies in ordinary beliefs by the method of cross-examination (*elenchos*); and we have seen why the different traditions expressed in ordinary beliefs make his task comparatively easy. The virtues are expected to include justice, making someone a good law-abiding citizen, and at the same time to be good for the agent himself; and both these expectations are liable to conflict with ordinary beliefs about virtuous action. Socrates simply exposes the conflict without trying to remove it or to find a satisfactory account of the virtues; and the natural result of his questions might seem to be moral scepticism, refusal to admit that any account of the virtues is more rationally acceptable than any other. The 'Double Arguments' (*Dissoi Logoi*) claim to offer equally cogent arguments for and against disputed moral principles; Socrates' method, applied to any account of the virtues, seems to be equally capable of refuting all candidates, and leaving no acceptable answer.[31]

6.4 *Socrates and the sophists.* Socrates and Plato have sometimes been contrasted with 'the sophists', as defenders of traditional morality against the solvent tendencies of sophistic criticism. Both sides of this contrast are wrongly drawn. There is no collective view of 'the sophists'; and Plato never suggests that all or most sophists are hostile to traditional morality. He rejects popular prejudices against the supposed dangers of sophistic education (*M.* 91a6–92c7); and he criticizes sophists for just the opposite reason, that they uncritically accept and defend ordinary beliefs about morality (*R.* 493a6–d7). The sympathetic presentation of Protagoras illustrates this objection; the sophist simply describes and develops conventional views, but cannot justify them, or show that what seems true to most people really is the truth about morals. Callicles the radical critic is no sophist; and even if Thrasymachus is one, Plato never suggests that his view is at all typically sophistic. Nor are Socrates and Plato obvious advocates of traditional values. The destructive scrutiny of ordinary beliefs seems much more likely to undermine confidence than any sophistic education would; and Socrates and Plato do not deny it.[32]

6.5. *Socrates and radical critics.* Socrates and Plato are often presented as opponents, not only of the sophists, but also of the radical critics (especially when sophists and radical critics are wrongly identified). But they agree with several of the radical critics' demands, and find it hard to reject the rest. Socrates assumes, and his interlocutors agree that each virtue is admirable (*kalon*) (*Ch.* 159e1; *La.* 192c5–7; *Pr.* 349e3–8, 359e4–5), good (*agathon*), and beneficial (*ōphelimon*) (*Pr.* 360b3; *Ch.* 160b6–13; *La.* 192c8–d8; *Eud.* 279b4–c1). But Socrates also assumes, and they agree, that virtue must be good for the agent and contribute to his happiness (*M.* 88b1–3; *Ch.* 175c9–176a1; *Eud.* 278e3–279a2). We have seen that this is a natural assumption about at least some virtues, when the agent's own expectations are considered. But Socrates applies it to all the virtues; he assumes that a real virtue will always be worth while, and infers that it must always benefit the agent.

Here Socrates agrees with the radical critics. And he must explain his attitude to the conventional virtues they attack. Their claim that justice benefits other people, not the agent, is quite plausible; we might think a defender of conventional virtue should concede this, and reject the assumption that someone has reason to do only what benefits him. While my benefit is one good reason for action, neither the radical critic nor Socrates shows it is the only good reason. He assumes that self-interested prudential wisdom and the other virtues do not conflict, and indeed imply each other; but he has no immediate support from ordinary beliefs. Since he criticizes conventional beliefs about the virtues, and requires real virtue to benefit the agent, it is hard to see why Socrates can avoid agreement with the radical attack on conventional virtues, especially the parts of them which benefit other people.

6.6. *Socrates' defence of virtue.* It is easy to miss these questions about Socrates' position, because he never expresses open scepticism about the recognized virtues. He regularly praises justice, temperance, and courage, and displays them in his own actions. But he does not show how his attitude is justified, or why he can accept so many of the radical critics' assumptions without being committed to their conclusions. Socrates' different views seem hard to connect, and even hard to reconcile; for he combines destructive criticism of ordinary moral beliefs and controversial assumptions about virtue and the agent's benefit with praise of the recognized virtues. Can he justify these claims, or even justify one from the other?

Socrates' prospects depend on the powers of his elenctic method; for he presents all three kinds of conclusions as though they were justified by elenctic argument; and we must see whether he can fairly claim to overcome the problems in other theories. Though we have seen that Socrates' contemporaries both raise and answer many of the questions which concern Socrates and Plato, Socrates uses a new method, elenctic inquiry. His method justifies the claim that he is the first to do moral philosophy; the others examined philosophical questions, but he is the first to treat them with a philosophical method. What this method is, and whether it will do what Socrates and Plato expect—these are the next questions.[33]

III SOCRATIC METHOD AND MORAL THEORY

1. Socrates' methods of ethics

1.1. *The problem.* Socrates' audience are confused about their own moral beliefs, and face radical criticism of the recognized virtues. But he seems to answer none of their questions about the virtues; he raises further questions, and seems to offer no constructive replies. He interrogates people by his method of examination (the elenchos); he asks them to say what a virtue is, shows that each definition they offer conflicts with their other beliefs about the virtue, and eventually reduces them to confusion. He wants to show their ignorance about morals, and professes to know nothing himself. The apparent result of this method would be further confusion about morality, or at least scepticism about the prospects of reaching justified and reliable beliefs (*Eu.* 11b6–e1). Socrates has positive moral convictions; he is recognized as brave (*La.* 181a7–b4, 188c6–189c7), and temperate (*Ch.* 176b5–8); he insists above all on justice (*Ap.* 28b5–9). But these convictions seem to be unconnected with his criticisms of other people's beliefs; apparently he violates his own disclaimer of knowledge about morals, and evades the critical scrutiny which would undermine his confidence. Still less could we expect his philosophical methods to support his beliefs; they expose inconsistencies and justify no positive conclusions. The negative criticism and the positive convictions are important in Socrates' life and practice, as far as it appears in the early dialogues; but only the negative criticism seems to be supported by philosophical argument.[1]

I intend to argue that Socrates is a constructive theorist, and that the constructive ethical theory both influences and is influenced by his critical methods. The elenchos—apparently just a devices for exposing confusion and inconsistency—is used to support positive doctrines. Not all the positive doctrines rely on the elenchos; some rely on the analogy between virtue and craft (*technē*), to be discussed later. But those which do rely on the elenchos deserve study by themselves, to see the powers of the elenchos and the strengths and weaknesses of the doctrines.

1.2 *Positive doctrines*. In most dialogues the negative view of Socrates' methods seems obviously correct. He professes no positive views. He asks the questions; the interlocutor proposes the definitions and rejects them when they conflict with his other beliefs. We learn that the interlocutor's beliefs are inconsistent; we seem to learn nothing about Socrates' beliefs, which appear irrelevant to the whole process.

Not all the dialogues are elenctic. The *Apology* and *Crito* present Socrates' own moral convictions. The *Apology* does not say how he would defend them, but the *Crito* does; he claims to follow the strongest argument found by examination (46b3–c1), and when several examinations of a question have reached the same conclusion, he accepts it. But still he invites Crito to re-examine the conclusion, and when Crito refuses, takes it as an agreed basis for further argument (48b3–6, b11–c2). Socrates claims that his positive views rest on agreements secured by the elenchos, and corrigible by an elenctic examination.

The elenchos can support these claims, even though Socrates always examines other people's beliefs and never his own (cf. *R.* 337e1–3; *Tht.* 150c3–7). For if the interlocutor denies a Socratic position, but is induced to reject his denial by a fair argument, and finally agrees with Socrates, Socrates can claim some (by no means conclusive) support for his position. He can defend the *Crito's* claims about his convictions, if he can show that his views will, and his opponent's views will not, survive the elenchos (*G.* 509a4–7).

Socrates values the negative, therapeutic function of the elenchos (*Tht.* 151c5; *Sph.* 230d6–e3), when it removes false pretensions to knowledge (*Ap.* 21 c3–e2, 29e3–30a2; *Ch.* 166c7–d2) and exposes the interlocutor's ignorance (*La.* 199e13–200a8; *Eu.* 15d4–e2). But this therapy should precede positive progress towards the truth (*Ch.* 166d2–6; *Sph.* 230c3–d4), which is Socrates' goal (*Ch.* 165b5–9). When he advises people to take virtue seriously (*Ap.* 30a7–b3; *Cri.* 53c6–8), and argue about it daily (*Ap.* 38c1–5), he promises not only that his methods will expose any lingering confusions, and produce a healthy moral scepticism in place of thoughtless dogma, but also that they will improve moral convictions. The negative procedure of the elenchos does not refute this claim.

1.3. *Agreed examples*. The critical dialogues (the *Euthyphro*, *Laches*, *Charmides*, and *Lysis*) end inconclusively with the rejection of all candidates for an account of a virtue, but with no positive answer.[2] Socrates, like everyone else, appears to take this conclusion seriously; but it does not show that no positive doctrine is accepted in the argument. Typically, an interlocutor's proposed definition of a virtue is refuted by counter-examples which do not satisfy the definition. If the elenchos were meant simply to expose inconsistency in beliefs, the interlocutor would be free to amend his position by retaining his definition and rejecting the counter-examples. But normally he is not allowed this freedom; the counter-examples refute the definition, because they express moral judgements accepted by Socrates and the interlocutor alike.[3] The interlocutor is required to answer sincerely, because the elenchos tests his moral judgements, and not simply his ability to maintain a consistent case (*La.* 193c6–8; *Cri.* 49d1; *Pr.* 331b8–d1; *G.* 495a5–b6; *Tht.* 154c7–e6). These agreements reached in a dialogue mark progress towards understanding a virtue, even if they do not yield an acceptable definition.

1.4. *Agreed principles.* Agreement is not confined to isolated examples, but includes general principles which control the direction of argument:

1. Socrates rejects efforts to define a virtue through types of action, and seeks an account of a state of the soul.
2. He insists that any virtue must always be admirable (*kalon*), good (*agathon*), and beneficial (*ōphelimon*); any definition which does not conform to this principle must be rejected. (*Ch.* 159c1, 160e6; *La.* 192c5–7; *Pr.* 349e3–5, 359e4–7; *M.* 87e1–3; *R.* 331c5–9.)

These Socratic principles accepted by the interlocutor are vital for the argument; the second one especially is always accepted, and never taken to be merely provisional. Socrates believes that an interlocutor who accepts these principles, and adjusts his other beliefs about virtue to fit them, will make progress, and reach positive results.

1.5. *The disclaimer of knowledge.* The 'negative' view of the elenchos might claim support from Socrates' repeated insistence that he does not know what any of the virtues is, and cannot answer his own questions. (*Ap.* 21b1–d7; *Eu.* 5a3–c7; 15c11–16a4; *Ch.* 165b4–c2, 166c7–d6; *La.* 186b8–c5, d8–e3, 200e2–5; *Lys.* 212a4–7, 223b4–8; *G.* 509c4–7; *M.* 71a1–7, 80d1–4; *HMa.* 286c8–e2, 304d4–e5; *Symp.* 216d1–4.) These repeated disclaimers of knowledge are too frequent and emphatic to be dismissed as ironical without strong reason; Aristotle takes them seriously (*SE* 183b6–8), and so should we.

However, a disclaimer of knowledge does not require a disclaimer of all positive convictions. Socrates observes strict conditions for knowledge, and allows knowledge about virtue only to someone who can answer the Socratic question and say what it is (*Eu.* 5c4–d1; *La.* 190c6; *HMa.* 286c8–d2). Failure in the elenchos is proof that someone has no knowledge (*Ap.* 21c3–22a5, 29e3–30a2). If Socrates demands this stringent justification for a claim to knowledge, it is not surprising that he claims no knowledge for himself. But he can still claim positive beliefs, which lack this stringent explicit justification, but are still reliable. Socrates does not explicitly distinguish knowledge from true belief; but his test for knowledge would make it reasonable for him to recognize true belief without knowledge, and his own claims are easily understood if they are claims to true belief alone. Though he has no knowledge, he is better off than his interlocutor; the elenchos exposes conflicts in an interlocutor's beliefs till they desert him and leave him confused (*Eu.* 11b6–e6), but Socrates' own beliefs do not conflict, and remain stable and reliable under examination (*Cri.* 48b3–e2, *G.* 508e6–509a4). His belief that it is better to suffer than to do injustice survives the elenchos (so he claims in the *Gorgias*) because the interlocutor finds that his denial of the Socratic belief conflicts with other more basic beliefs of his; Socrates, then, has *some* reason for confidence in his beliefs, even though he cannot find the account of justice or the good which would justify them.

1.6. *The priority of definition.* Our view of Socrates' disclaimer of knowledge will also decide our verdict on one of his basic and most puzzling procedural principles. Often he says or implies that we cannot know anything about, say, virtue until we know what virtue is (*M.* 71b3–7), and 'knowing what it is' requires us to say what it is, give a Socratic account of it (*La.* 190b7–c5). Now if 'know anything about *x*' includes all true beliefs about *x*, Socrates means that we cannot claim to recognize cases of virtue or virtuous action until we can define virtue. This requirement would be not only eccentric in itself, but disastrous for his method; for his refutations rely on the interlocutors' recognition of examples without a definition. And it would be no less disastrous for his own practice; for he claims positive beliefs about the virtues with no definitions, the very claim which his principle is supposed to reject. The principle justifies the search for a definition; but if no definition can be found without prior knowledge of examples, which itself depends on a definition, the principle also makes the search futile and misguided.

These consequences follow from Socrates' principles only if 'know' is taken to include all true belief. If he observes a distinction between knowledge and true belief, he avoids these objections; he can insist that without knowledge of what virtue is we cannot have fully justified beliefs about virtue, and still allow us true beliefs to recognize examples of virtue. Since 'know' in 'know what virtue is' requires the support of a Socratic definition, it is reasonable to infer that it will require the same support in 'know about virtue'. Socrates does not explicitly disown the self-defeating view of his principle; but he never explicitly or implicitly endorses it, and we have no good reason to ascribe it to him. He allows both his interlocutors and himself true beliefs without knowledge; his procedural principle still needs defence, but it is not self-defeating.[4]

1.7. *Consistency and truth.* Efforts to show how the elenchos yields positive doctrines face one powerful objection; whatever Socrates may think, the formal structure of the elenchos allows him to test consistency, not to discover truth. If I survive an elenchos with my original beliefs intact, I have some reason to believe they are consistent; but they may be consistently crazy. Why, for instance, should Laches not maintain his position by rejecting alleged cases of non-martial courage, or by denying that courage is always admirable? (*La.* 191c7–e7, 192c4–7.) Socrates does not allow this kind of defence; but is he justified?

The agreed beliefs about examples and about general principles allow Socrates to steer the elenchos in the direction he wants. The interlocutor will find a conflict in his beliefs between his definition of a virtue, his beliefs that particular actions and people are virtuous, and his belief that virtue is always admirable and good. Socrates expects him to resolve the conflict by retaining the second and third beliefs and rejecting any definition which conflicts with them; and he supposes that adjustment in this direction will lead nearer the truth. This is partly an empirical claim, about what particular interlocutors will do; but naturally Socrates tries to influence them in the direction he prefers; and we must see whether the assumptions which support his efforts can be defended.

Socrates looks for answers to his requests for definitions; though he does not expect they will be easily found, his questions are no mere opening gambits. He uses the elenchos to approach an answer. We have not yet found that his confidence is justified, but we have found no decisive objections. Aristotle recognizes Socrates' disclaimer of knowledge; but he sees no conflict with a search for definition to discover the truth (*Met.* 1078b23–30); we should see no conflict.

2. *Problems in defining virtues*

2.1 Socrates' demand. Socrates begins an examination by demanding a definition of the relevant virtue. Though some interlocutors think the demand is easily satisfied, they soon find they were overconfident (*Eu.* 5d1–e2; *La.* 190c4–7, e4–6; *M.* 71e1; *HMa.* 287d7–e6); but Socrates, who cannot answer the question himself, realizes its difficulty. Still he insists on it because he expects important results. He wants an answer to his question to show what the pious is, with a single character or form in all pious actions (*Eu.* 5d1–5); when he knows what character or form the pious has, he can use the character as a standard to decide whether an action is pious or not (*Eu.* 6d9–e6; 72c6–d1).

The interlocutor's first answer does not satisfy Socrates, and he often complains that it is not the right sort of answer. (*Eu.* 6d1–e1; *La.* 190e7–9, 191c7–192b8; *M.* 72a6–73c8; *HMa.* 287e5–289d5; *Tht.* 146d3–147c6, 148c9–d7.) He is dissatisfied because the interlocutor offers examples, and not a general definition. Why is this a reason for Socrates to complain?

Perhaps the interlocutors simply misunderstand Socrates' question, and do not know the difference between a definition of piety or the pious and an example of something pious. But Socrates never suggests that they cannot distinguish the two questions; he suggests that they are wrong to offer examples to answer his request for a definition. Here we might sympathize with the interlocutors; why would it not be useful to begin a search for a definition with examples which the definition must cover?[5] Perhaps Socrates' claim about the priority of definition does mislead him.

Some of this criticism is fair. Socrates' failure to consider a variety of examples makes it easier for him to assume that just one answer to his question can be found for each virtue, and there is a single character or form of piety and the rest; this 'Unity Assumption' (UA) must be criticized later. But he does not ignore examples altogether; objections to a definition depend on the interlocutor's recognition of examples, and definitions are gradually improved by exposure to these counter-examples. Socrates' main point is that examples do not answer his main question, about the common character which would provide a standard for judging whether something is pious. We may be able to identify examples of pious actions in ordinary conditions, and state rules to justify them; but Socrates wants a way to project these rules to difficult cases, where, like Euthyphro, we cannot easily decide what an example of a pious action would be. He is right to say that a mere list of easy cases or familiar rules about a virtue will not answer his question; if the question is legitimate at all, he must find the explicit understanding of a virtue which will allow projection to difficult cases.

2.2 *Behavioural accounts.* We might suppose that Socrates' request for an account of the pious or the brave would be answered by a single description of pious or brave actions applying to each of them. But he rejects attempts to define virtues by reference to virtuous actions, and indeed appears to think that UA, the demand for a single form, requires him to reject them. He refutes Charmides' effort to define temperance as 'gentle' or 'quiet' behaviour, by producing cases where 'gentle' or 'slow' behaviour would be bad (*Ch.* 159b7–160d4).[6] We are inclined to protest; Charmides never meant that running gently and slowly displayed the kind of gentleness found in temperance. But that is the point; if he means to define temperance as a certain way of behaving, the definition must restrict the behaviour to temperate behaviour. If Charmides cannot suitably limit the relevant kinds of gentleness, Socrates' objection is sound. Similarly, Laches did not mean that the 'flight' of Scythian mounted archers or of the Spartans at Plataea in a tactical retreat was the flight of cowards, and of course it is only cowardly flight he means to reject. But he identifies cowardly flight by relying on our views on courage, which are to be explained, not merely presupposed.

Some other accounts may be too narrow to capture the range of a virtue. (Some accounts may be both too narrow and too wide.) Socrates persuades Laches that courage can be displayed elsewhere than in battle; men can be brave in facing danger at sea, or disease, or poverty, brave in public affairs, and in resisting pains, fears, appetites, or pleasures (*La.* 191d3–e2). We might be surprised that Laches accepts all these examples at once; he might fairly object that Socrates stretches the ordinary concept of courage.[7] But Socrates shows him the common features shared by those actions and the original examples of courage; in all of them someone sticks to his resolve and does what he thinks best despite strong inducements to abandon his resolve. All these actions display the moral features

Laches saw in the original cases; and the limitation to certain kinds of situations comes to seem arbitrary.

A behavioural account may avoid these problems—but only, Socrates thinks, if it is too vague to be informative. 'A temperate man does his own' (*Ch.* 163b3–c8) is hard to refute (except for the problem about self-consciousness at 164a1–3); but it does not help us to identify temperate actions or men—and the explanation referring to 'the practice of good actions' (163e10) is no help. 'A just man gives men their due, or what is fitting' (cf. *R.* 332b9–c3) is irrefutable, but useless; when it is made clear, it can be refuted.[8] If we try to avoid objections with an amended behavioural account like 'The just man pays his debts when it is fitting', and try to specify the virtue with limited behavioural rules, we shall not cover the full scope of the virtue; for the just man may find scope for just action prescribed by no rules.

2.3 *Objections to behavioural accounts.* Socrates rejects behavioural accounts because he believes that virtuous actions cannot be identified by our ordinary ways of classifying actions. We tend to think that standing firm and running away, or returning what we have borrowed and keeping what we have borrowed are not the same kind of action. But from the virtuous man's point of view these will count as the same kind of action, acting bravely or justly, in the right conditions. The classification which matters to him depends on the point of a particular action, and two otherwise quite different actions with the same point may both be the brave or just thing to do. Unless we see the point of the virtuous man's actions, we cannot see what range of actions will count as doing the virtuous thing. Socrates shows Laches that when we see the point of very dissimilar (in one way) actions in war, public affairs, sickness, and so on, and see that they are all meant as ways of enduring against evils, we shall see why the brave man is right to count them all as doing the same thing. If we try to find what is the same about them by simply observing the behaviour without considering the agent's aims and intentions, we shall fail.

2.4. *Tendencies and states.* Socrates relies on a powerful line of objection to behavioural accounts; and if he were asked to show why a virtue cannot be just a readily observable pattern of action, that the 'one form' must be something other than a kind of action, he could defend himself. We can now see what is wrong with the argument he uses to defend his rejection of behavioural accounts, and how his position could be strengthened. He looks for a single 'power', bravery, displayed in all brave actions, and suggests that the UA requires this kind of answer. But his argument is confused. He offers the example of speed, which is the same in all speedy things, the power which achieves much in little time (*La.* 192a1–b3).[9] Is this the kind of 'single power' he wants?

We can speak of a single power in two ways:

(a) x and y have the same A-power when each of them does F (where F is some kind of behaviour); each of them has the power to F.

(b) x and y have the same B-power when each of them is in the same state, G, which causes their behaviour.

Socrates' term 'power' (*dunamis*) covers both A-powers, which might be called 'tendencies', and B-powers, or 'states'. A-powers are identified by their behavioural expressions; if x's and y's behaviour is the same their A-power is the same. Socrates' account of speed treats it as an A-power. But B-powers are not so directly related to behaviour. A type of behaviour may encourage a search for a B-power, if, say, we look for the condition which causes the symptoms of measles. But when we have found the condition, we may identify and examine it in chemical terms; we shall know that two people are in the same state without reference to their symptoms if we know their chemical condition. While an A-power can correspond to several B-powers, a single B-power can also cause different (from one point of view) kinds of behaviour, and so correspond to several A-powers.

Now if Socrates' objections to behavioural accounts were right, a virtue cannot be an A-power. With an A-power like punctuality (let us suppose), we can identify the behaviour to be expected of the punctual man apart from its aim—the actual or intended results of his normally arriving on time are irrelevant to his being punctual or not. But Socrates' objections to behavioural accounts of virtue have shown that there is no easy way of identifying the brave man's behaviour analogous to 'arriving on time' for the punctual man's behaviour; brave actions are identified as those a brave man with the brave man's aims would do. Neither the A-power of standing firm nor the A-power of fleeing can be bravery, since each of these powers may sometimes be expressed in both brave and cowardly actions. A virtue, then, should be a B-power; the power will not be identified by an observed similarity in behaviour, but brave actions will be those which would be produced by bravery. This does not mean that only brave people can do brave actions, but that an account of brave action depends on an account of a brave person.

Since a virtue is a B-power, and speed is an A-power, Socrates' defence of his approach to virtue by the example of speed is misguided. He assumes too readily that the UA licenses his demand for a single B-power; at most it requires a single A- or B-power, and does not decide which. Socrates' bad argument blinds him to his further claim, that the virtues are B-powers, and he does not argue for it as he should. But his negligence is not fatal to his position; for the arguments he needs can be found by reflection on his objections to behavioural accounts, which offer strong grounds for his implied claim that virtue must be a B-power.

2.5. *Characters and actions.* If this is Socrates' view, an apparent source of confusion can be removed. We are inclined to think he makes his task harder for himself by the unclarity of his questions—he does not decide whether he wants an account of the predicate 'pious' or 'brave' applied to actions, or of the virtue of piety or bravery in persons. The *Euthyphro*'s progress from questions about Euthyphro's allegedly Pious action to questions about piety in persons illustrates Socrates' regular move from predicates of actions to virtues in persons.[10] Whether or not he is clear about his move, it is defensible. If he is right to treat virtues as B-powers, then an account of a virtue in a person will be necessary for, and prior to, an account of virtuous action. It will not be prior to recognition of particular virtuous actions; they will be the material for discovery of a B-power, if there is one to be discovered, since we will look for the B-power which produces these actions or most of them. But rules about virtuous actions will not by themselves fix the scope of the virtue.

2.6. *States of character and wisdom.* When the interlocutor tries to define a virtue as a state of character, suggesting that courage is endurance or temperance is modesty, Socrates still objects. Laches agrees that courage is admirable and good; but endurance is sometimes disgraceful and harmful; so endurance cannot be courage (*La.* 192b9–d8). Charmides' suggestion is refuted in the same way (*Ch.* 160e2–161b2). A condition of feelings or emotions which is not guided by some kind of wisdom cannot produce the actions expected from a virtue (*La.* 192c8–d2).

The next problem is to specify the kind of wisdom needed to avoid Socrates' objections. He examines Laches' revised account of courage as wise endurance, and shows how a man's endurance may be irrelevant to his courage, if it is displayed when questions about what is good and bad over all are not at stake (*La.* 192e1–193a1). He then turns to trickier cases, where *A* (because he is an expert or for some other reason happens to know the right answer) knows enough to face the situation confidently, and *B* is ignorant of what *A* knows, but faces it anyhow (193a3–c5). Laches agrees that in these cases *B* is braver than *A* (193c6–d10). He now faces an awkward choice between the claims accepted:

1. Courage is wise endurance.
2. Courage is always admirable.
3. Socrates' cases were genuine cases of courage.
4. They show that sometimes the ignorant are braver than the wise.
5. Ignorance is always disgraceful and wisdom admirable.

Laches might resolve the conflict by denying (3) and (4), and rejecting these alleged cases of courage because they seem to conflict with (1), (2), and (5). But Socrates urges him to follow his initial judgement, (3) (193c6–8). Alternatively Laches might reject (2); but Socrates does not suggest it, and would not allow it. As usual, the judgements about particular cases, and the general belief that a virtue is admirable and good are held constant.

Socrates rejects (4). He has asked what kind of wisdom is needed for brave endurance (192e1); and (3) shows only that *B* can be braver than *A* even if he knows less about the present conditions, or about diving, if he dives to rescue someone drowning. (3) does not show that *B* knows less than *A* about what is best to do in these conditions.[11] If *B* knows enough about the good to know that this dangerous action is the best one, he will do it bravely and wisely (cf. *Pr.* 359c2–e1). Nicias avoids Laches' dilemma by replacing the vague reference to wisdom with 'knowledge of what is to be feared and faced with confidence' (194d1–195a1); and this knowledge is found to be identical with knowledge of good and evil (198b1–199c1).

2.7. *Socrates' conclusion.* Laches' problem suggests to Socrates that an adequate definition of a virtue cannot simply mention a character-trait. Unless it is controlled by knowledge of the good, that trait will not be virtuous. The same argument would apply if Charmides amended his account of temperance from 'modesty' to 'wise modesty'. In the argument with Critias Socrates shows that the relevant kind of wisdom is the knowledge of good and evil. To avoid the systematic failure of accounts referring to states of character, we must always qualify them by reference to knowledge of the good.

3. *Socrates' method of refutation*

3.1. *Definitions and reasons.* Socrates assumes that an explanation of why an action is virtuous must show why it is worth while. He rejects Euthyphro's account of the pious as the god-beloved on this score. To say that an action is god-beloved does not explain why the gods love it; and Socrates assumes that the answer 'because it is pious', when properly understood, should state the reason (*Eu.* 10d1–7)—though it will not give the complete account of the reason until we replace 'pious' with the right definition (10e9–11b1).[12] To defend his assumption that the gods love what is pious because it is *pious*, and not for some other reason, Socrates must rely on a general claim that any virtue must show what is worth while about it, and therefore an account which fails this test must be rejected.

3.2. *The general argument.* Socrates does not formulate the generalization of the *Euthyphro*-assumption. But it underlies his use of counter-examples; for he regularly argues that an account fails because it allows actions and states which would not be worth while, and therefore not virtuous. His argument looks simple and powerful; but it rests on controversial assumptions. To show, for instance, that courage cannot be mere endurance, Socrates must argue as follows:

L1.   Endurance is courage (*La.* 192b9–c1).

L2.   Courage is a virtue.

L3.   Any virtue is always a good and admirable state for a person to have (*M.* 87d2–3).

L4.   Anything good is beneficial (*M.* 87e1–2).

L5.   Therefore courage is always a good, admirable, and beneficial state for a person to have (*La.* 192c4–6).

L6.   Therefore, if endurance is courage, it is always a good, admirable, and beneficial state.

L7.   Any good and beneficial state will always produce the good and beneficial action (*M.* 87d8–e4).

L8.   The good and beneficial action will always be the best one to do.

L9.   Therefore the brave action will always be the best one to do.

L10. Therefore if endurance is courage, the enduring action will always be best.

L11. But sometimes the enduring action will not be best (if the endurance is foolish).

L12. Therefore foolish endurance is not good or admirable.

L13. Therefore endurance is not always good or admirable.

L14. Therefore endurance is not courage (*La.* 192d7–9).

In the Laches only L1, L5, L12, and L14 are explicit; but the other steps must be supplied to connect or defend the explicit steps. A parallel argument is needed to show that temperance is not gentleness or modesty, or to show that justice is not debt-paying. Since this form of argument does so much for Socrates, the steps deserve close scrutiny.

3.3. *'Admirable' and 'good'*. Socrates secures Laches' acceptance of L5 by pointing out that courage is admirable, and suggesting that the failure of endurance to be beneficial shows that it is not admirable (*La.* 192c4–d6). He shows at most that being beneficial is necessary for courage to be admirable. In the *Charmides* he argues more carefully, as follows:

C1. Temperance is admirable (160e6–7).

C2. Temperate men are good men (160e9).

C3. If anything makes men good it must itself be good (160e11).

C4. Therefore temperance is good.[13]

In the *Meno* Socrates assumes directly that virtue is good (*M.* 87d2–3). But even if we accept this, and support it by the *Charmides*'s argument, it shows only that virtue is some kind of good; it does not follow that every kind of good is admirable, or that an action which in some way fails to be good thereby fails to be admirable. Socrates never justifies his regular moves between 'good' and 'admirable' and back, and never explains why what is admirable cannot sometimes conflict with what is good.[14]

3.4. *'Good' and 'beneficial'*. The move from L3 to L4 is clearest in the *Meno* where Socrates argues:

M1. Virtue is good.

M2. Virtue makes us good.

M3. Everything good is beneficial.

M4. Virtue is beneficial and makes us beneficial (87d2–e4).

M5. Virtue makes us beneficial to ourselves (88b1–c3).

M1 could be defended by appeal to C1–C4; and the whole argument will support L5. But M3(=L4) is extremely dubious; if we agree with C4, we do not obviously accept M4, unless we refuse to recognize any conflict among goods. Nor does C2 obviously commit us to M4, or to the way Socrates interprets M4 in M5.

Until we know how 'beneficial' is to be understood, we do not know how strong a claim Socrates makes in M5. But at least we do not seem to be committed to it when we accept L3 or C2; we might protest that M3 explains the use of 'good' for artefacts and instruments designed for a particular task, but not its use for good men or good pictures, which are not instruments, have no task, and are not good for anything. To defend his assumption, Socrates must reply that the connection between being good, being virtuous, and being good for something applies no less to men than to instruments; though men are not designed for a task, their excellence or virtue still depends on some purpose and goal. Even if we agree, why should we accept Socrates' view of the goal? Why must a man's virtue always be beneficial to himself rather than to other people? Socrates' case needs fuller examination.

3.5. '*Always good*'. Whether or not we interpret 'beneficial' as M5 requires, should we accept L7? Socrates' attempted counter-examples collapse if we reply that courage is worth having because it is usually a good thing and leads to the best action, but may sometimes lead us astray. Socrates must insist that if an action is virtuous, a virtuous man will always have overriding reason to do it—otherwise his virtue will not guide his action as it should. He assumes that an action we have overriding reason to do must be good and beneficial, in a way not further explained by L7.

This same assumption that a virtuous man will always be guided by his virtue leads Socrates from L7 to L8. We might agree that a virtuous man always has *some* reason for doing a virtuous action, so that, with Socrates' view of a good reason, the virtuous action is always good and beneficial to *some* extent; but still we might deny that virtue is always supreme, that a man always has overriding reason to do the virtuous action. Socrates assumes that these limits on the rationality of virtue are wrong. He believes virtue is supreme, that we always have overriding and conclusive reason for doing the virtuous action, and that therefore the virtuous action must be 'the good one', not merely good to some extent, but the best on the whole. The belief that virtue is always worth while, explained by Socrates' view of what makes an action worthwhile, justifies L8.

These arguments and assumptions make the elenchos work for Socrates; he needs them to justify the conclusions he draws, that (e.g.) endurance is not courage, since otherwise he could conclude only that the interlocutor must give up some of his beliefs, without being able to say where he went wrong. Socrates assumes that any rational man confronted with the conflicts revealed by the elenchos will draw his conclusions; but this assumption itself rests on further views about virtue and action which need defence.

4. *The final good*

4.1. *Goods and the final good.* Socrates needs to explain and defend his claim that the virtuous action must always be best. The interlocutor removes conflicts in his beliefs by adjusting his moral rules and principles to his beliefs about what is best; but is he any better off? His unrevised beliefs created conflicts; but if his beliefs about what is best are chaotic, his moral beliefs will still conflict—if one action seems best from one point of view, another seems better from another, and he cannot decide between the two points of view.

To answer this problem Socrates explains the vague claim that virtue must always be good or beneficial, with the more definite claim that it must always lead to the agent's happiness (*eudaimonia*) (*M.* 88b1–3). He progresses from the apparently reasonable claim that nothing will be temperance which is not good, to the very strong and disputable claim that it must make the temperate man happy (*Ch.* 175c9–176a1). How has he a right to appeal to the agent's happiness?

The *Lysis*'s argument for the necessity of a 'primary object of love' (*prōton philon, Lys.* 219d1) exposes the general principles about desires and the structure of aims which guide Socrates' moral argument. Whenever A chooses x, his choice of x must be explained by his choice of some end—he chooses x for the sake of y; but his choice of y must in turn be explained by some further end, his choice of z ... and so on (*Lys.* 219c1–5). But now this process cannot continue for ever; we must recognize some object of desire not desired for any further end (219c5–d2). This primary object of desire is the good (220b–7); and it explains our desire for other objects; when we seem to want a subordinate object chosen for the sake of something else, and appear to be concerned about it, our concern is really for the primary object, or final good (219d5–220a6).

4.2. *The necessity of a final good.* Part of Socrates' claim is fairly easily understood; he means that A's seeking x is explained by a desire for x, and that this desire for x explains his action by showing what A sees in x—that he wants x for the sake of y. This is a familiar pattern of explanation by desire; but why is there a single end for all desires? Socrates offers only the lame plea that we must stop somewhere and a fallacious move to the conclusion that there must be just one terminus of all desire.[15] Aristotle's suggestion that a final good is required to prevent desire from being empty and pointless (*EN* 1094a18–22) perhaps explains Socrates' claim. If there were many termini for desire, goods would be just an inexplicable heap; it would not be clear why desire should reach a terminus in them, and there would be no way to decide priority among them. We could not know that something is really beneficial if it contributed to one good and deprived us of another. To decide if it is really beneficial we must know if it contributes to the rational structure of ends which achieves the final good. This defence is not offered by Socrates himself; and it clearly needs further support. But it explains why a rational order in desires must focus on a final good.

4.3. *Happiness and virtue.* The *Lysis* does not explicitly identify the primary object of love or final good with happiness, which is elsewhere taken to be the final good. But happiness is what we all want, and want for its own sake (*Eud.* 278e3–6, 280b5–6, 282a1–2), and subordinate goods are related to it as they were related to the final good in the *Lysis*—they are neither good nor bad in themselves, but contribute to happiness when they are rightly used (*Eud.* 281d2–e1; *Lys.* 220a1–5). Virtue must contribute to happiness, and must therefore include knowledge of what contributes to happiness; 'virtues' without knowledge of the good would sometimes harm us, because we would not always be sure of using them to achieve the good (*Eud.* 281c5–6; *M.* 88b3–6); if virtue is always a good, it includes knowledge of the good (*M.* 88b1–d3).[16]

Socrates will rely on this argument to show why virtue must contribute to happiness. Not everyone consciously pursues a final good; but anyone who knows what it means to pursue it will prefer to have his desires organized for its pursuit—virtuous and worthwhile actions or states of character will then be those which contribute best to the final good. Now a virtuous man will always regard virtue and virtuous action as worth while and will prefer them to anything else. His preference can be rationally justified only if his virtue and virtuous action can be shown to contribute to his final good. Socrates can now justify the procedure of the elenchos. Proposed accounts of virtues should be adjusted to beliefs about the final good, because they will then contribute to what a rational man will think most worth while; and the revised beliefs will be less prone to conflict than the original beliefs were, if beliefs about the good are not haphazard, but depend

on a rational order of goods converging on a final good. Socrates' interlocutors would be inclined to agree that virtues are good or worth
while from *some* point of view, the agent's or other people's, but not
necessarily all from the agent's. Socrates rejects this hesitation; he is
asking about the kind of life a man will find worth while for him, and
the kinds of virtues he will require in that life. The interlocutor and he
agree that a virtuous man will always have good reason to act virtuously; but Socrates apparently restricts the scope of 'good reason'
by insisting that someone has a good reason to do an action only if it
benefits him. We might have said that a virtuous man has good reason
to do actions which benefit others, not himself; but Socrates' account
of good reasons rules out this option.[17]

4.4. *The contents of the final good*. Socrates' demand that virtue
should contribute to the virtuous man's happiness is clearly controversial. But some controversy and some objections may rest on a misunderstanding of his demand. He is no less vague than I have been so
far in the exposition of his views about the nature of the final good; it
may be a single state or activity separate from all other goods, but it
could equally well be an ordered compound of more and less valuable
goods in themselves. Certainly Socrates implies in the *Lysis* and
Euthydemus that the recognized goods, such as health or wealth, will
not be part of the final good without proper use, since they may harm
us.[18] But this comment is still non-committal; he cannot be accused,
on this evidence alone, of refusing to allow a variety of goods in
themselves. The final good imposes a structure and hierarchy on
choices; but either a unitary or a compound good can do this.

4.5. *Hedonism*. To call the final good 'happiness' is not to insist on
any determinate content for it; for, as Aristotle says, we can agree that
the name for the final good is 'happiness' or (what is virtually the
same) 'living well', and still disagree about the contents of happiness
(*EN* 1095a14–26).[19] 'The final good is our own happiness' sounds
controversial; but it is not controversial because it implies some kind
of psychological or ethical hedonism, as it might in a later ethical
tradition. For Socrates, as for Plato and Aristotle, happiness has no
necessary connection with the agent's pleasure or contented
feeling—these might be important components of happiness, but some
further argument is needed to prove that they are.

4.6. *Egoism*. But still the question raised by Socrates' assumption

(M5) that our virtue must benefit ourselves can no longer be avoided. Even if we agree that some rational structure of goods is necessary to order our choices, why should we agree that the agent's good, rather than other people's good or some non-personal good, must be the ultimate end? When Socrates assumes that I have a good reason for doing only what benefits me, does he not rely on some psychological or ethical egoist thesis about virtue and motives? This question cannot be easily settled; but some unjustified attacks on Socrates can be avoided. If someone says that the final good is some desirable state of himself, his end will be purely self-confined; that is why a hedonist interpretation of Socrates will make it easy to think he is an egoist. But the mere claim that I have reason to aim at my final good does not say what the final good will be like; if all its components are self-confined, then my final good will be self-confined; but if they include concern for the good or harm of others for their own sake, my final good will be partly altruistic or sadistic. If we want to know if Socrates' final good is indifferent to the concern for others which we would take to be central in morality, we must see what its components are; we cannot simply reject the appeal to the agent's final good as clearly incompatible with morality.

We may agree that not all concepts of the final good are self-confined, but still maintain that the mere reference to the agent's final good is irrelevant to, and even incompatible with, a proper account or morality. This objection needs further discussion. So far I have only defended Socrates against one charge of egoism, and shown that the mere reference to the agent's happiness does not imply self-confined egoism. I have not shown that he is not a self-confined egoist; for I have not considered other beliefs of his which may commit him to more definite views on the content of the final good. But eudaimonism—reference to the agent's final good—by itself is not evidence of any straightforward kind of egoism.[20]

5. *The inseparability of the virtues*

5.1. *Socrates' argument.* Socrates' demand that virtue should contribute to happiness requires him to deny that the virtues are separable. He will argue as follows:

1. Bravery and brave action are always beneficial.
2. A man's character and actions will not always be beneficial unless he knows and pursues the final good.

3. A man will know and pursue the final good only if he has all the virtues.
4. Therefore a man will be brave and act bravely only if he has all the virtues.

In his defence of (2) Socrates agrees that a virtue without knowledge of the good would not be beneficial (*Eud.* 281b4–c7; *M.* 88b1–d3), but because of (1), he insists, this cannot be a real possibility. He rejects the ordinary view that courage is confidence in pursuing aims, and that temperance is control of desire, whether the purpose of the confidence and control are good or bad; the pseudo-courage separated from knowledge of the good will merely be some kind of boldness (*La.* 196e1–197c1; *Pr.* 350c1–5; *M.* 88b3–6). But if a brave man is to find what is really beneficial, he must evaluate his action from the point of view of all the virtues; and if he knows and achieves the final good, Socrates cannot deny him complete virtue, but must accept (3) and (4).

5.2. *Aristotle's argument.* This position is assumed rather than explained in the Socratic dialogues; it can usefully be compared with Aristotle's more systematic but strikingly similar argument embodied in the doctrine of the mean. Like Socrates, Aristotle denies that virtues like courage and temperance are traits like confidence and modesty which someone could display without knowledge of the good. The virtuous action must hit the mean, and avoid mistaken excess in these traits and their associated feelings (*EN* 1106b24–27); and the mean must be determined by the right conditions (1106b18–23), as the wise man would decide them (1106b36–1107a2). The wise man is needed because the virtue which hits the mean must contribute to the agent's happiness (1106a14–24), and the wise man knows what contributes to happiness (1140a25–8). A character trait without wisdom will not reliably benefit the agent; it will simply be a good natural capacity or 'natural virtue', not a real virtue (1144b8–14; cf. *M.* 88b1–c3. *Eud.* 281b4–d2). Real virtue requires wisdom (1144b14–17); a wise man has all the virtues; and so each virtue requires them all (1144b30–1145a2).

5.3. *Character traits.* Socrates' interlocutors assume that the virtues are separable because each requires a distinct character trait and the observance of a distinct set of rules. Socrates' view implies that there are no rules to define the scope of each virtue. He points to actions sanctioned by the recognized rules which would not be beneficial, and therefore would not be virtuous, or to virtuous actions which would not be sanctioned by the rule. Efforts to separate virtues by distinct sets of rules and character traits ignore the way a virtuous man aims at the best; to aim at the best he will need all the virtues, which may violate the rules and traits we mention to isolate one virtue.

5.4. *Conflicts*. We might insist on the separation of virtues which can conflict; sometimes the just action and the generous action may clash; or the endurance and confidence developed in the brave man may make it harder to show the temperate man's modesty—perhaps one virtue should not be developed too far when it clashes with others. Socrates and Aristotle must reply that these appearances of conflict are deceptive. Since virtues aim at the final good, they cannot conflict and cannot be pursued to excess (*MM* 1199b36–1200a34); reference to the final good will decide what is the virtuous action to do—and any real virtue will aim at the best action. The natural traits without knowledge may indeed conflict; but the real virtues will not (*MM* 1200a5–11). Conflicts, then, are signs of incomplete virtue; the justice which is overridden by equity is not real justice (*EN* 1137b11–14, b34–1138a3), and the temperance which leads someone astray is not real temperance.

The elenchos has reached a controversial conclusion. Socrates has argued that if someone agrees that a virtuous man always has good reason to be virtuous, and adjusts his beliefs about the virtues to fit his views about good reasons, he will not accept his old conception of isolated rule-governed virtues; he will prefer those reconstructed virtues which fulfil a man's rational aims. Here is a schema for identifying virtues and virtuous actions; until we know more about the composition of the final good, we do not know what kinds of traits or actions Socrates will prescribe, or how far he will reject ordinary views. But he can fairly claim that the schema is an important product of the elenchos—guided by Socratic assumptions.

6. *Virtue and other people's interests*

6.1. *The problem for Socrates*. So far we have discussed Socrates' arguments about two virtues, courage and temperance, which might be supposed to be at least partly self-regarding. His demand that virtuous action should be best for the agent, by contributing to his own happiness, is not uncontroversial; but it is at least not grossly implausible for these virtues. We may have more serious doubts about the virtues generally supposed to be other-regarding, and especially about justice, which meets the sharpest criticism from some of Socrates' contemporaries. Significantly, the Socratic dialogues do not discuss justice at length; but Socrates' general view of other people's interests, shown by his comments on love and friendship and his particular claims about justice, show that he faces serious questions about his general account of virtue.

6.2. *Friendship and love.* Socrates' treatment, in the *Lysis*, of love between persons conforms to his general eudaimonism. They soon agree that people are loved for their usefulness (212c5–d4); like other objects of love they must be loved because the lover thinks they are useful and needs them (214e3–215c3). Socrates thinks that the admirable (*kalon*) is what is loved; but then he moves from 'admirable' to 'good', and suggests that the good is loved (216c4–217e2). Now the good that is loved is loved for the sake of some further good (218d6–10), and this further good is eventually loved for the sake of the primary object of love, the final good (220b1–5). And so all concern for other people, as for other objects of love, has to contribute to the agent's own final good, which Socrates elsewhere identifies with the agent's happiness.[21]

Now we might have been inclined to sympathize with Socrates' eudaimonism about courage and temperance, which might plausibly be said to promote the agent's own good (though we might wonder if this is all they do). But his eudaimonist treatment of friendship is much more controversial; we may well be inclined to reject the reference to the agent's happiness which Socrates thinks is obviously necessary. But it is hard to decide how far we should disagree unless we know better how Socrates understands his comments on happiness.

6.3. *The problem of justice.* These assumptions about the relation of other people's interests and the agent's happiness raise hard questions about justice. No Socratic dialogue examines justice as critically as the *Charmides*, *Laches*, and *Lysis* examine other virtues; and this is no accident.[22] For the guiding principles of the elenchos are hard to apply; and Socrates' problems point to more general difficulties with the principles.

Part of his normal strategy will work. The easy account of justice as law-observance collapses for the same reasons as Euthyphro's account of piety as what the gods love collapsed. Socrates will argue that if something's being lawful and just is a reason for accepting it, what is lawful cannot simply be what is prescribed by a positive law—for sometimes that can be bad; he can show that what is lawful and just will be what is really best, and that someone needs knowledge of this to prescribe what is best (*Min.* 317b2–d1; *HMa.* 284d1–e9).[23] 'Best' here must mean 'best for the community' (*EN* 1129b14–19); but what Socrates usually means is 'best for the virtuous agent', and justice does not seem to meet this condition. Protagoras remarks that we benefit from each other's justice (*Pr.* 327b1–2); but this does not show that my justice benefits me—indeed, it tends to show that my justice is someone else's good, and not mine (*R.* 343c3–7, 367c2–5; *EN* 1130a1–5).

6.4. *Socrates' View.* Socrates will act justly at any cost to himself because injustice is always disgraceful (*aischron*) and evil (*kakon*)—and, quite exceptionally, he claims to know this (*Ap.* 29b6–7); we should decide whether an action is just, and then do it, not worrying about its consequences (*Ap.* 28b5–9, d6–10). Socrates appeals to justice to sanction his obedience to the god rather than to the Athenians (*Ap.* 28d10–29a4), and to sanction his compliance with the Athenian sentence of death instead of escaping (*Cri.* 54b2–5). If Socrates thinks he has an absolute obligation to be just which cannot be explained with other virtuous action, by reference to his own happiness, justice will be a serious anomaly in his moral theory, and awkward conclusions will be drawn. We might think, 'So much the worse for Socrates' theory, if it cannot show why we have reason to be just', or 'So much the worse for justice, if Socrates' theory shows we have no reason to pursue it'. Neither conclusion is welcome to Socrates.

6.5. *Socrates' defence of justice.* The theoretical defence of justice, to show it can be explained and vindicated by the general Socratic theory, is a major task for Plato in the *Gorgias* and *Republic*. But the line of defence is sketched in the *Crito*. Socrates maintains that justice is the healthy state of the soul, injustice its unhealthy state, so that justice is as worth while as health (*Cri.* 47d7–48a1); he infers that acting unjustly is as disastrous as doing what is unhealthy (47e6–48a1, 49b4–6).[24] This defence is regrettably cursory; Socrates admits this when he refers to the results of 'previous agreements' to support the position he assumes here (46b5–c5, 48b11, 49a4–b6).

6.6. *Difficulties.* But what kinds of agreements would support him? 1. How does he know a just soul is healthy? If he can show (a) a virtuous condition of soul is good and healthy, and (b) justice is a virtuous condition of soul, his conclusion will follow. We might accept (a) for courage and temperance, if we can show that they contribute to the agent's good; but if a virtue must contribute to my good, why should we accept (b)?

2. Socrates will presumably defend (b) by claiming (c) justice is admirable and good (implied, 49b4–7), and (d) whatever state of the soul is admirable and good is a virtue. But now he simply slides from 'admirable' to 'good' in his usual dubious way; and when 'good' here must mean 'beneficial to the agent', the slide begs the whole question about justice.

3. Even if justice is psychic health, how can Socrates show that unjust actions always damage the agent so severely that they are not worthwhile? Even if a single unjust action threatened my psychic health slightly, might it not have compensating benefits?

Socrates' defence of justice cannot be properly assessed, and certainly cannot be accepted, until he explains some of the central concepts. What is psychic health, and how is it related to happiness? Or when is someone benefited? These questions can be answered only by a fuller account of the final good and of the way virtue contributes to it. On some accounts, the moves required for the argument about justice might be defensible; but a large task faces Socrates. The *Crito* does indeed rely on 'previous agreements' in other Socratic dialogues which link virtue, admirability, benefit, and happiness. But the problem of justice seems to create a dilemma; either justice is a virtue and not all virtues benefit the agent, or virtues do benefit the agent, and justice is not a virtue. Socrates does not show he can avoid this dilemma with a suitable account of justice and benefit.

6.7. *Justice and harm.* Socrates argues that the just man will not treat anyone unjustly, even in retaliation (49b10–11), and then includes all harm under injustice (49c2–8), because it is never just to do harm to anyone (49c2–5). These are important consequences of Socrates' theory, rejecting traditional views about the legitimacy of retaliation. He argues that it is agreed to be just to benefit, and not to harm, other people; but my justice benefits my soul and my injustice harms it; and the benefit and harm to my soul do not vary with what the other person does, but with what I do; and so it is equally just and good for me to treat him well in all conditions.[25] This argument will be plausible only if Socrates explains what the psychic benefit will be, and how an intentional infliction of harm on someone else damages my soul. His defence is as weak as his overall defence of justice.

6.8. *Justice and obedience.* Socrates' defence of obedience to the law and refusal to escape is an important test-case for his view on justice; for if he recognizes an exceptionless obligation which could not plausibly be related to his concern for his own good, his moral theory does not explain his own moral beliefs. Much of his speech sounds like a defence of absolute obedience. He waives any right to object to a law because it is unjust, and therefore not really lawful at all (50a4–6; cf. *HMa.* 284d3–7), and any right to object to an abuse of the law (50c1–2, 54b8–c1). The laws and the state argue that disobedience to positive law is unjust when he owes them obedience in return for his birth and upbringing (50d1–51c4) and because he has freely agreed to keep the laws and abide by the state's verdicts (51c6–52a3), so that he will be acting unjustly on three counts if he disobeys (51e4–7).

Let us suppose Socrates is right to believe he has these reasons for obedience; do they rule out disobedience in any conditions? If he is right, and if he has no counter-claim of justice to defend disobedience, disobedience would be unjust. But his argument does not rule out a counter-claim. If he disobeys the law he will not benefit himself (53a8–54a1) or anyone else (54a1–b1), contrary to Crito's claims (45c8–d7), but he will have done his best to undermine the law (50a9–b5, 53b7, c1, 54c2–7); and so he has no counter-claim. But if the law required him to do something unjust, or some actions required by justice required disobedience to positive law, Socrates does not say that the law's claim would always be overriding; this kind of conflict arose when he did disobey the regime (*Ap.* 32c8–d3), and would arise again when he threatens to disobey any prohibition on his philosophical activity (*Ap.* 28d6–29a1). In the *Crito* the law does not require unjust action, and his philosophical activity gives no reason for disobedience (53c4–d1); and he does not say what it would be just to do if these conditions did not hold. The argument in the *Crito* can fairly be attacked on various grounds; but it does not by itself justify obedience in all conditions; to reach that conclusion Socrates must claim that the claims of obedience are always overriding in questions about justice, and he avoids any such claim, which would be inconsistent with his other convictions mentioned in the *Apology*. The *Crito* does not offer a complete account of when it is just to obey the law, and if it is taken as a complete account, it seriously over-simplifies Socrates' own views; but it leaves room for the essential qualifications.[26]

6.9. *Unanswered questions.* The *Crito* argues that a certain kind of disobedience would be unjust, and defends just action as a benefit to the soul. But none of Socrates' comments explains why it benefits the soul. It is not too implausible to assume that my brave and temperate actions benefit me, in allowing me to fulfil my rational plans without hindrance from irrational desires; but it is not at all clear that my just action directly benefits me the same way. Socrates tacitly acknowledges this; instead of claiming that my just action benefits me, he claims that my justice is good for my soul and requires just action. But he has not shown why justice benefits my soul, except by the question-begging assumptions that it is a virtue and all virtue benefits the soul. Though he claims that justice will fit his general pattern of moral argument and justification, he certainly fails to prove it. His comments on happiness, the good of the soul, and justice are not supported by a clear account of happiness or the soul's good; until a clear account is found, the large claims about justice cannot reasonably be accepted or finally rejected. These questions are raised in the Socratic dialogues; but only the *Gorgias* and *Republic* discuss them at length.

7. *Definition and knowledge*

7.1. *Conditions for a definition.* Socrates seeks definitions of the virtues; and though he never explicitly accepts a proposed definition, some necessary conditions are fairly clear.

1. Socrates rejects definitions whose consequences clash with the interlocutor's beliefs about particular virtuous actions; to avoid these kinds of counter-examples, the correct definition must match the true judgements, accepted in the elenchos, about examples of virtues and virtuous actions.

2. Definitions are rejected if they imply that a virtuous action is not beneficial; a correct definition must match judgements about what is beneficial. Now this condition affects the first. When the interlocutor's beliefs about examples clash with his beliefs about the good, Socrates rejects accepted examples. Nicias, with Socrates' clear approval, rejects Laches' belief that animals and others can be brave without wisdom; they are only fearless, not really brave (*La.* 196e1–197c4), since their fearless actions are not always beneficial.[27] The judgements accepted in the elenchos are not always accepted by the interlocutor before the elenchos; like Aristotle (*EN* 1145b4–6), Socrates overrides some of the common beliefs.

3. A definition should not merely be a true description of the virtue; it must also be explanatory. Socrates seeks a standard or paradigm for

deciding what is virtuous (*Eu.* 6e3–6); and Euthyphro's account of the pious as the god-beloved fails this test, since it is a true description of the pious but does not say what the pious is (11a6–b1). It offers no standard; for the gods have a reason for loving what is pious, that it is pious (10e9–11a6), and Euthyphro's account offers no reason. The right account should explain someone's reasons for calling something pious. Socrates' other arguments explain this demand. We have justified our belief that an action is virtuous only if we can show that we always have overriding good reason to do it; we can show that, on Socrates' view of a good reason, only if we show that it benefits the agent, contributes to his own happiness; and so an adequate account of virtuous actions or states of character must show how they benefit the agent. This was the argument which showed that the definition of one virtue must make it inseparable from all the others.

7.2. *Conditions for knowledge.* Socrates believes that someone who cannot say what a virtue is has no knowledge of the virtue; he suggests, though he does not say, that someone who could say what it is would have knowledge.[28] The Socratic dialogues do not discuss this question, but the nearest Platonic comments, in the *Gorgias* and the *Meno*, fit Socrates' demand neatly.

1. The elenchos finds a conflict between (a) the interlocutor's beliefs about what some virtue is; (b) his beliefs about examples of the virtue; and (c) his beliefs about the good; and this conflict makes some of (a) wander away (*Eu.* 11b6–c6). Someone who can define a virtue has adjusted (a) and (b) to (c). He will therefore not be liable to the doubt and confusion of the interlocutors refuted in the elenchos. His beliefs will be stable; and stability is recognized as one condition for knowledge (*M.* 98a).[29]

2. Stability alone does not make beliefs into knowledge. Socrates' beliefs are stable, but are not knowledge; they survive the elenchos, but he cannot show that they survive because they are true—perhaps a resourceful interlocutor could refute them, or some conflict has not been exposed. But if he could support his beliefs with definitions, Socrates could claim that they are stable because they are true. At least, they would be true as far as the elenchos could discover; for it exposes conflicts between pairs of beliefs, showing that at least one is false, and someone who can define the virtues will avoid that kind of conflict. In so far as someone is immune to Socrates' methods for detecting falsity, he can claim to satisfy a further condition of knowledge, that it should be true (*G.* 454c7–e2).

3. Someone who finds a Socratic definition of the virtues can justify his belief that something is virtuous, since Socrates requires an explanatory definition. He satisfies a third condition for knowledge; he can give an account, or work out an explanation, of his beliefs (*G.* 465a2–7, 501ab; *M.* 98a).

7.3. *The priority of definition.* Socrates' conditions for definition, justification, and knowledge show what is plausible in his claim that knowledge of what virtue is is prior to knowledge of anything else about it. Socrates does not mean, as we saw, that a definition of the virtue is prior to any belief about the virtue or recognition of examples. He need not deny that we can have confident and correct beliefs that this action is brave. But to know this, confidence and correctness are not enough; we must be able to justify the belief. Now Socrates claims that to justify a belief that something is brave we must (by the argument previously mentioned) show that it benefits the agent as a brave action should; we cannot show this without an account of bravery and its relation to the final good. We may find strong convictions opposed to ours and may be unable to justify our own convictions; Socrates demands an appeal to the general principles which determine whether something is virtuous at all, and so demands a definition of the virtue referring to the final good. He does not reject confident beliefs about a virtue, but denies that they count as knowledge unless they can be justified by being shown to meet a rational man's demands of a virtue.

7.4. *Definition and meaning.* A Socratic definition says what a thing is, and states an account which justifies our beliefs about it. It does not primarily analyse a concept or state the analytic truths which determine the meaning of a term. This should already be clear from the account of Socrates' arguments; but the point deserves further defence, since it is vital for avoiding mistaken criticism of his definitions. We need not enter disputes about the existence of an analytic-synthetic distinction; we need to show that, even if there are conceptual inquiries and analytic truths, Socrates' inquiries are not conceptual, and his definitions do not yield analytic truths. Socrates has no explicit notion of an analytic truth; someone might argue that while he confuses the analysis of concepts with positive moral prescriptions, one thing we find in the dialogues is conceptual inquiry. But even this version of the 'conceptual' view is wrong.[30]

1. If Socrates were analysing concepts, he should appeal to the interlocutors' linguistic intuitions. But he does not; he appeals to their

moral judgements. Laches' admission that courage can be displayed in a variety of conditions (*La*. 191c7–e3) does not depend on knowledge of what 'courage' means, which would produce the opposite reaction; he relies on his judgement that there is no morally relevant distinction between the cases. All the counter-examples require moral judgements; and Socrates never suggests that someone who rejected them would show his ignorance of what the word means.

2. An account of the meaning of '*F*' fails if it cannot cope with recognized paradigm examples of *F*s. But Socrates' account of courage rejects universally agreed examples of courage in animals (*La*. 196e1–197c4). He does not deny that they are universally agreed, but insists on a moral principle which rules them out. This kind of argument is legitimate if he means to discover the truth about courage, but not if he means to discover what 'courage' means.

3. A purely conceptual inquiry should have no moral implications. Socrates may prove to an interlocutor that he cannot consistently believe both (a) a just man always benefits other people; and (b) a just man benefits his friends and harms his enemies (cf. *R*. 335a–e). But then the interlocutor can give up either (a) or (b), and either approve or disapprove of justice, if Socrates has proved only that his concept of justice is muddled. But Socrates does not allow these options; the interlocutor is expected to decide for one alternative. This procedure is justified only if Socrates appeals to the interlocutor's moral judgements, as well as to his awareness of consistency or inconsistency.

4. A Socratic definition will not analyse the concept inarticulately grasped by the ordinary speaker. An analysis of a concept will not be sufficient, since the analytic truths about a virtue might not say that it is beneficial; nor will it be necessary, since a Socratic account may reject some analytic truths about a virtue—for instance, that it is separate from all the other virtues. Socrates does not want to know what the virtue-words mean; he wants to know whether ordinary beliefs about this or that virtue refer to a rationally acceptable virtue, and can be used to find a standard for judging something virtuous.

7.5. *The Unity Assumption*. Criticism of the UA should follow some decision about the character of a Socratic definition; for that will show what sort of unity Socrates assumes or demands. Critics are right to complain that he underestimates multivocity, as though it were a superficial and easily detected feature of names irrelevant to an examination of things (*Eud*. 277e3–278c1, *Tht*. 199a4–5). But this failure is not fatal; Socrates is not primarily interested in meaning, and a single meaning of a term '*F*' is neither necessary nor sufficient for the existence of a single form of *F*. It is not necessary; for health might be a single condition of the body, but 'healthy' applied to medicines (meaning 'productive of health') and applied to appetites ('indicative of health') may be differently related to this single condition. It is not sufficient; for 'speedy' may have a single meaning, but different B-states may underline the same A-state, contrary to Socrates' view that a virtue is a single B-state. Socrates does not qualify his claims this way; and his failure to qualify leads him and Plato into problems—we have seen one in the argument about speed as a single power.[31] But questions about univocity do not settle the merits of his case for UA.

Socrates looks for a single form to provide a standard by which we can decide whether anything is virtuous. Appeal to such a standard would be a useless account of initial learning of 'just' or 'pious' or of recognition of just or pious things; we would already have to recognize just or pious things to recognize their similarity to the standard.[32] But Socrates is not concerned with learning, but with justification; he wants to know whether our use of the term 'just' or 'pious' as a virtue-term is defensible. It will be defensible only if the term refers to a real virtue; and so Socrates legitimately asks for an account of piety and justice, to see if they are real virtues and benefit the agent.

The ordinary classification of persons and actions as just and pious depends on beliefs about justice and piety; and Socrates asks whether the beliefs are justified. He denies that the mere existence of a purported virtue-term shows that it refers to a real virtue, and tries to see if its use and the related beliefs about the virtue are justified. The question is fair when ordinary speakers and moral agents try to extend their use of virtue-terms to new or difficult cases. A consensus over easy normal cases allowed us to learn the term 'just'; but when difficult questions arise about the justice or piety of some action (Euthyphro's, for instance) an ordinary competent speaker and agent may not be able to go on, or may disagree with others. Socrates demands an explicit understanding of the principles guiding (not necessarily explicitly) our application of 'just' or 'pious', so that we can see whether they are consistent and justifiable, and can appeal to them to project our judgements to new cases. He does not distinguish this legitimate demand from the assumption that just one standard must underlie each virtue-term; but if we dismiss his demand for *one* standard, his search for a standard to justify the use of virtue-terms is not at all discredited.

7.6. *The Cratylus on names.* These claims about UA and Socrates' attitude to virtue-terms are derived from Socrates' practice in the early dialogues, not from a theoretical statement and justification of his position. But they can be supported from the explicit theory presented in the *Cratylus*; whether Socrates consciously relies on any such theory or not, a glance at the *Cratylus* will suggest how his practice in the early dialogues might be defended, and the further questions it raises.

Socrates insists against Hermongenes that the world contains things with stable natures (*Cra.* 386d8–e4), and that names can be correct or incorrect in so far as they do or do not reveal these stable natures (386d8–e4, 387b11–d8); names are instruments for distinguishing and teaching stable natures (388b7–c1), and will be correct in so far as they reveal them (387b11–c8, 389d4–390a2). Since correct users of a correct name '*x*' should have no false beliefs about *x* associated with '*x*', names in a natural language are not correct; but they can still be names *of*, and refer to, those stable natures (cf. 429b12–c5). A bad picture of Caesar can still be of him as long as it preserves his outline; similarly, an incorrect name of a stable nature *x* will remain a name of *x* as long as it preserves *x*'s outline (432d11–433a2).[33]

Some of this theory helps to explain the aims of a Socratic elenchos. Names of the virtues are not correct, since Socrates' interlocutors associate them with false beliefs about the virtues. But Socrates believes they are names of real virtues none the less. 'Horse' is a name of a real nature if horses belong to a real natural kind; 'whitehorse', referring only to white horses, does not qualify; nor does 'Athenocynohipp' referring only to horses and dogs in Athens. Socrates tests his UA by seeing whether 'courage' is more like 'horse' or the other two. It will refer to a single real nature if courage is a real virtue, a state which really contributes to the good. Socrates looks for the outline of a real virtue preserved in his interlocutor's beliefs about courage, and tries to discover the virtue imperfectly represented in those beliefs.

7.7. *Problems for Socratic definition.* How can Socrates decide if his interlocutor's beliefs refer to a real virtue? We can tell whether 'horse' refers to a natural kind if our taxonomy rests on some zoological theory; but Socrates has no access to the virtues apart from his own and his interlocutors' moral beliefs. How then can he follow the *Cratylus*'s advice to examine things, and not rely on names to discover the truth? (432d2–e3.) He must show that Prodicus' interests are not his (cf. *Pr.* 358a5–b2), that he asks, not merely what beliefs the interlocutor associates with the name, but whether the beliefs are true and refer to a real virtue.[34]

Naturally, if the interlocutor's beliefs preserve only the outline of a virtue, a correct account of it will require their revision. But then how can we decide if a word refers to a virtue, or what outline is preserved? If a picture depicts someone a bit like Caesar and a bit like Cicero, we might decide that it is of Caesar rather than Cicero if we know its history, and especially if we know that the painter was looking at Caesar. Socrates speaks as though the 'lawgiver' assigning names could offer some parallel for names of virtues (*Cra.* 390c2–d5; cf. *Ch.* 175b2–4); but how can he show, without begging the question, what nature the name is 'really' assigned to? If we thought all aquatic finned creatures were fish, and discover that some have lungs while others have gills, we do not decide that 'fish' refers to these two kind of creatures and not to a natural kind. Rather, we reject our previous beliefs that whales and so on are fish, and keep 'fish' as the name of the natural kind requiring least revision in our beliefs about the extension of the term. This over-simplified story may suggest how—in Socrates' terms—we might decide what nature a natural-kind term is really assigned to. But what is the ethical analogue?[35]

Socrates can appeal to three kinds of shared beliefs; (a) rules and definitions; (b) beliefs about examples; (c) theoretical connec- tions—e.g. the assumption that virtuous action is admirable and beneficial. Socrates and the interlocutor disagree about (a); Socrates relies on (b) and (c) against (a), and on (c) against (b). He and the in- terlocutor agree that courage is a virtue, and on the theoretical con- nections of virtues. To show that the interlocutor's beliefs 'preserve the outline' of the virtues, Socrates proposes quite extensive revisions. Ordinary beliefs do not immediately acknowledge that each virtue is inseparable from all the others, or that every virtue must benefit the agent. Socrates appeal to (c)—especially to the claims that virtuous action is worth while and that worth while action must benefit the agent—to force a revision which makes the 'outline' clearer. His revi- sion naturally requires the rejection of some supposed examples and rules of courage, so that they can identify more clearly the virtue they are both talking about.

But how far can the revision go, and still leave them talking about the same thing? Socrates does not alter the reference of 'courage' by revising some beliefs about examples of courage, any more than a scientist alters the reference of 'fish' by denying that whales are really fish; each of them discovers more about the real reference of the term. Since 'fish' was an accepted natural-kind term, a scientist discovers its real reference by discovering the real natural kind closest in extension to the supposed extension of 'fish'. Socrates can claim with equal justice that some revision in ordinary beliefs is needed to reveal the real reference of 'courage'.[36] But if the revision goes too far—and 'too far' is hard to specify clearly—so that appeals to (c) alter (b) beyond recognition, Socrates simply rejects the interlocutor's beliefs, and neither explains nor justifies them; he can hardly pretend to show why it is worth while to do recognized brave actions, and his assumptions will be at least as open to question as the rejected beliefs might have been. Socrates asks what the bravery is in the recognized brave actions; if he rejects all these examples, he will not answer his question.

Socrates never admits that he rejects ordinary beliefs wholesale; we will know if he should admit this only if we know his account of the final good. For some accounts might require the recognized virtuous actions; others clearly would not. Until we know Socrates' conception of the good, or why he thinks one conception should be preferred to another, we can hardly answer our question. Here as elsewhere, Socrates' theory raises an important issue, but does not decide it.

8. *The elenchos and moral theory*

8.1. *The possibility of knowledge.* We have found that the elenchos is not merely destructive and critical. It yields positive results. It should even yield knowledge to match Socrates' conditions. An account of courage, for instance, as 'endurance controlled by knowledge of the good' would meet the objections raised in the *Laches*, but it would not satisfy Socrates. For an account must provide a paradigm, to help us decide whether an action or person is brave; we need some clearer conception of the good to know when someone displays knowledge of it. But this should not be beyond Socrates' reach; further elenctic inquiry might produce some agreement on constituents of the good, which could be used to find the right definition.

Socrates should not believe, then, that the elenchos can never in principle meet his demand for definition and knowledge. Naturally the definitions it finds will rely on the agreement between Socrates and the interlocutor; one interlocutor might be wrong to agree, but his answers can be confirmed by other people's agreement. This all looks a feasible programme for Socrates; when he and his interlocutors, after repeated tests, are satisfied with an account, he can claim knowledge derived from the elenchos.

8.2. *The function of the elenchos.* Socrates uses the elenchos both for criticism and for discovery; that is why it is a new approach among Socrates' contemporaries to moral questions. He is critical; he does not accept the results of the ordinary moral education as a satisfactory moral condition. That education trains someone to follow willingly the social norms (*nomoi*) prescribing various virtuous actions; but it does not teach him to explain or justify those norms. Socrates' interlocutors show the effects of this training. They recognize several virtues, can state various rules for virtuous actions, and can recognize examples of virtuous actions and people. But they cannot show the relation or difference among the virtues, or state rules to cover all the cases they recognize, or explain how to recognize examples in more difficult conditions. Ordinary beliefs about the virtues include conflicts, but ordinary moral training does not explain the principles on which beliefs about virtues are meant to rest and which would show how to correct them. Protagoras' teaching simply added to the basic training, but did not correct its faults.[37]

Socrates' first task is critical, to expose the conflicts. But he does not stop there; nor does he try to justify ordinary beliefs by some more general theory like the Democritean theory, or reject them out of hand, as more radical critics choose to do. The elenchos will work only if ordinary moral beliefs are corrigible from within, if the interlocutor accepts the principles which allow revision and improvement. Socrates believes that principles connecting virtue with what is worth while and beneficial can be used to correct other beliefs, and to show that a coherent moral view can be discovered in ordinary beliefs, by the interlocutor himself. He expects the interlocutor to accept general principles about virtue and good reasons, and to adjust his other beliefs to suit. So far Socrates has only suggested what should be done; he has not shown what the moral results of his programme would be, and in particular he has not shown that they would support his own convictions about what is virtuous. But he has sketched a pattern of argument with reasonable prospects of reaching constructive results.

8.3. *Principles derived from the elenchos.* Socrates' positive moral doctrines do not just happen to emerge from the elenchos; he makes sure they will emerge. Certain principles about virtue and benefit guide the whole argument and heavily influence his conclusions; they are always assumed to be true; and he never conducts a full elenchos without them. They are not merely part of his moral theory, but guide his whole procedure in looking for a moral theory.

Now these principles are 'connected' with the elenchos, since their truth is assumed at the outset of elenctic inquiry; but surely any other principles Socrates might have assumed as true would be 'connected' with it no less? But this does not make Socrates' procedure trivial. He will claim that his principles are not an arbitrary selection from the many that might be assumed in an elenchos, but the assumptions needed to produce a coherent, rationally acceptable theory from elenctic inquiry. If the interlocutor believes that bravery is endurance, and also that the brave action is not always the enduring action, Socrates shows him how to decide which belief he should reject. He assumes that any rational man will agree that virtue is worth while, and that what is worth while benefits the agent; and these principles of practical rationality will guide the elenchos to a better account of the virtues. The guiding principles are not purely formal; they have disputable consequences about the content of morality, to be examined later. But Socrates will insist they are not arbitrary, that any reflective practically rational agent will accept them, and will correct his own beliefs by them.[38]

8.4. *Justification.* Can Socrates claim that his positive doctrines are justified by the elenchos, when the doctrines depend on principles presupposed in the elenchos? How can principles be justified by the elenchos which presupposes them? Socrates' defence of the principles by appeal to the elenchos will be circular, but not clearly vicious. For the elenchos is not doomed to success; an interlocutor might simply fail to decide in the way Socrates expects, even when the choices are clear to him; and then Socrates' theory would not be a good theory of *his* moral judgements. When the elenchos and the associated principles do work, Socrates can claim that to this extent they yield a correct account of the moral beliefs of this interlocutor and of anyone who agrees with him. Socrates tests the principles by seeing whether an elenchos relying on them will work on someone's moral beliefs. The test is perfectly genuine, not at all a foregone conclusion; and success in the test is some justification of the principles.

It should no longer seem absurd for Socrates to defend positive doctrines by appeal to the elenchos. They result from elenctic argument; the general principles on which they rely are required by the elenchos, for its constructive results; and the principles themselves are justified by the interlocutors' acceptance of them in the elenchos. So far Socrates' moral principles and his method of moral inquiry are inseparable; the principles are necessary for the method, and the method is powerful enough to defend the principles.

9. *Virtue as a craft; evidence*

9.1. *Gaps in Socrates' theory.* I have not told the whole truth about Socrates' moral theory; I have made his doctrines seem to be a reasonable product of the elenchos only by ignoring those doctrines which do not fit. I now want to explain these further doctrines by reference to a prominent feature of Socratic argument so far ignored—the craft-analogy (CA), which argues from the character of specialized crafts to conclusions about the character of virtues.[39] First, a review of some evidence will show that Socrates takes the CA seriously.

9.2. *Crafts and explanation.* Socrates tests someone's claim to knowledge by asking him to give an account. Only craftsmen show knowledge of their craft (*Ap.* 22b9–d4)—though not of other areas (22d4–e1)—by giving an account of what they do. The capacity to give an account distinguishes a real craftsman from someone who merely has a knack or technique which he cannot explain (*G.* 465a, 501a). It is worth while for Socrates to see why a craft satisfies his demand for an account; if moral knowledge could be a craft, it would also satisfy his demand.

9.3. *Experts.* The expert in a particular craft offers authoritative guidance, supported by a rational account; and Socrates argues that we should seek someone equally authoritative in morals (*Cri.* 47c8–48a1). In the *Laches* he demands an expert craftsman in moral training (*La.* 184e11–185e6). However, he does not claim to be the craftsman himself; his convictions rest on the elenchos (*Cri.* 48b3–c1) and on the interlocutor's agreement (48b3–c1), always open to re-examination (48d8–e1)—this is no expert's procedure.[40] Socrates does not think his elenctic method has made a craftsman out of him, but he does not say whether it could ever produce the kind of craft-knowledge he seeks.

9.4. *The concentration on knowledge.* These comments in the *Laches* and the *Crito* do not quite imply that any virtuous man must have the craft Socrates seeks; it might be confined to moral experts, and there might be non-expert virtuous men. Nor do they imply that craft-knowledge is sufficient for virtue. But both these implications are clear in other arguments, when Socrates abruptly and without defence converts the search for a virtue into the search for the craft, or the branch of knowledge, which is the virtue. In the *Euthyphro* he asks how piety is parallel with other crafts, and what its product is (*Eu.* 13a2–e11, 14c3–e7). In the *Laches* he moves abruptly from the proposal that courage is wise endurance, to Nicias' Socratic view that it is some kind of knowledge (*La.* 194c7–d9); he does not justify the elimination of any mention of an affective state. In the *Charmides* he argues that temperance is not modesty; he does not ask if it is wise modesty, but considers what kind of craft it might be (*Ch.* 165c4–e2); he must assume it is no more than a craft.

9.5. *Definitions and knowledge.* Socrates expects good definitions to provide paradigms or standards for deciding whether actions or persons are virtuous. He notices, though, that moral decisions raise peculiar kinds of disputes. Disputes about number, size, and weight are settled by measurement; but moral questions, involving the disputed terms 'good', 'just', and 'admirable', do not yield to this kind of decision procedure (*Eu.* 7b6–d7).[41] When we measure, we agree on a procedure to settle a question, and on how to apply the procedure, even when we disagree about the answer; our initial dispute about the weight of a cake rests on guesses superseded by the authoritative results of measurement. An account of a virtue which allows the use of measurement in reaching moral conclusions will satisfy Socrates' demand for a paradigm.

But an account including disputed moral terms prevents measurement. If we use a balance to decide the weight of a cake, our judgements about weight do not affect our seeing the same reading on the balance; but if we define a virtue in moral terms, no procedure will settle our moral dispute without relying on prior moral agreement. Measurement, or any useful analogue in morals, precludes disputed terms. Socrates must choose between two answers to this problem:

(ED) An adequate account must eliminate disputed terms and provide a paradigm which allows measurement.

(NED) No correct account of a moral property can eliminate disputed terms; therefore moral questions provide no paradigm which allows measurement.

Socrates endorses neither ED nor NED in the Socratic dialogues, though he endorses ED in the *Protagoras*. But he sometimes rejects answers which include disputed terms. Critias' account of temperance as 'doing well and admirably' is unsatisfactory because it does not identify the specific product of temperance (*Ch.* 163d1–e2). One of Gorgias' answers includes disputed terms and is not clear (*G.* 451d7–e5); and when Callicles replaces one disputed term with another he makes nothing clear (*G.* 489e1–8). Socrates, then, should accept Thrasymachus' and Cleitophon's demands for a clear and exact account of justice without disputed terms (*R.* 335c6–d4; *Clt.* 409b4–d2).[42] Now if he accepted NED, he might still reject some accounts which include particularly vague disputed terms; a general rejection of answers including disputed terms suggests ED, but the Socratic dialogues say nothing so sweeping.

Though Socrates does not explicitly accept ED, he has reason to welcome it if it could be achieved, if moral disputes could be settled by some analogue to measurement. Now if virtue is a craft, there will be good grounds for expecting such a solution. For a craftsman's methods are analogous to measurement in the right way; he uses a clear, authoritative procedure, which can be explained to non-experts (*Ap.* 22d2–4). If there were moral craftsmen, moral disputes could be settled without use of disputed terms; and Socrates will have solved an awkward problem if he can show that virtue is a craft, and that the solution of disputes only requires a craftsman. He never explicitly argues this way; but it would be a natural way to justify efforts to identify virtue with some craft.

This should be enough evidence that Socrates takes the CA seriously; much of his positive theory will be true only if it holds. Why does he find the CA so attractive, and what must he prove to show it applies to virtue?

10. *Advantages of a craft*

10.1. *Crafts and rationality.* A craftsman can satisfy Socrates' demand for an account of what he does; for he can explain each step in production by its contribution to the product. If the product is an artefact, each step will be justified by its contribution to an object separate from any exercise of the craft. Some crafts, however, produce no artefact; an expert flute-player or chess-player produces nothing but good flute-playing or good play in chess. But he still produces a product which can be identified without reference to his particular movements. When we can recognize a tuneful sound in music or a win in chess, we can decide if certain movements are good flute-playing and good chess-play; a tuneful sound is not a good product *because* it is the result of good production, but the production is good because of the product.

The rationality of a craft, then, depends on a definite subject matter and product which can be achieved by some regular and clearly explicable process. This is what distinguishes a craft, competent and authoritative in its own specialized area, from a pseudo-craft, which trespasses in the area of specialized crafts, but is incompetent in areas where it should be competent if it relied on real technical principles. Socrates attacks the pseudo-crafts of the rhapsode and the orator for their pretensions and failures. (*Ion* 537c1–538b6, 539d5–541c2; *G.* 451a3–d6, 455a8–456a6.) They cannot justify themselves with a rational account of their productive process, but must rely on the poet's or rhapsode's non-rational inspiration, or the orator's rules of thumb (*Ion* 533c9–535d5; *G.* 462b5–c7). Against these impostors, crafts legitimately appeal to Socrates.

10.2. *Crafts and teaching.* Since a craft proceeds by a rational, explicable process, it can also be taught rationally; someone can be told what to do, and why that is the right thing to do for the product he can recognize; and when he has properly learnt the craft, he can teach it to others. Socrates has reason to welcome this aspect of a craft, and to contrast it with ordinary moral 'teaching'; Protagoras recognized that someone 'learns' ordinary virtue in the way he picks up Greek, by growing up in society (*Pr.* 327e1–328c8; cf. *M.* 92e3–93a4, *Alc.* 110c3–111a4). Affective training, by rewards and punishments (325c6–d7) and appeals to someone's sense of honour (325e1–326a5) may produce law-abiding citizens; but it is hardly the teaching which will make someone a qualified expert able to explain his craft. The failure of someone with ordinary moral training to survive the elenchos shows Socrates the faults in this training. Now if virtue is a craft, it can be systematically taught and explained; someone who has learnt it the right way will be able to explain himself in an elenchos. The fault in ordinary virtue as recommended by Protagoras is not only that it is taught the wrong way, but also that it cannot be taught the right way; for that collection of rules and customs cannot be systematically justified without the revisions demanded by the elenchos. But if virtue can be made a craft, its procedure and products will have been adjusted to meet Socrates' criticisms.[43]

10.3. *Crafts and objectivity.* A craftsman is recognized as an authority in his field, as someone who knows, and is agreed to know, the right method for producing a particular product. If questions are treated by a craft, they are settled objectively; there is a right method, and answers do not depend on the prejudices of particular people; sceptical doubts about the possibility of objective answers in that area are removed. Socrates notices that moral questions raise disputes with no acknowledged authoritative arbitrator, and may cause scepticism about whether there is an authoritative answer to be found. The elenchos tries to remove some of the scepticism, by showing that some agreements can be reached. But it does not go far enough; for it requires concessions by one interlocutor which another might refuse, and so hardly answers a sceptic who sees no rational solution to the disputes. But if Socrates could show that virtue is a craft, these doubts would be silenced; for then he would have shown that there is one clearly correct method of treating moral questions to reach definite answers.

When he claims that virtue is a craft, Socrates does not mean that he himself or any recognized virtuous man practices a craft; for no one has the right knowledge to explain the really virtuous man's methods. But he has good reasons for thinking that real virtue—not fully embodied in anyone at the moment—will be a craft; for a craft will clearly satisfy some of his basic demands of virtue and moral knowledge, and he can reasonably look for an account of virtue which will show that the CA is apt. At the same time, not all of virtue looks easily reducible to a craft; and part of Socrates' task is to show that problems here do not undermine the CA.

11. *Problems in the craft-analogy*

11.1. *Subject matter.* If the CA holds, we should be able to answer about a virtue the questions we can answer about a craft; Socrates is right, then, to look for the subject matter and product of virtue. The question is discussed at length in the *Charmides*, and Socrates persists in his search, despite Critias' suspicions that virtue is not a productive craft. Critias defends badly his first suggestion, that virtue is concerned with activity and not production (*Ch.* 163a10–d8). Next he suggests that not all sciences need a subject matter and product separate from the science itself (165e3–166a2); Socrates replies that they do not all produce artefacts, but they do all have subject matters and products separate from themselves (166a3–b6).[44] The demand for a product is not abandoned in the *Charmides* (cf. 174e8–175a7), and elsewhere it is accepted (*Eu.* 13d9–14a10; *Eud.* 291d7–292a5; *Clt.* 409a7–d2).

We might think the *Charmides* hints at Aristotle's view that virtue and practical wisdom have no product, because they are concerned with activity and not production (*EN*1140b4–7); but though Aristotle accepts Critias' distinction, Socrates has good reason to reject it, and insist on a product. For if someone aims to make a product, his work can be tested for correctness, once we identify the product (cf. *EN* 1105a26–8), and the craftsman can explain what he does by reference to this identifiable product. Aristotle's wise man cannot justify himself this way, since the actions he prescribes are not productive, and cannot be justified by reference to a product, but aim at living well in general (1140a25–8). If he demands the same kind of justification from a craft and from a virtue, Socrates is right to seek the product of virtue.

11.2. *Superordinate crafts*. Socrates argues that a virtue cannot be just one craft co-ordinate with the others, with its own separate area of competence; a craft with such limited scope would not always benefit us as a virtue should (*Ch.* 174b11–175a3);[45] and so virtue must be a superordinate science of good and evil.[46] A superordinate science is needed to use other sciences' products (*Eud.* 289b4–c4), which are liable to misuse without knowledge of how to use them (*Eud.* 281d2–e1, II *Alc.* 146d7–e3). A kingly, ruling science is required (*Eud.* 291c7–d3; cf. *Ch.* 173a7–d5, 174b11–d1); but now what is its subject matter and product? Its product must be always good (292a7–11); but we have found that only knowledge is always good (292b1–2; cf. 281e2–5); the kingly science can produce nothing but itself, so that we still do not know its product or its benefit (292b4–c5).

The steps in this argument are highly dubious.[47] But Socrates rightly neglects the obvious answer—that the kingly science is the science of good and evil (*Ch.* 174c2–3; II *Alc.* 146d7–e3; cf. *Eud.* 281d2–e2), and produces happiness; this answer will not suit the CA, since it retains disputed terms, and does not clearly identify the product (cf. *Clt.* 409a7–d2). To explain and justify a productive process, we must identify the product apart from the process; we know someone is doing the right thing to make a table only if we can identify a table without knowing how it is produced. The *Euthydemus*'s argument does not at all reduce the CA to absurdity; but it shows the problem in making it useful.

11.3. *Misuse.* The *Euthydemus* assumes that the superordinate science of good will solve the problems of misuse and ensure happiness (cf. *Ch.* 174a10–c3). But how can any craft by itself exclude misuse? A craft is a rational procedure for producing a certain product when a craftsman wants to (*HMi.* 366b7–c4), but does not prescribe when he will want to, or how he will use the product. He can make his product badly, or use his craft to produce a non-standard product—so that if justice is a craft, the just man may show his craft-skill either in producing the standard product, virtuous action, or in a non-standard product, vicious action (*HMi.* 375d7–e1, 376a2–4, *R.* 333e3–334b6).[48] Even if he produces the standard product, he may misuse it; this is why Socrates demands a superordinate science. But why does the superordinate science not face the same problems? Even the final good produced by this science will be open to abuse if we sometimes want something else more strongly; and for the same reasons, we might work badly towards the final good, or use the science for something else. The craft itself cannot expect to proscribe these kinds of misuse; and another superordinate craft will begin a vicious regress.

Socrates might avoid the problem with Aristotle's answer; virtue is not a craft or capacity, but a state of character which includes the desire, not produced by a craft, to use knowledge to achieve the right results. For Aristotle, wisdom, unlike cleverness or ability, avoids misuse because of its correct grasp of ends (*EN* 1144a22–b1; *HMi.* 364e2–6; *R.* 333e3–4; *Def.* 413a8); and this grasp proceeds, not from another capacity which can be used well or badly, but from a state of character which cannot (*EN* 1106a6–13, 1127b14–15, 1129a11–17). A craftsman may have or lack the further excellence which uses his skill correctly; but a wise man needs no further excellence (*aretē*), since wisdom includes right use (1140b21–2); and the wiser man is not like the better craftsman, more capable of acting badly, since wisdom is a virtue, a state and not a capacity (1140b22–4).

Now Aristotle's answer will wreck the whole CA, and Socrates avoids it. He suggests that the good man will go wrong intentionally, if anyone does (*HMi.* 376b4–6), hinting that no one does. An Aristotelian solution claims only that the virtuous man does not go wrong intentionally; but Socrates goes further. He rightly hints at a general claim that knowledge is sufficient for virtue and virtuous action (KSV). To defend the CA he must show that all we need for living well is a craft; virtue must have a product which everyone will want when he knows it, and the product must be incapable of misuse.

12. *Desire and rational choice*

12.1. *Desire and the good.* The CA requires Socrates to claim that if A knows what action is best, A will do it. He must rule out two other options:

1. Indifference; A knows that x is better than y, and still has no desire to do x rather than y.
2. Incontinence; A's knowledge that x is better than y creates some desire to do x, but he still wants more to do y.

He rejects indifference by arguing that some good is the only goal; all desires aim at some good, and at nothing else (*G.* 467c5–468a5).[49] Socrates relies on a general view of how desires explain actions. We explain why A does x by a desire of his; but 'A did x because he wanted to do x' does not explain much. For a real explanation, we must know why A wanted to do x, what was the point of x, what end x seemed to advance, or what was the good of x. Socrates takes all these questions to be equivalent; if A believes x advances y, y is the good A seeks in doing x. We can still ask what is the point of y, and look for some good advanced by y; but all these goods converge on an ultimate end, the final good (*Lys.* 219c1–5, 219d5–220a6). The belief that x contributes to the final good he desires will be necessary and sufficient for A to desire and choose x.

12.2. *Socrates' assumptions.* This account requires all desires to be rational or good-dependent; if A wants x, he wants it for its contribution to some good y, and ultimately to the final good, and if he ceases to believe that x contributes to the final good, he will cease to want x.[50] Socrates will argue that a desire is explanatory only if it relates an action to this structure of means and ends, and thereby shows how the agent acts rationally, within the limits of his factual beliefs and views of ultimate ends. If we can find no systematic pursuit of stable goals in a creature's behaviour, we shall not know what desires to ascribe to it at all; if we cannot assume that a bird wants to protect its young, we have no reason to suppose that it means its wing-flapping to divert predators, rather than to attract suitors, or for self-defence or exercise. Similarly, Socrates might argue, we must assume rationality in a man's actions to have any systematic way of ascribing desires at all. The agent's own reports offer no way out unless we suppose they are correct; but Socrates has no reason to allow us incorrigible access to our own desires, and will accept our reports only if they also make our behaviour rational. Reference to a desire, on this view, will explain an action only in so far as it shows how it is rational, and could be chosen to achieve the agent's ultimate ends—if it did not show this, it would not show the point of an action at all.

12.3. *The denial of incontinence.* Socrates believes that the final good we all desire is happiness (*Eud.* 278e3–279a1, 280b5–6). To reject indifference, he has strengthened this assumption so that we all desire whatever we believe to contribute to happiness; to reject incontinence, he strengthens it further, so that we never desire anything more strongly than we desire what contributes to our happiness. He rejects Meno's suggestion that *A* might know that *x* is evil and still choose *x*; no one, Socrates replies, wants to be unhappy, and so no one wants what will make him unhappy (*M.* 77b6–78b2).[51] The reply is invalid; *A* may not want *x* *because* it makes him unhappy, but he may still want *x* *although* it makes him unhappy. To rule this out, Socrates must assume, as he assumes in the *Gorgias* and *Lysis*, that incontinent action is excluded because the *strongest* desire is always focused on the final good, and incontinent desires are excluded because *all* desire is focused on the final good.

12.4. *Defence of Socrates.* Socrates rejects incontinent actions because they must be explained by incontinent, non-rational desires, and a non-rational desire fails his conditions for being explanatory. If I say *A* chews light-bulbs because he wants to chew them, and can say nothing more about why he wants to, I am none the wiser; I will doubt whether his action is explicable by his reasons at all. Similar doubts arise if *A*'s acting on that desire would be intelligible in some contexts, but not in this context; if *A* always refuses to eat because he does not want to dirty his plates (so he says), his action is not fully understood or explained, when we cannot see why this trivial inconvenience should matter so much to him in this context. *A* is not acting 'contrary to reason' in the sense of having false beliefs about the situation; but we still have not properly explained his action by his reasons, when we do not see the point of action on that desire in that situation.

Now Socrates might well argue that his opponents' alleged cases of incontinence ought, on their view, to be like these cases where rational explanation breaks down, which are (to put it anachronistically) the concern of the psychiatrist rather than the moralist; for the choice of what is known to be worse is no more intelligible than a fixation on clean dishes. We should be equally at a loss to see the point of such an action in these conditions, and ought to be equally inclined to seek explanations independent of his reasons. And Socrates will correctly insist that alleged incontinent actions are not at all inexplicable; if *A* has another drink even though he says he knows he will have a hangover in the morning, his desire for another drink fully explains his action, leaving us quite unpuzzled and normally disinclined to ask the psychiatrist. Now, Socrates will maintain, if the desire explains *A*'s action, we must see the point of it; and therefore *A* cannot be acting against his desire for the final good. If alleged incontinent actions were really incontinent, they would be inexplicable; since they are explicable, they are not really incontinent.

Socrates' objection to incontinence does not depend on alleged analytic truths, claims about the meaning of 'desire' or the self-contradictory character of 'desiring what we believe to be bad for us'; it is presented as a claim about 'human nature' (*Pr.* 358c6–d2). And yet it would be naïve to suppose he has simply overlooked the alleged cases of incontinence he would have found by further empirical investigation; he is well aware that people do the actions normally called incontinent. He relies on general and basic and (he thinks) obviously true assumptions about the explanation of human action, connecting desires and reasons with rationality and the pursuit of the agent's good; if these assumptions were rejected, he implies, we could not understand what we learn by explaining an action by desires and reasons, and we could hardly claim to explain an action at all. The whole argument depends on Socrates' view of desires; it does not imply that knowledge or reasoning can cause action independently of desires. He agrees entirely with Hume that reasoning moves us only because it depends on some previous desire for an end, and disagrees with Hume only in rejecting desires independent of the final good. This line of argument is not explicitly presented by Socrates; as usual, he uses the assumptions and we have to see how they might be defended. But it supports his view of incontinence by strengthened versions of principles about choice, rationality, and the agent's good which we have already seen in the conduct of the elenchos; and that is some reason for thinking that Socrates would accept the argument as an explicit version of what he implicitly accepts.

12.5. *Objections to Socrates.* Socrates is right to insist that normal alleged cases of incontinence do not verge on insanity, and are not unintelligible or inexplicable. But still his case is open to objections.

1. He is right to demand some broad over-all rationality in the actions of a creature to whom we ascribe desires; if any desire makes his

actions as a whole equally pointless and chaotic, none explains anything. But the minimum rationality that prevents chaos may fall far short of what Socrates wants; and though it may be required in someone's actions as a whole, it allows some deviant actions. Socrates is wrong to suppose that the general explanatory assumption requires the rationality of every single desire.

2. He rightly insists that a mere reference to desire will often fail to explain an action if we cannot see why the agent should have acted on that desire. He wrongly infers that any irrational desire is non-explanatory because we cannot see why the agent acts on it. Sometimes we explain why A does x because he wants y by saying that he wants y because he wants z, and so on, citing further reasons; this is Socrates' method. But the explanation need not refer to A's reasons; we can explain and understand why A follows his desire for food, by reference to the primitive and basic character of this desire, or why he sticks slavishly to a moral rule he has learnt, by reference to his upbringing and training. These causal explanations will make action on a desire just as intelligible as further appeal to the agent's reasons would make it. We can explain why someone should persist in his desire for food, drink, or sex, even against his rational plans; and though these are not the only sources of incontinent action, it is no accident that they are star examples, because of their intelligibility—a kind of intelligibility overlooked in Socrates' concern with the agent's reasons.

Socrates might still fairly insist that (to put it vaguely) the ascription of a desire to someone should set an action in some pattern, and allow us to see some system in his actions—we should prefer this over an account which reduced them to chaos. But he wrongly assumes that incontinent desires fail this test. To take the star examples again—we can systematically explain and see a pattern in many of a man's actions if we suppose he wants to satisfy his desire for food, drink, or sex, for its own sake. This remains true if the pattern in these actions conflicts with a larger pattern in the man's rational aims.

Socrates' arguments against incontinence rest on correct, or at least defensible, principles about the explanation of actions. But these principles are vaguer than he thinks; and he is wrong to suppose they rule out explanations referring to incontinent desires.

12.6. *Results of Socrates' argument.* Socrates' denial of incontinence rests on the account of rational desires in the *Lysis*; since all desires are rational, they all conform to this pattern derived from the

CA.[52] The choice of medicine is explained by the desire for health, and ultimately by the desire for the final good (*Lys.* 219d5–220a1); if I know aspirin contributes more to health and my other goals than penicillin, I shall choose aspirin, and the medical craft will determine which I choose. If virtue is a craft, then all a man's choices must conform to this pattern; for if all his desires aim at the final good, and moral knowledge tells him what contributes to the final good, then this knowledge is sufficient for virtuous action.

13. Knowledge and rational choice

13.1. *Crafts and products.* The denial of incontinence frees Socrates from any problems about non-rational desires; but to defend KSV and the CA, he must also show that rational desires create no problems, and that the CA works for all the rational desires associated with virtue.

Now crafts show clearly how knowledge can be sufficient for right action. If I want a bed, have no conflicting desires, and acquire the carpenter's craft, I shall make a bed and achieve my end. The carpenter can justify himself, and show that this is the right way to make a bed because he can show how each step contributes to the product I recognize. The same is true if the product is not an artefact; a violin-teacher can show that these are the right movements for a tuneful sound; and someone who wants to make a tuneful sound and knows that these are the right movements will try to make them.

Our interest in a craft depends on our previous interest in the product; if it is an artefact, we must already want it as a means to some end of ours, or if it is not an artefact, we may want it as an end in itself. The craft does not decide what the product will be like, or convince us to want it; the user must decide what product he wants (cf. *Cra.* 390b1–4). Some users may rely on a second craft which requires the product of the first (cf. *Eud.* 289c4–d4) to produce its own product; but if all products are chosen by crafts with further products, a vicious regress results.

13.2. *Varieties of means and ends.* For Socrates moral knowledge is a superordinate craft (*Eud.* 289c1–4, 291c3–d3) which seems to halt the regress of products and crafts. For its product, happiness (cf. 289c6–8), is required by no further craft; it is what we all want (278e3–279a2). Socrates' position comes to this:

V. We all want happiness, and virtue produces what contributes to happiness.

Socrates seems to have shown that (with incontinence ruled out) if I know what virtue requires I shall do it—a vindication of the CA.

But V alone does not show that virtue is a craft. For something may be 'a means to' or 'contribute to' or 'promote' some end in different ways. Both an exhausting journey to a resort and swimming every day contribute to a good holiday; but the first may be a purely instrumental means, and the second is a component of having a good holiday.[53] These two ways of contributing to an end allow two ways in which A and B might pursue the same end by different means:

1. A and B may pursue the same determinate end x; they agree on components of x, and on examples of achieving x; they can still disagree about instrumental means to x.

2. A and B may pursue an indeterminate end x; they both call the end they pursue 'x', and agree on some of its properties, but not far enough to specify the same components, or to agree on examples of achieving x; their disagreement cannot be confined to instrumental means.

These distinctions raise awkward problems for a defence of the CA relying on V. For some examples will show that a craft is competent when A and B pursue the same determinate end, and disagree only about instrumental means, but much less clearly competent when then they only pursue the same indeterminate end and disagree over its components.

1. If I want health, and a doctor prescribes a medicine, I shall (in suitable conditions) want the medicine. The doctor and I aim at health as a determinate end, and he prescribes instrumental means to it.

2. If I want to be healthy, and a doctor tells me that being healthy consists in a certain balance of bodily elements, I shall want this balance. He tells me that a component of health, which I recognize as a painless and undisturbed physical condition, is identical with the condition in which elements are balanced a certain way; he provides another description of the same components of health. The examples support Socrates' connection between knowing and wanting, not only for instrumental means but also for components of a determinate end already chosen under some other description.[54]

3. Suppose I look for a worthwhile job. A careers adviser cannot help me until I decide what I will count as a worthwhile job, or what criteria will be relevant. He can tell me what to do if I want a well-paying, socially useful, or intellectually absorbing job; but I must decide how far I ought to care about these things, and no expert is

readily available to help me, since 'a worthwhile job' is an indeterminate end.

13.3. *Problems for virtue.* Socrates must choose between two versions of his principle V; let us call them the technical and the non-technical conceptions of virtue (TV and NTV):

TV.   Happiness is a determinate end to which virtue prescribes instrumental means (as in the first example) or components already chosen under another description (as in the second example).

NTV. Happiness is an indeterminate end for which virtue prescribes components not already chosen under another description (as in the third example).[55]

Socrates' claim, that virtue is craft-knowledge which will make a non-virtuous man choose virtuous action, depends on TV. For KSV is plausible if the virtuous and the non-virtuous man agree on the components of the final good, and the non-virtuous man is persuaded that the virtuous man's craft uses more efficient means to achieve this determinate end. But if the end is indeterminate, and virtue prescribes both instrumental means and components, Socrates has not shown how the non-virtuous man will be persuaded that these are the right components, or that his persuasion will result from knowledge, without a change of view on the ultimate end. We can understand KSV and the CA applied to the choice of instrumental means; for a craft is a rational, systematic, objectively defensible procedure just because it can relate its actions to a recognizable determinate product, artefactual or non-artefactual. But there is no determinate product to justify the actions of a craft when the end is indeterminate; Socrates has not shown that a craft has any rational method for prescribing the components of an indeterminate end. NTV does not strictly exclude KSV; someone might reply that some other kind of knowledge besides a craft will change someone's views about the components of the final good and alter his desires. But this option is not open to Socrates: for his defence of KSV is explained by the CA, and he recognizes no moral knowledge which is not a craft; and so NTV destroys his defence of KSV, since it destroys the CA.

Someone might reject this insistence on TV as pedantic literalism in the interpretation of the CA; why would some broader notion of craft not cope with NTV? This would be misplaced charity to Socrates, because of failure to see why he justifiably thinks the CA worth while.

It is no empty metaphor; we have seen that if its main points can be satisfied by virtue, then Socrates will achieve one of his aims—he will have found a rational account of virtue which will show beyond reasonable doubt what the virtuous action is and why it should be done. But the CA achieves this aim exactly because a craft prescribes instrumental means to a determinate product; if 'craft' is extended so that the CA can include NTV, the assurance of rationality, explicability, and objectivity is lost, and with it the whole point of the CA for Socrates. The CA will prove something important and controversial about virtue, if the virtuous man is like the craftsman in our first two examples; but Socrates has not shown how a craft will help with the problem of choosing a worthwhile job, in our third example, unless he can show that a worthwhile job really contributes to some determinate end. Socrates would be right to reject any dilution of the CA to cover NTV; either TV is right, or the CA is wrong.

13.4. *Socrates' solution.* The *Lysis* commits Socrates to the rejection of NTV, and to a strong version of TV. NTV assumes that components 'contribute to' and are 'chosen for the sake of' the final good, and also, unlike instrumental means, are goods in themselves. But Socrates maintains that no good chosen for the sake of the final good is chosen for its own sake or is a good in itself (*Lys.* 219c1–d5, 220a6–b5). Health might seem to be desirable both for itself and for some further end; but Socrates argues that since it is chosen for some further end it cannot be good in itself, but only an 'image' of what is really good (219c1–5, d2–5). Socrates commits himself to two principles:

LC. If *A* chooses *x* for the sake of *y*, *A* does not choose *x* for its own sake.

LG. If *x* and *y* are goods, and *x* contributes to *y*, *x* is not good in itself.

These two principles rule out component means; and since virtue prescribes what contributes to happiness, LG implies that it cannot prescribe goods in themselves. Socrates cannot accept NTV, or even the limited prescription of components conceded to virtue by TV. The *Lysis* recognizes only the pattern of rational choice displayed in a craft; and this pattern demands TV.

13.5. *Socrates' task.* Acceptance of TV does not require Socrates to accept what people say about the character of the final good. He defends none of the popular accounts of the supreme goods; indeed he recognizes that people seem to disagree radically about worthwhile pursuits (*Cri.* 47c11–d5). It might seem reasonable to infer that happiness, the final good, is an indeterminate end (*EN* 1095a14–26). But Socrates can still defend TV as an account of what everyone really pursues, not an account of what everyone claims to pursue; these claims are proved wrong when they do not explain a man's choices. People wrongly claim, Socrates thinks, that they pursue recognized goods, health, wealth, and so on, as the final good (*Eud.* 280b5–281c5); Their claims are refuted when their choices show that these do not constitute the final good they seek. Neither Socrates nor his interlocutor can specify the components of the determinate end they both pursue; but if they will agree on the components when they understand their choices better, TV will be vindicated.

Socrates can reasonably maintain that it is difficult but worth while to find the agreed conception of the determinate end everyone pursues. When it is found, TV will satisfy Socrates' demands for rationality; for we can decide and justify our decision that something is virtuous by reference to an agreed conception of the final good. The CA will then perfectly match Socrates' demands. Now Socrates does not try, in the Socratic dialogues, to specify the determinate end everyone pursues; but he need not think his task is so hopeless as to discredit TV—and the *Protagoras* offers an answer.[56] If TV is true, knowledge of virtue ensures virtuous action, and the paradox of the *Hippias Minor* need not worry Socrates; since the product of virtue is a determinate end everyone pursues, someone who knows what virtue produces and requires will act virtuously. The virtuous man still differs from the non-virtuous only in his knowledge of what contributes instrumentally to the good. Socrates accepts those assumptions about all human choice (in his denial of incontinence) and the character of the final good and virtue (in TV) which allow him to retain the CA.

14. *The unity of the virtues*

14.1. *Knowledge and the unity of the virtues.* The *Laches* concludes with an argument to show that all the virtues are really a single virtue, knowledge of good and evil; other dialogues strongly suggest the same conclusion. So far we have seen Socrates argue for only the reciprocal implication of the virtues:

RV. A man has any of the virtues if and only if he has them all.
But eventually he defends the stronger unity thesis.

UV. All the virtues are the same virtue.

Now RV does not commit Socrates to UV. Like Socrates, Aristotle accepts RV (*EN* 1144b32–1145a2) and will not allow the virtues to be separated. But two possible objections to UV remain.

1. Aristotle distinguishes the virtues by their subject matter, finding courage primarily displayed in danger in battle (1115a10–35); though the brave man will need wisdom and therefore the other virtues, still the conditions make his action an expression of courage. Similarly, temperance is displayed primarily in the control of certain basic appetites (1118a23–6). Socrates rejects this division. He persuades Laches, who tries Aristotle's moves, that the same state of courage is found in all kinds of conditions; appeal to some favoured external conditions produces arbitrary and misleading boundaries for courage (*La.* 191d3–e2). The *Charmides* mentions control of appetites only once (*Ch.* 155c5–e3); but Socrates never even argues against the restriction of temperance to desires for bodily satisfaction; he assumes that temperance is unrestricted in its scope. He cannot divide the virtues by Aristotle's method.

2. Aristotle also insists that complete virtue results from the training of different emotions, feelings, and desires; though it is a single state of character and intellect, the constituent virtues can still be distinguished by their causal origin. Socrates' defence of RV allows, and even requires, these distinctions. Laches is convinced by the first move because he sees that in all these cases someone has trained himself to act on his resolution despite desires which hold him back. Later he sees why ignorant divers are braver than, not merely as brave as, the experts; since they have no factual knowledge to remove their fears, they need courage to withstand the fears and stick to their purpose (cf. *La.* 193a3–c11). Socrates might equally have generalized from his own display of temperance in the *Charmides* to temperate men in various conditions who restrain desires urging them to do what they rationally reject. These accounts of virtues reflect the belief that they are necessary and worth while partly because they control and direct desires and emotions which would divert a man from what he rationally approves.

But this belief about the virtues collapses when Socrates accepts KSV and the CA. If no one is incontinent, there are no conflicting desires to be controlled, and if each virtue is just knowledge, they cannot be distinguished by the different non-cognitive tendencies involved. Aristotle explains why Socrates accepts UV and he himself does not; Socrates thinks all the virtues are cases of knowledge (1144b17–21, 28–30). In the Socratic dialogues Socrates assumes the truth of KSV before he defends UV; and in the *Protagoras* the defence of UV rests explicitly on the defence of KSV (*Pr.* 353a4–b3).[57]

14.2. *The* Charmides. Socrates examines a Socratic view which associates temperance with self-knowledge and knowledge of one's own knowledge and ignorance (*Ch.* 167a1–7; cf. 166c7–d2; *Ap.* 21d1–7). Now Socratic self-knowledge is an important component of temperance; it will free someone from the mistaken conceit of knowledge which produces unreflective intemperate action; and it explains some of the truth in the earlier definitions—it will make a man calm and modest, never impulsive or brashly self-assertive, so that he acts appropriately and 'does his own work'. But Socrates never justifies his exclusive concern with cognitive conditions for temperate action; he simply assumes the truth of KSV.[58] And then the argument continues:

1. Only knowledge of good and evil always benefits us (174b11–c3).
2. Therefore, if temperance is separate from the knowledge of good and evil, it does not always benefit us (174d4–7).
3. But temperance always benefits us (175e2–176a5).
4. Therefore temperance is the knowledge of good and evil.

The first step, like the previous discussion of self-knowledge, assumes the truth of KSV; otherwise Socrates would have no reason to believe that knowledge of the good could avoid misuse, or that it would be sufficient for happiness (174b11–c3). Once KSV is assumed, he can readily infer that temperance must be the superordinate science of good and evil; something else would be required for temperance if it included some distinctive affective condition, but KSV rules that out. The last step of the argument is not explicit in the *Charmides*; but Socrates offers no reason for doubt about the first three steps, and they allow no escape. The argument works for any virtue, with Socrates' usual assumptions about virtue and happiness plus KSV, and commits him to UV.

14.3. *The* Laches. Like the *Charmides*, the *Laches* begins with common beliefs about non-cognitive aspects of a virtue, rejects them to examine a Socratic account confined to knowledge, and finally shows that this account implies UV.[59] The strategy is the same; Socrates shows that the favoured kind of knowledge—knowledge of what is to be feared and faced confidently (*La.* 196d1–2)—must collapse into knowledge of good in general. He could show this by the *Charmides*'s argument; but he uses another one:

1. Courage is knowledge of future goods and evils (198b5–c7).
2. Knowledge of any goods and evils must be knowledge of them all (198d1–5, 199b9–c1, c7).
3. Therefore courage is knowledge of all goods and evils (199b9–c1).
4. But knowledge of all goods and evils is complete virtue (199d).
5. Therefore courage is complete virtue.

The crucial move is (2). Socrates' claim concerns knowledge or science, not mere belief. True beliefs about future goods and evils do not obviously require beliefs about past and present. But Socrates implies that someone who claims knowledge of future goods should be justified by general principles about goods and evils without temporal restrictions.[60] One (2) is granted, KSV disposes of objections to (3) and (4), and (5) follows.[61] Socrates' conclusion would be absurd if it were meant to analyse the ordinary concept of courage. But we know Socratic definitions are not meant as analyses. He looks for the single state of the soul which is the same in all brave persons and actions; and now he has found that this state is identical with knowledge of the good.[62]

14.4. *The unity-thesis and the definition of the virtues.* If Socrates believes UV, he seems to have found an account of the virtues:

KG. Courage (temperance, etc.) is knowledge of the good. However, this does not mean he is wrong to disclaim knowledge or to deny that he has found a satisfactory answer to his question. KG will not reveal much about brave actions or provide the paradigm Socrates seeks in a definition, unless some further account of the good is found. When its components are specified we shall be able to decide whether an action is brave or not; but KG alone will not help if we are as confused about the good as about courage.

UV rests on KSV, which in turn rests on TV. Socrates' argument shows that if the CA is accepted, the hardest task is not the discovery of an account like KG, immune to refutation in the elenchos; once KSV is accepted and Socrates' normal assumptions about the virtues are applied, KG emerges easily. The hard tasks are to defend KSV and to make KG useful; each task requires a proof of TV from an account of the components of the final good. Not surprisingly, these tasks occupy Socrates in the *Protagoras*.

15. *The value of moral knowledge*

15.1. *The implications of the craft-analogy.* Socrates takes the CA seriously enough to explore the consequences of treating virtue as a craft, and to argue that they are acceptable. The rejection of incontinence, the defence of KSV and the argument for UV are all used to defend and exploit the conception of virtue as a craft. We must now consider whether his views on the value of knowledge and virtue are consistent with the CA.

If virtue and moral knowledge are simply a craft, they will be valuable for its results in producing the right product; its efficiency, however, gives us no reason to value it for its own sake. And so if Socrates values either moral knowledge or virtue for its own sake, he will show that he thinks it is more than a craft; if he values them only for their results, he can still treat them as a craft. Though moral knowledge and virtue will be identical if the CA is right, it will be easier to consider Socrates' views on knowledge and on virtue separately, since they raise different questions.

15.2. *The necessity of knowledge.* First, Socrates believes that knowledge is necessary for virtue (KNV). Someone's ability to give an account will decide not only whether he has knowledge, but also whether he has virtue (*Ap.* 29d2–30a2). A man who cannot say what courage is casts doubt on his own courage (*La.* 193d11–e6);[63] and if he does not know what a friend is, he cannot have the virtue of friendship, or be a real friend (*Lys.* 212a1–7, 223b4–8).[64] Socrates does not say why he believes KNV; but some reasons can be inferred from what he says.

15.3. *Stability.* Moral beliefs may desert a man under scrutiny (*Eu.* 11b6–e1; *La.* 194b1–4; *R.* 334b7–9); but knowledge is stable. The instability of beliefs might seem unimportant; a man's convictions may be quite reliable, even if the elenchos could refute them. But they may not always be reliable; if he has to decide what to do in conditions beyond the scope of ordinary rules, and has no reasoned principles to guide him, he may be at a loss—this is Nicias' problem. Or he may be strongly induced to act viciously, and if his moral beliefs do not rest on reasoned conviction, he may find no good reason to follow them—this is the failure of Charmides and Critias.[65] The reasoned conviction of someone who can give a Socratic account of a virtue is not just intellectually desirable; unless moral situations are predictable and decisions easy, the justification a man can offer himself for his beliefs may well affect his practice.

15.4. *Disputes.* A man's beliefs may be unstable because of his own doubts, and because of disputes with other people. Someone with moral knowledge can state the principles that justify his beliefs; and if two people agree on the relevant principles they can settle a dispute more easily than if they cannot justify their beliefs at all. A Socratic account will help to solve disputes, and most of all if it conforms to TV and ED; for all disputed terms will be removed from the principles, which will justify actions by reference to a determinate end. If the end is agreed, the principles and the suitable actions will be more easily agreed. Socrates does not examine moral disagreement in the Socratic dialogues; but he could fairly offer this solution to the problem recognized in the *Euthyphro*.[66]

15.5. *Motivation.* Socrates' solution to the paradox of the *Hippias Minor* applies to virtue only if someone believes virtuous actions benefit him; otherwise he may believe that *x* is virtuous and still choose *y* because he believes *y* benefits him. But Socrates can ensure that anyone who *knows x* is virtuous will also know it is beneficial; for if he knows it is virtuous, he can explain how it is, by showing how it contributes to his own happiness; and therefore, by KSV, he will always do *x* when he knows *x* is virtuous.[67] Without Socratic knowledge the belief that a virtuous action is beneficial may be unstable; but a Socratic account of a virtue will ensure virtuous action. Knowledge about virtue will not be the only source of the necessary belief that virtue benefits the agent; but it will be the most reliable source.

15.6. *The importance of knowledge.* Socrates believes knowledge is a common benefit to everyone (*Ch.* 166d4–6; *G.* 457e3–458b1, 505e3–6); an unexamined life is not worth living, and it is a supreme good to argue daily about virtue (*Ap.* 38a1–6); and Socrates would think it the height of happiness to go on examining the heroes in Hades (*Ap.* 41b7–e4). None of these comments shows that he values inquiry and knowledge, or deplores the unreflective acceptance of conventional beliefs, apart from the results. Self-examination is worth while because of the importance of correct beliefs about morals. (*Ch.* 157a2–b11; *La.* 185b9–c1; *G.* 472c4–d1, 500c1–4; *R.* 352d4–6).

15.7. *Influence of the craft-analogy.* All these reasons for valuing knowledge are consistent with the CA; they never require us to value it except for its results. Like other crafts, moral knowledge is worth while for its efficient production; the product determines the excellence (*aretē*) of the craftsman (*EN* 1105a27–8). Socrates might well appeal to other crafts for examples to show why moral knowledge is worthwhile.

But if these are Socrates' only reasons for valuing knowledge, his defence of KNV must rest entirely on an appeal to results. If someone with right belief could not give an account of his actions as one of Socrates' favoured craftsmen can, but could reliably produce equally good products, he should be counted as good a craftsman as the man with knowledge; similarly, if someone with only correct moral beliefs could be as reliably efficient in action as a man with moral knowledge, he would apparently refute KNV, since only the results are alleged to make knowledge necessary. Socrates does not consider this possibility; but if he accepts the CA he should recognize it as a limit on his defence of KNV.

16. *The value of virtue*

16.1. *Instrumental value.* If virtue is a craft, the reasons for saying that moral knowledge is instrumentally valuable will show that virtue is instrumentally valuable. And Socrates' principles about virtue and happiness restrict virtue to instrumental status.

1. TV requires happiness to be a determinate end; the virtuous and the non-virtuous must agree on its components. The non-virtuous man does not agree that virtue is a component of the end, and Socrates does not try to persuade him; therefore virtue should be only instrumentally valuable.[68]
2. Socrates often says that the virtues are 'useful' or 'beneficial' (*ōphelimon*) and therefore to be chosen for the sake of happiness. These remarks do not show that they are only instrumentally valuable; for he might still say either that they contribute to happiness as components, not as instrumental means, or that they are both instrumental means and goods in themselves. However, LG insists that nothing which contributes to the final good is a good in itself, and rules out both these options.

If Socrates stands by these central principles, TV and LG, he cannot value virtue for itself, but only as an instrumental means to the final good. This is what we would expect anyhow, if virtue is simply a craft.

16.2. *The care of the soul*. Socrates regularly associates his call to virtue with advice to care for the soul, since virtue is the best state of the soul. If he thinks virtue is only instrumentally valuable, he ought to believe this about the good condition of the soul too. Nothing in the Socratic dialogues requires any other view.[69]

Moral education should improve the soul, because an improved soul will improve the whole man, just as a healthy head will improve the whole body—all the goods and evils for a man flow from his soul (*Ch.* 156d5–157b1). Training in courage should aim to improve a man's soul (*La.* 185b9–e6), because the condition of his soul is determined by his moral training (*Pr.* 313a1–314b4), and will decide whether he lives well or not. Socrates demands care for the soul, not mere habituation to right action, because be believes virtue is a state of the soul, knowledge of the good, and not a habit of rule-following; rules do not always prescribe the best action, but it must be found by knowledge. A good state of the soul, on this view, will be desirable for its results in action. Socrates advises the Athenians to take care of their souls (*Ap.* 29d7–e3) or of themselves (35c5–6), before they pursue the recognized goods, wealth and so on, which do not produce the virtue needed for their correct use—virtue will secure these goods and other benefits for individuals and states (30b1–3; cf. *Eud.* 282a1–7). Socrates' advice implies no more than that virtue is the superordinate craft which uses recognized goods for the best results.

Socrates claims that life with a bad soul is even less worth while than life with a corrupt and diseased body (*Cri.* 47c8–e1). If virtue is the soul's health, is it not good in itself? This is certainly the *Republic*'s view (*R.* 357c1–3).[70] But there Plato insists that something can be both good in itself and good for its consequences; this is exactly what LG denies, and the *Lysis* treats health as one of those subordinate goods which are not good in themselves (*Lys.* 219c1–5). Our view of the *Crito* depends on whether we read it with the *Republic* or with the *Lysis*. Socrates might, consciously or unconsciously, contradict LG here; but nothing in the text requires it. The *Crito*, like other Socratic dialogues, allows the soul's perfection to be only instrumentally valuable.

16.3. *Virtue and action*. Socrates believes that virtue is a state of the soul—the possession of knowledge of what contributes to the final good. A virtuous man needs this state of soul because it produces the right results; and any state with the same results will be as good a candidate for virtue. The principle that a craftsman's excellence is determined by the excellence of his product applies here, just as it applied to moral knowledge, since virtue and moral knowledge are just the same craft. Socrates has no reason to claim that being a virtuous man or acting for a virtuous man's reasons and motives has any value apart from efficiency in action; and LG even forbids any such claim. This consequence of the CA is not rejected by Socrates—but Plato rejects it in the *Phaedo*.[71]

17. *Craft and elenchos; problems*

17.1. *Socrates' theoretical principles*. Socrates has no elaborate, carefully argued position defended against objections; but he has a coherent set of mutually supporting principles for understanding the virtues and moral choice; and to this extent he has a positive moral theory. His use of elenctic inquiry is too systematic to result from haphazard negative criticism; and when he finds that the CA has controversial implications for the nature of virtue, he defends the CA by showing that these implications are acceptable; this is evidence of a fairly systematic theory.

I have separated Socrates' arguments into those which rely on principles presupposed and confirmed by the elenchos and those which rely on principles derived from the CA. Arguments relying on both kinds of principles are combined in the dialogues, and Socrates may not have separated the principles. But a separation will be useful. For the craft-principles cannot be defended as necessary assumptions for reaching positive results from the elenchos; nor are they defended in the Socratic dialogues by elenctic argument. To defend his assumptions Socrates might argue that we expect virtue to be rationally justifiable and to include knowledge, and that our paradigm of rationally justifiable practical knowledge is a craft; and his rejection of incontinence claims to rest on beliefs about motives and actions which we all accept though we say things incompatible with them. He might believe, then, that the craft-principles are no less secure and legitimate than the others presupposed in the elenchos. But the craft-principles create problems of their own; though they strengthen elenctic argument, they also demand results hard to achieve by the elenctic method.

17.2. *Value of the craft-principles*. The craft-principles answer questions raised by the elenchos-principles.

1. Socrates argues that a virtue must be some single state of the soul; the CA shows what state it must be—knowledge and nothing more.

2. The elenchos-principles require virtue and virtuous action to contribute to happiness; the CA shows how—virtue is the knowledge of what is instrumental to happiness, and is therefore itself instrumental to happiness.

3. Socrates assumes that the final good is happiness; the CA tells him more about happiness—that it must be a determinate end.

4. The elenchos seeks an account of a virtue to say what the virtue is and why it is worth while. The CA makes this demand more precise; it requires an account to show how a virtue contributes to the achievement of a determinate product, the final good. If this kind of account is reached, it will satisfy Socrates' search for an objective answer, a proof that virtue is worth while; for virtue will be found to produce something we all want, and (by KSV) we will then act virtuously. The craft-principles show why Socrates is right to seek an account of the virtues, and what an account will say. Doctrines which would be ambiguous and ill defined without the CA become relatively clear and precise when the CA is applied. But these results raise their own problems.

17.3. *Rationality.* The elenchos is guided by the *Lysis*'s doctrine that goods are chosen for their contribution to the final good; Socrates assumes that an interlocutor forced by the elenchos to decide will prefer his choices to converge on a final good, though they need not have previously converged on it. But to deny incontinence and to show that someone desires only what he believes to be good, Socrates must insist that all desires as they are—not just as someone under examination would prefer them to be—already converge on a final good. The *Lysis* and *Gorgias* accept the strong principle Socrates needs; but only the weak principle is needed for, or confirmed by, the progress of an elenchos. The strong principle needs further defence.

17.4. *Virtue and happiness.* Socrates' assumption that virtue is beneficial rests on his principle V. But V is compatible with NTV, since it does not restrict the components of the final good. The CA needs TV, which restricts the permissible components; since happiness is a determinate end, only agreed components—those which a virtuous and a non-virtuous man alike pursue—should be mentioned in its definition. TV is needed to make moral choice conform to the pattern of a craft; but it is not defended in the Socratic dialogues, or required by the elenchos.

17.5. *Craft and definition*. A good definition of a virtue should yield a standard for moral decision; but Socrates does not decide whether or not it should eliminate disputed terms. When he accepts the CA, though, he must accept ED, which makes moral disputes soluble by some analogue to measurement. The CA requires KSV, which requires TV, which requires ED. A craftsman seeks instrumental means to some determinate, identifiable end—that is why he can explain and defend his procedure as the right way to make the product; TV makes virtue a craft by making the final good a determinate end. But the final good will not be a determinate end, recognized by the virtuous and the non-virtuous man, unless ED is true. For NED would allow accounts of the final good to include disputed terms, which virtuous and non-virtuous men might apply differently; then they might disagree on the components of the final good, if they cannot remove disputes about what is (say) good and admirable; and then they do not share a determinate end, so that TV is false. If Socrates sees these consequences of the CA, he should seek definitions satisfying ED.

ED imposes strict conditions on acceptable definitions; the *Laches*'s proposal KG clearly fails ED, though for NED it might not be so unsatisfactory. But while the elenchos offers reasonable prospects of finding NED-definitions, its success in meeting ED is much less assured. Nothing in principle prevents it from finding ED-definitions; but the Socratic dialogues never find them. The CA, and especially TV, seems to ask more than Socrates can confidently expect from the elenchos.

17.6. *Sources of knowledge*. If virtue is a craft, Socrates has clear answers to central questions in his theory. But he ought to show how the precepts of the craft can be discovered. Normally we might decide what we want to produce, and look for the most efficient way to produce it. To find the parallel, Socrates must first prove TV. But he does not; he suggests no source of moral knowledge outside the elenchos. It looks difficult to prove what a craft requires by the elenctic method; and if Socrates realizes this, it is not surprising that he offers no examples of moral knowledge resulting from the elenchos. His modesty is partly justifiable from the character of the elenchos; but partly it rests on his demand for the craft-knowledge which does not emerge from the elenchos—and here either the elenchos or Socrates' demand may be at fault.

17.7. *The status of the elenchos.* If moral knowledge is a craft, valued for its results, the elenchos should be valued for its contribution to more efficient action, by its removal of false beliefs and its progress towards knowledge. But when the knowledge is found, the elenchos should no longer be an essential method of moral instruction. It would be eccentric for any expert to instruct his pupils through the elenchos; he ought to use the systematic exposition proper to a craft. Since Socrates is no moral expert, the Socratic dialogues never threaten the elenchos with obsolescence; but if moral inquiry and knowledge are valued for their results, the value of the elenchos must be strictly limited.

This conclusion follows from the craft-principles; it does not conflict with any elenchos principles. And yet, if Socrates considered the value of the elenchos without reference to his craft-principles, would he reach the same restricted view of its value? He might reasonably insist that the elenchos stimulates someone to hold his moral convictions in the right way, rationally and autonomously, so that he can defend them for himself against objections; and he might argue that the right way of holding moral beliefs is good in itself even apart from its results. Similarly he might value knowledge reached from elenctic examination because it shows that someone's moral beliefs are justified by the right kinds of reasons, and that he has reached them by his own reflection on his beliefs. But if knowledge is to be valued just because it has been reached by the elenchos, it cannot be simply craft-knowledge valued only for its results. If Socrates agrees, he should not treat moral knowledge and virtue as a craft; the way someone holds his convictions will matter, apart from their results.

Socrates strongly believes elenctic inquiry is worth while, and has no reasoned theoretical argument to show why it is. He must accept the defence offered by the CA, if he thinks virtue is a craft. But this defence may not fully explain what Socrates, if he faced the issue clearly, would think valuable in the elenchos; and if he attached some further value to elenctic inquiry and the knowledge founded on it, he should say what virtue is, if it is not just a craft. The Socratic dialogues never hint at any conflict between the craft-principles and Socrates' interest in the elenchos; but in the *Meno* Plato finds a conflict, and rejects Socrates' view that virtue is a craft.

18. Problems in Socrates' theory of virtue

18.1. *The content of morality.* Socrates' theory provides answers to central questions that face any moral theory, and to that extent satisfies his demand for a rational account.

1. He can say what the content of virtue is. TV requires a determinate end, and virtue prescribes the means to the end. The virtuous man does not differ from the non-virtuous in his description of the final good, but in what he knows about the instrumental means.

2. He can show why the content of morality gives someone a reason to choose virtue; virtue prescribes means to an end we all pursue.

3. He can explain what will justify an action and show it is virtuous—its contribution to the determinate end of happiness. This account of the content of morality will allow Socrates to show what he wants to show, why morality is important and deserves to be taken as seriously as he demands; if it promotes human aims and interests as they are, it is worth while for anyone. The immediate problem facing Socrates concerns the specification of the final good and the defence of TV. But attempts to settle this problem raise other questions.

18.2. *The link with recognized virtues.* As soon as Socrates specifies the components of the final good, he can test ordinary virtuous actions to see if they really contribute to that determinate end. At first sight, it looks quite likely that they will not; he may well find that his reconstructed virtues overlap hardly at all with the recognized virtues; and can he then claim to have presented a theory of those recognized virtues, or to have found the single virtue of courage, say, in recognized brave actions? This question was raised earlier about Socrates' method in general; but it is far more acute if TV is accepted. For while we might agree, or at least find it plausible, that the virtues should contribute to some kind of final good, why must they contribute to a determinate end? The general principle V might be defensible; but if it is defined by TV and ED, it might well seem to demand the wholesale rejection, and not merely the revision, of beliefs about the virtues.

18.3. *Happiness.* We previously defended the concept of happiness against objections that it made Socrates' theory of virtue egoistic or unacceptably restricted the content of virtue. But if he accepts TV, these objections are more powerful. His theory still need not be egoistic in an obviously unacceptable way—his position would be clear only if he said what happiness consists in; but the scope he allows for virtue is no longer clearly acceptable. For if recognized virtue does not contribute to the determinate end Socrates call 'happiness', is that good reason to reject it? Only if the pursuit of the determinate final good is preferable to everything else; but Socrates has not proved that. 'Happiness is the supreme good, preferable to all else' may sound almost tautologous, with Socrates' normal view of happiness. But it is plausible, at most, for 'whatever is really happiness'; it is far less obviously plausible for 'the determinate end we all pursue as happiness'. For we might be wrong in our universal pursuit of some determinate end, and our beliefs about virtue might alter our view of the final good. Socrates' claims about virtue and happiness are controversial enough even if happiness is taken to be an indeterminate end; but we are tempted to retract even our initial sympathy if it is taken to be a determinate end. Perhaps Socrates thinks there is no choice of final good, that there is some determinate end which it is psychologically necessary to pursue; but he has not proved it.

18.4. *Courage and temperance.* The problem Socrates faces can be illustrated from the *Laches* and *Charmides.* Throughout each dialogue he never suggests that he will fail to act in ways recognized as brave and temperate (*Ch.* 155c5–e3; *La.* 188e5–6). He tests various definitions by appeal to the interlocutor's recognition of what is brave and temperate. But his final account is divorced from the normal affective aspects of these virtues; and if TV is assumed, will someone with knowledge of the good regularly do what is normally counted brave and temperate? Socrates has not specified the final good or shown what actions it will require; but he has no right to assume that it will require most of the recognized virtues. He might argue that some of the actions recognized as brave and temperate will benefit any rationally prudent man; but it is not clear how much of the recognized virtues will be included.

18.5. *Friendship.* If TV and LG are applied to the *Lysis*'s discussion of friendship (and LG is formulated in the *Lysis* itself), the conclusions are highly disputable. We have noticed Socrates' insistence that *A*'s love for *B* should contribute to *A*'s happiness; and if TV applies, friendship must contribute to what *A* already wants—love for *B* cannot add a new component to *A*'s conception of the final good. If LG is accepted, no person's interests can be valued for their own sake, but only for the sake of some separate good—indeed, Socrates suggests that someone needs subordinate objects of love only until he has achieved the final good, and then needs them no longer (*Lys.* 215a6–c2). All his examples of benefits from objects of love mention only instrumental benefits (217b1, 218e3–219c3), and he treats love of persons no differently (219d5–220a5). The mere reference to the agent's happiness does not by itself convict the *Lysis* of egoism, or of subordinating other people's interests to the agent's; but TV and LG make these charges more plausible.

18.6. *Problems with justice.* Now if a virtuous man's concern for other people's interests is so strictly limited, Socrates will face still more difficulties in applying his principles to justice. He is certain that a correct account of justice will recognize the kinds of just actions he defends in the *Apology* and *Crito*; and he believes he can show that just action benefits, and unjust action harms, the agent's soul. He might have defended this claim by showing that a just state of soul is somehow good in itself—if he could show this; but that line of defence would conflict with the rest of his account of virtue and of the soul's good. For if justice is the same craft-knowledge as all the other virtues, it must be instrumentally beneficial like other crafts. TV has the same result; for it requires justice, like any other virtue, to promote some determinate end accepted by the non-virtuous man, and injustice must do the soul some harm he will recognize. Any 'justice' passing this test will be far from recognized justice—or at least Socrates has shown nothing else. If he accepts the CA, and expects TV to decide what is just, he should not advocate recognized just actions so confidently. Some account of a man's good and of his soul's health might support Socrates' views on recognized justice; but the account required by the CA will not support them. The demand to be told what craft justice is and what its product is will cause Socrates some embarrassment, though it is a perfectly legitimate demand on his theory of virtue (cf. *Clt.* 409a7–d2).

18.7. *The self-sufficiency of virtue.* Socrates' defence of justice leads him to a stronger claim, that justice and the other virtues are not only necessary, but also sufficient, for happiness. A good man cannot be harmed (*Ap.* 30c6–d5, 41c8–d2; cf. *Lys.* 215a6–7); being virtuous is not simply our best prospect for happiness, but in itself ensures happiness; the virtuous man will not fail to achieve happiness for reasons beyond his control. Socrates wants the achievement of happiness to depend on us, not on chance; and he is attracted by the extreme view, which writes off all the alleged components of happiness which are not guaranteed by virtue.

But can virtue be self-sufficient if TV is true? Socrates must prove that the final good has no components which are not infallibly secured by virtue; and while TV does not rule this out, it makes the task look rather unpromising. Socrates might argue that virtue is self-sufficient because it is the supreme constituent of happiness; but TV and LG rule out this defence. The CA suggests no obvious way to defend the claim of self-sufficiency; if virtue is like any other craft, how can it be protected against defects in the material or against external interference which might frustrate its aims? Both the self-sufficiency of virtue and the CA are important to Socrates; but they are not easily reconciled, and he does not reconcile them.

18.8. *Implications*. Socrates' difficulties about justice and about the self-sufficiency of virtue are not isolated problems; for the easiest answers to them threaten the rest of the CA. If he can show that justice and the other virtues are goods in themselves, some of his problems will be reduced; but then he must deny TV; the rejection of TV, however, brings down KSV and the CA with it. The difficulties show how the CA forces Socrates into positions hard to defend with a plausible moral theory.

It would be wrong to lay all the blame for Socrates' troubles on the CA. The elenchos-principles raised serious questions, which still remain for Socrates if the CA is rejected. But the CA commits him to claims which do not merely raise questions, but seem to be beyond his resources to prove, or to imply unacceptable results about virtue. It is the CA, through TV, which severely restricts the content of morality and requires a kind of justification which threatens to sever any connections between Socratic virtues and recognized virtues. Socrates must show that the CA can avoid these unacceptable results, or abandon it and tackle afresh the question it was meant to answer. The *Protagoras* and *Gorgias*, in their different ways, try the first approach; the middle dialogues and the *Republic* try the second.

IV THE *PROTAGORAS*: A HEDONIST DEFENCE OF SOCRATIC ETHICS

1. The issues

1.1. *Virtue and teaching.* The *Protagoras* contains Plato's first systematic defence of Socratic ethics. We have noticed some of the disputable assumptions underlying Socratic doctrines; the *Protagoras* states and defends these assumptions. Quite appropriately, the dialogue is concerned with Socrates' initial question, whether virtue can be taught (319a5–c2); since virtue can be taught if and only if it is knowledge (361a5–c2), the initial question demands an examination of the claim that virtue is knowledge. 'Teaching' here requires more than just any inculcation of social norms. Protagoras describes that kind of 'teaching' in the Great Speech, but Socrates is not satisfied; he asks whether virtue can be taught as a rational discipline, systematically explained and justified. As usual, his paradigm of a rational discipline is a craft. And so the initial question requires examination of the CA.[1]

The early dialogues did not ask Socrates' initial question; but they assumed an answer. The *Charmides* promised that Socrates' words would improve Charmides' psychic health (*Ch.* 157a3–b1); and the *Laches* explicitly sought the craft which someone could learn to become virtuous (*La.* 185e4–6). Socrates did not justify his assumption that a craft of virtue could be taught, or that it was sufficient for virtue; but he certainly relied on this assumption when he accepted the CA. He must show, then, that virtue can be taught as a craft; and in the *Protagoras* he tries to show it.

1.2. *The unity of the virtues.* The *Protagoras* leads no less naturally to a defence of UV. Socrates accepted this doctrine in the *Charmides*; but he argued for it only in the *Laches*, and without explicitly endorsing it. Protagoras' account of the virtues spoke vaguely of the virtues cultivated by his method of moral training; sometimes he mentions 'the virtue of a man', sometimes he mentions particular virtues without explaining their relation. Socrates' question about the relation of the virtues is quite fair (329c2–d2).[2] Protagoras did not say whether the virtues contributed to any overall end, or whether they required each other. Socrates accepts both these claims.[3]

But to defend the full UV thesis Socrates needs to prove more than that the virtues reciprocally imply each other's presence (RV). He also wants to show that learning some craft is sufficient for virtue; and his defence of KSV is a necessary preliminary to the defence of UV. In the early dialogues he assumed the truth of KSV without argument;[4] but in the *Protagoras* he presents the final defence of UV only when he has argued for KSV. If KSV is true, Socrates must deny the existence of incontinence; he must deny that in alleged incontinent actions the agent really acts against his knowledge of what is best. In his argument for KSV Socrates duly denies the existence of incontinence.

1.3. *Hedonism.* Here Socrates relies on doctrine without precedent in earlier dialogues. For he defends KSV and UV by a hedonist account of choice and decision which raises a major question of interpretation. It is often supposed that if Socrates accepts hedonism, the *Protagoras* is a strange anomaly among the dialogues; for the earlier dialogues do not endorse hedonism, and later dialogues, the *Gorgias* and the *Phaedo*, strongly repudiate it. To remove the anomaly, some have suggested that Socrates does not seriously endorse the hedonism, but assumes it only for the sake of argument, to prove to 'the many' that even on their view of the final good KSV is true.

I shall argue that the hedonism is Socrates' own view, intended, like the rest of the *Protagoras*, to support positions assumed without defence in the Socratic dialogues. Hedonism explains the rather indefinite talk of the final good, provides a clear subject matter for the craft of virtue, and removes one possible objection to Socrates' defence of KSV. The earlier dialogues have neither endorsed nor rejected hedonism, and Socrates has good reason to invoke it here. Questions about the *Gorgias* and the *Phaedo* must be postponed; but I shall deny that they demand a non-literal view of the hedonism in the *Protagoras*.[5]

2. Hedonism and incontinence

2.1. *Socrates' problem.* To reject Protagoras' account of the virtues Socrates defends UV in a series of unsatisfactory arguments, and eventually by the argument from hedonism.[6] The last of the unsatisfactory arguments isolates the problem exactly; Protagoras denies that knowledge is sufficient for courage, insisting that 'nature and good training of the soul' are also required (350a4–b2).[7] This 'good training' will supply a non-cognitive component of courage necessary to produce the right degree of 'endurance' (cf. *La.* 192b8), to prevent either mad daring or lethargy; the Protagorean moral training described earlier is designed for this kind of non-cognitive modification of character. If courage needs a non-cognitive element, temperance may need one too, and UV will collapse. Protagoras denies KSV, assumed in the earlier dialogues, and could reasonably defend himself by citing cases of incontinence; if knowledge does not prevent conflicts of desire, the virtuous man needs further non-cognitive training to overcome them.[8] Socrates defends KSV; he expects that an examination of the many's reasons for denying KSV will help them to decide about UV (351b1–3). He is right; if KSV is true, then each of the virtues includes the same knowledge of good and evil, and nothing more—they are all the same virtue.

2.2. *The introduction of hedonism.* Socrates' next moves are rather surprising; but his strategy soon becomes clear. First he suggests the identity of the pleasant and the good, and Protagoras dissents (351b3–e11).[9] He abruptly turns to incontinence (352a1–353b5), but then returns to hedonism (353c1–354e2), and uses it to defend KSV (354e3–357e8). We must see exactly what the hedonist thesis is, and what Socrates takes to be its role in the argument. Then we can see if it is superfluous, or easily replaced by an equally plausible defence of KSV.

2.3. *Socrates' hedonist thesis.* Socrates' examples persuade the many that they will always reject actions which promise present pleasure outweighed by future pain, and accept actions which promise present pain outweighed by future pleasure (353c9–354c5); maximum pleasure is the goal of all their actions (354c3–e2). This is a fairly clear statement of hedonism, both psychological and ethical. Socrates and the many agree that we choose something as a good for its pleasure, and that we choose pleasure as the good (354c5–e2).[10] Socrates claims, not that the many consciously accept this form of hedonism, but that elenctic examination will show that their deliberations and choices are hedonistic; then he considers whether these deliberations and choices allow room for incontinence. The many defend the possibility of incontinence before they realize that they are hedonists (353c1–8, 354a2–7); and Socrates argues that when they accept hedonism, they can no longer recognize incontinence. They have agreed that maximum overall pleasure and pain are the only considerations determining choice, and so committed themselves to a principle of hedonistic prudence:

> HP: When A chooses x over y, he chooses x because he believes x will yield greater over-all pleasure than y.

When the many accept HP, Socrates argues, they must reject incontinence.

2.4. *The argument against incontinence.* Socrates now substitutes 'pleasure' and 'good' for each other in contexts which reduce the many's position to absurdity. He argues as follows:

1. (The many's claim.) Sometimes A knows x is worse than y, but still chooses x, overcome by the pleasures in x.[11]
2. (Substitute 'good' for 'pleasure'.) Sometimes A knows x is worse than y, but still chooses x, overcome by the goods in x.
3. (Substitute 'good' for 'pleasure' in HP.) When A chooses x over y, he chooses x because he believes x will yield greater over-all good than y (i.e. will be better than y).
4. (Apply (3) to (2).) Sometimes A knows that x is worse than y, but still chooses x over y, because he believes x is better than y.

Here (4) is internally inconsistent, and the many's position is indeed, as Socrates says, 'ridiculous' (355c1–d3).

When 'overcome' in (1) and (2) is replaced by the clearer formula in (4), the many's case collapses. (4) depends on (3), and (3) on HP. For (3) is a familiar Socratic principle, but flatly opposed to the initial claims of the many; and if Socrates simply assumed its truth without argument, he would merely beg the question against the many. But his argument is fair, since he can defend (3) from HP, already accepted by the many.

2.5. *The conclusion of the argument.* Socrates now tries to identify and explain the phenomenon which the many inconsistently call 'being overcome by pleasure', now that he has exposed the inconsistency. Similarly, a non-believer in witches might try to explain 'bewitchment'. Though the initial description reflects a mistaken theory, there is something to be explained; and someone might decide that what was called 'bewitchment' is only hysteria. Socrates concludes that what the many call 'being overcome by pleasure' is really only ignorance of what is pleasantest. First he infers from the previous argument that 'being overcome' is simply choosing actually greater evils in return for actually smaller goods (355d3–e3). Substituting 'pleasure' for 'good'

(355e4–356c3), Socrates explains the choice of actually smaller instead of actually greater pleasures, by ignorance of the relative size of the pleasures, and lack of the right science of measurement; that is why 'being overcome' is only ignorance (357c1–e2).[12]

Socrates relies on HP to persuade the many that the choice of pleasures is affected only by consideration of their relative size. If anything else is allowed, his arguments collapse at once. But the many cannot both accept HP and also allow that someone can choose against his belief about what is best and pleasantest.

2.6. *The role of hedonism.* This analysis of the argument implies that hedonism is vital for Socrates' case; for the argument shows only that hedonists—those whose choices conform to HP—cannot be incontinent, and will apply to everyone only if psychological hedonism is correct. If the many were not hedonists, their initial objection to KSV would not be refuted. For they suggested that some of a man's desires—for food, sex, revenge, and so on—might move him apart from his beliefs about the good; and only HP showed that they could not recognize such incontinent desires. To refute the many Socrates needs (3); to justify (3) he must appeal either to HP or to some other defence; but another defence is hard to find. If he needs HP for the rejection of incontinence, Socrates cannot afford to reject hedonism.[13]

2.7. *Objections.* When the many accept HP, they accept three assumptions, about the measure of value, hedonism, and prudence:

M. When A chooses between x and y, he values them by a single measure.

H. When A chooses between x and y, he values them only for their pleasure.

P. When A chooses x over y, he chooses it because he values x more than y.

These principles rule out different kinds of incontinence; and if the many examined them separately, they might not be so ready to concede them all to Socrates.

1. We might be incontinent because we recognize incommensurable standards of value, or 'measures'; this was part of the many's original view. We can rank various things, including pleasures, as goods, and various things, including goods, as sources of pleasure; but when our ranking of goods and ranking of pleasures prescribe incompatible actions, we have no third standard to measure both goods and

pleasures authoritatively, and sometimes we want the goods more, other times the pleasures. H removes this source of conflict by denying that there are two standards; there is one standard, of good and pleasure alike, and the conflict imagined by the many cannot appear. If we accept H, we accept M, and cannot allow this kind of incontinence.

2. But we might accept H and M, and still allow incontinence. If *A* has another drink too late at night, we might show why his action was incontinent by denying M; he believed that taking the drink would be pleasantest, though not best for him, and chose the pleasant over the good. But we might equally accept M, and agree that *A* knew that abstention would be pleasanter over all than drinking, but still say that he could not resist the drink. Socrates claims that *A* must falsely believe that drinking is pleasanter over all, because he is misled by the nearness of the pleasure it promises (356c4–8, 357a5–b3). But this explanation is required only if we accept P; and P follows neither from M nor from H nor from both together.

Socrates' reply to the many concentrates mainly on H, to prove that pleasure is the standard which guides their choice. But to justify his principle (3), and reject the second kind of incontinence, he must assume P, which does not follow from H; and though the many accept all of HP, they are offered no separate argument for P. We might reasonably advise the many to reject P, which clearly conflicts with their initial acceptance of incontinence; and then Socrates' argument against the second kind of incontinence collapses. Though H excludes some cases of incontinence, Socrates' case still depends on the unjustified assumption P.

2.8. *The proof of the unity of the virtues.* The rejection of incontinence meets the objection to KSV which threatened UV. Protagoras insisted that courage requires nature and good training of the soul, not knowledge, because someone might have knowledge and use it badly, without these non-cognitive components of courage. But Socrates has now argued that no one will fail to pursue what he believes to be best; and since all virtues aim at what is best, no one will fail to be virtuous except through ignorance. 'What is best' is taken to mean, as usual in Socratic ethics, 'what is best for the agent' (359e4–360a6). Socrates can easily prove now that all the virtues are exactly the same science—the knowledge of good and evil, now more informatively described as the science of measuring pleasure and pain. This science is not simply one component of virtue, but necessary and sufficient for

each of the supposedly separate virtues, now found to be indistinguishable; the five virtue-names are names of the same condition
of the soul, knowledge.[14]

3. *Results of the argument*

3.1. *Hedonism and the final good.* Socrates defends hedonism only
by showing that the many implicitly accept it in their choices. But to
defend the truth of KSV and UV, hedonism must be true, and not
only the many's belief. And indeed pleasure is a plausible candidate for
final good. Since everything is done for the sake of the final good,
some common end should be discoverable. '*A* did *x* for the sake of
happiness' is true for all actions, but uninformative, since 'happiness'
implies no more than 'doing well'. '*A* did *x* for the sake of pleasure'
seems more promising; it seems to allow some better description of
what happiness consists in. And we might plausibly argue that it is
the universal goal of all action and desire; for satisfaction of a desire
yields pleasure; everyone seeks the satisfaction of his desires; it is easy
to conclude that what everyone seeks is the pleasure consequent on
the satisfaction of his desires.

Pleasure seems admirably suited to do what Socrates expects of the
final good. We should be able to decide by reference to a single end,
the final good, which of two actions is worth while, and therefore virtuous; this is our way of avoiding those apparently insoluble ethical
disputes which worried Socrates in the *Euthyphro*. If we know only
that the final good is happiness, we are no further forward; but if we
know it is pleasure, we seem to make progress. For if we can
recognize cases of pleasure and tell when one pleasure is greater than
another, we can apparently estimate the probable yield of pleasure or
pain from this or that action, and choose between different possible actions. These are the benefits Socrates expects from the science of
measurement, to realize the science of good and evil which he hoped
for in earlier dialogues.

3.2. *The teachability of virtue.* The *Protagoras*, and especially the
hedonism, including HP, offers solutions to central problems in
Socratic ethics; and this is one reason for Plato to find the hedonist
theory attractive. Most clearly of all, Socrates can now show that virtue is teachable, as the early dialogues assumed. The *Protagoras* not
only defends KSV against objections, but also specifies more clearly
what is to be taught—a craft with a definite subject matter and
procedure, the measurement of pleasure and pain. Protagoras

described only the inculcation of the unsystematic beliefs of the many, with no guarantee of their truth. Socrates' measuring science offers the prospect of truth and objectivity, against the beliefs of the many offered by Protagoras.[15]

3.3. The defence of the craft-analogy.

In assuming that virtue is teachable knowledge, Socrates assumes that it is a craft. A craft can be taught and guarantees right actions because it prescribes ways of producing a product already accepted as desirable; the carpenter's craft does not teach us that it is desirable to make beds, but how to make them, given that we want to make them. To show that virtue is unproblematically teachable, Socrates needs to show that it is concerned with instrumental means and not with the choice of ends—for crafts are his only examples of teachable disciplines, and they offer no rational method for choosing ends. This is why Socrates needs to prove TV, that the final good is a determinate end, not disputed between the virtuous and the non-virtuous, and that virtue is concerned only with disputes about instrumental means.

Socrates argues that there is no real dispute about the character of the final good; the end which everyone looks to is pleasure, and people disagree only about ways to achieve it. The measuring craft does not persuade people to pursue pleasure, but shows them how to satisfy their desire for it. Socrates' defence of KSV, and his whole conception of virtue in the early dialogues, required TV; but he did not defend TV. He defends it in the *Protagoras*.

This account of the final good and the way virtue contributes to it also supports Socrates' earlier view of the status of virtue, that it is itself only an instrumental means to happiness.[16] Happiness is maximum over all pleasure; virtue is the craft of measuring pleasures and pains so as to find the action which yields the largest surplus of pleasure over pain. On this view, virtue both prescribes instrumental means and is itself instrumental to happiness; there is no reason to treat it as a good in itself, and the *Protagoras* never suggests that it is.

The defence of TV requires a strong hedonistic thesis, which we may call *epistemological* hedonism. Socrates needs to claim not only that everyone pursues as good what he takes to be pleasant, but also that we can decide whether anything is good only by deciding whether it is pleasant, and not conversely. He claims this when he tells the many that they decide what is good by looking to what is pleasant, and does not suggest the converse (cf. 353c9–e1, 354b5–e2). In the order of knowledge and decision pleasure is prior to good; for correct judgements about what is pleasant are independent of correct judgements about what is good or virtuous. That is why virtue acquires a definite subject matter and procedure when its object is no longer specified merely as 'good and evil', but as 'pleasure and pain'.

3.4. *Elimination of disputed terms.* If the Socratic elenchos is to provide accounts of the virtues which satisfy TV, it must eventually eliminate such disputed terms as 'just', 'good', 'admirable' from definitions of the virtues. For TV requires happiness to be a determinate end, and to be determinate it must be definable without disputed terms. If virtue must contribute to this determinate end, it must also be definable without disputed terms. In the *Euthyphro* Socrates contrasted those questions where a measurement-procedure prevented the outbreak of rationally insoluble disputes with ethical questions, where such disputes seemed to be inevitable (*Eu.* 7b–d).[17] The *Protagoras* offers exactly the measurement procedure which removes the disputes, by freeing us from the puzzles created by conflicting appearances (356c6–e2). The disputes are removed because the final good is defined by reference to pleasure, a determinate end; now all the virtues can be similarly defined without disputed terms.

3.5. *The replacement of the elenchos.* Socrates' view of virtue as a craft seemed to suggest that a virtuous man, like other craftsmen, would not need the elenctic method to settle moral questions; the elenchos would be useful for the discovery, not for the practice, of the craft.[18] The *Protagoras* commits Socrates even more clearly to this position. The virtuous man's craft will not be the habit of rule-observance prescribed by Protagoras; nor will it be Socrates' ability to justify his claims and reach moral conclusions by the elenchos; a craft infers its procedures from a clear conception of its product, and does not rely on the elenctic treatment of common beliefs. The elenchos, Socrates believes, shows that virtue must be a craft; and in the *Protagoras* it also shows what the product of the craft must be; for the agreed conception of the final good is reached in an elenctic inquiry. By identifying the craft and the product, the elenchos promises its own obsolescence.

4. Problems

4.1. *Conceptions of pleasure.* Hedonism solves some of Socrates' earlier problems; and doubts about hedonism itself raise doubts about the solution. First of all, Socrates does not say what he supposes pleasure or enjoyment to be, whether 'acting for pleasure' is acting for the sake of a certain kind of sensation consequent on the action, or is simply performing the action with absorbed interest for its own sake, or requires some other account. But his use of the appeal to pleasure restricts the views he can allow.

1. The pleasure of doing x seems to be a condition of the agent which is distinct from doing x. Socrates remarks that health, good physical condition, safety of cities, rule over others, wealth are good because they result in pleasure and the removal of pain (354b3–7). He does not suggest that we gain pleasure from health and from wealth in different ways, or that the pleasure of health is simply a way of being healthy; pleasure always seems to be separate from the action.

2. The pleasure and pain of different actions should be uniform and homogeneous; for the measuring science must compare them without reference to their source (351c2–6), and decide their relative quantity (356a1–6). If different kinds of pleasure came from different sources, the measuring science could not decide the best action simply by measuring quantities of pleasure.[19]

3. Socrates' epistemological hedonism requires judgements about quantity of pleasure to be independent of judgements about what is better and worse. Otherwise the science of measuring pleasures would depend on a prior science of good; and accounts of virtue would still include disputed terms.

A standard 'empiricist' view of pleasure as a uniform sensation resulting from various activities and conditions would meet these three conditions. Socrates may not definitely endorse this or any other view of pleasure. But if he cannot defend any view satisfying the three conditions, hedonism will not show how virtue is a craft; for other views will not show how the science of pleasure is simply a craft for finding instrumental means to a determinate end.

4.2. *Problems in hedonism.* It is not necessary to review all the arguments against hedonism here; but a critical reader of the *Protagoras* might fairly raise some issues.

1. We need not deny that (a) we do some actions to gain pleasure, and (b) we gain pleasure from the satisfaction of any desire; but it does not follow that (c) the ultimate aim in all our desires and actions is pleasure. We may take pleasure in having satisfied a desire, or in having attained some good, but the pleasure supervenes on the achievement of the primary end we sought, and does not replace it. Even if pleasure supervenes on all desire-satisfaction, it does not

become the ultimate end of desire; but without some such illicit move, Socrates can hardly defend his claim about pleasure.

2. We may fairly doubt whether pleasure is really a uniform sensation, and whether we can judge that one pleasure is preferable to another apart from any other judgements of value. Perhaps pleasures differ in quality as well as quantity; or perhaps quantity cannot always be assessed apart from our views of the value of an activity producing the pleasure. Someone may enjoy painting more than drinking because he thinks painting is more worthwhile, not the other way round. We may still agree that everyone does or should seek maximum pleasure; but we must now reject Socrates' epistemological hedonism. For if judgements of pleasure sometimes depend on other judgements of value, they will not always settle conflicts of values; and then Socrates loses the measuring science which settles disputes about good and evil and the virtues.

3. Though Socrates does not describe the measuring science in detail (357b5–7), he expects objective knowledge to replace the power of appearance. The science must offer generally reliable principles about the pleasure following different actions, apart from disputed claims about good and evil. But if different people's pleasures depend on their other beliefs and preferences, the hedonic science will not escape the power of appearance; it will be no objective science at all.

These criticisms of hedonism do not refute the claim that everyone pursues pleasure, or that every desirable action must promise some pleasure; but they do refute the doctrine which solves problems in Socratic ethics. When Plato accepts the criticisms of the *Gorgias*, the problems return.

4.3. *Hedonism and recognized virtues.* We noticed that if the CA, and especially TV, is accepted, Socrates faces some problems in showing that the virtues recognized by his theory are the same virtues as those normally recognized, that when people speak of 'courage', 'justice', and so on, they really refer to what he calls by those names.[20] The problem is still more acute in the *Protagoras*. Socrates relies on his normal assumption that any virtue contributes to the agent's final good; since the final good is pleasure, virtue must contribute to the agent's pleasure. Hedonism will justify the recognized brave action of standing firm in danger and facing battle (359e1–4), but only when it is admirable, therefore good for the agent, therefore pleasant for him (359e4–360b3); and Socrates does not suggest how often a really brave man (on hedonistic principles) will do the recognized brave action.

4.4. *The problem of justice.* As usual the problem is especially serious with justice, both for Protagoras and for Socrates. Protagoras promised to teach his pupil good deliberation about his own affairs and the state's (318e5–319a2), and to make men good citizens (319a3–5). Now perhaps a good citizen needs justice; but why does someone need it for good deliberation about his own affairs? Protagoras comments that we benefit each other by our justice and virtue (327b1–2); I benefit by your justice, and you benefit by mine. But he does not show why I benefit from my justice. I have reason to do the just actions necessary for you to benefit me, but no reason to do all the actions of a just man. Socrates' demand that all the virtues should promote the agent's good, and therefore his pleasure, only sharpens the problem. A hedonist 'just' man has reason to do the recognized just actions necessary to avoid the pain which follows the detection of injustice; but this policy seems to demand only the appearance and reputation of recognized justice—as Glaucon remarks in the *Republic*.[21] Socrates' defence of justice in the *Crito* already faced problems from the rest of the Socratic theory; the problems are still more acute in the *Protagoras*.

4.5. *Care of the soul.* Socrates claimed that it is never worth while to be unjust, because injustice is a vice and all vice damages the agent's soul. Hedonistic arguments do not make these claims any more plausible. If Socrates claims that injustice harms the soul by weakening its capacity to pursue pleasure, his account of pleasure does not support his claim. Alternatively, he might claim that injustice damages the soul's capacity to gain pleasures of the soul, more valuable than the ordinary pleasures of the body. But these superior kinds of pleasure undermine the uniformity of pleasure assumed in the rest of his argument; and even then he must show how recognized unjust actions incapacitate the soul for these pleasures—his task is not easy.

Socrates could argue that temperate actions directly benefit the agent; since just actions all too obviously seem to harm him, Socrates replied that still they benefit the agent's soul. The reply was hard either to reject or to defend while 'a man's good' and 'the good of the soul' were left unexplained. But the reply seems to collapse if the soul benefits by being more capable of pursuing pleasure; Socrates does not show that justice strengthens, and injustice weakens, this capacity; his hedonism undermines his defence of justice.

4.6. *Conclusion*. The *Protagoras* represents a reasonable development of the Socratic theory outlined in the early dialogues, and to that extent, we have no reason to doubt that the hedonism is Socrates' own doctrine. The craft-principles in the early dialogues needed defence; and the *Protagoras* defends them.[22] Hedonism was not implied in the early dialogues, but strongly—and perhaps indispensably—supports the claims implied in those dialogues which make virtue nothing more or less than a craft. The hedonism of the *Protagoras* need not be weakened, excused or explained away. However, the hedonist doctrine is open to objections; we will find that Plato thinks the objections demand the rejection of the doctrine. Then he faces further problems. He might not regret the failure of hedonism if some other theoretical support for Socratic ethics will do just as well. But what other candidate is available? Hedonism answered specific questions about KSV and TV; if Plato rejects hedonism he must find other answers, and it is not clear where they are to be found. If they cannot be found, Plato should ask how much of Socrates' craft-theory of virtue can be accepted if its hedonist defence fails. These questions should help to explain the progress of the argument in the *Gorgias* and later dialogues.

V THE *GORGIAS*: PROBLEMS IN SOCRATIC ETHICS

1. *The questions*

1.1. *The* Gorgias *and earlier dialogues.* The *Gorgias* frequently recalls earlier dialogues; it defends Socrates' life and philosophical position; it often echoes the *Crito* in particular; even more than earlier dialogues, it emphasizes the powers of the elenchos.[1] However, it needs separate discussion. For Polus and Callicles are a new kind of interlocutor, more critical and less co-operative than the others; and Socrates replies with new doctrines. An account of Plato's moral theory which finds conflicts and developments in his views must explain both the similarities and differences between the *Gorgias* and earlier dialogues, identifying the changes, and show what problems they might be expected to solve.

1.2. *The issues.* The careful construction and varied subject matter of the *Gorgias* advance two connected lines of argument.

1. Socrates wants to show that virtue is a craft. The *Protagoras* contrasted a Socratic craft with sophistic education, a refinement of ordinary moral training. In the *Gorgias* rhetoric is the rival candidate for the superordinate craft (452e4–7). Socrates argues that rhetoric does not, and Socratic moral science does, satisfy the conditions for a craft; he still defends the CA.

2. The *Gorgias* faces a question overdue for Socrates' attention, about the kinds of actions which this moral craft will recommend. The dialogue examines the recognized virtue which seemed hardest to defend as a craft aiming at the agent's own interest—justice; both Polus and Callicles, in their different ways, argue that a rational man has reasons in his own interest to be unjust rather than just, and Socrates tries to refute them from his own views on virtue and self-interest. This question affects the CA. For if Polus and Callicles are right, and Socrates' rational craft designed for the agent's self-interest precludes justice, then either we have reason to reject this craft, or we have no reason to be just; either way, Socrates should not claim to reduce the recognized virtues to a craft, or to explain and justify common morality. Socrates has criticized common accounts of the virtues in earlier

dialogues; he has not said he intends wholesale rejection of common beliefs about virtuous actions; indeed, the *Crito* demands scrupulous respect for the common view that justice requires obedience to law. Socrates maintained that all the virtues, including justice, are in the virtuous man's interest, but did not show why recognized virtuous actions would be in his interest. In the *Gorgias* he at last faces the radical critics' objections.[2]

1.3. *The* Gorgias *and the* Protagoras. I have argued that the *Protagoras* accepts a hedonist view of virtue and the good; and I will argue that the *Gorgias* rejects it. Either Plato's development is curiously anomalous, or my account is wrong, or Plato has good reasons both for accepting hedonism in the *Protagoras* and for rejecting it in the *Gorgias*.[3] I have tried to show his good reasons for accepting it; and I must now show his good reasons for changing his mind. If he does change his mind, he faces a problem with the CA. We saw how hedonism appeared to be the most plausible defence of the CA; either we were wrong, and the *Gorgias* has some defence at least equally plausible, or the CA will raise difficult and unanswered questions.

It would in some ways be most helpful to comment on the argument step by step. But for brevity, and to emphasize the important points, I shall select only some parts of the arguments with Polus and Callicles, and then suggest how some other parts of the dialogue are relevant.

2. *The first defence of justice; the argument with Polus*

2.1. *Tests for a craft.* Rhetoric is a rival for Socrates' moral craft because it seems to have the same supervisory role, dominating the other crafts to achieve the agent's goals (456a7–8). Socrates disagrees; rhetoric is non-rational, a mere technique acquired by experience, no real craft; it seeks the pleasant, not the good; it can give no account of its method (464e2–465a7). These charges are puzzling. Why can rhetoric not be systematically taught and explained like a craft? Why can no craft aim at pleasure? The *Protagoras* seemed to describe a science of pleasure and pain, which Socrates now apparently rejects. These questions are answered only later in the dialogue.

Socrates criticizes rhetoric because an unjust man can learn it and use it for his unjust purposes. We might think this is no fair objection to rhetoric in particular, since it applies equally to every craft, as Gorgias insists (456c6–457c3). But Socrates implies that rhetoric cannot be the superordinate craft he seeks; if it were, it would teach a man justice, and he would be just and act justly (460a5–c6).[4] The rule that every craft can be used for good or bad purposes has one exception—the superordinate craft which includes all the virtues, and which is sufficient for virtuous action. Socrates assumes that the *Hippias Minor* paradox can be answered without rejection of the CA. He relies on two Socratic doctrines:

1. All a man's desires aim at his own good (the denial of incontinence).
2. Justice contributes to a man's own good.

It will then follow that someone who knows what justice requires will do it.[5] Socrates defends both of these doctrines, and thereby defends the CA, in the argument with Polus.

2.2. *Desire and the good*. Socrates rejects Polus' claim that the skill of rhetoric is really good for the orator because it allows him to act like a tyrant and do what he pleases; it still does not allow him to do what he really wants, and so it is not good for him (466c9–467a10). What everyone really wants when he does an action is the good to be achieved (he believes) by that action; and someone who achieves what he really wants must achieve the good (468b1–4). This is simply a statement of the Socratic assumption denying the existence of good-independent desires. But why could unjust and tyrannical action never be chosen by someone who knew the good? Why would it never achieve the good he really wants? Polus and Socrates agree that 'good' here means 'good for the agent', in Socrates' usual way.[6] Socrates must now show that justice is always better for the agent than injustice would be (470e4–11).

2.3. *Justice and benefit*. Polus' objection to Socrates is—we might think—long overdue in the Socratic dialogues. He tells Socrates that justice is more admirable than injustice, but still may be worse than injustice, because it is worse for the agent; he denies the identity of the good (*agathon*) with the admirable (*kalon*), and of the bad (*kakon*) with the shameful (*aischron*) (474c4–d2). In earlier dialogues Socrates often assumed the identity denied by Polus; when the interlocutor agreed that a virtue was admirable, Socrates at once inferred that it was thereby good, and in particular good for the agent, conducive to his own happiness.[7] Polus reasonably objects that we may have grounds for admiring an action or state of character without thinking it is beneficial to us. There is nothing immoral in his suggestion; indeed, we might think it is necessary for any genuinely moral point of view. But Socrates does not agree.

2.4. *Socrates' reply*. Polus agrees that what is admirable is pleasant or beneficial *for someone*; but Socrates infers that if the victim of punishment finds it less pleasant for him, and yet more admirable than unpunished injustice, he must find it more beneficial *for him* (475b3–e6).[8] To avoid gross fallacy, Socrates must rely on the previous argument. He asks whether Polus would *choose* something admirable and beneficial (475d4–e6); they are concerned with different possible objects of choice. Polus agrees that he would choose what is admirable (475d4–6); they assume that if a possible object of choice is admirable, I thereby have reason to choose it, and will choose it. But it is agreed that whatever I choose, I desire, and whatever I desire, I desire for its expected benefit to me. And so, if I have reason to choose what is admirable, I must expect it to benefit me, either because of its expected pleasure or because of some other benefit to me; and then, on this assumption, Socrates' argument is fair.[9] Polus' position is inconsistent; if I desire whatever I desire for my own good, I cannot desire something admirable which I do not believe will benefit me. Polus has five choices. He can either (a) deny that I desire whatever I desire for my own good; or (b) deny that something's being admirable is a reason for choosing it; or (c) deny that justice is admirable; or (d) deny that justice excludes acting like a tyrant; or (e) agree with Socrates. Socrates assumes that he will choose (e); but other options seem at least equally plausible.

3. *The Argument with Callicles*

3.1. *Objections to Socrates' method*. Callicles sees one assumption which damaged Polus' case. Socrates had assumed that law-abiding, non-tyrannical behaviour is just, and therefore admirable and beneficial; in fact, Callicles replies, that kind of behaviour is not really just, but merely conventional justice, which is neither admirable nor beneficial (483a2–b4, c 6–484a2).[10] A really just man pursues his own interest, with none of the concessions to other people which conventional justice demands.

Socrates' method relies on the interlocutor's agreement, sometimes about disputable moral questions (cf. *Cri.* 49a4–b6). He can defend the accepted virtues to a compliant interlocutor accepting common views on what is really just and admirable; Polus agreed without question that law-breaking is unjust and shameful. But without these concessions, refused by Callicles, the value of the Socratic method can be challenged; if the elenchos relies on such concessions, it will surely not alter someone's general views about virtue, and though it may make his beliefs more consistent, it will apparently not convert him from being a Calliclean to being a Socratic. Socrates has not previously faced this challenge to the elenchos; he needs to show that even Callicles must concede enough for constructive elenctic argument (487d7–e7).

3.2. *Objections to Socrates' doctrine.* Callicles notices a conflict in ordinary beliefs about justice and virtue:

1. Justice is a virtue.
2. My virtue always benefits me.
3. My justice benefits other people (cf. *Pr.* 327b1–2).
4. What benefits other people sometimes harms me, and what benefits me sometimes harms other people.

Like Socrates, Callicles accepts (1) and (2), and, like Socrates, he claims the right to adjust common beliefs about justice to these general principles; the apparently plausible claim (4) then requires the rejection of (3). Now how can Socrates disagree? Callicles' argument suggests that if the elenchos can reach any positive conclusions about justice, they will be Calliclean and not Socratic conclusions. In the *Crito* Socrates accepted (1)–(3); but he did not show how his position could be defended by elenctic argument. He needs to show that (4) is false, that my justice benefits other people but never harms me; otherwise normal elenctic argument will vindicate Callicles and refute Socrates, on Socrates' normal assumptions which control the elenchos.[11]

3.3. *Callicles' hedonism.* Before he replies, Socrates presses Callicles to explain and defend his case, and eventually to accept hedonism, which Socrates then tries to refute. A refutation of hedonism damages Callicles' original case only if hedonism follows from his case; and so we must first see whether it does follow. The argument proceeds in three stages.

1. Callicles rejects conventional justice because it restrains the superior man's pursuit of his own interest. The superior man is wise and brave; he will fulfil his plans without shrinking through weakness of soul (491a4–b4); and so he will reject conventional just action as far as he can since it conflicts with his plans.[12]

2. How do we know that conventional just action will conflict with his plans? Callicles replies that a man cannot be happy if he is enslaved to anything; he must be free, and freedom is the power to do what he wants without restriction (491e5–6; cf. *Lys.* 207e1–3). These restrictions may be imposed by himself, if he is self-controlled and temperate, as well as by other people; and Callicles rejects this self-imposed restriction on desire-satisfaction (491d4–492a3). The superior and wise man will cultivate his desires until they are as demanding and extravagant as possible, and then will seek satisfaction for them. This rejection of temperance supports the previous rejection of justice; Callicles suggests that the many approve justice and temperance alike because of their own weakness; they have no power to satisfy their desires, but make a virtue out of powerlessness (492a3–b1). The superior man's plans will conflict with justice; they require unrestricted freedom for desires, and justice restricts this freedom.

3. How do we know that happiness requires the unrestricted satisfaction of desires? Callicles has to say what conception of the good underlies his claim; and he replies that maximum pleasure is achieved by cultivating extravagant desires which produce large satisfactions (494a6–b2). Pleasure must be the good for Callicles, because the only good reliably secured by his policy is the pleasure of maximum desire-satisfaction (494b6–495d5); on any other view of the good, his policy could not be relied on to achieve the good. And so Callicles' defence of unrestricted satisfaction of desire requires a hedonist conception of the good.

So far Plato's presentation of Callicles' position is fair. Callicles defends his rejection of conventional justice by his rejection of temperance, and his rejection of temperance by his acceptance of hedonism. If the hedonism is refuted, Callicles' defence of the first two positions will collapse. But it does not follow that the two positions themselves will collapse, or that the first will if the second does. For Callicles may not have presented the best possible defence of his own initial rejection of conventional justice. We must first examine Socrates' arguments against Callicles' hedonism and then ask how effectively he can reply to the two positions which Callicles defended through his appeal to hedonism.

3.4. *Socrates' objections.* Socrates presents two arguments against Callicles' identification of pleasure and good. The first (495e1–497d8) is bad. He shows that enjoying *some* pleasure is not the same as doing well on the whole; but he does not show that doing well on the whole is not simply having more pleasure than pain on the whole.[13] The second argument (497d8–499b3) claims that the coward has pleasure equal to or greater than the brave man's, so that the coward is at least as good and wise as the brave man, contrary to Callicles' previous claims.[14] This argument appears to strangely ignore the obvious reply in the *Protagoras*. We could agree that sometimes the coward may enjoy no less pleasure than the brave man enjoys, and still maintain that the brave man enjoys more pleasure on the whole, over his whole life, because of his brave action. Why would this not be a fair defence of hedonism for Callicles to offer?

First of all, Callicles' previous defence of hedonism excludes this reply. For he accepted hedonism just because he rejected any restraint of desires; but if he agreed that the brave man gains more pleasure on the whole by restraining his cowardly desire to flee, he must agree that some restraint is justified. This argument shows that Callicles cannot both reject all restraint and advocate a way of life which requires courage (491b1–3, 492a2, b1); for courage, even as Callicles understands it, requires some restraint of desires. Any hedonism useful for Callicles' purposes must be open to Socrates' attack; for to accept the defence we have suggested, Callicles must abandon his own previous position and allow restraint of desires. Socrates' objection, then, is a fair *ad hominem* argument, revealing an inconsistency in Callicles' position—he both advocated a superior man's life, which demands courage, and rejected any restraint of desires. This rejection of restraint requires the version of hedonism refuted here.

3.5. *Objections to the* Protagoras. But Socrates goes further, and speaks as though he had refuted hedonism and shown that there are good and bad pleasures (499c6–7). He has only refuted Callicles' version of hedonism. Why should he not still agree with the *Protagoras*, that pleasures are not bad in themselves, but only in so far as they cause more pain than pleasure on the whole? (Cf. *Pr.* 351c2–6, 353e5–354a1, 354b5–c2). If Socrates means to reject hedonism, he should also argue against the *Protagoras*'s solution.

He has reason to dispute the epistemological hedonism of the *Protagoras*, and to deny that hedonic judgements are independent of other judgements of value and themselves determine judgements about the good. The *Protagoras*'s defence of courage over cowardice values the brave man's prudent arrangement of his life over the chaos in the coward's life. The coward may reply that the pleasure of avoiding danger is so great, or the pain of facing danger so severe, that he prefers to run and face the consequences. Like the brave man, he feels pain when the enemy approach and pleasure when they withdraw (*G.* 498a5–c1); both the pain and the pleasure are more intense; and it is not clear, on purely hedonic grounds, which life is to be preferred. We may believe the coward's life is more painful, if we already value the goods secured by the good man. But now we have abandoned epistemological hedonism; we find the pleasanter life through our other values; our hedonic judgements offer no independent standard of good and evil. The coward cannot easily be refuted on purely hedonistic grounds; he may still prefer the pains he faced because of his cowardice over the pain he avoids by running away. Socrates implies in the *Gorgias* that unrestricted hedonism alone does not require the order and structure which, Callicles agrees, any satisfactory life should embody. Callicles wants a superior man's life which requires a rational plan, and courage to pursue it; and the mere policy of maximizing pleasure does not justify that plan.

Socrates now believes that there are good and bad pleasures (498c6–7; contrast *Pr.* 351c2–6), and that our final good is not pleasure, but the good for which we choose good pleasure (499e3–500a3; contrast *Pr.* 354c5–e2). The *Protagoras* denied both claims, arguing that all pleasure, in so far as it is pleasure, is good, and that the good is maximum over-all pleasure. Socrates does not explicitly reject those answers; but he never relies on them in the *Gorgias*; doubts about them are justified by his doubts about epistemological hedonism.[15]

3.6. *Pleasure and science.* Socrates' attack on rhetoric as a pseudo-science concerned with the pleasant without the best (465a1–2) raises further questions about hedonism. Rhetoric's concern with pleasure seems to disqualify it as a science or craft because it cannot give an account or explanation of what it does (465a2–7, 500e4–501e5). Apparently the measuring science of the *Protagoras* must be rejected as a pseudo-science because it is a science of pleasure. It is not certain, though, that Socrates means this; for a hedonist will deny that the measuring science is concerned with the pleasant *without* the best; he will say it is concerned with the best because it is concerned with maximum over-all pleasure. Now if Socrates means to endorse this reply, he will seriously weaken his case against rhetoric; to avoid his attack, an orator must simply consider maximum over-all pleasure.

Socrates' case is stronger if epistemological hedonism is false; in that case mere measurement of pleasure and pain will not identify the most desirable action without appeal to other values. A science or craft appeals to these other values; it aims at some definite product, with some objective standard of success apart from the opinions of the craftsman or the particular customer. The expert user's verdict, not just anyone's, decides if a bridle is well made (cf. *Eud* 289c1–4; *Cra.* 390b1–e4; *R.* 601c10–602a1). Even if there is no expert user of, say, beds or clothes, the carpenter or tailor must satisfy objective conditions for a well-made bed or coat; a good raincoat is waterproof, and we can know that a coat is waterproof or not apart from the beliefs of a particular user. But the fashion designer or rhetorician or any technician of pleasure has no objective conditions of his product which show that it is well made. There are no expert users; Socrates has argued that the virtuous and brave man is no more expert about maximum pleasure than the cowardly and foolish man. And the producer has no way to show he has made the right product apart from the opinions of his customers, all equally authoritative. Since he can appeal to no objective standard of correctness, he relies on memory and experience of what has pleased his audience in the past (500e4–501c1). When he tries to produce maximum pleasure in his audience, he depends on his audience's values, and has no definite objective principles to define his aims, as a proper craftsman should. This criticism will explain why Socrates thinks concentration on pleasure excludes the kind of science he seeks.[16]

3.7. *Non-rational desires.* Why should Plato change his mind? What did he not see in the *Protagoras*? Callicles himself raises one problem; his choice of pleasures will be far different from, and antagonistic to, Socrates' choice, and Socrates cannot rely on immediate agreement that one way of life is pleasanter than another. It would be hard to show that some neutral measuring science of pleasure could settle their dispute about what is pleasanter, and the dispute suggests that judgements about comparative pleasantness depend on nonhedonic values. But if Plato agrees with this, epistemological hedonism collapses; the science of pleasure will no longer settle moral disputes, in the way Socrates expected in the *Protagoras*.

But in the *Gorgias* Socrates has a further objection to Callicles not available in the *Protagoras*. He begins his argument with the wise men's story mentioning an unrestrained and insatiable part of the soul and its appetites (493a3–5, b1–3).[17] He does not explain the character of these desires, or how they make this part of the soul insatiable. But it is fair to assume that they are appetites which simply demand more and more satisfaction without concern for the good or bad results. If this is what Socrates means, he has a powerful objection to Callicles. If Callicles rejects temperance, he must advocate the unrestricted satisfaction of these desires which will cause conflicts in a man's purposes and destroy the rational order which Callicles himself has admitted to be necessary for a well-planned life. This argument was not available in the *Protagoras* and so could not be used to refute hedonism, because Socrates denied the existence of these non-rational desires which would conflict with a man's desire for the over-all good; he denied the possibility of incontinence.

Acceptance of non-rational desires is not necessary for the *Gorgias*'s attack on epistemological hedonism. Even if all someone's desires are for the good, he may, like the coward, plan his life imprudently, or fail to plan it at all; and Socrates will deny that measurement of pleasure alone will refute the coward. But recognition of non-rational desires strengthens the attack on Callicles' version of hedonism; if Callicles allows the satisfaction of all desires, his policy will not be merely strange or imprudent, but destructive of any rational plan for a life at all, since these non-rational desires are unconcerned with someone's over-all good. Socrates relies on this objection when he defends the psychic order and harmony which prevents control by non-rational desires; but his defence causes other problems for his theory.

4. *The second defence of justice*

4.1. *Psychic order.* The argument with Callicles raised three issues: (1) Callicles' rejection of conventional justice; (2) his rejection of temperance and self-control; (3) his acceptance of hedonism. Hedonism was required for the reason we saw, to justify the rejection of temperance. But then Socrates argued that Callicles could not accept hedonism without rejecting courage as a virtue; and if he cannot accept hedonism, he cannot defend his rejection of temperance. For if anything else besides unrestricted desire-satisfaction is recognized as a good, Callicles cannot show that it may not require restriction of desire-satisfaction. Once he is forced to recognize that restriction of the pursuit of pleasure and desire-satisfaction is legitimate, because there are good and bad pleasures (499a6–e5), he cannot reject temperance altogether.

Callicles cannot easily deny that courage and resolution in pursuit of rational aims is a virtue. For his superior man has a rational plan for his life which he follows with resolution and without flinching; to develop his demanding and expensive desires and find resources to satisfy them, he must restrict the satisfaction of other desires, especially those insatiable non-rational desires which might divert him from his main aims. If Callicles agrees that a rational plan of life requires courage in pursuit of rational plans, he has an equally good reason to demand temperance, to restrain non-rational desires. He thought that courage excluded temperance; Socrates has shown that a brave man has reason to be temperate too; indeed the temperance is hard to distinguish from the courage, when both virtues prescribe pursuit of rational aims without distraction from conflicting non-rational desires. We have not yet decided which actions will really be temperate—that depends on what the right rational aims are; but Socrates can fairly claim to have shown Callicles that temperance should not be rejected altogether. He has not relied on the consent of an interlocutor with conventional moral beliefs, who will agree without argument that temperance and self-restraint is a virtue; he can argue that even a critical interlocutor will accept general conditions for an acceptable plan of life which require temperance.

4.2. *Psychic order and justice.* Now all this argument against Callicles was meant to refute his initial rejection of recognized justice—or so it appeared; at any rate, Socrates offered to convince him that it is better to suffer than to do unjust action (482b2–6), and claims to have proved this (508a8–c3). But his argument is as bad as the argument he offered Polus. Socrates has shown that someone who aims at the good—as usual, his own good—will require order in his soul (506c5–e5); and he has some reason to identify this order with temperance or self-control (506e5–507a7). But when he says that the temperate man will do what is 'fitting', and will thereby embody the other virtues, including justice (507a7–c7), we must hesitate.

In one way, Socrates' inference is justified; a man with an orderly soul will do what is fitting for his own benefit; and since (Callicles and Socrates agree) real virtues are the conditions which benefit the agent, such a man will have all the real virtues, including real justice. But Socrates has not shown why someone with this 'Socratic' justice (s-justice) will have commonly recognized justice (c-justice), and so benefit other people, contrary to Callicles' view.[18] C-temperance requires c-justice; that was one reason why Callicles rejected c-temperance. But Socrates has not proved that a rational man need c-temperance; the s-temperance required is some restraint of non-rational desires, but Socrates has not shown why an s-temperate man will not act tyrannically. S-temperance no doubt requires s-justice, but it does not clearly require c-temperance and c-justice. If Socrates can show that our s-unjust action promotes s-injustice in the soul, and thereby harms us more than other people's unjust action against us ever would, he will have shown it is better for us to act s-justly than to act s-unjustly; but for all he has shown, Polus' tyrant does not act s-unjustly—the required connection between s-injustice and c-injustice has not been proved.

4.3. *The reply to Callicles.* Socrates originally sought to refute Callicles' defence of c-injustice, and to defend c-justice. He has completed the first task more successfully than the second. Callicles originally advocated c-injustice for the sake of a man's own desire-satisfaction; c-justice was bad because it restrained a superior man from the unrestricted pursuit of his own satisfaction and pleasure. Socrates has undermined that defence of c-injustice, by showing that some restrictions are necessary for a satisfactory life; a man's rational pursuit of his own happiness has not been shown to conflict inevitably with c-justice. But while Socrates has disarmed one case against c-justice, he has not shown that the restriction of desire it demands is necessary, or even tolerable, for a rational man. He has undermined one argument for c-injustice, but offers no further arguments against it or in defence of c-justice.

Socrates need not reject c-injustice altogether. People may be wrong about justice, as they were wrong about temperance and courage. But if he cannot preserve some sufficient number of the common beliefs, is he still talking about the same virtue?[19] And apart from these worries about co-reference, it will be disturbing if his theory allows a s-just man no good reason for the reliable concern about other people's interests demanded of a c-just man.

4.4. *Justice and other people's interests.* The problem is clear when Socrates contrasts the attitude of the orator and of the real politician. The orator cares about pleasure, both his own and other people's (503c4–6), and Socrates suggests he cares about other people's for the sake of his own (cf. 462b11–c2). The good politician is a craftsman with his eye on the good (503d5–504a5), and concerned to make the citizens better (504d5–e4, 507a8–e3). Socrates needs to show that this treatment of the citizens is just—that their 'improvement' really benefits them, and that the s-just man has reason to benefit them. He suggested that a man's own good requires friendship with others (507d6–e6); but he has not defended steady and reliable concern for other people's interests; why should a wise man not 'improve' people for his benefit, not their own? Socrates told Polus and Callicles that happiness excludes tyrannical treatment of other people; but Thrasymachus' objections in the *Republic* show that the claim has not been proved.[20]

5. *Results and problems of the* Gorgias

5.1. *Knowledge and virtue.* We have examined the *Gorgias*'s defence of Socratic doctrines, and its challenge to the distinctive doctrines of the *Protagoras*. It is useful to see how satisfactory this defence is, and what doubts or lines of further inquiry it might reasonably suggest to Plato.

First of all, Socrates relies on KSV; the man who has learnt justice is just, as the man who has learnt carpentry is a carpenter (460a5–b7). We might object to this analogy; 'carpenter', in the relevant sense, is a capacity-word, meaning 'someone capable of making beds, tables, etc., if he wants to', so that we could easily say, 'He is an excellent carpenter, though he has been a bus-driver for twenty years and done no carpentry.' 'Just man', we might insist, differs from 'carpenter' in referring to a state and disposition which will reliably produce just actions; it means not 'capable of doing just actions if he wants to', but 'reliably doing just actions when they are called for in normal circumstances'. And in this sense, it seems Socrates has no right to assume that learning about justice is sufficient for being just. This would be an Aristotelian objection to Socrates' argument (cf. *EN* 1106a6–9, *MM* 1208a31–b2).

Since Socrates attacks rhetorical training because a pupil can misuse it, he must defend someone who has learnt justice against the same attack. He argues, as we have seen, that everyone always seeks the good for him, and that justice is good for the just man. The first step requires the denial of incontinence; but Socrates suggests no reply to the counter-examples offered by the many in the *Protagoras*. In the context (467c5–468c8) this was not surprising, since Polus would hardly defend rhetoric because it satisfies incontinent desires. But the failure to answer the many's objections casts serious doubts on Socrates' over-all defence of KSV, and on the initial claim about learning justice as a craft. The *Protagoras* appealed to hedonism for a non-question-begging defence of KSV against the many. But once the hedonism is rejected, Socrates has no defence to replace it; and he certainly offers none in the *Gorgias*.[21]

5.2. *Non-rational desires*. The *Gorgias* not only fails to argue, as the *Protagoras* did, against the existence of non-rational desires, but even seems to recognize them. For the insatiable part of the soul needing control and restraint should consist of non-rational desires; why else would the control and restraint be needed? (Cf. 493a1–b3.)[22] Socrates advocates self-control (491d4–e1) and temperance; Callicles' view is rejected partly because it allows freedom to the non-rational desires which a prudent man would restrict. The account of virtue assumes the existence of non-rational desires; a virtuous man needs order in his soul, producing s-justice and s-temperance, to control his non-rational desires and achieve his own good.

Elsewhere, however, Socrates has assumed or argued that there are no non-rational good-independent desires to conflict with desires resting on belief about the good; and if there are none, we need not control them. On this view, the central element in the *Gorgias*'s account of virtue, self-control, must be unnecessary. That is why the *Charmides* ignores self-control; the one apparent example of psychic conflict (155ce) is never discussed in the dialogue. The *Laches* excludes endurance from the account of courage, and, like the *Charmides*, treats knowledge as the whole of virtue. Reasonably enough, Socrates in the *Protagoras* is sceptical about talk of being 'overcome' by pleasure—the result of a failure of 'control'—and argues that it is simply ignorance (*Pr.* 357e2). Even in the *Republic* Plato recognizes that there is something paradoxical in this talk of controlling oneself and being overcome, and tries to justify it (*R.* 430e3–431b2).[23]

The *Gorgias* first claims that whoever has learnt justice is just, implying the truth of KSV and the rejection of good-independent desires. It claims later that justice is psychic harmony, implying the existence of good-independent desires and the falsity of KSV.[24] Socrates must reject at least one claim; but he can reject neither without serious damage to his position. He tells Callicles that to avoid unjust action we need a craft which will tell us how to avoid it (509d7–e7); but he does not explain how a craft will produce psychic order. His argument has not supported the CA, but undermined it.

5.3. *Virtue and the final good*. We noticed that the CA and KSV rested not only on the denial of incontinence, but also on the truth of TV, that virtue secures the instrumental means to a determinate final good accepted by virtuous and non-virtuous alike. The hedonism of the *Protagoras* described this determinate end; but when the *Gorgias* rejects hedonism, it offers no alternative answer. A determinate end is needed for Socrates' argument against the tyrant; for he assumes that the tyrant lacks only the knowledge of how to attain happiness, and that the removal of his ignorance will alter his practice. But then what is this conception of the final good on which Socrates and the tyrant agree? Polus is surprised at the suggestion that justice and culture (*paideia*) are necessary for happiness (470e4–11).[25] Socrates and the tyrant do not seem to share the necessary common conception of the final good. But if the tyrant lacks knowledge of the components of happiness, he will not save himself by acquiring some craft. For crafts are rational, systematic procedures just because they rely on some agreed conception of the product; and that is just what Socrates and the tyrant apparently do not share. If Socrates admits this, he must also agree that crafts cannot be the model for virtues, and that the virtuous man's actions cannot be defended by the kind of argument which would defend a competent craftsman.

5.4. *The status of the virtues.* Socrates' account of the virtues allows him some defence against this charge. Though he has described no determinate and accepted final good, he has argued that the virtues are worthwhile for any conception of a final good which will satisfy a rational man; someone who accepts a rational order in his choices has reason to control and order his desires, whatever ultimate end he pursues. This is why justice can fairly be compared with health (479a5–c4). Whatever goals someone pursues, he has reason to want a healthy body; and Socrates believes—though his reasons only become clear later, in the discussion with Callicles—that someone with any rational plan has equal reason to want a healthy soul, with rational desires controlling non-rational desires. It is not clear whether he means that this is a useful instrumental means to happiness, or both an instrumental means and a component. In the Socratic dialogues, we argued, virtue was treated only as an instrumental means to happiness, and the *Gorgias* nowhere rejects this view.[26]

The snag in this defence of virtue should already be clear. Callicles overstates his case against the recognized virtues; Socrates shows the inconsistency in his advocacy of a life which both conforms to a rational plan, requiring courage and endurance, and rejects all restraint of desire; and he defends some parts of temperance. But someone might apparently accept this defence, and still advocate a Calliclean way of life, aiming at the expansion and satisfaction of appetites, if he planned it carefully and restrained his desires to avoid future frustration. Socrates would not regard this as a temperate way of life; but his defence of temperance shows nothing wrong with it. Someone else might reject this Calliclean ideal of extravagant desires and intense satisfactions, but still advocate a disciplined life aiming at his own benefit at other people's expense. Socrates would not call this life 'just'; but if justice is simply the psychic order of someone who does what is fitting for his own happiness, why is it not a just life?

Socrates claims, as in the *Apology* and *Crito*, that it is always worth while to be just, and that just action matters most for happiness (512d6–e5), as though the just man were self-sufficient, and independent of other dangers to his happiness. But the account of justice as mere prudential psychic order does not support this claim; that order has been shown to be useful, not to be intrinsically good; and it does not clearly require the kind of just action Socrates defends in the *Apology* and *Crito*, and again in the *Gorgias*. He has refuted Callicles' argument that my good necessarily conflicts with other people's, because it requires unrestrained desires; but he has not argued against the possibility of conflict. He has not shown that a s-just man with an orderly soul, seeking his own good, will always find it worth while to benefit others.

The problem here concerns TV and the determinate character of happiness. To argue for more than some weak prudential self-control Socrates cannot remain neutral or agnostic about the character of the final good. For any conception of the final good accepted by Callicles will apparently require the violation of c-justice; and to defend c-justice Socrates must show that Callicles has the wrong conception of the final good, and the virtuous man has the right conception. But now we lose a major benefit of the CA. If virtue is a craft, ethical disagreement is rationally soluble, because it is concerned with instrumental means to a determinate end—some agreed product. Once we allow disputes about components of the end as well, we lose the previous assurance that disagreements are rationally soluble; for we have not been convinced that the choice of an ultimate end, not guided by the principles of any craft, is a rational choice. Apparently Socrates must either fail to justify the recognized virtues or lose his argument for the rationality of the virtuous man's choices.

5.5. *Elenchos and craft*. The *Gorgias* emphasizes a problem in Socrates' programme about the relation of the elenctic method to the moral craft which Socrates hopes for.[29] The powers and limits of the elenchos are displayed; it relies on the interlocutor's agreement, and reaches conclusions which justify confidence (508e6–509a4), but support no claim to firm knowledge (509a4–7). The moral craft, on the other hand, should not suffer from these limitations; it will have a definite conception of the product, and explain each step in production by reference to the product. This moral craft assumes agreement on the product; and if the elenchos is to show the possibility of a moral craft, it should reach an agreed conception of the final good. The *Protagoras* solved this problem, if the elenchos showed that pleasure is the final good, and that a science of pleasure is possible. The *Gorgias* abandons both claims without replacing them with other claims to solve the same problems. Socrates still treats the elenchos as a method of discovering the principles which will belong to a moral craft. But he finds no agreed conception of the final good; and without it, the moral craft cannot begin.

5.6. *The results of the* Gorgias. The *Gorgias* is a puzzling and unsatisfactory dialogue, because it attempts ambitious tasks with the inadequate resources of the Socratic theory. Unlike the Socratic dialogues, it faces the awkward questions raised for Socrates by the recognized virtue of justice and by radical criticism of it; it tries to defend Socratic method and doctrine without the dubious support of the *Protagoras*'s doctrines. Success is far from complete. The *Protagoras*'s views are rejected, but the questions they tried to answer are still unanswered. The Socratic defence against Callicles shows the incoherence in Callicles' defence of an unjust way of life, but does not vindicate justice; and that whole argument is plausible partly because Socrates recognizes non-rational desires, and so undermines his basic doctrine of KSV.

The *Gorgias* shows the problems arising for any defence of Socratic ethics which cannot count on support from the *Protagoras*. Plato eventually decides that these problems are too severe, and that the theory itself needs radical revision. We will see the revision most clearly in the *Republic*; it presents a different theory, intended to cope with some of the problems arising from the *Gorgias*. But first it is useful to consider some arguments in the middle dialogues; for they attack some of the *Gorgias*'s assumptions about moral knowledge and virtue, and they underlie the new theory of the *Republic*.

VI THE MIDDLE DIALOGUES: CRITICISMS OF SOCRATIC ETHICS

1. *The significance of the middle dialogues*

1.1. *New doctrines.* At first sight, the middle dialogues could be ignored in an account of Plato's ethics; unlike the dialogues we have discussed so far, they do not concentrate on moral questions; their interests in metaphysics and epistemology and their startling and ambitious conclusions contrast sharply with the silence or agnosticism of
earlier dialogues. I shall argue that none the less they are important for
our purposes, and that they explain some of the crucial differences we
will find in comparing the *Gorgias* with the *Republic*. Important parts
of the metaphysics and epistemology are not mere extravagances or
products of Plato's un-Socratic interests; I shall try to show how they
are intelligible answers to legitimate questions that a critic of Socratic
ethics might raise.[1]

The middle dialogues are concerned, as Socrates was, with the
search for a definition. The search leads Plato to three metaphysical
doctrines with no earlier parallel:

1. The *Meno* defends Socratic inquiry into virtue with the Theory
   of Recollection.
2. The *Phaedo* argues that the final objects of recollection and of
   Socratic definition are separated Forms.[2]
3. The *Symposium* argues that the Form of Beauty is the final
   object of all desire for the beautiful and the good.

The Theory of Recollection connects (1) and (2); the Theory of Forms
connects (3) with (2), and therefore also with (1); and the *Phaedrus*
confirms the connection by its appeal to recollection in its account of
desire. We must see why Plato's Socratic aims and methods must be
explained by these new doctrines.

1.2. *Conflicts with Socrates.* The middle dialogues appear not only
to explain and develop Socrates' views, but also to reject them:

1. The *Meno* rejects the Socratic defence of KNV, and argues that
   for right action true belief is just as useful as knowledge.

2. The *Phaedo* criticizes people with 'slavish' virtue, who act virtuously for the sake of some recognized good separate from virtue. Socrates never attacks this motive for virtuous action.

3. The *Symposium* does not openly reject any Socratic doctrine; it re-examines the questions answered by the *Lysis*'s account of the primary object of love, and we must see whether the very different and far more complex apparatus of the *Symposium* reaches the same answers.

4. The middle dialogues never claim that virtue is a craft, and never argue from features of a craft to features of a virtue. It is not easy to explain this silence about the CA; it might be an accident, since the middle dialogues do not discuss the virtues at length. But still, silence about such a central feature of Socratic ethics is striking; and we can reasonably ask whether the new doctrines of the middle dialogues give Plato reason to reject or fail to emphasize the CA.

1.3. *Explanations.* We might try to resolve these apparent conflicts and argue that Plato means to supplement, and not to reject, Socrates' views, or that he addresses different questions outside Socrates' concerns. Instead I shall suggest that the conflicts are genuine and explicable; Plato's defence of Socratic inquiry through his metaphysical doctrines conflicts with other Socratic views, especially on the three points above. We have examined some questions raised by Socrates' theories, and the different solutions of the *Protagoras* and *Gorgias*. And though Plato discusses metaphysical and epistemological questions far more in the middle dialogues than in most earlier dialogues, he is still concerned with the same questions in Socratic ethics.

2. The Meno; the Unity Assumption

2.1. *The procedure of the* Meno. The first part of the *Meno* (to 80e) looks like a standard Socratic inquiry; Socrates insists as usual that a definition of virtue is prior to any knowledge of what it is like (71b1–8);[3] and Meno's various definitions are proposed and rejected. But Plato is far more self-conscious about his aims and methods than he was in the Socratic dialogues, or even in the *Gorgias*.[4] First he sets out criteria for a good definition; then he raises Meno's basic objection to the whole elenctic method, far more serious than Callicles' attack in the *Gorgias* (G. 482c4–483a2). Normally Socrates practises his method without reflection; this radical criticism, requiring examination and defence of the method itself, is unparalleled in earlier dialogues.

2.2. *Definition and the Unity Assumption.* Socrates' insistence on the priority of definition justifies his elenctic search for a definition. But this search is harder than it looks because he is as selective as ever about acceptable definitions; in the *Meno* he repeats the UA, but realizes it is not self-evident or unproblematical, and tries to defend it. He wants, not 'many virtues', many examples and types of virtuous behaviour, but the single form found in all virtue (72a6–d1). His defence in the *Laches* appealed to the unsatisfactory example of speed (*La.* 191d9–192b8); but here he realizes the UA is not equally obvious for all predicates. For (A) predicates like 'bee', Meno is convinced, and Socrates presumably thinks also, that a single definition could easily be found in such unproblematic cases (cf. *Tht.* 147c4–6). Meno then accepts UA for (B) 'health', 'strength', and 'bigness' (72c6–e8); and Socrates thinks he will more easily accept it for (C) 'virtue'.

(B) is not so obvious; Meno might reply that a strong or healthy woman or child cannot do what a strong or healthy man can do, and a big woman or child would not be a big man. Socrates will presumably insist that none the less a single account of health, strength or bigness can be found; health may be (say) a single condition of the bodily elements, though producing different effects, and bigness or strength may be (say) dimensions or physical capacity exceeding the norm, though the norms may differ (cf. *HMa.* 294b2–4).

2.3. *The Unity Assumption and virtue.* Socrates might have offered a similar answer for virtue; in all the different cases virtue is good performance of function. But he does not offer this answer; and if he did, he would not be correcting Meno, who accepts it at the same time as he insists on the diversity of virtue (72a2–5). Now Socrates denies that this is the kind of unity he wants; he is concerned, not with the meaning of 'virtue' which would apply to the virtue or excellence (*aretē*) of men, women, horses, and hammers, but with the nature of human virtue, and he implies that it must be a single state or conjunction of states of a person. The state must be 'single', not as a single A-power might be, producing the same type of behaviour, but as a single B-power, a single state producing perhaps quite different kinds of behaviour.

Socrates defends this claim inadequately. Meno agrees that all his virtuous people need to act justly and temperately; Socrates infers that they need temperance and justice to become virtuous, and that therefore virtue is the same in them all (73a6–c6).[5] But he does not defend the claim that temperate and just action must be explained by the same virtues in all cases, temperance and justice; why should Meno not say that same kinds of actions—temperate and just actions—are explained by different B-powers in different people? To refute him and to show that a single virtue is needed, Socrates would have to show that they are the same actions in so far as they have the same causation; the temperate actions of men, women, and children, or of old and young people, may be very different from every other point of view than that they are the actions that would proceed from the same state of the soul—they are actions that a temperate person would do (though they need not always be done by a temperate person; cf. Ar. *EN* 1105b5–9). Here as in the Socratic dialogues Socrates needs this claim, though he does not argue for it.

2.4. *Problems for the Unity Assumption.* Socrates' argument was meant to show that the UA applied to C-predicates like 'virtue', as well as to A-predicates like 'bee' and B-predicates like 'health'. He does not himself say how these predicates should be distinguished, though he implicitly recognizes that they are steadily harder cases for UA. For (A), we might suppose, a single set of agreed features defines what it is to be mud or a bee. (B) might be those predicates which allow disputes to be settled by an agreed measurement-procedure (cf. *Eu.* 7b6–d5); we might accept UA for health, strength, or bigness if we allow a single kind of agreed procedure in each case, though with different norms or standards of comparison.

But (C) still raise a problem, more evident in the *Meno* than in earlier dialogues. Socrates has rejected Meno's many virtues because the virtuous person will always act 'well', and 'well' must be explained by 'justly and temperately', and that in turn by 'with justice and temperance'; he rightly ignored 'performing its function well' as a general account of virtue, because 'well' would have to be explained the same way, and the general account by itself would be uninformative about human virtue. He claims that the only coherent standard for our classifying people as virtuous refers to states of character, justice, and temperance. But is this a proof of UA? Hardly; since 'justice' and 'temperance' like 'virtue' are disputed predicates (in the *Euthyphro*'s terms), and we do not know they refer to a single condition until we define them, we still do not seem to know that 'virtue' refers to a single condition. And yet Socrates has managed to defend UA for 'virtue' only by appeal to the other disputed predicates; we need to know whether they can be eliminated from the account of virtue. The initial explanation of virtue does not satisfy his aim of eliminating disputed terms (ED), and he does not show that he can both satisfy ED and defend UA.[6]

3. Problems of definition

3.1. *Conditions for a good definition*. When he has persuaded Meno to accept UA, Socrates explains the kind of single account he wants. Two of his conditions are easily accepted; the *definiens* and *definiendum* must be coextensive (75b8–c1);[7] and the account must not be unintelligible to an interlocutor without specialized knowledge (76e3–4).[8] But the third condition is more difficult. Meno rejects an account of shape as 'the only thing which always goes with colour', because it will not help anyone who is as puzzled about colour as about shape (75c4–7); and Socrates agrees that it is 'more dialectical' to answer 'through those things which the questioner previously agrees he knows' (75c8–d7). Meno did not know about colour because he could not give an account of it (75c5–7); and Socrates' 'dialectical requirement' (DR) implies that if *A* defines *x* for *B* as '*yz*', and *B* does not know about *y* and *z*, *A*'s definition is a bad one.

3.2. *Implications*. What kinds of predicates will pass the DR? A-predicates are good candidates; Socrates suggests it is easy to say what is a bee or mud, and so these could readily be mentioned in a definition.[9] B-predicates might violate the prohibition on specialized knowledge, if only an expert knew the right account (cf. *Alc.* 111e4–6). C-predicates clearly fail the DR; Socrates rightly rejects any interlocutor's claim to know about any moral property (cf. *Eu.* 7b2–e4). The DR makes sure that the predicates mentioned in a definition are understood, on Socrates' normal test for understanding—that a definition can be found; and definitions including moral terms seem to merely replace one ill-understood predicate with another. An account of courage as 'knowledge of good and evil' or of virtue as 'performing one's function well', or with 'well' replaced by 'with justice and temperance', will fail the DR, and Socrates does not allow them as adequate accounts. The DR requires ED.

3.3. *Meno's definitions*. Socrates' criticisms of Meno's definitions show that the DR is not easily met. First Meno suggests that virtue is the power to rule over men (73c9–d1); Socrates easily shows that this account is too narrow, since virtue need not be displayed in ruling (73d2–4), and too wide, since virtue requires ruling justly (73d7–9). Socrates develops the second objection when he examines Meno's more promising account of virtue, as the power to acquire goods (78b9–c1). This account is also too wide, because a virtuous man will only acquire goods justly, and too narrow, because someone who acts justly, but fails to acquire goods, is still virtuous.

Socrates' objections are surprising; he normally thinks virtue is a craft, a power to acquire goods (cf. *HMi.* 375d7–e3); and his rejection of incontinence (*M.* 77b6–78b2) seems to rule out abuse of this capacity, since everyone who knows he has it will use it to acquire goods. So far Socrates should accept Meno's definition; though Meno has mentioned only recognized goods open to abuse (78c5–d3; cf. 87e5–88a5; *Eud.* 280d1–4), real goods require psychic order and justice (cf. *G.* 505a5–c7), and, this granted, Meno's account should be right.[10] But Socrates does not agree; he insists that since (a) a virtuous man will acquire goods justly, therefore (b) virtue cannot be only a capacity to acquire goods (78d3–e3). But (b) does not follow from (a) if justice and virtue are only instrumental to the final good; for then if I have the capacity to acquire the good, I shall use it to obtain the good, and just action will be required. To prove (b) from (a) Socrates must show that someone who acts justly cannot simply choose just action for the sake of its instrumental benefits, but most choose it the way a just man would choose it (cf. *EN* 1105a23–6). That would show why virtue could not simply be a capacity to acquire goods, but must include acquiring them the right way. Perhaps it is wrong to press the argument so far; but to justify his objections to Meno's account, Socrates must raise doubts about the assumption of the Socratic dialogues, that a virtue is simply an instrumental means to good results. This line of objection to the previous Socratic view remains relevant later in the dialogue.

3.4. *A dilemma.* To avoid the objections to his account of virtue as the capacity to acquire goods, Meno is persuaded that he must mention justice in his account (78e7–79a2; cf. 73d6–10); but now the amended account is faulty because it mentions a part of virtue in the account of virtue (79a7–b3; cf. 74a7–10).[11] There are two faults in the account; (a) it is circular (79b4–c10), and (b) it violates the DR (79d1–e4). But Socrates proves (a) only through the DR. If virtue is defined as 'acquiring goods with justice', the account is not circular until we substitute 'the part of virtue which . . .' for 'justice'; and it is the DR which demands that substitution, to show we know justice; without the DR Socrates could not make the account appear circular. He can also appeal to (b) alone to reject less evidently circular accounts of any disputed property which mention other disputed properties; he uses the DR to insist on ED.

But the DR makes the task of definition harder. When Meno's list of the goods acquired by virtue satisfied ED and the DR (78c5–d1), Socrates found counter-examples to the account; but when the account was protected against the counter-examples, it failed the DR. The insistence on ED also casts doubt on Socrates' initial claim, UA. For no account of virtue or virtuous action in ED-terms has seemed at all likely to show the single state common to all virtuous action. Socrates finds accounts uninformative if they violate the DR; but those which satisfy the DR do not satisfy his demand for a single standard for classifying virtuous actions and people. These problems might suggest that not all his demands can be satisfied.

4. *The Theory of Recollection*

4.1. *Meno's paradox.* Socrates' insistence on the DR reasonably leaves Meno puzzled about whether he can answer the Socratic question at all. But he does not attack the DR alone, but a more basic Socratic principle, the priority of definition (71b1–8), because it rules out any search for a definition (80d5–e5):

1. If I don't know what x is, I know nothing about x.
2. If I know nothing about x, I can't identify x.
3. If I can't identify x, I can't recognize x as the subject of my inquiry.
4. If I can't recognize x as the subject of my inquiry, I can't inquire into x.
5. If I don't know what x is, I can't inquire into x.[12]

Meno suggests that if I know nothing about x, I can't even pick it out from the undifferentiated mass of things I don't know so that I can inquire into it (80d6–7); and even if I could somehow collect a body of truths which in fact apply to x, I could not tell they apply to x if I do not know x (80d7–8).

The argument seems to be hard for Socrates to evade. (1) is his own principle; (3) and (4) are hard to challenge. He must show that (2) is false. Now we found that the Socratic dialogues did not explicitly or implicitly endorse (2); but the demand for knowledge of the constituents of a definition satisfying the DR might excusably lead Meno to suppose that Socrates relies on (2) here. Certainly the earlier dialogues did not explicitly reject (2); and they offered no account of inquiry and definition which would support (1) without (2). Socrates should clarify his position against Meno's objection.

4.2. *The examination of the slave.* The *Meno* again displays its self-conscious attitude to Socratic method. For the examination of the slave is a scale-model of a Socratic elenchos, with a commentary to explain and justify the procedure. First the slave's initial confident beliefs are refuted, and he is reduced to confusion (84a3–b8); but further interrogation shows that he can correct his beliefs to reach the right answer.

Socrates claims that he does not teach the slave the answers (84c10–d2; cf. *Ap.* 19d8–e1). Naturally, he asks leading questions; but the slave is expected to accept only the answers which seem reasonable to him, justified by beliefs he already accepts; he is not taught anything he can see no reason to accept. This progress to improved beliefs from his own resources is compared to recollection; in each case someone reasons from his present beliefs to an answer which seemed beyond him until he realized he had the resources to find it. The slave and Socrates' other interlocutors discover the resources they need in their present beliefs, through Socrates' questions, and find answers which require rejection of some other beliefs.[13]

4.3. *The answer to Meno's paradox.* Socrates describes an elenchos to answer Meno's attack; though the slave does not know, he has true beliefs about the questions discussed (85c6–7).[14] Socrates agrees that if we do not know what x is, cannot give a Socratic account of x, we do not know anything about x; but we can still have true beliefs about x. To inquire into x we need only enough true beliefs about x to fix the reference of the term 'x', so that when the inquiry is over, we can see we still refer to the same thing. This reply rejects Meno's step (2).

Socrates confirms his answer when he explains his initially rather vague distinction between knowledge and belief (85c9–d1). The Socratic dialogues implicitly demanded a Socratic account for knowledge; the *Gorgias* explicitly demands an account (*logos*, G. 464e2–465a7) or explanation (*aitia*, 500e4–501b1) as well as truth (454c7–e2). In the *Meno* too true beliefs are converted into knowledge by 'reasoning out the explanation' (*aitias logismos*, 97e2–98a8). A Socratic definition of virtue will satisfy this condition; it will explain and justify a man's belief about virtue. But Socrates' interlocutors have true beliefs about virtue without this justification. Plato's explicit distinction between knowledge and true belief disarms Meno's paradox and its attack on Socratic inquiry.[15]

4.4. *Conditions for success.* Socrates must convince Meno that an account of virtue is an account of the same thing Meno asked about at first (80d7–8); but if some of Meno's initial beliefs are rejected, how can Socrates show they are beliefs about the virtue he wants to define? Or, in the *Cratylus*'s terms, how can Socrates show that Meno's name 'virtue' preserves the outline of (what Socrates calls) virtue plus false beliefs about virtue, and is not really the name of something else than (Socratic) virtue? This question has already arisen about the elenchos.[16] Socrates must show that his definition offers the best rational account of the original beliefs, because it explains how recognized cases of virtue converge on a final good; recollection will reconcile someone's views about virtue and about the good. These conditions, and their severe difficulties, apply no less to recollection than to the Socratic elenchos—naturally enough, when the two methods are the same.

5. Recollection and Socratic knowledge

5.1. *The scope of recollection.* The Theory of Recollection formulates and explains some of the principles of the Socratic elenchos. We may find this a disappointing result from Plato's promise of a new and exciting theory; but our reaction would be premature. The method Plato discusses is familiar; but his claims about it are not.

Plato claims that all knowledge and all learning about virtue require recollection (81c9–e2).[17] In the *Republic* this claim (without mention of recollection) supports his attack on those non-rational methods of instruction which inculcate new beliefs in someone without appeal to reasons which convince him, as though they were producing sight in blind eyes; the correct method uses his reasoning capacity and rationally convinces him to revise his beliefs (*R.* 518b6–d1).[18] Plato demands recollection for correct moral instruction.

5.2. *Moral knowledge, elenchos, and craft.* This demand ought to surprise Socrates if he thinks moral knowledge is a craft.[19] The moral craft will include truths first discovered by the elenchos; but elenctic instruction in a craft looks inept, if not absurd. A shoemaker does not teach his apprentices by cross-examining their previous beliefs on how to make shoes—they may have none. Neither Socrates nor Plato in the *Meno* recommends the elenchos for teaching a craft. If Plato accepts the CA, he ought not to claim that all moral knowledge and instruction is recollection; conversely, this claim justifies some scepticism about the CA.

5.3. *The Dialectical Requirement and the Craft-Analogy*. The account of recollection raised doubts about one argument for the DR. *A*'s definition of *x* as '*yz*' is useless to *B* if *B* is wholly ignorant of *y* and *z*. But this alone does not justify the demand for *knowledge* of *y* and *z*. Socrates' account of inquiry would allow *B* to have true beliefs about *y* and *z* without knowledge; and if recollection resulted in such an account of *x*, what would be wrong with it? Once knowledge and true belief are distinguished, the requirement looks less legitimately dialectical, demanded by sound elenctic method. If true belief is enough, Socrates loses his objections to accounts of disputed properties which mention other disputed properties not yet known; for true belief about these unknown properties may be all a definition needs.

Now the defence of the DR undermined by the account of recollection is not the only possible defence. The DR requires elimination of disputed terms; though we may sometimes agree in applying these terms, and share some true beliefs about their referents, we have no agreed standard, and without that we cannot fully explain or justify our beliefs. We shall solve the problem when disputed terms are replaced by those with agreed standards of application. This project must succeed if Socrates is to maintain TV, on which the CA depends. He can still defend the DR by this line of argument, despite recollection.

None the less recollection raises a question about the DR. For it may produce informative definitions which fail the DR; and we have seen that the definitions which satisfied the DR failed the elenchos. The account of recollection revives an earlier question about a craft's demands on the elenchos. If recollection produces definitions which fail the DR, and fails to produce those which pass it, Socrates cannot satisfy ED from the elenchos; and then it is hard to find the ED-definitions needed by TV and the CA.

5.4. *Virtue and craft in the* Meno. Later Plato perhaps suggests why he never endorses the CA in the *Meno*. Craft-teachers teach us the craft of making a product we already recognize and want (90b7–e8); and the teacher of virtue should teach us the virtue by which men govern houses and cities admirably, and look after parents, citizens, and foreign guests in the way worthy of a good man (91a1–6; cf. *Pr.* 318e4–319a2). When Anytus denies that the sophists teach this virtue, Socrates is surprised; for they are well patronized, and surely craftsmen who could not teach us to make the right product would be out of business (91c6–92a6).

Normally we can tell if someone is a real teacher or not, because we can recognize the right product, even before he teaches us how to make it, and test his success. But it is harder to identify the product of moral knowledge; if it is 'admirable' government, and the actions of a 'good' man, some firm criteria are needed to decide what is admirable and good—or else TV is not satisfied, and the morally inexpert cannot tell who really teaches virtue. In the *Protagoras* and the *Gorgias* Plato wants to find the moral craft by finding a product which satisfies TV.[20] In the *Meno* he is silent—and rightly, if he rejects TV, and thinks moral knowledge is recollection, not a craft. Plato does not explicitly question the CA. But it is striking that he raises this problem about agreement on the right product of a moral craft, in this dialogue, and in none of the others we have discussed. It is equally relevant to raise this question if he is sceptical about the DR. For if the DR and ED cannot be satisfied, we cannot explain in undisputed terms what a good man will do, and cannot prove TV and the CA.

The *Meno* itself mentions none of the objections we have found to Socratic knowledge. We have only raised some questions a reader might reasonably ask, and suggested what their consequences might be for Socrates' theory of virtue and moral knowledge. Plato may not see these consequences himself, and the *Meno* does not show whether or not he does. We can decide the issue only when we see if he uses the *Meno*'s argument elsewhere to reject Socratic views.

6. *Knowledge, right belief, and virtue*

6.1. *The argument.* After the account of recollection has introduced the distinction between knowledge and belief, and has partly shown how knowledge is acquired, Socrates considers the role of knowledge and belief in virtue, and in particular examines a Socratic doctrine, KNV. He clearly rejects one argument for KNV, and has often been taken to reject KNV altogether.[21] This further claim is unjustified, and Socrates leaves room for some defence of KNV; the previous account of knowledge as recollection, and the questions about CA, show why Plato might still want to defend KNV.

The central objection to KNV rests on the distinction between knowledge and belief anticipated in the slave passage. Socrates stresses this distinction strongly (98b1–5), and though he has used it in earlier dialogues, it is first formulated clearly in the *Meno*. If there is right belief as well as knowledge, knowledge will not be the only true guide to action; right belief will be no less useful. Now this defence of right belief refutes KNV only if a defence of KNV must rely wholly on the results of knowledge in action—for this is the only function of knowledge which right belief performs equally well. Now Plato's initial argument for KNV did indeed rest wholly on the good results of knowledge; since virtue is always beneficial in action, and since only knowledge is always beneficial in action, virtue must be knowledge. And Plato recognizes that a refutation of this argument will show only that *perhaps* virtue is not knowledge (87d4–6)—that is, it will only remove one defence of KNV. Now can he expect to find some other defence?[22]

6.2. *The objection to Socrates.* The *Meno*'s argument for KNV from the good results of knowledge is entirely Socratic (cf. *Eud.* 282a1–7, *Ch.* 174b11–c3). We saw that Socrates accepted KNV and defended it, in so far as he explicitly defended it, within the restrictions of the CA. Any craft is valuable because of the good results in its product; and Socrates offers no other reason for valuing knowledge and virtue. The objection in the *Meno*, then, is quite suitable. Plato's explicit account of knowledge and belief exposes a question implicit in Socratic method. Socrates wanted knowledge; that was why he demanded an account of their beliefs from the interlocutors; he could defend his demand by appeal to the good results of craft-knowledge. But was that all? If the good results of knowledge could be secured without the explicit understanding of moral beliefs required for a successful elenchos, then would the Socratic method be superfluous, or no better than some other method producing equally good results? Socrates' conviction of the value of the elenchos is clear; but like other convictions of his, it is not defended at length, and he does not face these questions. The *Meno*'s challenge to KNV forces a defender of the Socratic method to face the questions; like Meno's paradox it questions one of Socrates' presuppositions.

6.3. *Plato's position.* Plato expresses no doubts about the Socratic defence of KNV, and presents no other defence. However, he has reason for doubt, if he doubts whether virtue is a craft, a reliable tendency to do good actions, valuable only for the results. His earlier rejection of the account of virtue as a capacity to acquire goods (78c3–79a2) is justified if he doubts that virtue is only a reliable tendency to produce good results. The Theory of Recollection may strengthen these doubts. By itself it does not imply that virtue or knowledge is valuable for anything but its results; but we have seen that it suggests some doubts about the CA in general; and these doubts will justify doubts about whether good results exhaust the value of a craft. If virtue is not a craft, then it may not be valuable only for its results; and so knowledge might still be necessary for virtue, even if it does not improve the results. Because knowledge includes an explanation and justification, it is more honourable, though perhaps no more efficient, than right belief (98a5–8).[23] Plato's conclusion, that we must know what virtue is before we can decide for or against KNV, is exactly right; to know whether the *Meno* has refuted KNV, we must know if virtue is valuable only for its results. Plato does not reject Socrates' view of the value of knowledge and virtue; but he does not endorse it, and does not reject KNV.

6.4. *Results of the* Meno. The last part of the *Meno*, like the other two parts, is a self-conscious examination of a central Socratic doctrine. If our account is nearly right, the Theory of Recollection is central in the dialogue. It raises questions about the earlier requirements for a definition, and more general questions about the CA, if all moral knowledge is to be recollection. These possible doubts about the CA are relevant for the argument about KNV; for that argument explicitly ignores any special features of recollection (87b6–c1), and if we do not ignore them, KNV may still be true, because moral knowledge is recollection, not craft-knowledge worth while only for its results. I have tried to display the questions about Socratic ethics that might reasonably be provoked by the *Meno*; I have not pretended that Plato explicitly raises them, or definitely rejects the CA. But I shall try to show that arguments in other dialogues follow naturally from this line of thought found in the *Meno*.

7. *Definition and observation*

7.1. *Origins of the Theory of Forms.* Further discussion of the Theory of Recollection leads to the *Phaedo*; and since the objects of recollection there are separate Forms, we must consider why they are separated, and why recollection is supposed to lead to knowledge of them. Aristotle suggests that Plato was stimulated to separate the Forms by Socrates' search for definitions in ethics (*Met.* 987b1–8, 1078b17–32, 1086b2–7); and since we have seen how the Theory of Recollection has the same origin, the separated Forms naturally belong in a further account of recollection. To see if Aristotle is right, we must look beyond the *Phaedo*, and find the kinds of problems which separation is meant to solve. This inquiry will sometimes lead away from ethical questions. But that cannot be helped; we cannot fix the effect of the Theory of Forms on Plato's moral theory without deciding some disputed questions about the point of the theory in general.

7.2. *The problems.* Plato advises the philosopher to avoid the senses which belong to the body, and tell him nothing clear or accurate (*Phd.* 65a9–b7), and to seek the truth by reasoning with the soul by itself (65c2–d2). The soul should examine the just itself and the other forms—the natures of things, or what each thing is (65d4–7, d12–e1)—because they are inaccessible to the senses and known only by pure thought (65e1–4). These forms seem to be the familiar, unseparated essences which Socrates sought to define (*Eu.* 5d1–5, 6d9–e1; *M.* 72c1–d1); if we believe just men are just by justice, we must recognize something called 'justice' or 'the just' (*HMa.* 287c1—d3; *Phd.* 65d4–7).

But the *Phaedo*'s unfamiliar claims about these familiar forms raise questions:

1. Why should we examine objects inaccessible to the senses? If the senses confuse us about sensible objects, why should intellect not avoid this confusion in dealing with sensible objects? But if sensible objects confuse intellect too, why should the senses be criticized?

2. Why does Plato, unlike Socrates, believe these forms are inaccessible to the senses?[24]

3. Which forms are inaccessible to the senses? Plato mentions the just, the admirable and the good (65d4–7), and then 'all' the natures, and what 'each' thing is, bigness, health, strength and the rest (65d12–e1; *M.* 72d4–e9). But these examples of 'all' include only the *Meno*'s classes (B) (e.g. health) and (C) (e.g. justice), whereas Socrates also recognized forms for (A) (e.g. bee) (cf. *M.* 72a8–c4, 74d4–75a1; *Cra.* 389a5–b6; *G.* 503e1–4). Does Plato believe that all forms, or only forms for (B) and (C), are inaccessible to the senses?

7.3. *Types of predicates.* Plato's contrast between the three types of predicates (implicit in the *Meno*) may influence his view in the *Phaedo*. Sometime he contrasts the agreed decision-procedures for (B) with the rationally insoluble disputes over (C) (*Eu.* 7b6–d5). Sometimes he contrasts agreement about (A) with disputes and confusions about (C) (*Phdr.* 263a2–b5). In general, (A) do not arouse disputes; (B) may arouse disputes, but with a recognized decision-procedure; (C) arouse disputes with no such procedure (*Alc.* 111a1–112d9).

The severe problems arise for (C). Plato explains why:

1. We 'think the same' about A-predicates (*Phdr.* 263a6–7), but about C-predicates we disagree with each other and even with ourselves (263a9–10).
2. We therefore become confused about C-predicates, and even infer that injustice and the other C-properties are as unstable as our own beliefs about them (*Cra.* 411b3–c6). Plato rejects this inference (*Cra.* 386d8–e4, 440b4–d2).
3. This instability of belief leads to disputes (*Phdr.* 263a2–4, b1–4); and disputes about (C), unlike disputes about (B), lead to violence (*Eu.* 7c10–d7; *HMa.* 294c8–d3; *Alc.* 111e11–112c7), because they allow no rational decision-procedure.

7.4. *C-predicates and definitions.* The origin of the trouble is in definitions, not in examples. Plato does not say that we have trouble in agreeing on whether Aristeides was just, but that we cannot explain why he was, as the Socratic dialogues show. This failure leads to disagreement over difficult or unusual examples, since we lack the agreed explicit understanding of our judgements which would help us to project from easier to harder cases. With C-predicates the problems cannot be solved by a simple description of common beliefs. An A-predicate is associated with the same correct set of descriptions by everyone, but a C-predicate is associated with different sets of incorrect descriptions by different people, though each set still preserves the outline of the C-property. We are not short of beliefs about C-properties; an ordinary man with some experience of temperance has beliefs about it associated with the name 'temperance' (*Ch.* 158e7–159a10), and his beliefs may be quite confident (*La.* 190e3; *M.* 84b9–c2; *Alc.* 110b1–6); but they still may not yield an adequate account of temperance.

Plato emphasizes this trouble with (C), as opposed to (B). He defines the large, a B-property as 'the exceeding', but still seeks a similar account of the beautiful, which will show when something really is beautiful whether it appears to be or not (*HMa.* 294a6–c2). If we know what is supposed to exceed what, the account of the large will provide a decision-procedure; for we can measure to see whether or not this exceeds that. But no equally good account can be found for the beautiful, the subject of undecidable disputes (294c8–d3). An account should identify the beautiful which will never appear ugly to anyone (291d1–3), and will make everything which has it beautiful (289d2–5, 292c8–d5).[25] But each candidate proposed is no more beautiful than not-beautiful (289c3–5, 293b10–c7); similarly, Charmides' candidate for temperance, modesty, was no more temperate than not-temperate (*Ch.* 161a6–b2), and Laches' candidate for courage, endurance, was no more brave than not-brave (*La.* 192c3–d8). A correct definition should resolve these problems.

7.5. *Inadequacy of the senses.* So far we can explain why the *Phaedo* might distinguish (A) from the rest. In *Republic* VII Plato explains how this distinction is relevant to questions about the senses, when he shows which predicates do or do not provoke the soul to the kind of reflection which begins recollection. The soul is not provoked to ask what a finger is, since the senses never tell it that a finger is the opposite of a finger (*R.* 523a10–b2, b9–c1, c4–e1). But the senses do nothing sound with 'large', 'small', 'hard', 'soft', and other pairs of contraries (523b3–4). Sight sees that the same length which is large in a finger (compared with a smaller finger) will also be small in a finger or in anything of equal length (compared with a metre rule); and so it reports that the largeness or the large in the finger is also small (523e3–524a10). The senses mingle largeness and smallness, and the soul must distinguish them by reason (524b3–c8; cf. 475e9–476a7); to distinguish them, it seeks definitions (524c10–13).[26]

Here Plato separates (A), where the senses give adequate answers, from (B), where they do not. They will report that something is large or small, but we will not expect to understand largeness or smallness from what they report. This argument justifies Plato's advice in the *Phaedo* to turn away from the senses if we want to learn about (B) and (C)—and also his restriction of the advice to these predicates (cf. *R.* 523b2–4 with *Phd.* 65b1–7).

7.6. *Sensible and non-sensible.* Plato wants to distinguish observation from examination and interpretation of what is observed (*R.* 524b1–2)—this is a fair description of his distinction, though not an explanation or defence of it, since lines are notoriously hard to draw here. He will argue that we can decide when something is a finger by a fairly uniform set of observations, and settle doubts by further observation. But no uniform set of observations decides when something is large—things of confusingly various sizes count as large, and the same size will be no more large than small. We shall not settle disputes by closer observation; we can observe that x is larger than y, but we do not know the standard of comparison by looking at x and y; if y is a normal-sized F, x's being larger than y may show that x is a large F, but x may still be a small G. For correct interpretation, we must know the relevant standard of comparison. If we could explain what a finger is through a fairly uniform set of observations, Plato is right to say that 'large' is different from 'finger'; if this account of 'finger' is oversimplified, there will be fewer non-observational predicates than Plato thinks, but his claim that 'large' is non-observational may still be right.

8. *Arguments for separation*

8.1. *Types of flux*. According to Aristotle, Plato's Heracleitean views, applied to Socrates' search for definitions stimulated him to separate the Forms; since sensible things are always in flux, there can be no knowledge of them, and Socratic definitions must therefore apply to something else (*Met*. 987a32–b7, 1078b12–17, 1086a32–b13). We have seen Plato's interest in Socratic definition; but how is this talk of flux to be understood?

A Heracleitean doctrine of flux might refer to either or both of two types of change:

1. S(=self) change; at time t_2 x is more or less F than it was at t_1 (e.g. it becomes hotter than it was, or moves further from y than it was).
2. A(=aspect) change; x changes from being F in one aspect to being not-F in another (e.g. x is big compared with y, small compared with z).

We might think A-change is at best a reduced and metaphorical kind of change; but Heracleitus illustrates the unity of opposites and universal flux, not only by S-change, but also by the compresence of opposites, in the up-and-down road, the straight and crooked writing, good and bad food (good for some people, bad for others). A doctrine of flux might be found in a concern with A-change as well as in a concern with S-change.[27]

8.2. *Flux in Plato*. In the arguments stimulated by Socrates' ethical interests, Plato never claims that sensible particulars suffer the constant total S-change which would make them unknowable.[28] But a doctrine of A-change in sensibles follows naturally from the problems with B- and C-properties. Plato finds a Heracleitean unity of opposites in a beautiful (*kalē*) girl who is ugly (*aischra*) compared with gods (*HMa.* 289a2–c6), and later in being buried by our children and burying our parents, which is sometimes admirable (*kalon*), when done by some people, other times disgraceful (*aischron*), done by others (293b5–e5). Neither the girl nor the action-type will answer our demand for the beautiful which is never ugly, because they suffer A-change from beautiful to ugly.

Republic VII associates this A-change with the senses; the only properties they pick out as 'the large' are both large and small. Aristotle's remark applies naturally here; sensible properties allow us no knowledge of the large because they are always A-changing from large to small. Now A-change or compresence of opposites is useless for Plato's purposes if the opposite aspects can be easily distinguished on any occasion; a centaur may be a man and not a man, but if the human aspects can be distinguished from the others, no problems arise. But Plato insists that problems do arise if we rely on sensible properties to understand largeness; for they always present largeness confused with smallness (*R.* 524b4–c8), and reasoning is required to find the right principles for distinguishing the two properties. The finger-passage finds Heracleitean flux in sensible properties; if Aristotle is right we would expect Plato to use this argument in separating the Forms; and so he does.

8.3. *Compresence of opposites.* The *Phaedo* uses the argument from A-flux to justify the separation of Forms. Plato does not mention flux; but he relies on the division between sense and intellect mentioned earlier (74b5–6, c13–d1, d9–10, 75a1, a5–b2), and appeals to the compresence of opposites found by the senses, to show that the forms must be separate. The results of reliance on the senses, described in *Republic* VII, justify separation. Plato argues that the form of equal is apart from equal sticks and stones (74a9–12):

1. Equal sticks and stones sometimes being the same appear equal to one man, and not to another (74b7–10).
2. But the equals themselves have never appeared to you unequal, or equality inequality (74c1–3).
3. Then these equals (sc. the sticks and stones) and the equal itself are not the same (74c4–5).[29]

Plato considers whether equal sticks and stones are good guides to the equal itself. It might seem simply a mistake to offer examples when a definition is needed; but in the *Hippias Major* too he asks whether examples (girls, gold, accepted kinds of good fortune) are a guide to the beautiful itself.[30] Like the initial answers offered by interlocutors in the Socratic dialogues, these answers are not at all absurd, and do not imply confusion. Sometimes it may seem reasonable to suppose that examination of standard examples will be a good guide to the property under discussion. We might say that a bee is what a bee is—meaning that the observable properties of this bee taken by itself are a good guide to the properties of bees. Similarly, we might try to treat the observable properties of sticks and stones as a good guide to 'the equal in' something, the properties which make something equal. But observable properties do not help; the sensible equals are deficiently equal (*Phd.* 74d5–8), because the senses reveal equality deficiently (cf. *R.* 523e6–7)—the equal sticks may be three inches long, but a three-inch length is no guide to equality. Some will say that the equal sticks and stones are equal, others, thinking of them in other relations, will say they are unequal; this variation is ruled out in what is really equal (cf. *HMa.* 291d1–3; *Symp.* 211a2–5). The argument is continuous with Socrates' interest in definitions, and with *Republic* VII.

The argument which has separated the Form of Equal is also meant to yield Forms for the greater and the lesser, B-properties, and for the admirable, the good, the just, the pious, and all the things we call 'what *F* is itself' in our questions and answers (*Phd.* 75c10–d3), all the C-properties examined in the Socratic inquiries.[31] Here as earlier in the *Phaedo*, no Forms for (A) are mentioned; and if the argument about equals relies on the problems raised in *Republic* VII, Plato should not require them.

8.4. *Rejected explanations.* Later in the *Phaedo* Plato tries to show why the senses cannot yield knowledge of B- and C-properties, and why separated Forms are needed. He fixes on one aspect of knowledge mentioned but hardly clarified in the *Meno*, that someone who knows can produce an explanation and justification of his beliefs (*M.* 98a1–8). An explanation requires an answer to Socrates' demand for a definition; and Plato argues that the senses and observation do not yield an adequate answer, because sensible properties suffer from A-flux, or, as *Republic* VII said, they have opposite B- and C-properties compresent and confused. Plato rejects definitions of B- and C-properties in observational terms because they do not adequately explain why things have those properties. The rejected accounts mention some observable features (e.g. 'by a head') of what makes x larger than y (*Phd.* 96d7–e1), or some observable operation (e.g. 'add two') to make x more numerous than y (96e1–3). An observable feature O of x may show us that x is F, but O will not provide the right account of x's being F; for the correct account should apply always and only to Fs, whereas (a) O might be present in non-Fs (100e8–101b2), and (b) O might be absent in Fs (97a5–b3). As in *Republic* VII, Plato means that we can never generalize from O to know what F is; he defends his previous claim that observation of equal sticks and stones yields no adequate account of the equal.

Plato prefers a 'safe explanation'; 'x is F by the presence of the Form The F' (100b3—101c9). By itself this is too safe to be useful, and since Plato believes the Forms are known by definitions (75d1–3, 76d7–9, 78d1–3). 'The F' should be a place-holder for a definition of the Form.[32] But the definition should not be confined to observable properties; things will not be beautiful by the presence of bright colours or a pleasing shape or anything of that kind (100c9–d3), but only by the presence of The Beautiful Itself (100d3–8); cf. *HMa.* 289c9–d5, 292c9–d3). The Form of Beauty must be separated from all observable properties which will be both beautiful and not-beautiful. As earlier in the *Phaedo*, Plato exploits the argument in *Republic* VII to find separated Forms for B- and C-properties.

8.5. *The sight-lovers. Republic* V explicitly insists, as the *Phaedo* implied, that reference to separated Forms is necessary for knowledge of B- and C-properties; and it shows, as the *Phaedo* also implied, that the separated Forms are required because of faults in the senses and observation. Plato argues that those who love sights and sounds, and recognize 'many beautifuls' but no single Form, The Beautiful, cannot escape the *Phaedo*'s objections to defective explanations. Each of the forms is one, but appears to be many because it appears in different conditions, associated with actions, bodies and other forms (*R.* 475e9–476a7). Meno supposed that the many types of virtue would show what virtue is (*M.* 782c6–d1, 74c6–10); and the sight-lovers suppose that many observable properties will be the beautiful in different things—sometimes bright colours, sometimes symmetrical shapes, and so on (476b4–6; cf. *Phd.* 100c9–d3)—or that justice in promises is truth-telling and debt-paying (331c1–3), a citizen's justice something else, and so on. They believe there are many answers to Socrates' question, but no single account of one property, the F

(478e7–479a5; cf. *Pm.* 132a3).[33]

Plato argues that the observable properties will not yield the right answer; for observation presents opposite B- and C-properties confused in the same observable property (524c3–4), and each of the sight-lover's many Fs will be both F and not-F (479a5–8). Plato must show that even within their chosen areas the sight-lover's accounts fail, that (e.g.) the bright colour alleged to be the beautiful in temples is beautiful in the Parthenon but will not save a crude Boeotian effort from being ugly.[34] In the *Meno* he argues appropriately; ruling a state, one of Meno's alleged many virtues, will not always be a virtue unless it is done 'justly and temperately' (*M.* 73a6–9, d6–8); but this qualification requires. C-predicates in the definition and a single form of virtue. Similarly, only beneficial debt-paying counts as justice (*R.* 331c3–d3); and a C-predicate like 'beneficial' destroys the sight-lover's clear and exact account (cf. 336c6–d4) of the many justices in observational A-predicates. The sight-lover must recognize a single property, justice, and a Form of Justice, apart from observable properties.

8.6. *Inferences about flux.* Plato's arguments about the compresence of opposite B- and C-properties in sensible properties justify claims about flux; quantity (e.g.) in sensibles changes and fluctuates constantly and is not definite (Alex. *In Met.* 83.9–10), because the senses confuse large and small (*R.* 524b4–8); the same observable size is large in one thing, small in another, and A-changes from large to small.[35] Plato can ascribe flux to these sensible properties or to classes of things described by them; 'the many beautifuls are in flux' many mean (1) 'bright colour (e.g.) A-changes from being beautiful in x to being ugly in y'; or (2) 'bright-coloured things, in so far as they are bright-coloured, A-change from being beautiful to being ugly, because some of them are beautiful, others ugly'. Plato assumes (2) when he relies on the argument from compresence of opposites (*Phd.* 74b7–9) for his claim that the many beautifuls and equals, men, horses, and so on, are in flux and the Forms are not (78c6–78a4).[36] If he were ascribing radical S-change to sensible particulars, he would be completely unjustified; but if he ascribes only A-change, he is justified by the previous argument.

8.7. *Becoming and perishing.* Like the *Phaedo*'s argument, the argument in *Republic* V relies on the compresence of F and not-F in the many Fs (*R.* 479a5–b10); but it will justify the apparently surprising inference that the many Fs suffer becoming and perishing and therefore allow us no knowledge of the F (495a10–b3, 508d4–9, 518e8–9, 525b5–6, 534a2–3). Since the many Fs are sensible properties (507b2–10), both F and not-F, the F in them comes to be in some conditions and perishes from them in others (cf. *Phd.* 102d5–e3). If any sensible property alleged to be the F gains and loses the F in it, it cannot yield the right account of the property which is always F.

Neither here nor in the *Phaedo* does Plato's doctrine of flux obviously claim more than his arguments warrant. The separation of the Forms relies as Aristotle says, on a doctrine of flux; this is no strange doctrine unsupported by the arguments about compresence of opposites, but a fair summary of these arguments.

8.8. *The senses and the sensible world.* We can now explain two puzzling claims in the *Phaedo* (65a9–b7):

1. The senses are inaccurate and confusing.
2. Sensible things are unstable and confusing.

Each of these two claims might seem to undermine the other. But Plato has argued that sensible properties suffer A-flux, and if 'sensible things' in (2) are these sensible properties, (2) is justified. And now (1) is justified; the senses confuse us about the F (some B- or C-property) by presenting observable Fs which are F and not-F. (1) and (2), suitably understood, are consistent, and indeed equivalent, consequences of the separation-argument, and imply no general attack on the reliability of the senses or the stability of the physical world.

I have discussed Plato's arguments for separated Forms, Aristotle's comments associating these arguments with a doctrine of flux, and Plato's own remarks about flux, to show how they can be interpreted as parts of a coherent position which Plato argues for, rather than a set of extravagant claims undefended by argument. If we interpret flux as A-flux of sensible properties, we can explain why the flux of sensibles precludes knowledge of B- and C-properties from them; why flux should be part of an argument for separated Forms; why Aristotle talks about flux, while Plato's arguments mention compresence of opposites; and why Plato's arguments justify his remarks on flux. To show that his position is coherent, we have had to combine various comments and arguments in different contexts; though the resulting pattern of argument cannot be found all at once in any one Platonic passage, it explains better than other accounts both what Plato says and what Aristotle thinks Plato says.

9. *Questions about Plato's theory*

9.1. *Two views of separation.* However, it may not be clear how these arguments explain why Plato believes the most striking and apparently extravagant of his doctrines about Forms, that 'separation' which Aristotle takes to be the decisive difference between Socrates and Plato (*Met.* 1078b30–3; *Pm.* 130a1–5). In the middle dialogues Plato does not mention 'separation'. He insists on the non-identity of the Form of *F* and the many *F*s (*Phd.* 74a9–12, b4–7; *R.* 476c9–d3; *Symp.* 211a1–b5). This might imply nothing more than non-reducibility:

> NR: The forms of B- and C-properties are not definable through sensible properties alone, and not identical with these properties, or with sensible objects as described by their sensible properties.

NR is a legitimate conclusion from Plato's arguments.

However, 'separation' for Aristotle implies a stronger claim about independent existence:

> IE: Forms exist for B- and C-properties; for any property *F*, if *F* sensible particulars exist, the Form the *F* exists; and it is not the case that if the *F* exists, *F* sensible things exist.

Plato does not clearly formulate IE in the middle dialogues; but he suggests it, and Aristotle's view that he holds it is normally, and rightly, accepted.[37]

9.2. *A connecting argument.* IE does not follow from NR or any of the arguments for separation; but Plato offers no further argument in its defence. To reach it from NR he could argue as follows:

1. The justice (or some other B- and C-property) of sensible objects exists independently of their sensible properties.
2. Justice exists independently of sensible objects, as described by their sensible properties.
3. Sensible objects are simply bundles of sensible properties.
4. Justice exists independently of sensible objects.

(1) follows from NR, provided it means only that no one set of sensible properties makes something just; it does not follow that something with no sensible properties can be just; (2) will be true only if it is similarly restricted. But even an unjustifiably strong version of (2) does not imply IE, except relatively to a particular description of sensible objects by sensible properties. To drop this restriction and

assert (4), Plato must rely on (3). But he cannot accept (3) without undermining the arguments supporting (1). He has argued that we cannot explain how to ascribe justice (even imperfect justice) to sensible objects if we describe them in observational terms alone; the argument would be absurd if (3) were true. It is not easy to find good reasons for believing (3), or even to say what exactly it means, how non-observational predicates could never in principle be applied to sensible objects. This argument is relevant because Plato himself never offers any argument for IE besides those for NR, and the argument here suggests why he might confusedly believe, what he would like to believe anyway, that NR is enough for IE. The confusion might be partly explained by indiscriminate talk of 'sensibles' or 'what the senses reveal', meaning sometimes 'sensible properties' and sometimes 'sensible objects' (which might also have non-sensible properties); to justify conflation of these two uses of 'sensibles' and move from (2) to (4), (3) is required. Plato does not distinguish IE from NR sharply enough to see this fatal objection to the argument he would need to prove IE from NR. (He might still argue for IE on other grounds; but he offers none in his arguments for separation of Forms.) His attitude to separation confirms our claim that the arguments for NR are his real arguments for separation; he offers no further argument for IE, and if he argued from NR, he would have faced an awkward choice. His unclarity about NR and IE is best explained by his failure to formulate (2) and (4) clearly enough to display their vital difference.

9.3. *The two doctrines about Forms.* It would be foolish to deny or underestimate the importance of IE to Plato, or to suggest that its influence can easily be removed from the Theory of Forms. But it would be equally wrong to suggest that it exhausts the interest or importance of the theory. NR, a legitimate conclusion from fairly clear and defensible arguments, is important in its own right for Plato's moral theory, quite apart from IE. Naturally Plato cannot be expected to distinguish arguments from NR and arguments from IE, since he does not distinguish NR and IE themselves. But NR rests on arguments about Socratic definition; to see what ethical view follows from these arguments, and what alterations, if any, Plato can fairly demand in the Socratic theory, we should concentrate on NR. If we set aside IE, we will set aside some of Plato's moral beliefs, but we will retain the beliefs he can fairly claim to have supported by argument; and it is worthwhile to see what these are.

9.4. *The range of Forms.* Plato requires separated Forms for non-observable properties, (B) and (C).[38] We may be surprised at the prominence of (B) in his arguments; for while Socrates sees that (C) are difficult, he shows no concern about (B), which raise no insoluble disputes. The prominence of (B) in the arguments shows that Plato does not want separated Forms primarily as devices for solving disputes, or because no definition can readily be found. He displays no fear of violent disputes over the large or the equal, and can easily find fairly plausible accounts of them (*HMa.* 294b2–5; *Pm.* 140b7–8). But still he must think they clearly require separated Forms, or else they would not be so prominent in the arguments.

B-properties clearly display features Plato finds in C-properties. The star cases are relative properties which obviously, Plato thinks, cannot be grasped by observation; we must know the relevant standard of comparison. It does not follow that he thinks (B) and (C) are all somehow relative properties; he does not show that health, justice, and bravery, for instance, are. He needs to show only that (C) are like (B) in being deficiently revealed by the senses, so that a definition in observational terms cannot be found.

An observational account of a moral property does not clearly succumb to Plato's attack on observational accounts of largeness and so on, since moral properties are not all obviously relative. Our question (1) 'Is Fred brave?' is not ill-specified as (2) 'Is Fred big?' might be. 'Big' needs to be completed as 'a big man' or 'a big animal' or the like before we can look for answers to (2); and our beliefs about his observable properties will not help until we learn or assume the relevant completion. But a study of Fred's observable properties would not be so absurd a response to (1); no completion of 'brave' is needed. Plato needs further arguments to show that the failure of observational accounts which is so obvious with (B) applies to (C) as well.[39]

9.5. *Plato's arguments.* The objections to observational accounts of C-properties (*M.* 73a6–9, d6–8; *HMa.* 293b10–e5; *R.* 331c3, 479a5–8) follow the standard Socratic method of counter-examples (cf. *Ch.* 161a6–b2; *La.* 192c3–d8). To separate moral Forms from sensibles, Plato must believe that these accounts always allow clear counter-examples because of systematic weaknesses. Socrates did not say whether observational accounts failed because the interlocutor happened to think of the wrong observational answer, or because no right answer in observational terms could be found. Plato commits himself to the second view; this is why his separation of the Forms has no precedent in the Socratic dialogues. His line of argument is Socratic; but his conclusion is not.

9.6. *Socrates' Unity Assumption.* The separation-arguments answer a question raised in the *Meno*. Socrates' defence of UA and a single account of virtue against Meno's fragmented account of many virtues required a description of virtue to include the C-predicates 'justice' and 'temperance' (*M.* 73a6–c5, d7–8, 78d3–6). The separation-arguments imply that this is no temporary concession to ignorance; even in the right definition C-predicates are ineliminable. Without a separated Form we will find no 'one' in the 'many' at all; since there is no single observational account of the beautiful, the sight-lover will be right to admit many beautifuls and no one 'the beautiful'. But without a single form, a survey of the many beautifuls will yield no adequate account of the beautiful, since we correctly judge that each of the many is not beautiful; they will yield a series of rules with exceptions but no account or explanation of the exceptions. Plato's separation-arguments display what he takes to be necessary conditions for Socratic inquiry; a rational account of a moral property requires a single form; the single form cannot be described in observational terms, and must be a separated Form.

10. *The Theory of Forms and moral theory*

10.1. *Socrates and non-reduction.* Though Socrates is silent about the separation of Forms and the imperfection of sensibles, these doctrines are defended by standard Socratic methods of argument; this may suggest that when IE is neglected, the rest of the separation-thesis, NR, is just a Socratic commonplace. But this conclusion would be wrong. Though Socrates provides the method of argument Plato needs to defend his claims, only Plato draws the general conclusion, that ED-accounts can always be expected to fail. The application of virtue-terms cannot be understood by reference to observable similarities—this is Plato's inference from Socratic refutations. By itself, this would not distinguish virtue-terms from many others which Plato finds unproblematic; observably diverse actions in the right context can also count as making a contract or passing a message, because some accepted convention (in the first case) or the intended result of the actions (in the second case) makes the actions share (as Plato would say) 'one form'. Plato believes that moral terms cause a special problem; the 'one form' in various virtuous actions includes their tendency to contribute to the good; just as conventional agree-

ment on conditions which validate a contract is required for agreement about when contracts are made, so agreement about the good is
required for agreement that an action-type or action-token is virtuous.
But this agreement about the good is harder to secure.[40]

10.2. *The disputed questions.* Socrates tries to solve the problem by
showing that virtue is a craft; and this claim requires an ED-account
of the final good. He offers a hedonistic account in the *Protagoras*,
rejected but not replaced in the *Gorgias*.[41] Plato rejects this reply, and
denies that the good can be removed from the disputed properties—otherwise no separated Form would be needed for it. He does
not defend his rejection of the Socratic view; but Socrates' failure to
find an acceptable ED-account might well persuade Plato that the
search is misguided. If a virtuous man can rely on no agreed account
of the good, but has to set his own standards, moral properties cannot
be wholly explained by undisputed properties; for the virtuous and the
non-virtuous man will not agree in their account of the components of
the good. Socrates supposed he could prevent this kind of dispute by
treating the virtuous man as a craftsman, who may disagree with a
layman about the instrumental means to production of the product,
but is not required to show that the product is worthwhile. Plato's
separation of the moral Forms shows he rejects this Socratic solution.

10.3. *Hypotheses.* Plato's rejection of ED explains his interest in
accounts of a virtue which will survive an elenchos, but do not include
a full account of the final good. His account of hypothetical method in
the *Phaedo* applies to ethics too. When he abandons his search for a
general teleological account of nature and turns to what people say
(*Phd.* 99c6–e5), he relies on piecemeal hypotheses, accepted as long as
they leave our beliefs consistent (100a3–7, 101d4–5), and assumes the
existence of Forms with partial definitions not confined to observational predicates (100c9–d3).[42] In ethics non-observational accounts of virtues will be admissible hypotheses, even though they include no account of the final good.

Though Socrates might easily find these hypotheses—Nicias' account of courage would be an example—he never admits their value.
His neglect is reasonable; if he demands an observational account of a
virtue to solve disputes, a hypothesis will not meet his demands at all.
But if Plato rejects observational accounts, hypotheses will not fail so
badly; an account of the final good will revise and co-ordinate the
hypotheses, but will not remove moral predicates from them. Socrates

could have found some limited use in hypotheses; but for Plato their use is much less limited. In particular, a hypothesis will be a worthwhile, though second-best, result of elenctic inquiry; Plato offers definitions in *Republic* IV more freely than Socrates ever did, because he does not claim they are more than hypotheses.[43]

10.4. *Consequences for Socratic doctrine*. Socrates needs ED for his central claims about virtue and happiness. The connection can be displayed briefly: CA → KSV → TV → ED.[44] The consequences of NR are easily seen: NR → not-ED → not-TV → not-KSV → not-CA. TV is the vital point. If virtue is a craft, recommended for its product, the final good must be a determinate end, and since moral predicates are sources of dispute, our account of the final good must eliminate these predicates and provide an external standard for testing the correctness of moral judgements. NR rules out this external standard and TV collapses. Socrates at once loses his argument for KSV, and the problems solved by the CA all return.[45]

10.5. *Moral knowledge as recollection*. The arguments for separation show why all moral knowledge must be recollection. Plato examines one part of recollection left vague in the *Meno*—'reasoning out the explanation'—and argues that only an account of a Form in non-observational terms will yield the right explanation. The method of recollection will not yield the ED-definition which a craft requires. The Socratic dialogues treated moral knowledge both as the result of the elenchos and as the content of a craft; but the second condition required the kind of account of moral properties which the elenchos could not readily provide.[46] Plato decides in favour of Socrates' first condition, and rejects the second. In the other middle dialogues, just as in the *Meno*, he never suggests that virtue or moral knowledge is a craft; and he has good reason to avoid this claim.

Plato agrees with Socrates that there is objective moral knowledge, that some people's moral judgements can be rationally justified; he still looks for the 'one form', to and the standard which explains and justifies beliefs about a virtue. But Socrates looked for some external guarantee of correctness; virtuous action had to contribute to some final good accepted as a determinate end by virtuous and non-virtuous alike. Plato rejects the external standard; moral beliefs cannot be tested for correctness except by the procedure of the elenchos, which may yield a systematic, coherent account of moral judgements, but may not link them to any external standard. When Plato rejects Socrates' guarantee of objectivity for moral beliefs, and offers no substitute, he rejects the demand for such a guarantee as illegitimate.[47]

I have spoken as though Plato noticed these consequences of the separation-arguments, but have not shown that he does. To see whether he does or not, we must examine his ethical arguments, especially in the *Republic*; but other doctrines of the middle dialogues suggest that he realizes the conflict between Socrates' views and his own.

11. Genuine and spurious virtue

11.1. *Knowledge and virtue.* The *Meno* refuted the argument for KNV from the usefulness of knowledge in action, and showed that right belief is just as useful; but Plato also suggested that acting virtuously might require more than simply doing virtuous actions (*M.* 78c3–79a2). In the *Phaedo* he attacks people who do the virtuous action, and have the necessary right beliefs, but are not virtuous. The separation-arguments alone do not justify his attack, since they do not imply any value in knowledge apart from its results; but if they show that virtue is not a craft, they remove one reason for believing that, like a craft, it is valuable only for its results. The *Phaedo* reopens the question.

11.2. *Care of the soul.* The context is the psychophysical dualism of the *Phaedo*. Different men's goals depend on their concern for the body or the soul; those who care about the body want wealth (*Phd.* 66b7–d3) or honour (68c1–3, d8–9), while the philosopher who cares for his immortal soul will have a desire (*erōs*) for wisdom (66d7–67b5), but no concern for the body. Like the *Gorgias*, the *Phaedo* recognizes conflicts of desires rejected by Socrates; but, unlike the *Gorgias*, it ascribes them, not to two parts of the soul, but to the soul and the body (94c9–e6). Different people with these different concerns have different ultimate ends; the *Phaedo* does not suggest that the philosopher and other men simply choose different means to the same determinate end they all pursue. Disputes about the components of the end—discernible though not recognized in the *Gorgias*—are now recognized.[48]

11.3. *Slavish virtue.* Plato claims that only the philosopher concerned with his soul will have real virtue, while other reputedly virtuous men are simply brave because of cowardice and temperate because of intemperance, with only an illusion of real virtue (68c5–69a4). In their

brave actions they restrain their fear only from fear of worse consequences from cowardice, and in their temperate actions they forego
pleasure only for the sake of greater pleasures (68d5–9, e2–7; cf. *Pr.*
356a8–c3, 359e8–360b8); this whole method of balancing consequences and comparing pains and pleasures like sums of money
should be abandoned for real wisdom, which will reject these
calculations (69a6–c3).[49]

11.4. *Plato's criticism.* Plato attacks slavish virtue for two reasons
not clearly separated in this compressed passage:

1. These pseudo-virtuous people choose virtuous action for the
   ends which a non-virtuous man would accept, pleasure or
   honour; they believe virtue and not vice will secure these
   desirable consequences, but their ultimate aims are no different
   from the non-virtuous man's.
2. They choose virtuous action for its consequences and not for
   itself.

Both criticisms are needed to show that the slavish men are at fault in
being brave because of cowardice; for someone who was brave only
for the sake of some admirable consequences—perhaps in defence of
his philosophical vocation—might still choose to be brave only for
these consequences, and therefore, on Plato's test, would be brave
because of cowardice. Now a brave man must consider the likely consequences of different actions in deciding what will be the brave thing
to do; but he will value the action he chooses for itself, as wise endurance in the face of danger for some overriding good—not because
this kind of action produces consequences welcomed from some other
point of view. Plato's treatment of virtue requires reference to consequences in deciding what the virtuous action is; but here he rejects
consequentialist grounds for *valuing* the virtuous action when it is
chosen—it must be chosen and valued for itself.

Both of these criticisms would surprise Socrates. He sees nothing
wrong in (1); for he believes that all men pursue the same determinate
end, and differ only on instrumental means. He sees nothing wrong in
(2); for he thinks virtue is craft-knowledge, and virtuous action is the
production of desirable results—he has no reason to value either virtue or virtuous action apart from its consequences. Socrates' ready
acceptance of (1) and (2) is clearest in the *Protagoras*; its conception
of virtue as a measuring-craft concerned with pleasures and pains is a
clear target for the *Phaedo*. But (1) and (2) are ineliminable parts of

the CA, not just of the *Protagoras'* hedonistic defence of it; Plato's attack on them is a rejection of the whole CA.

Plato recognizes that slavish men have right belief; as the *Meno* said, it is no less useful than knowledge in action, since all the slavish men do the actions a virtuous man would do (or at least Plato never suggests they do not). But here he shows why the *Meno*'s refutation of one argument for KNV did not refute KNV; knowledge is not necessary for virtuous action, but is necessary for virtue, since everyone but the philosopher is slavish.[50] The option left open in the *Meno*—that knowledge might be necessary for virtue apart from its results in action—is exploited in the *Phaedo*.

11.5. *Real virtue.* It is easier to understand Plato's criticisms than to see how someone can avoid them; he must expect virtuous men to value virtue and virtuous action for itself, but does not explain why they should. He perhaps means that a virtuous character is not worth while only as a reliable source of virtuous actions desirable for their consequences; to decide whether someone is virtuous or not, we must consider both his actions and his reasons; and if his reasons attach no value to virtue and virtuous action for itself, he is not a virtuous man. To decide whether someone has acted generously and shown himself generous when he does a generous action, we must consider the reasons for his action; but if his virtue were valued only as a device for securing good consequences, we should care only about whether he will regularly perform these desirable actions; the generous man's reasons are one source of regular generous action, but not the only one, and our high estimate of them would be inexplicable if we cared only about the actions for their good consequences. We must take an interest in virtuous character as an intrinsic good for the virtuous man or for other men associated with him; this interest is explicable if association includes association in attitudes, aims, reasons, pleasures, and sentiments, and not merely co-operation in action. Socrates' rejection of behavioural accounts of virtue might have suggested that he saw this point. But his reasons are different; he believes knowledge is necessary for the right results, and for that reason only is necessary for virtue.

Socrates sees no further reason for accepting KNV, because the CA allows none.[51] Aristotle sees the difference here between virtue and craft; efficiency in production of the right product decides whether someone is a craftsman, but efficient action does not make someone virtuous unless he chooses virtuous action steadily, knowingly, deliberately, and for its own sake (*EN* 1105a25–b9, 1144a13–20). Plato does not state this view clearly; but he must accept it to justify his attack on slavish virtue. This view explains why knowledge is necessary for virtue, and recollection for knowledge. A virtuous man chooses virtue for the right reasons, because he can explain how it is a good in itself; and to find the explanation, he will need an account of virtue reached through the elenchos. The *Phaedo* defends the position suggested without defence in the *Meno*.

11.6. *The virtuous man and the philosopher.* Plato's account of virtue is complicated by his belief that the only virtuous man is the philosopher who cares for his soul and seeks knowledge of the Forms. He accepts Socrates' view that the virtuous man will care for his soul, but, unlike Socrates, thinks he will care for the soul's good in itself, not only for its efficiency in action.[52] A non-slavish man will regard virtue as a good state of himself, and will choose virtuous action for the right reasons. If Plato is right to insist on the right reasons, and these require philosophical knowledge of virtue, to give an account of it, he will be right to insist that moral wisdom requires philosophical wisdom. He can also show why the virtuous man will resist some physical desires when he exercises justice and temperance.

However, Plato claims that a virtuous man will also be a contemplative philosopher who renounces all unnecessary concern for the body, and seeks knowledge of disembodied Forms. And this does not follow from the previous arguments. Even if a virtuous man needs some philosophical knowledge, he need not advocate a life devoted wholly to philosophy; indeed, he may repudiate it as incompatible with the recognized virtues. Nor does his care for his soul and restraint of physical desires obviously require exclusive concern for the wholly non-physical part of him; he is concerned with his moral, rational, and affective personality, and it is not clear how much personal identity is left in Plato's purely intellectual soul. Plato needs to show that only the purely intellectual soul has any intrinsic value at all; but if he shows that, he has no right to assume the value of the recognized virtues as easily as he does. Both the virtuous man and the philosopher can be said to 'care for his soul' and to display 'wisdom'; but the moral and the contemplative uses of these terms cannot be identified as readily as Plato suggests.

11.7. *Results of Plato's argument.* Plato's position, then, is not free of confusion. His dualist psychology helps him to see that the soul is a proper object of moral concern for its own sake; but it also misleads him into thinking that the soul recognized by a moralist must be a non-physical pure intellect. He therefore argues illegitimately that real virtue and care for the soul makes a man a contemplative philosopher. This mistake must not be glossed over; for Plato's tendency to identify the demands of virtue and of his own contemplative ideal influences his theory more than once in the *Symposium* and the *Republic*. But not all of the argument depends on the *Phaedo*'s metaphysics. The distinction between genuine and spurious virtue rests on independent argument; and we might agree that the virtuous man should choose virtue for its own sake and care for his soul, without accepting Plato's views about the soul and its proper care. Though Plato thinks his demand for genuine virtue supports his ascetic ideal, we need not agree. Quite apart from the *Phaedo*'s ideals, the argument is Plato's development and revision of Socrates' views on the care of the soul. Socrates' views were consistent with the CA; but Plato's are not. Plato believes that virtue cannot be assessed or recommended, as a craft can, by some external standard. When a man acquires virtue, he recognizes different intrinsic goods; and one of them is a virtuous state of character itself. A man's virtue determines what ends he pursues and what kind of man he is, with reference to no further end. Once again, I have ascribed to Plato a more explicit view than the text will justify; but some other arguments will confirm that he sees the force of his attack on slavish virtue.

12. *The* Symposium; *desire and the good*

12.1. *Rational desire.* The separation arguments attacked Socrates' principle TV, and the CA which depends on it. But if the CA fails, Socrates loses his account of virtue and rational choice. He argued that someone rationally chooses virtue when he finds that it contributes instrumentally to the final good he already desires and recognizes; LG ensured that virtue would always be only an instrumental means to the final good.[53] Now if TV is rejected, Socrates cannot show, on his account of rational choice, that someone can rationally choose to be virtuous; his paradigm of rational choice is the choice of medicine for the sake of health; but if the final good is not a determinate end, the choice of virtue does not conform to the paradigm. If Plato denies the determinacy of the final good, he must either accept that virtue is not open to rational choice, or show that Socrates' account of rational choice was too narrow.

The *Symposium* recalls the discussion in the *Lysis* of the primary object of love and its relation to subordinate objects, when Socrates presented his technical model of rational choice, and insisted on LG. But the *Symposium* uses some new apparatus in its account; the primary object of love is the separated Form of Beauty (*to kalon*), and someone comes to know and love it through a puzzling process of ascent. To decide whether Plato has a Socratic or a non-Socratic account of rational choice, we need to know whether this apparatus simply elaborates a basically Socratic view, or represents non-Socratic doctrine.

12.2. *Desire, beauty, and good.* Diotima examines the the love of what is beautiful or admirable (204a2–3).[54] But she also means to include desire for goods (204e1–3), and for happiness (204e5–7), the final good (205a1–3); and the later discussion is meant to apply to the good as well as the beautiful (206e8–207a2). She considers all and only desires for the beautiful and the good (205e10–206a12), taking these all to be focused on happiness.[55] The *Symposium*'s position on the relation between the beautiful and the good is never clear; but to justify his substitution Plato must believe at least that whenever we pursue goods we pursue them as being beautiful, and vice versa; goodness and beauty might be distinct properties of pursued objects, but pursued objects must have both of them.

12.3. *Socrates' view.* This close connection between the beautiful or admirable and the good is not clearly Socratic. Socrates often assumes that whatever is admirable is beneficial, and uses this assumption to show that any virtue agreed to be admirable must also be beneficial. In the *Gorgias* he answers the objection that 'good' and 'admirable' might refer to conflicting standards, by arguing that the admirable is either pleasant or beneficial or both (*G.* 474d3–e1). All the admirable things which are beneficial are, in Socrates' view, useful as instrumental means to some further end; and though he does not say that the admirable is what is pleasant or *instrumentally* beneficial, he needs no more in his argument.

12.4. *The* Hippias Major. Plato implicitly criticizes both parts of the *Gorgias*'s account. If 'pleasant' is restricted to the pleasures of some senses, the account of beauty seems arbitrarily restricted; but it is not naturally extended to all pleasures (*HMa.* 298e7–299b3). The suggestion that the admirable is beneficial pleasure (303d10–e10) is open to an earlier objection against an account of the admirable as the useful, which treated something as admirable when it performed its function well (295c1–e3). Socrates rejects this view; something is useful when it confers some power or capacity; but powers can be used well or badly, and what confers a power with bad results can hardly be admirable (296c5–d3). The amended account of the admirable as what produces the good is also attacked; since the producer and its product are separate, the admirable and the good must, on this view, be separated (297a2–d1).[56]

The last criticism is important because it rejects a consequence of the account proposed, that the final good cannot be called admirable, since it produces no further good, and that therefore nothing admirable could be the final good; if LG is accepted, nothing admirable could even be a good in itself. The rejected account suits Socrates' treatment of the virtues; they are admirable, but they contribute to the final good, and therefore, by LG, are not goods in themselves. If the rejected account of the admirable were right, we could decide what is admirable by deciding what contributes to the final good, already identified as a determinate end. 'Admirable' and 'good' would not, on this view, be two conflicting standards, but the first would be reducible to the second.

12.5. *The question in the* Symposium. Whether or not the *Hippias Major* attacks a Socratic view of the admirable, the *Symposium* must agree in denying that the admirable is simply what produces the good. If the rejected account were right, we could explain how various admirable things are admirable—bodies, laws, and wisdom—by their contribution to some separate final good (*HMa.* 296d6–e6; cf. *Symp.* 211c2–6), but the final good itself would not be admirable. The *Symposium*'s inter-substitution of 'admirable' and 'good' precludes the restriction of 'admirable' to instrumental goods; the final good itself must be admirable. If the final good itself is admirable, then something admirable is not thereby a purely instrumental good; and Plato implies that the non-final goods which are admirable are not all purely instrumental goods. If they were purely instrumental, he could explain why they are admirable in the *Hippias Major*'s terms, as instrumental means to some separate end. But he does not do this. The means–end relation is replaced by the ascent from different embodiments of what is admirable and beautiful to the Form; though the non-final beautifuls are imperfectly beautiful, Plato never claims that they are purely instrumental.

Plato does not treat the final good as a determinate end, as the

Socratic claim TV requires; nor does he accept LG, the claim that subordinate goods are not goods in themselves. He agree with Socrates that everyone pursues happiness (205d1–3), and men pursue money, gymnastics, or philosophy for the sake of happiness (205d3–8). But he does not suggest that these ends are only instrumental to some separate end called 'happiness'; they may express different people's views of what constitutes happiness. The *Lysis* treated the subordinate goods as instrumental means to the final good, not real goods in themselves (*Lys.* 219d2–5); the paradigm of choice suited a craft aiming at a determinate end. Neither of these views can be found in the *Symposium*; this is not surprising, if Plato refuses to explain 'admirable' in terms of instrumental benefit. Instead of technical reasoning about means and ends, he presents his puzzling account of the ascent of desire from the various beautifuls to the Form of Beauty.

13. *The ascent of desire*

13.1. *The procedure.* Plato insists that a pupil beginning the ascent must already be 'pregnant in soul'. Like other people, he wants to create whatever will preserve for ever what he values most; since what he values most are excellences of the soul, wisdom, and the rest of virtue (208e1–209a8), he tries to create these in himself and in other people he loves (209a8–c7). These are excellences of soul because the soul must be developed to produce them; and the pregnant man looks for someone suitably beautiful in whom he can develop these virtues (209a8–b7). His conception of what is beautiful or admirable will be reflected in his choice of persons to love, and what to love about them, and in his choice of offspring—the virtues, laws, and so on, he tries to propagate. Both of these desires are altered by the development of his conception of the beautiful through the ascent. The account has six stages with corresponding objects: S1 = a single beautiful body; S2 = the beauty in all bodies; S3 = the beauty of souls; S4 = the beauty of practices and laws; S5 = the beauty of sciences; S6 = Beauty Itself.

13.2. *The first stage.* The transition from S1 to S2 makes clearest the kind of process Plato finds in the ascent. The pupil at S1 loves a single body for its beauty and already tries to bring forth beautiful discourses, because he is anxious to propagate virtue (210a6–8). He realizes that the beauty in all beautiful bodies is akin, and becomes a lover of them all, thinking less of this one (210a8–b6). He has been induced to move from S1 to S2 by his own reasoning; if he loves the first body for its beauty, he sees that he has equal reason to love any body of equal beauty; and since beauty is the same in all beautiful bodies, he has reason to love them all. This conclusion is reached by elenchos, just as Socrates overturned Laches' initial narrow definition of courage by showing him that courage can be displayed in all kinds of conditions (*La.* 191c7–e7). The pupil gradually comes to realize his own demands on an adequate object of love when a candidate is found unsatisfactory.

13.3. *The later stages.* The movements between S2 and S6 are not so fully described by Plato, and reconstruction must be more speculative. But the same account will work for them as for the first movement:

1. To pass from S2 to S3 the pupil must see that the beauty of souls is more honourable than the beauty in bodies (210b6–7). He is himself pregnant in soul, anxious to propagate virtue; he reasonably decides that a beautiful soul is a more suitable object of his attention than a beautiful body.

2. When he reaches S3 he looks for the suitable discourses to improve his beloved; he must know how he wants to improve him. Naturally he will think of the admirable practices and norms or rules he wants observed; and so he will aim at this kind of beauty, which leads him to S4 (210c1–6).

3. Beautiful practices express knowledge, and someone should aim at this knowledge, rather than solely at the practices. When the pupil realizes this, he moves to S5; he will want this knowledge for himself, and to decide how he should educate his beloved; and he will want his beloved to have the same knowledge (210c6–d6). In the Socratic dialogues Socrates shows the interlocutor should aim, not simply at good actions, but at a good state of the soul (*La.* 185d5–e2), which is found to be knowledge. In the *Phaedo* Plato suggested that this knowledge is to be valued for itself.

4. When the pupil values knowledge, he will come to value knowledge of what is beautiful; for this will be the best guide for his efforts to create virtue. When his search for this knowledge is over, he will have reached S6.

13.4. *Rationality in the ascent.* Throughout this sequence the pattern of elenctic argument can be discerned. Plato does not mean to describe just a curriculum, where the pupil sees no reason to pass from one stage to the next. We might suppose that just as we need to learn some mathematics to learn physics, we must see the less abstract kinds of beauty at the lower stages before we see the more abstract at the higher stages. But this alone will not satisfy Plato; for it would still require compulsion to move a pupil from the lower to the higher stages. In Plato's ascent, a pupil at each stage has to be shown, from principles he already accepts, that he has reason to move to the higher stage.

13.5. *Higher and lower stages.* We might think the ascent is like a curriculum which begins with reading children's books, but abandons them when they have served their purpose; does the pupil similarly cease to love the objects at lower stages when he reaches higher stages? Plato does not commit himself to this view, and could not justify it from his account. When someone reaches the Form of Beauty he finds a reliable account of what beauty is, since the Form's beauty, unlike the beauty of the 'many beautifuls' recognized by faulty observational accounts, does not suffer exceptions (211a1–b5).[57] The correct account allows us to love the lower objects to the right extent, and for the right reasons, in so far as they are really beautiful; but we have no reason to stop loving them altogether. The lower stages are means to the higher (210e5–6, 211c1–3), but Plato does not suggest they are only means. The lower beautifuls partake in the Form, and embody it imperfectly; but Plato does not claim they are imperfect because they are purely instrumental, but only because they are incomplete expressions of beauty.[58]

13.6. *Propagating virtue.* One strong reason for doubting that the Form is meant to replace all the other beautifuls in the lover's affections is Plato's treatment of the 'propagation of virtue'. At each step the pupil has been anxious to produce virtue in his beloved; and what he wants to produce depends on his conception of the beautiful (210a7–8, c1–3, d5–6). When he has the right view of the beautiful, he will produce real virtue, and no mere images (212a2–7). Success in the ascent does not make him think the lower beautifuls are useful only as steps to contemplation of the Form and otherwise useless; he still thinks it worth while to produce virtue, and to express his conception of the Form in men, laws and institutions (cf. 209c7–e4).

14. *The significance of the* Symposium

14.1. *Rejection of the craft-analogy.* The easiest way to see what is important in the ascent theory is to ask why Plato needs it at all. If he agreed with Socrates that beautiful things are all subordinate goods instrumental to the final good, he could easily explain how we can move from one to another; we would simply discover that this is more efficient than that as a means to the same final good. Such an account would be free of any strange talk about ascent; it would be the *Lysis*'s account of rational desire.

Plato rejects this solution. Not only instrumental goods are admirable, and subordinate goods are not all simply instrumental. Nor is the final good a determinate end, by which we can decide whether or not anything is really admirable; it is itself indeterminate, and people dispute about its content. A problem avoided by Socrates' theory now arises for Plato. If the final good is an indeterminate end, its constituents must be decided somehow; but what is the procedure? Socrates allowed a rational procedure for choosing subordinate goods, advising the choice of whatever one contributes best to the chosen end, but no procedure for deciding on the components of the good, since for him the final good is a determinate end, and its components are not open to rational choice.

14.2. *Plato's alternative.* The ascent-theory is meant to show how there can be rational choice of components of the good. In Socrates' view a rational desire is formed by deliberation about instrumental means to the final good; and therefore no desire for components of the final good can be rational. Plato rejects this view, and tries to show how the desire for something as an end in itself can be a rational desire formed by deliberation. He considered desire for the beautiful or admirable rather than desire for the good, because we are inclined to regard something as admirable and worth while in itself even if it contributes to no further good. Aristotle recognizes that virtuous action regarded as worth while in itself is done 'because it is admirable' (*EN* 1115b11–13, 1169a20–22); and the admirable has the same role in the *Symposium*. The ascent requires progress through various candidates for what is ultimately worth while in itself until the right candidate is reached.

The progress is elenctic. At each stage the pupil tests his aspirations against his present objects of admiration, and though he was not previously aware of it, finds the objects inadequate to the aspiration, in discovering that the reason he offers for choosing this object really justifies the choice of something else. As he reaches each new object, he finds it does not fully satisfy his criteria, as they become more explicit, for something admirable, and continues until he finds the right criteria. This process does not reveal more efficient means to a single determinate end, but allows a conception of the final good to emerge from rational reflection on the inadequacy of various candidates.

14.3. *Choice and knowledge.* When he rejects TV Plato rejects Socrates' defence of KSV. Socrates defended KSV by arguing that a man's choice of ends could be taken as fixed, and virtue could be confined to the knowledge of instrumental means. Plato cannot agree that virtue is confined to instrumental means; when someone becomes virtuous, his choice of ends does not remain fixed, and virtue requires changed desires for ends, as well as changed beliefs. Plato still believes with Socrates that knowledge alters action; but he now believes that it alters action only by altering desires for ends; the development of virtue is not, as it was for Socrates, purely cognitive, but both cognitive and affective. In Socrates' view, the desire for happiness and its components would have to be non-deliberative, since deliberative desire rested on deliberation about instrumental means to happiness. Plato argues that desire for the components of happiness can be deliberative too, though the deliberation follows a different pattern—it does not require reasoning about instrumental means, but elenctic discovery of the best conception of the end. Though Plato does not think knowledge alone constitutes virtue, he thinks it has more extensive tasks than Socrates allowed it in finding the right ends for vitue.

14.4. *Recollection.* The *Symposium* does not mention recollection; but it supports Plato's view that moral knowledge requires recollection and not craft-knowledge. The Form of Beauty is irreducible to observable properties, and therefore cannot be the object of a craft. It can be known only by gradual development and examination of beliefs about beauty, without the external standard of corrections sought by Socrates. All this argument in the *Symposium* supports the view that moral knowledge can only be recollection—for the elenctic treatment of desire and aspiration in the *Symposium* recalls the method called 'recollection' in the *Meno* and *Phaedo*.

14.5 *Virtues and motives.* Though the *Symposium* does not repeat the *Phaedo*'s criticism of slavish virtue, it suggests how the 'real virtue' vaguely advocated in the *Phaedo* might be possible. Socrates recognized action aimed at achieving the final good; and the pursuit of virtuous action for its consequences is condemned in the *Phaedo*, with no clear picture of the alternative. But the *Symposium* distinguishes action aimed at reaching the goal from action aimed at expressing it; someone can try not only to find the Beautiful, but also to express his conception of it in action; he will value virtuous action not only for its consequences in achieving one of his other ends, but also for itself, as part of the life prescribed by his view of the final good. This account of moral motives requires further examination; but at least it suggests a way to defend the *Phaedo*'s claim; someone who knows Beauty propagates real virtue, not just an image (*Symp.* 212a2–5), whereas the slavish man could produce only an image and illusion (*Phd.* 69b6).[59]

14.6. *The* Symposium *and the criticism of Socrates*. If this is the right account of the *Symposium*, it confirms to some extent the earlier account of the *Phaedo*; Plato discusses exactly those problems about desire and choice which he ought to discuss if the Theory of Forms demands rejection of the CA. Admittedly, the text is brief and obscure; but its view is not the *Lysis*'s view, and its striking peculiarities need some explanation. An explanation can be found in the questions about Socratic ethics which underlie the Theory of Recollection and the Theory of Forms.

15. *Recollection and virtue in the* Phaedrus

15.1. *The relevance of the* Phaedrus. So far the Theory of Recollection, the theory of ascent and the criticism of slavish virtue have been developed separately; only the reference to separated Forms in the *Symposium* has connected the first two. But the *Phaedrus* shows that Plato sees the connections between all three. It presents an account of ascent of desire and Platonic love in the language of recollection; and it uses this account to attack slavish virtue. A brief sketch of the relevant doctrines will show that our account of the argument in the *Phaedo* and *Symposium* has some textual support.[60]

15.2. *Slavish virtue*. The first two speeches contrast the sanity of the non-lover who does not sacrifice his own benefit for present gratification, with the madness of the lover whose passion (*erōs*) damages his own and other people's future good (*Phdr.* 233b6–c6);

the non-lover is a rational planner who deliberates about his best interests and acts on his deliberations (234b1–5), apparently the paradigm of a Socratic rational agent. Nor does he reject conventional virtuous action; the actions he chooses would all normally be accepted as temperate, and he avoids recognized intemperate action.[61] In his choice of virtuous actions for their beneficial consequences, he resembles the slavish man in the *Phaedo*; and Plato duly denounces him because he has only 'mortal!' temperance, and not the real 'divine' temperance of the Platonic lover, who is temperate because of madness (256e3–257a2). Plato sets Socrates the same problem here as in the *Phaedo*, to explain why the slavish man or the non-lover is not virtuous if virtue is only what Socrates says it is, knowledge of the instrumental means to a determinate end.

15.3. *Recollection.* Plato contrasts the Platonic lover with the non-lover by explaining how the lover acquires his knowledge and desires, through the method of recollection, proceeding from the many perceptions of *F*s to the one *F* grasped by reasoning (249b5–c4). Someone who is (in the *Symposium*'s terms) 'pregnant in soul' is stimulated by a perceptible instance of beauty (250c7–e1) to look for fuller understanding of beauty, and to express his conception in his actions, by trying to change his beloved (252d5–e1). As in the *Symposium*, his progress to knowledge of Beauty alters his view of how he should 'propagate virtue' (252e1–253b1).[62] The single process of recollection includes both cognitive and affective changes.

15.4. *Effects of recollection.* Plato's account of the lover shows that he does not disagree with the non-lover simply about instrumental means. The non-lover with his slavish virtue pursues the same kinds of ends a non-virtuous man might pursue, but believes that virtuous action will secure these ends, honour, wealth, pleasure. But the virtuous man who knows the moral Forms by recollection does not pursue the same ends as a non-virtuous man, because he and the non-virtuous man will not agree on a description of the final good as a determinate end. Because he accepts NR, and believes that what is admirable can be understood only by recollection, Plato rejects a Socratic view of virtue as knowledge of the right instrumental means; the virtuous man and the slavish dispute, not about instrumental means to a determinate end they both pursue, but about the components of the final good.

15.5. *Madness.* This dispute about ultimate ends partly explains why other people think the really virtuous man is mad; they neither share nor sympathize with his ultimate ends, but prefer the non-lover's virtue; and the virtuous man's madness makes him indifferent to the consequences of his actions (cf. 238a7–b4), so that other people think he is imprudent (256e3–257a2). Here as in the *Phaedo* the virtuous man chooses virtuous action for itself, apart from its consequences, to embody his conception of what is admirable. The *Symposium*'s treatment of propagating virtue explains why the virtuous man in the *Phaedrus* should reject the slavish attitude to virtuous actions.

15.6. *Knowledge and virtue.* The *Phaedrus* defends KNV; the lover with real virtue reaches knowledge through recollection, while the non-lover has only 'belief aiming at what is best' (237d8–9). Someone with slavish virtue has the right beliefs which produce virtuous actions; but a virtuous man needs the knowledge of virtue which shows him how virtuous action is worth while in itself, apart from its consequences. Here as elsewhere, the *Phaedrus* connects the middle dialogues' arguments about knowledge, in the Theory of Recollection and the Theory of Forms, with the arguments about desire and choice in the *Symposium*, and suggests their implications for a theory of virtue.

16. Problems for Plato's criticism of Socrates

16.1. *Results of the middle dialogues.* These brief remarks on the *Phaedrus* summarize what Plato has tried to prove in the middle dialogues about the Socratic theory. His attitude is not wholly negative; on the contrary, the account of recollection and the ascent of desire is meant to represent the Socratic elenchos; and it is reflection on the elenchos which suggests that separated Forms are needed. But Plato criticizes the CA. Socrates assumed the truth of TV; the separation-arguments reject it; the *Symposium* tries to replace the Socratic view of rational choice which supported KSV; and Plato insists that the CA misrepresents the proper status of virtue by making it worth while only for its consequences.

The result of this criticism is that Plato rejects those parts of Socrates' theory which depend on craft-principles, and retains the parts which depend on elenchos-principles.[63] Moral knowledge will emerge from, and will be justified by, the elenchos; but it will not meet the conditions for a craft. But if Plato sacrifices the craft-principles, he must face the problems which these principles answered for Socrates.

16.2. *Definition.* Plato rejects ED for definitions of virtues. If a definition satisfied ED, it would be illuminating, and would provide the kind of paradigm Socrates seeks; we could use sure and undisputed judgements, independent of problematic moral issues, to settle our problems about the virtues. But NR threatens a circle of moral terms in definitions; we may define the just and the admirable by reference to the good, and the good by reference to them. Too small a circle will be vicious, and our definition will explain nothing. Plato must show how a definition which fails ED can still be illuminating.

16.3. *Objectivity and justification.* Socrates' appeal to the CA, and especially to TV, showed how virtue could be justified to anyone. If he could prove his case, the virtuous man's choices would not simply be his personal preferences; they would aim at an end which everyone would agree he had reason to pursue. This account of virtue would show how moral beliefs could be more than mere Protagorean conventional norms, and could be rationally and systematically taught. But if TV is false, and the virtuous and non-virtuous disagree about components of the final good, Socrates' justification fails. For if the virtuous man has reached his view through recollection, he has simply found an account which makes sense of his own moral beliefs; how can he show he began from the right place and reached the right terminus? A craft would correct this apparent subjectivity of the elenctic method, by showing a determinate end for virtue to aim at. When he rejects the CA, Plato loses this external test of correctness; and questions about objectivity and justification return.

16.4. *Motivation.* Socrates' views on justification reflect his desire to show that anyone has a reason to be virtuous, and thereby to provide a motive for a non-virtuous man to choose virtue. If Plato's account of definition and justification confines them within moral beliefs, and does not allow appeals to ends that the non-virtuous man accepts, how can he persuade a non-virtuous man to be virtuous? Apparently he must either agree with Protagoras against Socrates that there is no rational method for acquiring virtue, or show that he has a different way of satisfying Socrates' demands.

16.5. *Plato's tasks.* These problems confirm the value of the CA; it is not a naïve mistake, but an important set of doctrines for solving central problems of interest to Socrates and Plato alike. And yet, Plato should be praised, not blamed, for finding fault with Socrates. His major criticisms show that the CA's demands cannot plausibly be met, and that its view of moral knowledge and virtue is intolerably over-simplified. If the CA must be rejected, so must the argument of the *Gorgias*. For its defence of justice relied on TV and KSV; Socrates claimed that the virtuous man has a craft which achieves a determinate end, which will persuade the non-virtuous man that he has reason to be virtuous. Plato rejects this argument, but offers no systematic theory to fill the gaps left by the rejection of the CA. Instead the middle dialogues offer pictures and metaphors—recollection, separation, non-slavish virtue, ascent of desire, madness—which fall short of a systematic theory. These pictures raise our problems clearly enough, but do not resolve them. The middle dialogues are far more tentative and exploratory, despite their superficial appearance of dogmatism, than the Socratic dialogues. But in the *Republic* Plato tries to combine the pictures into a sketch (unfortunately only a sketch) of an alternative theory.

VII THE *REPUBLIC*: PLATO'S NEW THEORY

1. *Introduction*

1.1. *The inquiry into justice.* I shall discuss selected topics in the main ethical argument of the *Republic*, to show how it contributes to the questions examined so far. The best way to isolate the main thread of argument, for this purpose, from the diverse interests of the *Republic* is to show how Plato treats the problems examined in earlier dialogues. The main problem is clearly Socratic. An account of justice is expected to show what Socrates assumed, that justice is a virtue and therefore contributes to happiness. Plato defends the *Crito*'s claim that justice benefits, and injustice harms, the soul. Books II and IV might be treated as a standard Socratic inquiry elaborating the similar argument in the *Gorgias*.

1.2. *New arguments.* But even these books are not as Socratic as they might look. Some features of the argument show that Plato rejects those Socratic principles which supported the CA.

1. He recognizes the possibility of incontinence and rejects KSV; if KSV is false, justice cannot be simply a craft.
2. The accounts of justice and the other virtues are hypotheses, which do not satisfy Socrates' condition for a definition.
3. The demand for a proof that justice is a good to be chosen for itself and not merely for its results is foreign to the Socratic dialogues and the *Gorgias*, but follows naturally from the *Phaedo*'s attack on slavish virtue. These claims in the apparently Socratic inquiry of II–IV show already the influence of the middle dialogues.

But the later books of the *Republic* must be examined to see the effects of the middle dialogues on Plato's ethical argument. Books V–VII defend the Theory of Recollection, both the epistemological and metaphysical theory of separated Forms and the *Symposium*'s theory of rational desire. I shall argue that these doctrines are essential for the main argument of the *Republic*, and especially that they radically affect the division of the soul used in Books VIII–IX to support the defence of justice in Book IV. The Theory of Forms explains why knowledge is necessary for virtue, and the *Symposium*'s account of desire shows the fault in the Socratic view.

1.3. *Attempted solutions.* The *Republic* tries to answer the hardest problem for Socratic ethics, to show how justice is a virtue because it benefits the agent; but now Plato avoids appeal to the CA and relies instead on the views we have seen defended in the middle dialogues. These revisions of the Socratic position do not make his task easy, and we may reasonably doubt if they go far enough; perhaps Plato should simply have rejected the basic Socratic assumption that virtue benefits the agent. The account of justice as psychic harmony in Book IV revives a problem in the *Gorgias*; what has the psychic harmony concerned with pursuit of my own interest to do with justice and its concern for other people's interests? In Books IV and VIII–IX Plato argues that someone with a harmonious soul directed by reason is just. Different views of 'direction by reason' can be found in IV and in later books; but will any of them prove Plato's case about justice? That is the question to be examined.

2. *Problems in* Republic *I*

2.1. *The opening moves.* Book I is a test case for our view that Plato abandons the CA. It is Socratic in style and content, and it appeals regularly to the CA. The return of the CA after its absence in the middle dialogues is surprising; perhaps Plato's silence did not indicate a change of mind.[1] I shall try to explain why the attention to the CA fits the general purpose and Socratic character of Book I, even though Plato himself has rejected the CA. The discussion reminds us of the Socratic dialogues because it is meant to expose the weaknesses in Socrates' views on justice, and in the CA, a central part of those views; the criticism exposes weaknesses in the *Gorgias*'s defence of Socratic views through the CA. We need to show the weaknesses Plato identifies for us, and to show that he identifies them for himself. To prove this second point, we need to see if the rest of the *Republic* criticizes or abandons the Socratic principles of Book I.

A behavioural account of justice is rejected for the normal reasons (331c1–332c4).[2] Then Socrates demands to know the subject matter and product of justice which distinguish it from all other crafts, and Polemarchus cannot oblige (332c5–333e2). This is a fair demand, on the assumption, accepted in the Socratic dialogues, that justice is a craft, to be valued for some product distinct from its exercise. The next argument raises the paradox of misuse (333e3–334b6). The

Socratic answer to the paradox depended on KSV and TV, to show that the product of justice is a determinate end which everyone wants and no one will misuse. Plato must decide whether or not to accept this answer.

2.2. *Justice and harm.* The last argument against Polemarchus (334e5–336a7) defends a vital Socratic claim, equally vital in the *Republic*, that the just man will always benefit and never harm other people. Socrates' main claim is that (a) the just man will never harm anyone, because (b) he will never make anyone more unjust. If (b) is at all relevant to (a), Socrates must assume (cf. *G.* 470e6–11) that the most serious harm for someone is to be unjust; and so he must show how justice supremely benefits the agent. The account of justice as psychic harmony was intended to show that it instrumentally benefits anyone concerned with his own interests. But if Socrates can show how justice benefits the agent, he threatens the rest of his argument. For why will a 'just' man on this account (someone who benefits himself) reliably benefit rather than harm other people, or treat them justly rather than unjustly?

The *Gorgias* had no satisfactory answer to this question; and it is hard to answer within the CA. The CA and TV require justice to promote some determinate end accepted by the non-virtuous man; but it is hard to see how that kind of justice can always be expected to benefit other people too, since most plausible candidates for this determinate end may be indifferent or hostile to other people's interests. The CA makes Socrates' task harder; but even without the CA it is not easy. This argument exposes the claims Plato should defend in the rest of the *Republic*.[3]

2.3. *Thrasymachus' criticism.* Thrasymachus challenges the basic assumption in the argument with Polemarchus—that justice benefits both the agent and other people. Like Callicles and Socrates, he identifies a conflict in ordinary beliefs about justice:

1. Justice is a virtue.
2. My virtue always benefits me.
3. My justice benefits other people.
4. What benefits other people sometimes harms me, and what benefits me sometimes harms other people.

Callicles removed the conflict by rejecting (3) as a part of merely conventional justice. Socrates then rejected (4); and he must reject it to defend his last argument against Polemarchus. Thrasymachus rejects (1) (348c5–349a3). He does not accept Callicles' revised criteria for justice, but sticks to ordinary beliefs about just actions; he agrees that justice is concerned with other people's interests and expectations, and claims that this feature of common beliefs excludes Socrates' view of justice, because of (4).

Thrasymachus presents a new challenge to Socrates. No previous interlocutor persistently rejects the normal list of virtues; and in the *Crito* Socrates exploits this agreement, arguing from (1) and (2) that justice benefits the agent. Polus rejected (2) for justice, but Thrasymachus avoids that move (348e5–349a2). Socrates cannot rely on common beliefs (*ta nomizomena*, 348e9) that justice is virtuous or admirable. Normally Socrates retains (1) and (2) and rejects other beliefs about any virtue to suit (2). Thrasymachus suggests that this procedure applied to justice will require Socrates to reject (3); and then it will not be clear that he is talking about justice at all. Wholesale rejection of ordinary beliefs will apparently leave Socrates with no reason for his 'just' man to benefit others.[4]

2.4. *Justice and craft.* The CA, as applied by Thrasymachus, reaches awkward conclusions for Socrates. Thrasymachus agrees that just action is prescribed by a craft; but for him the craftsman is not the just man himself, but his superior, the ruler who prescribes the just action; and the just man's actions are designed neither to benefit himself nor to benefit other people, but to benefit the ruler (338e3–6, 343c1–d1). The *Gorgias* assumed that a just man would be a good ruler, and that his practice of the ruler's craft would make other people just, and thereby benefit them—Socrates still assumes this in his reply to Polemarchus. Thrasymachus answers that the ruler is not just, since justice applies only to his inferiors, and that his craft prescribes just actions as beneficial to him, not to the subject—as the shepherd fattens sheep for his benefit, not theirs (343b1–c1). Socrates needs to defend his way of applying the CA to justice. He presents two lines of argument. First he accepts Thrasymachus' view that justice is what is prescribed by the ruler, and argues that even so it is in the subject's interest. Then he argues (from 347d8) against Thrasymachus' general claim, apart from his claim about the character of rulers, that the unjust man has a better life than the just man.

3. *Socrates' Defence of Justice*

3.1. *Crafts and objects.* Socrates argues that a ruler will rule in the subject's interest if he is a real craftsman; for a craft in itself is not concerned with the interests of the craftsman, but with the object. When Thrasymachus objects that shepherds fatten sheep for themselves, Socrates finds a confusion between the various crafts and the money-making craft which uses them for its purpose; a shepherd practises his craft competently if the sheep are well tended, whether or not he makes money. Socrates wants to argue from the necessary features of any craft to its concern with the interests of its object; but he fails. He shows that competence in a craft requires the perfection of the object rather than benefit to the craftsman; but concern for the object does not require concern for its interests—a shoemaker is concerned with the perfection, but not the interests, of leather. Though skill at money-making is separate from skill at a particular craft, the criteria of excellence in a craft may be fixed by money-making considerations—good care of sheep requires their fattening because that is profitable. And in any case Socrates does not show why ruling is not a compound craft—administering and money-making; or even if ruling is a simple, non-compound craft, why should Thrasymachus not invent a compound craft of 'druling' (ruling plus money-making), and say that justice benefits the druler?[5]

The result is the failure of Socrates' project, begun in the *Gorgias*, of appealing to features of a craft to argue that if virtue is a craft it will pursue the right goals. He argued that a craft, as opposed to a mere technique, aims at some good (*G.* 503d5–504a5, 504d5–e5), and confidently inferred that a ruler or just man who is a craftsman aims at other people's good. Thrasymachus' replies show that this appeal to a craft will not work; any specialized craft can be used by the money-making craft for the agent's enrichment, and this problem seems to arise equally for virtue, if virtue is a craft. To show that virtue is not liable to misuse if it is a craft, Socrates must defend KSV; but we will see that this is not his reply to Thrasymachus later in the *Republic*.

3.2. *Overreaching*. Socrates now attacks Thrasymachus' claim that the unjust man is better off than the just man (347e2–6), and argues that the just man is a craftsman, not merely the object of the ruler's craft aiming at the ruler's interest. The just man is like other good and wise craftsmen who do not try to overreach other craftsmen, and the unjust man is like bad and incompetent craftsmen who try to overreach everyone (349b1–350c11). The argument rests on an equivocation in 'overreach' (*pleonektein*); the good craftsman will not try to 'overreach' another good craftsman, by adding to the right prescription of the right amount, while the unjust man will 'overreach' in a different way, by trying to get more benefits for himself.

Here again 'equivocation' is not quite right; Socrates will insist that the unjust man's overreaching is just a case of the first kind of overreaching—a foolish effort to grab more than the right amount, because he does not know the right amount, like an incompetent doctor who prescribes a whole bottle of pills because he does not know the right dose. But this account of the unjust man is meant to be supported by the 'overreaching' argument, and cannot fairly be used in its defence. Thrasymachus' unjust man is not devoted to pointless excess, but to securing the best results for himself—and Socrates has not proved that they are not acquired by injustice. To prove that the unjust man is simply incompetent at some craft, Socrates should show that he pursues the same determinate end as the just man, but less efficiently; but he has never found it easy to show that the final good is a determinate end. In any case, the argument does not show what Socrates wanted, that a just man is better off then an unjust (348b8–10). Like Socrates, Thrasymachus insists that a virtue should benefit the virtuous man (348c2–e4). If justice is some craft or other, it is some kind of wisdom and virtue (just as the shepherding craft is a man's virtue as a shepherd); but it has not been shown to be the virtue which contributes to happiness.

3.3. *The results of justice*. Socrates argues that injustice cannot be a craft because it allows no coherent rational plan to guide action. The argument has two parts:

1. If members of a gang of thieves treat each other unjustly, they will be incapable of any co-operative activity, even to fulfil their unjust ends (351c7–10); and so it is the work of injustice to cause hatred, strife, and incapacity for combined effort wherever it is present (351d8–e1).
2. Injustice will have the same result when it is present in an individual; he will quarrel with himself and be incapable of coherent action (351e6–352a8).

Now what is injustice in an individual? Socrates might mean either (2a) the injustice which makes A quarrel with B will also make A quarrel with himself; or (2b) if the parts of A quarrel with each other the way A quarrels with B, A will be incapable. Now Socrates can argue for (2b) from (1), that the analoguous condition of groups and individuals is equally harmful; he will rely on the *Gorgias*'s conception of justice in an individual as psychic harmony. But this argument does not show what Socrates wants, that it is bad for A if he is unjust to B. The 'injustice' in (2b) is only analogous to the 'injustice' in (1), not the same condition; the same condition is mentioned in (2a), but Socrates has not argued for (2a). He has previously claimed that injustice harms the soul of the agent (*Cri.* 47e6–48a1; *G.* 477b3–c5, 506d5–507a3); but his argument here does not support him—only the state causing internal dissension in a man, not the state causing injustice to other men, has been proved to harm the agent. The problem of defending (2a) from (2b) has arisen in the *Gorgias*, and will be prominent in the *Republic*.[6] Socrates' argument depends on TV; he suggests that injustice in the soul will cause some recognized harm to the individual, parallel to the recognized harm of injustice among thieves; then justice will secure some recognized good to the soul. But it is hard to prove (2a) on these terms; an unjust man has not been shown that the condition which makes him harm others also inflicts a recognized harm on him.

In any case, neither part of the argument proves more than that some justice (of either kind) is necessary for some limited purposes. Members of a gang should not be unjust to each other; but they may not give up injustice to non-members. Similarly, a man should prevent the internal strife which frustrates his aims; but he may still be unjust to other men. Thrasymachus might be persuaded that complete injustice would be unwise; but he can reply that justice is wise only if it is controlled and limited by over-all injustice. This weakness in the defence of justice undermines Socrates' last argument, that since justice is the virtue of the soul, it will make the soul perform its work well and so live well (353d3–e11).[7] He needs to show that justice produces some instrumental benefit which makes it sufficient for living well. But (2b) has shown only that psychic harmony has limited instrumental value. Socrates has chosen to argue from the instrumental benefits of justice for some recognized end; but that form of argument has not achieved what he wants.

3.4. Plato's attitude.

Does Plato accept Socrates' arguments in Book I? Certainly he accepts some of the conclusions: (1) Justice benefits the just man; (2) The just man benefits others; (3) Just men are unwilling to rule, but will rule well (347d1–6); (4) Justice is the soul's virtue. These conclusions are defended later in the *Republic*, but with different arguments. In particular no later argument suggests that justice is a craft, or appeals to its instrumental benefits. Socrates' conclusion, that we should know what justice is before we examine these questions, is fully justified (354b8–c3); until we know whether justice is a craft, whether it is instrumentally beneficial, and how justice within the soul is connected to justice between people, we cannot evaluate the case against Thrasymachus. But the weakness of Socrates' arguments as they stand raises doubts about a defence of justice which relies on the CA.

Plato's exposure of the CA and its weaknesses casts doubt on the *Gorgias*'s defence of justice, as a craft which benefits the just man and other men; Thrasymachus replies that nothing commonly recognized as justice can belong to a craft which benefits the just man. Socrates defends justice within the *Gorgias*'s views, which in turn defended the strong but unargued claims in the Socratic dialogues. His failure in Book I suggests that the *Gorgias*'s and the Socratic dialogues' assumptions allow no satisfactory defence of justice. The rest of the *Republic*, and especially Glaucon's initial objections in II, show that Plato draws this conclusion.

4. *Glaucon's objections*

4.1. *Types of goods.* Glaucon begins his criticism of Socrates' defence with a threefold division of goods into (a) goods chosen for themselves ('a-goods'); (b) goods chosen for themselves and for their consequences; (c) goods chosen only for their consequences (357b4–d2). This division already conflicts with Socrates' view in the *Lysis*; for he denied that anything chosen for the sake of something else could also be a good in itself, and therefore denied, contrary to Glaucon, that health is a good in itself (*Lys.* 219c1–4, 220a6–b5). The *Lysis* excluded b-goods, and *Republic* II frees Plato from this restriction. He can now recognize that x can be good in itself and for the sake of y, either as an instrumental means to y (as justice contributes to its rewards) or as a component of y (as justice, in Glaucon's view, contributes to living well). Glaucon exploits both of these options.

4.2. *Glaucon's complaint.* Glaucon has two objections against Socrates' previous arguments: (1) The refutation of Thrasymachus was too brisk (358b2–3). (2) He wants to hear what justice is, and what its power is when it is in the soul, not about its rewards and consequences (358b3–7).[8] The objections are connected; if justice is only a c-good, a version of Thrasymachus' position will be irresistible (359b7–c6), and in Book I justice was praised only for its consequences, in terms suitable for any craft. Socrates argued that the just man is the expert in producing some product which the unjust man wants but pursues inefficiently; and he advocated justice for its benefits in promoting aims which an unjust man shares. These arguments are open to Glaucon's criticism that they praise justice as a c-good, for its consequences. When Socrates agrees that justice is a b-good, (357d4–358a3), he rejects the position of Book I, and equally of the *Gorgias* and the Socratic dialogues, which all treat justice as a c-good. The rest of the *Republic* drops the CA, and uses none of the arguments, so frequent in Book I, which assume justice is some kind of craft. The two changes are connected. The CA suggests that the product of justice is desirable, and makes justice desirable for its product; once this suggestion is rejected, the CA becomes more misleading than helpful. Though Plato does not explicitly attack particular arguments of Book I and does not say that the CA caused the trouble, his claim that justice is a b-good requires the rejection of the CA and of the strategy of Book I. And there is reason to believe Plato sees this; he no sooner treats justice as a b-good than he says no more about the CA.

Like Socrates at the end of Book I (354b3–c3), Glaucon thinks a definition of justice is needed (358b4–7); he follows Cleitophon's demand to know what justice is and why it is worth while (*Clt.* 408d1–e3). If he accepted the CA, he should also accept Cleitophon's way of fulfilling that demand—an account of the subject matter and product of justice (*Clt.* 409a4–410e4). But that kind of account would imply that justice is a c-good, and Glaucon insists on a proof that it is a b-good; he rejects the account required by the CA. He challenges Socrates' conviction, displayed in earlier dialogues, that justice is always worth while, and implies that if it is a c-good, as earlier dialogues have assumed, Socrates' conviction was wrong (367d5–e1). To refute Socrates' earlier position, Glaucon must show that no account of justice as a c-good makes it always worth while for us to be just. He must eliminate two types of consequences; (1) natural consequences, which result from someone's justice apart from anyone's attitude to it, and (2) artificial consequences, which depend on other people's favourable attitude to his justice and their desire to reward him. Glaucon must show that neither kind of consequence will allow an adequate defence of justice.

4.3. *The social contract.* The account of the origins of justice explains why it is a c-good. Glaucon defends Thrasymachus' view that it is the advantage of the stronger; for it is prescribed by individuals too weak to resist injustice separately, who are collectively strong enough to coerce aggressors (359c3–6). Since each man is too weak to do what he would like most, unpunished injustice, they agree on mutual non-aggression and just action (358e3–359b5). This defence of Thrasymachus looks too plausible for Glaucon's purposes. For he defends Protagoras' claim that justice is necessary for social and political life (*Pr.* 324d7–325a2), by a Humean argument; though a system of justice requires me to forgo my advantage in particular cases, the system itself benefits me, and I have good reason to observe its rules.[9] Why does this defence of justice as a c-good not show why it is worth while for its natural consequences?

4.4. *Gyges' ring.* To show why the contract-theory gives no good reason to be just, Glaucon introduces Gyges' ring, which removes the bad artificial consequences of unjust action; anyone who accepts the contract-theory will use Gyges' ring if he is wise (359b6–c6, 360b3–d7), and show that he thinks justice is not a good for him (360c6–d2). Now Glaucon seems to refute himself with his own account of justice. For Gyges' ring removes only the artificial consequences of unjust action; but the contract-theory shows that unjust action has bad natural consequences, when it upsets the system of justice which benefits me; therefore I apparently have good reason to refuse Gyges' ring, and to stick to justice for its good natural consequences. Glaucon is hasty and careless in suggesting that a contract-theorist has no reason to refuse Gyges' ring.

But Glaucon's main point is still sound, if he distinguishes my interest in maintaining the system of justice, and my interest in acting justly. The two are not entirely separable. The survival of the system may require rules prescribing just action for everyone, including me, and then I have an interest in the enforcement of the rules. If I had to choose between mass production of Gyges' ring and no production at all, the second decision would no doubt be right. But this defence shows that I have reason to act justly only when an unjust action would damage the system too severely to be outweighed by the good results of the action; I will have no reason to avoid unjust action when it benefits me and does not damage the system so severely—for not all unjust actions will destroy the system. Glaucon is still right to say that a contract-theorist will use Gyges' ring; though his use will be more restricted than Glaucon alleged, it will still be frequent enough to show that a Humean theory, appealing to the bad natural consequences of unjust action for the system of justice, provides no reason to be just.

On this view, my justice benefits other people, as Protagoras agreed (*Pr.* 327b1–2), but harms me (*R.* 343c1–6, 367c2–5)—though Protagoras does not say this, he cannot refute it. The harm might sometimes be worth while for the sake of the system, but often this defence of just action will fail. This criticism also damages Socrates' defence of justice in I; limited just action may be needed to secure psychic stability in individuals or co-operation within groups (351c7–352a8), but that is no reason to avoid any injustice which does not conflict with these goals.

4.5. *Artificial consequences.* Now that Glaucon has rejected a defence of justice for its natural consequences, only artificial consequences are left—the rewards and honours attached to justice and the penalties of injustice; and Adeimantus easily shows that these justify apparent justice, but secret injustice. People regard injustice as being disgraceful only by convention, and think unjust action more beneficial than just action (364a1–6). They are wrong, if they do not qualify their preference for injustice by recognizing the bad natural consequences of some unjust actions for the beneficial system of justice; but for other unjust actions their preference is justified—they have reason to pursue the good natural consequences of these unjust actions and the good artificial consequences of apparent justice. Adeimantus criticizes defenders of apparent justice who praise justice for its artificial consequences, for two reasons familiar from the middle dialogues.[10] (1) They pursue the same ends as the unjust man (362b1–c8, 362e4–363e4), so that their defence of justice collapses against a proof that the same results are secured by apparent justice with secret injustice. They do not believe just and unjust men should pursue different ends. (2) They do not think justice is a good in itself; they can justify nothing more than an illusion of justice designed to secure the artificial consequences of justice (365c3–6). The same two criticisms apply equally to the contract-theorist; they recall the *Phaedo*'s criticism of slavish virtue (*Phd.* 69b5–8).

In the *Phaedo* slavish men chose courage and temperance for their natural consequences; why then does the *Republic* not recognize a separate class, apart from those denounced by Adeimantus, who choose justice for its natural consequences? Plato will reply that the benefits of temperance require slavish men to do temperate actions for the sake of these benefits; but the natural consequences of justice depend on a system, and only require a slavish man to do what is necessary to maintain the system—his own just actions do not benefit him except in so far as they uphold the system. Since someone can be a partial free-rider, benefiting from the system while acting unjustly, his only reason not to act unjustly rests on the artificial consequences of just action. And so, if we initially choose justice for its *natural* consequences, we can be forced to admit that often we have no reason to act justly apart from the *artificial* consequences. Plato's argument is over-simplified; but his conclusion is justified, provided always that we have no good reason to act justly unless it benefits us.

5. *Restatement of the problem*

5.1. *Glaucon's demands.* Glaucon wants an account of justice to show that it is good in itself apart from its consequences (358b4–7, d1–2, 363a1–2, 366e3–5) and contributes to the just man's happiness (367c5–d5, 368b6–7, 358c2–6, 361c3–d3). These two demands make justice a component of happiness; for its instrumental benefits are ruled out of the argument. It must be the supreme component of happiness, so that anyone who is just is thereby happier than anyone who is not.[11]

It is important to see what question Plato asks, and what he does not ask. He assumes previous knowledge neither of justice nor of happiness; no fixed conception of either will constrain the argument.[12] When Glaucon asks for a definition of justice, he cannot suppose that he knows, or that the people he criticizes know, what justice is. And when he criticizes them for pursuing the same ends as the unjust man, he cannot reasonably suppose they know what happiness consists in. People deny that justice by itself contributes to happiness because they have false beliefs about both justice and happiness; we should not expect Plato to prove that the actions they regard as just will contribute to what they regard as happiness, or even to what he regards as happiness; perhaps their beliefs about which actions are just are quite mistaken. And if Glaucon's demand is met, Plato will show that our beliefs about justice influence our conception of happiness; for when we find that justice is good in itself, we will find that it is a component of happiness, contrary to most people's view.

Here as elsewhere Glaucon's demands show the influence of the middle dialogues.[13] Socrates would agree with him that our account of justice must show how it contributes to happiness; but the Socratic dialogues assume that happiness is a determinate end describable without reference to moral properties, and that a suitable description will decide the truth of our account of justice. Plato's procedure in *Republic* II reflects his view that justice and the good cannot be explained without reference to disputed moral properties. For since justice is a component of happiness, and since no previous definition of happiness is allowed to control the inquiry into justice, beliefs about justice and about happiness must influence each other, and neither can be adequately defined without the other. Plato must then reject any attempt to find definitions which eliminate disputed terms, which would eliminate the mutual influence he finds between beliefs about justice and beliefs about happiness. Though he does not defend the general claim here, his arguments in this book support his claims about the non-reducibility and (to that extent) separation of the moral Forms.

5.2. *Problems in Plato's question.* The rejection of Socratic conditions for definition leaves Plato with the problems we noticed earlier. A Socratic might ask what will be the point of proving that justice is a component of a final good defined so as to include justice; that proof will convince someone whose view of happiness includes reference to justice, but how will it convince anyone with views about happiness which do not value justice that he should treat justice as a component of happiness? Plato's argument seems to lose the objectivity sought by Socrates. He must appeal to common judgements about justice and about happiness to make any progress at all; though these judgements are liable to correction, they cannot be revised wholesale without allowing purely arbitrary accounts of justice and happiness.

These vague standards of proof in the *Republic* make it hard to see what Plato proves or where he goes wrong. At least he should not be attacked for failing to prove what he never promises to prove; he does not mean to show that recognized justice pays, or that justice, correctly defined, contributes to recognized happiness. But the question he chooses to ask still leaves him open to criticism.

5.3. *Teleologists' criticisms.* First of all he is open to attack from teleological theorists who sympathize with Glaucon's initial utilitarian argument. The critic will insist that there is nothing wrong with appeals to the natural consequences of morality, since they make it worth while, and it is real, not illusory, justice they recommend.[14] Plato's efforts to prove that justice is good apart from its consequences simply deprive us of any clear way of showing why someone who is not already just has reason to be just. A utilitarian critic can choose between two replies to the problem of Gyges' ring:

1. He may agree with Plato that my justice is worth while for me only if it benefits me, and accept the consequences; he will still observe rules of justice to maintain the system, and what would be unreasonable in taking advantage of Gyges' ring when the system is undamaged? Plato may react with pious horror to such infringements of recognized justice; but recognized justice may not survive his theory either.

2. Alternatively, the utilitarian may reject Plato's assumption that something is worthwhile only if it benefits me, as a mistaken egoist restriction on possible reasons for valuing justice. A utilitarian may agree that my justice benefits other people, not me, but insist that I can be concerned for other people's good for its own sake, apart from any benefit to me. Benevolent sentiment, on this utilitarian view, will support justice no less surely than the egoistic sentiment invoked by Plato, and we need not be trapped into Plato's unreasonable demands if we want to show that justice is worth while.

5.4. *Deontologists' criticisms.* A deontologist will agree with Plato in rejecting a defence of justice for its consequences. But he will also reject any demand, including Plato's, for a proof that justice benefits us at all. If we have a moral obligation to act justly, the obligation is unconditional; the action is right and obligatory quite apart from any benefit to anyone. But if we accept Plato's demands we remove the distinctively moral, unconditional character of the obligation, and reduce it to a prudential, hypothetical imperative, depending on some further good.[15] This critic will also attack Plato's ethical egoism, but he will be no more satisfied with the utilitarian alternative; if the obligatory character of morality for me depends on my happening to have benevolent sentiments, the unconditional obligation is undermined just as surely as by Plato's egoism. Plato's major fault, on this view, will not be his appeal to my interest or my own good as opposed to other people's, but his appeal to any interest at all.

These criticisms need further scrutiny; but it is already clear that Plato satisfies the defender of neither standard ethical view. His position may simply be a hopeless conflation of the errors of both views; or it may be a worth while third option. But his questions are more complicated than appears at first sight; and so, we will find, are his answers. In Book II he grasps the problem raised by justice for the two Socratic assumptions, that justice is a virtue, and that my virtue contributes to my happiness. Like Thrasymachus, Glaucon has argued that a correct account of justice requires the rejection of the first assumption; no one disputes the second. Plato tries to justify both assumptions. But, unlike Socrates, he does not demand a proof that justice contributes to some determinate end; and therefore it is less clear what kind of answer will, or should, satisfy him; he wants to prove that justice is a component of an indeterminate end, not that it is instrumental to a determinate end. These un-Socratic demands make Plato's answers harder to assess than Socrates' would have been. Since Cleitophon's clear method of justification (*Clt.* 409a4–410c4) is rejected, Plato tries another method.

6. *The Division of the Soul*

6.1. *The purpose of Plato's division.* Plato's criticism of Socratic ethics begins with a basic support of the CA, the doctrine that knowledge is sufficient for virtue. Socrates accepted KSV because he rejected incontinence, and therefore had no use for talk of conflicting desires or of self-mastery. The *Gorgias*'s interest in self-mastery was hard to reconcile with earlier dialogues, and the *Phaedo* recognized conflicts of desire between the soul and the body.[16] But in *Republic* IV Plato tries to justify his talk of conflict more systematically by showing that three parts within the soul have different, and possibly conflicting, desires; if he is right, then KSV is false, and there is room for self-mastery, and for affective as well as cognitive training in virtue. The division of the soul is a necessary preliminary to the account of the virtues in Book IV.[17]

6.2. *The argument.* Plato wants to show that the soul has different 'aspects' or 'parts'. He explains his claim by showing how it might be refuted; if Socrates is right, and all desires aim at the good, then the different tendencies in the soul will not belong to different parts (438a1–6); and so Plato's claim requires the rejection of the Socratic thesis. To reject it, he describes someone who desires drink, and yet something in him refuses to drink because it is better not to drink (439c2–7). The example shows the weakness in Socrates' reduction of alleged conflicts of desire to misjudgements about the good; our desire to drink need not rest on a belief about what is best over all (e.g. that the pleasure of the drink will compensate for the future ill health), but may persist even though we decide rationally that it would be better not to drink (439c8–d3).

These are genuine conflicts between different kinds of desires, Plato now claims; they are not simply the results of doubts or conflicting beliefs about the good. Nor are they urges which just happen to be opposed; an aversion to gin might be opposed to a desire to drink, if all I have to drink is gin, but the aversion includes no attitude to the desire to drink gin, but only an attitude to gin; but in Plato's case the rational desire includes an attitude of refusal to the desire to drink. When these different kinds of desires are accepted, Plato loses the Socratic argument against incontinence, which required the reduction of conflicts to mistaken belief about the good; if not all desires are desires for the good, Socrates' reduction fails. Plato shows he realizes the force of his argument against Socrates; for he mentions the case of Leontius, as a case of incontinence where the non-rational desire persists and moves the man even when he is well aware he is doing the wrong thing (439e6–440a3).

6.3. *Plato's principle of division.* Plato's division concerns desires, and especially Socrates' claim that all desires are for the over-all good, and alter their objects with altered beliefs about over-all good. Plato recognizes desires which are, and desires which are not, rational and good-dependent in the Socratic way. But Socratic desires have two features; they are concerned with goods, and they are rationally concerned with them, so that they seek the over-all good. These two features allow Plato three kinds of desires:

1. The appetitive part (*to epithumētikon*); entirely good-independent and non-rational, uninfluenced by beliefs about goods.
2. The emotional part (*to thumoeides*); partly good-dependent, influenced by beliefs about some kinds of goods.
3. The rational part (*to logistikon*); entirely good-dependent and rational, influenced by beliefs about the over-all good.

Plato's description of the three parts must be examined; for it is not as clear and systematic as it should be, or as this division might make it look. He tends to distinguish the parts, not by explicit description, but by offering striking examples of desires belonging to the parts; and he does not show which features of these examples he means to generalize. These obscurities matter when he tries to draw moral conclusions from the division.[18]

6.4. *The appetitive part.* Plato's account of appetite must be constructed from various unsystematic remarks: (1) Appetite is opposed by something which proceeds from reasoning; and so presumably it is somehow independent of reasoning (439c9–d2). (2) It proceeds from 'affections and diseases' (439d1–2), and includes basic biological drives for food, drink, and sex (439d4–8). (3) It is contrasted with the rational part, which reasons about what is better and worse (441b7–c2), and about the good of the whole body and soul and each of its parts (442b5–9, c5–8). If (1) alone were meant to define appetite, we might suppose that it is entirely non-inferential, or that no desire resulting from reasoning is appetitive; if, say, I reason that to satisfy my desire for a smoke, I must walk to the shop to buy cigarettes, or that I must put my hand in my pocket to remove the cigarettes, then my desire to walk to the shop or reach into my pocket is rational. But if (3) is applied, these desires are not rational, because they are un-related to deliberation about the good of the whole soul. In that case (2) cites examples of appetitive desires, but does not exhaustively specify them; any good-independent desire, whether or not it is one of these primitive urges, will be an appetite. Plato does not explicitly decide between these different views of appetite; but if he is primarily concerned with Socrates' views on incontinence, it should include all good-independent desires. If a desire resulting from deliberation about appetite-satisfaction belongs to the rational part, there will be conflict within the rational part; for this appetite-directed desire may conflict with desire resulting from deliberation about over-all good.

Plato is right to think that the basic biological urges are useful paradigms for incontinent action. Socrates believed that no action is explicable unless it reflects the agent's beliefs about the good; but, con-trary to Socrates' view, we can explain without reference to the agent's reasons why he pursues food, drink, or sex, even when he sees overriding reason to avoid them. For we understand someone's desire for food and find a coherent pattern in some of his actions by referring them to this desire; it is not an isolated quirk, as a desire to chew up a newspaper might be, which either leads us to ask what good the agent thought he saw in it or seems to provide no explanation by reasons at all. Basic appetites show most clearly why Socrates was wrong to identify intelligible, explicable action with rational action. Elsewhere, however, Plato wants appetite to include all good-independent desires, not just basic urges. Leontius' appetite for corpse-gazing is not one of the familiar urges (439e6–440a3); nor is the oligarchic man's desire for money in Book VIII (and cf. 436a1–3). Plato needs to show how these desires resemble the basic urges in being both intelligible and good-independent; this question will concern us in Book VIII.

6.5. *The emotional part.* If appetite and rational desire differ in their relation to beliefs about over-all good, they leave room for a third kind of desire, depending on beliefs about some kind of good, but not about over-all good. Now the emotional part is a slightly odd candidate for this role, since in IV it seems to be restricted to anger; but perhaps this restriction, like the restriction of appetites to primitive urges, is meant to display clear examples of emotional desire, not to fully specify their scope. Anger is a good example for Plato's purpose. If *A* wants to hit *B* out of anger at him, he does not want to hit *B* only because he enjoys it, or wants to release his frustration on *B*; he believes *B* has done something bad enough to deserve retaliation. If *A* is angry, some conception of good and evil will influence his desires, while it need not influence those other desires which might explain his hitting *B*; and so anger is good-dependent. Leontius makes this clear. His anger at his desire for corpse-gazing is not just an appetitive aversion; he thinks his desire is bad and condemns himself for it (439e9–440b4). At the same time anger need not rely on a rational consideration of over-all good. Odysseus is outraged at the misbehaviour of his maids with the suitors, and wants to kill them at once, which would ruin his plan to kill the suitors; and so his rational and emotional desires conflict (441b2–c2; cf. 390d1–5). This example illustrates Aristotle's comment on the emotional part, that it listens a bit to reason, but not always carefully, like an over-hasty servant (*EN* 1149a25–9); it is aware of some injury, at once decides the injury should be avenged, and seeks revenge (1149a29–34). This is exactly Plato's view; the emotional part recognizes some considerations of good, and can reason about them, but it does not recognize all the relevant considerations.

The emotional part's concern with some goods explains why Plato finds two other kinds of motive in it:

1. In VIII–IX (550b1–8, 581a9–b4) and the *Phaedrus* (253d6–7) he ascribes love of honour to the emotional part. This aim suits the emotional part because it requires a close attachment to a certain kind of good—a man's good opinion of himself and other people's good opinion of him. A complete honour-lover who is attached to this kind of ideal will pursue it against appetite, and also against his rational judgement that some more important good requires different action.

2. In IV the emotional part is the source of moral sentiments, and its training is especially important in moral education (440a8–e6). Children are 'full of emotion' at an early age (441a7–b1), and their moral beliefs are associated with emotions producing anger at

offenders (cf. *Alc.* 110b1–6), shame at their own failures, and desire for honour in success (cf. *Phdr.* 253d6, 254e4). This aspect of emotion appears in Odysseus' moral indignation against the slave-women (440b2–c2). These emotions are not inherently virtuous , but need to be attached to real goods, which will be good and admirable goals (cf. 403c4–7). An emotion is attached to its goal by habituation; it depends on fairly constant beliefs about the goodness or badness of something; it is not wholly flexible when rational beliefs about over-all good require different kinds of choices; and so it must be attached to the right kinds of objects to reduce conflicts with rational desires.

The common feature in these activities of the emotional part is its attitude to the good. Someone with an emotional part needs some conception of a good or harm to himself or someone else, and therefore some conception of someone's good, so that he recognizes honour, say, as a part of his good. But he does not pursue this part of his good because of his beliefs about its contribution to his over-all good; he may believe honour is one part of his good among others, but pursue honour more than the others because of his close attachment to honour. Plato does not say what his different examples of the emotional part's desires have in common; as usual he leaves us to guess from the examples; but his account is defensible.[19]

6.6. *The rational part.* Plato's practice of offering examples without explanation makes his view of the rational part especially obscure. Our view of the other two parts has required some view of the rational part already. It is parallel to the other parts, a further division of desires, rather than reasoning as opposed to desires—consisting of rational desires for the over-all good; Plato does not suggest that just any deliberative reasoning associated with a desire makes the desire rational. Sometimes rational desires are displayed in cases of continence (439c5–d8). But Plato also says that the rational part deliberates about the better and the worse (441b7–c2) and about the good of the whole soul and body (442b5–9, c5–8). It is not clear what these further deliberative tasks imply, or whether they require more than the prudent ordering of goals displayed by a continent man. These questions will become important later.[20]

7. The Virtues

7.1. *Results of the division of the soul.* When Plato allows the possibility of incontinence, he removes Socrates' defence for the claim that virtue is no more than knowledge; and so he rejects the Socratic view of the virtues which emerged from arguments in earlier dialogues. Now this rejection in one way makes Plato's task easier; he is free to accept those non-cognitive aspects of the virtues considered in the Socratic dialogues, but eventually eliminated because of KSV—the relation of temperance to self-mastery and of courage to endurance. The divided soul suggests a general pattern for explaining the virtues. If conflict between the parts is one reason for failure to act virtuously, virtue will require the removal of the conflict; and if the rational part's control is necessary for virtue, virtue will require the removal of the conflict to result in rational control. The conceptions of the virtues as a harmony between different parts of the soul controlled by the rational part was first suggested in the *Gorgias* (506e1–507a3); but it relied on no satisfactory account of the parts, and on no clear view of the role of knowledge in virtue. *Republic* IV tries to remove these defects in the *Gorgias*, and to exploit the division of the soul systematically.[21]

7.2. *Plato's procedure.* Book IV itself does not argue satisfactorily for its accounts of the virtues. But this failure is not to be explained simply by Plato's dogmatic and un-Socratic character. The combination of positive claims and slight argument can be explained by theoretical differences:

1. Plato can reasonably dispense with detailed argument if he thinks Socrates has already presented it. We noticed that some of Socrates' arguments relied on elenchos-principles, those which could be defended as presuppositions of his method of ethical inquiry, while others relied on craft-principles, resting on the CA. Now the CA depended on KSV, which required the rejection of incontinence. When Plato allows incontinence, he has reason to reject these Socratic arguments which rely on the CA and KSV. Above all, he can admit the non-cognitive aspects of the virtues eliminated by Socrates. The *Laches* and *Charmides* excluded endurance and self-control, and eventually treated each of the virtues as knowledge alone, because of KSV. If Plato rejects this move, the normal course of elenctic argument will yield an account of the virtues mentioning both cognitive and non-cognitive components. This is the kind of account reached in *Republic* IV; some of the work has already been done in the Socratic dialogues, and if Plato appeals to elenchos-principles rather than craft-principles, he can claim support from those dialogues.

2. Socrates assumed that an account of a virtue should eliminate moral terms—and thereby made his search for a definition harder.

Plato rejects the assumption, and is free to endorse the accounts in Book IV, though they retain moral terms.

3. Socrates required an acceptable account of a virtue to include an account of the final good—otherwise it would not eliminate all moral terms. Plato, however, recognizes the value of hypotheses, accounts which do not include an account of the final good, but still survive the elenchos. This is a further concession besides the acceptance of moral terms in definitions, and Plato exploits it in IV. The accounts offered are hypotheses, not complete definitions; and to Socrates they would be as unacceptable as an account of courage as 'knowledge of the good', without an account of the good.[22]

On all these points Plato shows he is influenced by the doctrines of the middle dialogues; his apparent facility in finding definitions is not the result of dogmatism; he uses Socrates' arguments, interpreted to suit his own views about definition. Book IV, like Book II, does not say that virtue is a craft, and avoids arguments from the CA. Plato has the reasons found earlier in Book II for rejecting the CA, and a further reason, since the acceptance of incontinence undermines a central part of the CA. Once again it is reasonable to suppose that Plato's silence, compared with the prominence of the CA in Socratic discussions of the very same virtues, is no coincidence.

7.3. *A problem about courage.* Laches suggests that courage is wise endurance; but his reference to endurance is dropped when Nicias proposes a Socratic account of courage as knowledge of what should be feared and faced with confidence (*La.* 194c7–d2, e11–195a1). But the elimination of endurance raises questions about the previous argument. Laches was first persuaded to extend the scope of courage beyond danger in battle because Socrates pointed to other examples of men sticking to their resolve despite inducements to break it (*La.* 191c7–e7); they display what he calls 'endurance of the soul'. Later he considers the non-experts who seem to be braver than experts; the brave man who dives to save a drowning man knows more about what is good than the expert diver who does not bother to dive. But now suppose A and B are equally expert on the good, and satisfy Nicias' definition, but A is an expert diver and B is not, and each of them dives to save C. Laches suggested, and Socrates did not refute him, that B would be a braver man than A.[23] But Socrates' theory cannot explain this belief; if knowledge of the good by itself decides that a man is brave, A and B should be equally brave whatever else they know or do not know.

Laches' judgement rests on his view of courage as endurance. If *A* is an expert diver and has no cause for fear when he dives to save *C*, he shows some evidence of being a virtuous man. But if *B* has good reason to be afraid because he is no expert and still dives to save *C*, he displays the courage which *A* does not need; for he endures in his desire to save *C*, even with powerful inducements against diving. Endurance is necessary for *B* because other desires are liable to conflict with his desire to do what he rationally judges best, whereas *A* faces no conflict and therefore needs no endurance. *B* need not be suffering a conflict of desires every time he acts bravely; but he must be liable to conflicts; his efforts and training prevent their occurrence when he has good reason to be afraid. If people were not liable to this kind of conflict, and did not need to remove or overcome it, endurance and courage would be unnecessary; this is the truth in the charge that when Socrates accepted KSV he made the virtues pointless (*MM* 1183b8–18). Aristotle agrees with Laches against Socrates on the superior bravery of the non-expert who has no expertise to give him confidence, and must rely on his endurance in the desire to do what he thinks best (*EN* 1115a35–b4).

7.4. *Plato's account*. Laches' belief was neither refuted nor accepted by Socrates in the *Laches*; but in the *Republic* Plato makes room for it in the account of courage. A brave man retains his belief that this is a brave action, and acts on his belief despite pleasures, pains, fears, and appetites (429c7–d2, 429e7–430b5). These conflicting desires can cause someone to lose his belief that an action is good (413a4–c4), or cause him, like Leontius, to do what he knows to be bad (439e6–440a3), or to fail to do what he knows to be best. Odysseus endured against this temptation (390d1–5). Since a man's rational and non-rational desires may conflict, his rational part needs to be enduring; and it will endure best with the support of the emotional part, when it is attached to bravery as a source of pride and honour, so that a man feels shame and anger at himself when he fails to be brave (442b11–c3). The emotional part is a lover of honour and a follower of right belief (*Phdr.* 253d7). If its sentiments are attached to brave action, a man will have a strong desire to act bravely; if they were attached to the wrong values, he would always suffer a severe struggle. No doubt a brave man will still have some desire to avoid danger; but if his emotional part is rightly trained, it will not cause severe conflicts.

This account stretches the ordinary concept of courage; like

Socrates' original suggestion to Laches, it allows courage to anyone who sticks to his virtuous resolve against contrary inducements, beyond the boundaries drawn by common sense or by Aristotle's favoured cases (*EN* 1115a32–5). Plato makes no concessions to the common-sense concept. But he does limit brave actions to situations where some kind of endurance can be shown—so that, in our previous example, *A* would not act bravely in rescuing *C*, though *B* would. Plato need not follow Socrates in collapsing courage into the rest of virtue, since he does not accept Nicias' Socratic definition which allowed the collapse.

7.5. *Temperance*. The *Charmides* is harder than the *Laches* to connect with *Republic* IV; it says less about the recognized connections between virtue and non-cognitive states, partly because the recognized virtue of temperance includes not only 'self-mastery', but also some vaguer notion of 'good sense' or prudence, so that in the *Charmides* this view eclipses all the others. Socrates concentrates on self-knowledge, one important component of temperance, but does not justify his assumption that it is the sole component. The initial example in the *Charmides* suggests that temperance is connected with the control of powerful and possibly harmful desires (155d3–e3); but in the *Protagoras* Socrates considers the notion of self-mastery and finds it incoherent. In the *Gorgias* he is much more sympathetic to it, and treats temperance as an order in the soul (*G.* 506e1–507a3).[24] If this suggestion is pressed, it makes Charmides' initial suggestions about temperance more plausible; he suggested that acting in an orderly (*kosmiōs*) and calm way is temperance (*Ch.* 159b2–3), and the *Gorgias* thinks an orderly (*kosmia*, 507a1) soul is temperate. He suggested that temperance is shame (or modesty; *aidōs*, *Ch.* 160e3–5); and a well-ordered soul would reasonably feel ashamed at the prospect of intemperate action. But these suggestions do not appeal to Socrates in the *Charmides* or *Protagoras*, because he recognizes no divided soul that would require any psychic order involving non-cognitive states for temperance.

In the *Republic*, however, Plato appeals to his division of the soul to justify his account of temperance as self-mastery, recognizing that talk of self-mastery will seem ridiculous to a Socratic (430e6–431b2). If the division is allowed, then some appetites may conflict with rational desires, and a temperate man who does not suffer constant internal struggle must have some psychic order producing calm and quiet in the soul. Whereas a brave man needs to continue his rationally desirable projects despite possible interference, a temperate man needs to inhibit his rationally undesirable projects however tempting they might be. But not every action will be done temperately. If *A* knows it is better not to drink turpentine, which he knows is in the bottle, has no desire to drink it, and does not drink it, he displays correct belief about the good, but no temperance; but if *B* thinks the stuff is gin, which he likes, and leaves it alone because he knows it is better not to drink it, he displays temperance. *B* need not suffer any struggle this time; but if he never had to train himself to avoid temptations of appetite, he would not be temperate, but beyond temperance, like Aristotle's gods (*EN* 1145a25–7).

7.6. *Conditions for temperance.* Beyond its association with self-mastery, Plato's account of temperance is less clear, especially when he suggests three non-equivalent conditions for being temperate:

1. In a temperate man the rational part of the soul dominates the other two parts so that they follow its desires (430e6–9).
2. The other two parts accept the rule of the rational part (431d9–e2).
3. All three parts are in friendship and concord (442c10–d1).

A merely continent man would satisfy (1) if he continually struggled against his appetites, but always overcame them. To satisfy (2), his appetites might be weak and submissive; but they might not display the friendship to the rational part required by (3). Aristotle's distinction between continence and temperance separates (1) and (2) from (3) (*EN* 1102b25–8, 1151b32–1152a6). Plato fairly clearly demands (3) for temperance, though he leaves no separate place for (1) and (2).

But how is (3) to be satisfied? If Plato's talk of friendship and concord is to be taken seriously, the appetitive part must somehow be induced to believe the rational part treats it well. We may think Plato's anthropomorphism goes too far, and that nothing can be made of these personal attitudes ascribed to a part of the soul. But Plato disagrees; for he suggests that the rational part will prescribe what is best for the whole soul and for each part (442e7), and this will no doubt induce the appetitive part to be friendly. Plato's position does not emerge at all clearly until Books VIII–IX.[25]

8. *Reason and Virtue*

8.1. *Wisdom.* The rational part's knowledge of the good seems to be closer to a Socratic virtue than Plato's courage and temperance have been; it is not one of the specialized crafts (428b10–d3), but is concerned for the good of the whole soul. But Plato does not say it is any kind of craft, and never appeals to the CA. When he says it seeks the good of the whole soul and of each part (442c5–8), Socrates could not have agreed, since he did not recognize a divided soul. It is not clear what this extra demand means for wisdom, until it is clearer what the interests of the rational part are; but at least Plato means that a wise man will recognize that his final good must satisfy him, not only as a rational planner, but also as a possessor of emotional and appetitive goals. This condition is not explained or illustrated in IV; but it becomes important in VIII–IX.

Plato agrees with Socrates in thinking wisdom necessary for any virtue, though he thinks the other virtues require more than wisdom. In his account of an individual virtuous man it is clear that the rational part must have knowledge (441e4–6, 442c5–8); a man is brave when his emotional part preserves the orders of the rational part with its knowledge (442b3–c5), and temperate because the other two parts agree with the wisdom in the rational part (442c10–d1). Though Plato does not renounce Socrates' demand for knowledge in a virtuous man, he does not defend it adequately. In the *Meno* and *Phaedo* he rejected the Socratic defence of KNV, and replaced it with another in the criticism of slavish virtue. But in *Republic* IV he neither defends KNV nor even explains what kind of wisdom the rational part has; his remarks leave several unanswered questions for later books of the *Republic*.[26]

8.2. *Moral education.* The account of courage and temperance suggests that purely cognitive training will not produce these virtues; Plato agrees with Protagoras that virtue requires 'nature and good training', and not simply knowledge (*Pr.* 351b1–2; *R.* 430a4–5). Socrates recognized no value in non-cognitive training; but in the *Republic* elementary education follows the traditional affective and emotional training accepted by Protagoras (376e2–4). Plato never appeals to the CA, any more than in IV, and never suggests that moral training should be like learning a craft. In Book I he asked why justice would not be liable to misuse if it were a craft (333e3–334b6). Socrates could answer this paradox with KSV; if someone knows that justice contributes to his good, then, since he always pursues what contributes to his good, he will pursue justice. On this view justice could be learned like any ordinary craft (cf. *G.* 460b1–c3).[27] Plato must reject this solution if he rejects KSV; and he does reject it, offering instead an answer consistent with the affective training prescribed in II–III. A just man must learn justice and be habituated to practice it in his youth, but learn about injustice only late in life (409b4–c1, d7–e2). His learning justice requires more than learning *about* justice, acquiring information about it; in the rest of II–III Plato insists on training to make someone enjoy and admire justice and to find injustice painful and shameful.

8.3. *Education and reason.* We might expect Plato to reject Socrates' emphasis on cognitive training, and to identify virtue with the harmonious condition of a soul trained by affective 'musical' training to choose the virtuous actions it admires and enjoys. But Plato finds this training inadequate; it only trains someone to take pleasure, suffer pain, feel shame, anger, and pride in the right objects before he acquires reason. He has true belief, and when reason prescribes actions he will welcome it as something akin to him (401e1–402a4), following it without conflicting desires; but until then he lacks wisdom, and therefore lacks all the virtues. He is still dominated by appetite and emotions, not by the rational part's deliberation about the good of the whole soul. If any deliberation about desire-satisfaction implied control by reason, the musically educated man would be controlled by reason, since he decides calmly and deliberately and is not diverted by conflicting desires. But Plato should not identify this harmony with the harmony resulting from rational deliberation about the good of the whole soul.[28]

8.4. *Education and moral motives.* Plato's emphasis on affective training leads him to qualify his charge in the *Phaedo* that all non-philosophers, including well-trained citizens, have only slavish virtue. A slavish man chooses virtue only because it produces the kinds of honours and pleasures he already seeks; but a musically educated man has learned to find virtue a source of pleasure and honour in itself; he enjoys and esteems virtuous action for itself and not for its previously desired consequences. His attitude to virtue, produced by his education, distinguishes him from the slavish man; and Plato suggests that musical education produces the love of what is fair and admirable (*kalon*, 403c4–7), apparently the kind of love expected of the Platonic lover in the *Symposium*, which would free him from slavish virtue (cf. 430b6–8).

But it does not follow that the musically educated man chooses virtue, as Glaucon demanded, for its own sake and not for its consequences. He still regards virtue as a source of pleasure or honour, and that is why he chooses it; he would not choose it without these consequences, and so he does not choose it for its own sake. He does not regard it as a source of pleasure and honour because of some further beliefs about what virtue is and why it is good and admirable, and so he does not meet Glaucon's condition, or the condition imposed on genuine non-slavish virtue. The musically educated man's 'love of the beautiful' is not the kind of love demanded of the virtuous man, though Plato does not explain the difference as he should.

8.5. *The demand for knowledge.* A careful reading of *Republic* III–IV shows that despite obscurities and possible confusions, Plato does not abandon KNV; he still accepts Socrates' criticism of Protagorean moral education, that it does not teach someone a rational account or justification of his beliefs. He avoids the Socratic defence of knowledge for its results, refuted in the *Meno*; the true and stable belief resulting from moral education (430a1–b5) may be just as useful as knowledge in action. But Book II has already implied that the really virtuous man will choose justice as a good in itself; and Plato's acceptance of KNV in Book IV is justified by the *Phaedo*'s claim that choice of virtue for the right reasons, and real virtue, requires wisdom (*Phd.* 69b1–3). Plato does not face or answer the question about KNV in Book IV, but his claims in the middle dialogues and in Book II explain his attitude.

If virtue requires knowledge, then the rational part which controls the virtuous man must have knowledge, not just right belief; and Plato needs to describe further the rational part which includes both moral knowledge and prudential deliberation. For Socrates the task would be easy; the knowledge would be a craft, producing some already desired product, and it would easily produce rational desires to do what it prescribed. Plato cannot explain the character or motive power of moral knowledge the same way; he denies that moral knowledge is a craft prescribing instrumental means to a previously desired goal. He has to show, then, how the rational part can acquire and justify its knowledge; information about some productive craft will not be enough for him. Socratic knowledge did not depend on non-rational training since it showed how a virtue would contribute to ends everyone accepts. Plato cannot so easily claim this; he suggests that previous affective training is at least necessary for someone to have enough psychological balance to act on his moral knowledge. It is not clear whether non-cognitive training is also a logical pre-condition for moral knowledge, to determine the ends for which moral knowledge finds means. Socrates believed that everyone has the same non-rational desires for ends. When Plato denies that, he must either admit that there is no rational decision between different ultimate ends, that moral knowledge is incompetent to deal with them, or show how a man can have reason to pursue one end rather than another. If Plato held the first view, that there is no rational decision about ends, he could not claim as he does (401e–402a) that a virtuous man's reason and feeling will reach the same view about the same questions—for if reason is concerned only with means, it will deal with different questions. He seems to believe that moral knowledge prescribes ends; but he does not show how someone could justifiably claim knowledge about ends.

9. *The definition of justice*

9.1. *The task.* The *Republic*'s account of justice has no Socratic precedent as helpful as the Socratic discussions of the other virtues. Socrates insisted that justice benefits the soul, without explaining how. The *Gorgias* tried to defend the Socratic claim, relying on an account of justice as psychic harmony; but it did not explain the relation between psychic harmony and KSV, or the connection between it and commonly recognized just actions. Efforts to fill the gap by appeal to the CA have collapsed in *Republic* I. In Book IV Plato tries to repair the *Gorgias*'s faults, for justice as for the other virtues. His task is hardest for justice, and his success is by no means complete. Unlike the *Gorgias*, the *Republic* has definitely rejected KSV and described the parts of the soul, so that it is easier to see what psychic harmony involves, and why it is worth while; but it still remains to be seen what this has to do with Thrasymachus' question, why a rational man should care about other people's interests.

9.2. *The argument.* The definition of justice is defended by the analogy of soul and state.[29] Plato argues that justice in the state is the condition in which its rational, emotional, and appetitive parts all do their own work; he infers that justice in a soul will be its analogous condition. The political analogy has two functions:

1. It is meant to identify a virtue in the soul corresponding to justice in the state. We might initially doubt whether justice is a virtue; but when we see that the order of the three parts of the state in which each does its own work benefits the state and is readily called justice,

we can infer that there is an analogous virtue of the soul, since soul and state are composed of the same psychic elements, and will benefit from the same order.

2. It is meant to show that this condition of the soul deserves to be called justice, since the analogous condition of the state is called justice too.

9.3. *Psychic justice.* These two functions of the political analogy are meant to solve two separate problems about justice:

1. Plato needs to find a psychic virtue corresponding to the state's justice, and can call this 'psychic justice' (p-justice) without begging any questions, as long as he does not assume that this is the virtue we commonly refer to in speaking of justice.
2. He also wants to show that p-justice is justice, that it is the virtue we normally refer to; that is why his argument is meant to answer Thrasymachus.

The political analogy is some use for the first problem, in suggesting that there may be an unnoticed virtue of the soul corresponding to justice in the state. When we have found a virtue for each of the three parts of the soul, we may think we have found all its virtues. In one way, Plato agrees; but still he thinks there is room for p-justice. While the political analogy may be helpful for discovering the extra virtue, it is not logically adequate to prove its existence. Unless we can show for reasons independent of the analogy that p-justice is really a virtue, the analogy must be rejected for misleading us; and if we can find the independent reasons for believing p-justice is a virtue, we do not need the political analogy to prove it. Whether or not Plato clearly sees the powers and limits of the analogy, he suggests the independent reasons he needs.

The analogy is much less useful for Plato's second problem. He cannot fairly assume that justice refers to just the same condition of souls and states. Here indeed we might find the crucial difference between justice and the other virtues. Temperance and courage are conditions aiming at the happiness of the whole soul; their analogues can easily be found in the state. But an individual's justice is other-regarding; we might say it is the condition which causes a man to produce a just order in which everyone does his own, and that a just state realizes that order. An individual may also be p-just, but it does not follow that his p-justice is justice or causes him to produce a just order. Plato's argument for the definition of p-justice does not try to show that p-justice is justice; he assumes over-confidently that 'justice' must refer to exactly the same condition of state and soul. Though this assumption is unjustified, he might be able to find the connection he needs between p-justice and justice; we must consider later how he could find it, and whether he finds it. His success or failure in finding the connection is irrelevant to his claim that p-justice is a virtue; and this claim should be considered first.[30]

9.4. *Psychic justice and other virtues*. P-justice may look a superfluous virtue. A p-just soul has parts doing their own work; but surely if someone is temperate, brave, and wise, all the parts have been covered. In a virtuous soul they will all do their own work, because they will all be in a virtuous condition; why then do they need some further virtue to make them do their own work? To see why Plato thinks p-justice necessary, two aspects of each of the other virtues should be distinguished. Each includes (a) a certain condition of the parts of the soul; (b) the contribution of this condition to the soul's good.

1. Courage requires endurance of the soul, with the emotional part's help. But someone might have an enduring soul with a bad rational part, and be resolute in fulfilling his bad decisions. Or he might have a bad appetitive part left unrestrained—he might be enduring in battle, and still see nothing wrong with indulging his appetites. If his endurance is to be complete courage, it must be used correctly to avoid these defects.

2. Temperance requires agreement of the parts. But they might agree in the rational part's bad policies. Or if the rational part is not vicious, but sluggish, they may agree to be idle, and lack the brave man's resolution.

3. Wisdom requires knowledge in the rational part; but if this is not used correctly, and produces no rational desires, it will not benefit a man.

If these psychic tendencies are to be real virtues, they must be used correctly, qualified by knowledge of the good and the appropriate desires; and then each virtue will need the others to avoid the defects allowed by each single psychic state. When a soul has each psychic state qualified so as to aim at the over-all good, each part does its proper work, and the soul is just. Psychic justice is a further condition apart from the psychic tendencies underlying the other three virtues; but it is not a further condition besides the three virtues themselves; when these psychic conditions have been modified by justice, they are the whole of virtue.

9.5. *Plato and the unity of the virtues.* To decide Plato's attitude to UV, we must distinguish the same two aspects of each virtue. Someone with the complete virtue of courage must use his endurance rightly; right use requires the other virtues; and so courage requires the other virtues. Similar arguments apply to temperance and wisdom. Justice clearly demands the other virtues; for they specify 'doing its own work' for each part (441d12–442b3). Plato, then, accepts the reciprocity of the virtues. But he does not accept the stronger Socratic unity-thesis; the virtue-names are not all names for just the same cognitive condition. Nor are they merely names (as the *Gorgias* might have suggested) for a single condition of psychic harmony.[31] In a fully virtuous man each of the four virtue-names refers to exactly the same condition of him, but indicates a different part of its causal origin. Temperance is complete virtue derived from agreement of the parts; courage is complete virtue derived from endurance; wisdom is complete virtue derived from moral knowledge; justice is complete virtue derived from the correct balance of endurance, agreement, and knowledge. Different affections and conditions of the three parts of the soul are required for the virtues (435b4–7), and the virtue-names mark these differences, though the complete training of the affections and conditions includes complete virtue.

Plato does not follow Socrates, because he does not accept KSV. A wise man will also have the other virtues; but he does not acquire wisdom just by acquiring knowledge, as Socrates thought, but must also acquire the desire to use his knowledge in the p-just way—only then will he have a virtue. Plato's views on the relation of the virtues is extremely close to Aristotle's; complete virtue, expressed in Plato's p-justice or Aristotle's wisdom, includes all the virtues (*EN* 1144b14–21, b32–1145a2), but different emotional and affective states must be trained, to produce the different virtues in which they are most prominent. This is what Plato means by his claim that justice ensures the growth and preservation of the other virtues (433b7–c1); none of the psychic states produced in moral education will become or remain a real virtue unless it is controlled by justice.

When Plato makes the virtues consist in psychic justice, he avoids the mistake of treating them simply as aspects of self-control or continence, though he does not clearly dissociate himself from this mistaken view. For there could be continence in which the rational part controlled the other two without the results Plato counts virtuous; the control might not amount to harmony and what Plato calls 'friendship', or it might be used wrongly.[32] If the parts must each do their own work and stay in the *right* order, a man must achieve the *right* kind of self-control, which cannot be simply the supremacy of the rational part over the others. Plato refuses to explain the virtues in undisputed, non-moral terms; they are not merely order in the soul, but the *good* order which achieves the person's happiness. By insisting on justice in the soul, Plato avoids over-simplification; but he also raises the legitimate demand for a further account of this good order.

9.6. *Justice and moral education.* Endurance and self-control, the psychic conditions required for courage and temperance, could be acquired by musical education. Plato has not said how wisdom is acquired. Justice is the hardest case of all. A man does not develop control by his rational part, or a desire for each part to do its own work, simply from musical education; and no Socratic craft looks adequate to produce the right knowledge and the right motives for a just soul. Plato rightly sees that affective training and technical knowledge alone will not produce the psychic order which is necessary for p-justice and complete virtue; but he has not explained what else is needed.

10. *Problems in Plato's definition*

10.1. *Psychic justice and common justice.* So far we have discussed p-justice, the psychic virtue corresponding to justice in the state. But how should we decide if p-justice is really the justice we refer to when we talk of justice? We should not insist that p-justice should cover all and only those actions and omissions which compose the common conception of justice ('c-justice'). Glaucon did not insist on this in II; indeed, he stressed that the nature of justice itself was still unknown, and that most people, thinking it consisted in non-aggression, believed it could be beneficial only for its consequences. Plato need not deny that justice as they conceive it is worth while only for its consequences; but real justice is worth while for itself.

Plato's account of justice, like any other Socratic definition, should not be expected to preserve all ordinary beliefs about justice, since it is not an analysis of the common concept, but an attempt to explain and, as far as possible, justify ordinary beliefs, by identifying the virtue they refer to; this justification may well require rejection of some of the original beliefs. Suppose someone asks whether measles is harmful, and explains 'measles' by 'whatever produces these red spots'. Investigation might lead us to classify measles by the virus (say) which causes certain harmful internal disturbances, and which also produces red spots; and at the same time, other conditions may cause red spots but no harmful disturbance. The answer to the original question will be that measles is harmful; but we will have changed our belief about the extension of 'measles'.[33] Plato might claim a similar licence to revise ordinary beliefs about justice. The example makes it clear why people were referring to measles; the virus-related condition was present in most of the cases they originally believed to be cases of measles. But what similar assurance can Plato offer about justice?

10.2. Plato's defence. Plato appeals to various points where p-justice is recognizably the virtue referred to in ordinary beliefs about justice.

1. He has defended the common belief that justice is 'doing our own work' or some form of it (433a1–b4); the form endorsed by Plato tries to make this condition clearer. Doing one's own work in a state is only an image of really doing one's own work (443c4–7); if it is simply the work the laws or the rulers prescribe, Thrasymachus' objection, that it is in the ruler's interest, not the agent's, is unrefuted. We might say that it would be unjust for me to do, or to demand of me, what is not 'my own work', meaning 'the work appropriate for me'; and Plato explains 'appropriate' by reference to the divided soul. What is appropriate for me is in my interest; and my interest requires p-justice in the soul; and so Thrasymachus is wrong.[34] Really doing our own work is concerned with good order in the soul, because that good order is most appropriate for us (443c9–e2). Plato has incorporated the common belief into his theory with an interpretation meant to support and clarify it.

2. Justice is an unspecialized virtue; as Aristotle says, in one sense justice includes all the demands on a virtuous man, and covers the whole of virtue (*EN* 1129b25–31).[35] Plato's p-justice explains this belief; for a p-just man has the other three virtues too, and his p-justice ensures their growth and preservation.

3. Plato mentions 'commonplace and vulgar tests' to show how the just man will refrain from some c-unjust actions (442d10–443b2); he will be innocent of the more flagrant acts of theft, murder, lying, adultery, promise-breaking, and so on. His p-justice will save him from crimes committed to gratify appetites, or such emotions as a desire for revenge, and the other unruly desires which would incite a p-unjust man to crime.

4. Plato's theory shows how justice fits with the other virtues and contributes to happiness. By itself this argument would have begged

the question against Thrasymachus, who rejected the belief that (a) justice is a virtue, because he accepted (b) virtue contributes to happiness, and (c) justice does not contribute to happiness; he argued that no correct account of justice could include both (a) and (b). Since both (a) and (b) are common beliefs about justice, Plato can claim that his account is better if it preserves them—as long as it has been shown on other grounds to explain common beliefs about justice and just action.

10.3. *Psychic justice and just actions.* For some clearer test of the co-reference of 'p-justice' and 'justice', we need to know what actions can be expected of a p-just man. Plato's answer is strange. He identifies justice with psychic health; like the other virtues in *Republic* IV it is a state of a person not defined in behavioural terms. Just actions are taken to be parallel to healthy, health-preserving actions; they produce a condition of justice in the soul (443e4–444a2, 444c10–d11), and all admirable actions produce psychic virtue (444d13–e5). Now Plato might argue that some just actions produce p-justice because we become just by doing just actions (cf. *EN* 1103a31–b25). But his claim that promotion of psychic health is necessary to make an action just (443e4–6) seems to misuse the analogy with health; no doubt a healthy medicine is productive of health, but healthy appetites and complexions are not productive, but indicative, of health (cf. Ar. *Met.* 1003a34–6). It seems much more promising to claim that the just man's just action expresses his p-justice than to insist that it must always produce or maintain it.

10.4. *The just man's motives.* Whose psychic health is considered here? Plato does not say that the just man's efforts to produce p-justice will be confined to his own soul (but cf. 589d5–590a2); but he has no reason to promote anyone else's. He will seek moral self-education and exercise, to make sure that he becomes and remains p-just. It does not follow that the desire for self-improvement will be his only motive for being just; it may be the criterion (good or bad) for just action, but he may have other reasons for doing the actions. Plato does not exclude these other reasons; but he does not say what they might be. The p-just man has reason to aim at the preservation of his own p-justice, but apparently no reason to aim at anything more.

Plato rejects the Socratic view that justice is only instrumentally valuable. Just actions were difficult for Socrates; when he could not show that they directly benefit the agent, he claimed that they made his soul just; but then he had to claim that justice in the soul is instrumentally beneficial, like other virtues, and could not readily justify his claims.[36] Plato insists that justice is a condition of soul valuable for itself; but then he seems to agree with Socrates that just actions are worth while only because they produce this condition of soul. He corrects Socrates' underestimation of states of character, and insists that justice is valuable for itself; but he still seems to believe that just action is valuable only for its contribution to p-justice—or at least he offers no better defence of just action.

10.5. *Justice and other people's interests.* One central belief about justice is that it promotes other people's interests; this is what leads people, including Thrasymachus, to think it is a good to other people and a harm to the agent (*EN* 1130a3–5), but it is also what makes justice complete virtue—for a man's virtue is tested by his exercise of it towards others (1129b35–1130a1). Now will a p-just man's p-just actions benefit other people?

Plato has disarmed some of Thrasymachus' reasons for believing that virtue, which both Plato and he expect to benefit the agent, is incompatible with justice. Thrasymachus and Glaucon alike assumed that a rational man will seek power and pleasure in ways contrary to other people's interests, which require the restriction of his desires; though they did not advocate expansion of all desires for its own sake, as Callicles did, they assumed that a rational planner would find his plans clashing with other people's interests. Plato has described goods in themselves which do not necessarily produce conflict; if he has shown that we have reason to value p-justice for itself, he has shown that sometimes we have reason to restrict our own desires, when they would damage our p-justice. Thrasymachus was therefore wrong to reject c-justice because it requires restriction of our own desires; someone who values p-justice will also avoid the c-injustice which would damage his p-justice by satisfying non-rational desires. Thrasymachus cannot show so easily that a rational man's goals will exclude c-justice.

However, this defence is very limited. Plato needs to show not only that p-justice rules out some c-unjust actions, but that it definitely requires a p-just man to benefit other people, and that p-justice is such a major good in itself that no other goal would compensate for its loss. As it is, he has not shown why a p-just man's rational plan of life would not include some c-unjust actions needed to fulfil it. And if the p-just man avoids c-unjust actions only for his soul's good, his desire for moral exercise will not obviously prescribe regular c-justice in other people's interests. If Plato cannot defend a virtue which benefits other people, he has not defended the virtue of justice challenged by Thrasymachus and Glaucon. But so far he has offered no good reason for a p-just man to benefit others; either we must agree that no sound moral theory can offer a better reason, or we must find Plato's theory altogether inadequate to explain a primary aspect of virtue.

It is quite fair to insist that Plato answers none of these objections in IV, and does not show why his theory is not exposed to them. But to show that it *is* exposed to them, we would need to know exactly what p-justice involves; and we cannot expand Plato's talk of 'control by the rational part' until we know what the rational part is like, which Plato does not explain in IV. All he has said about the rational part's concern for the good of the whole soul is too vague to rule out the compatibility of unjust actions with p-justice; but he has not committed himself to a view of the rational part which shows he has no defence against unjust action. Though these objections are fair and serious, they show what Plato has failed to say, not what he has wrongly said.

11. *The benefits of justice*

11.1. *Justice and health.* To answer Glaucon, Plato's account must show that justice is the greatest good in itself for a man. He compares justice with health. Health is the good order of elements in the body, so that the right ones rule and are ruled (444d3–6), and none of them upsets the proper function of the body by being too dominant. Justice is the corresponding order in the soul (444c2–d11). Plato has already assumed that justice is good for the just man, by maintaining that it is a virtue; but this analogy with health, and the appeal to a natural hierarchy in the soul (444d8–11) raises questions. Roughly, we can tell that a particular condition is physically healthy because it is necessary for the proper functioning of a normal human being, animal, or plant, and we agree on what that normal functioning is—since that is an acknowledged good, so is health. To identify mental health is notoriously more difficult, the harder it is to find an agreed conception of healthy functioning; some minimal kinds of prudence or rationality might be thought necessary for any sustained complex activity at all; but further judgements of what is and is not healthy require decisions about the value of different activities and ways of life. It need not be improper to speak of mental health in these cases—but it requires some previous proof that the activities of the allegedly healthy person are worth while. Has Plato passed this test?

11.2. *Plato's problem.* The answer depends on his view of the rational part's control.

(1) If a rational desire simply requires some reasoning, and someone who follows rational desire against appetite or emotion avoids incontinence or psychic chaos, Plato might well argue that a man must follow rational desire to be psychically healthy, whatever his aims in life may be, because he cannot pursue them constantly or effectively if he often follows appetite or emotion against his cooler reflective view of what he wants to do. Someone who needs this minimal prudence has reason to choose a just soul, if that is all there is to a just soul.

(2) However, Plato suggests that he means more than this—not simply that some reasoning should influence desires and action, but that reasoning about what is best over all, and about the good of the whole soul, must influence them. Someone might refuse another drink now so that he will be fit for boxing tomorrow without ever asking if it is best over all for him to be a boxer; he would display minimal prudence, but not psychic justice, on Plato's stricter conditions.

The second view of p-justice leaves it much less clearly a healthy state of the soul. Why should we not be content with minimal prudence, and doubt whether we will be better off controlled by the deliberation advocated by Plato? He needs some further argument for the importance of deliberation about the soul's over-all good; perhaps such an argument could be found. But at least he has no right to treat p-justice as such an obvious good that it can be identified with psychic health without further argument. The account of p-justice which makes it an obvious good is not Plato's normal account.

11.3. *The value of justice.* P-justice is compared with health to suggest that like physical health it is good for itself as well as for its consequences, as Glaucon wanted to be shown (357c1–3). We can roughly show that health is a good in itself by asking whether we would be fully satisfied with a life including all the consequences of health and all the other components of the final good, but without health; we would fairly insist that health must be added to the other components to make a complete final good. A sign of the status of health is the way we can enjoy good health—we do not enjoy it the way we can enjoy a symphony or a warm bath, but there is no metaphor in 'enjoy'. Does p-justice have analogous features?

Minimal prudence seems less obviously good in itself than physical health. Someone might accept it as a strategic measure, to secure the components of the final good; but if he could achieve the other components, protected against the consequences of imprudence, and lack minimal prudence, would he have reason to regret his position? Plato does not show why. The answer is still less clear for Plato's own normal conception of p-justice. If someone chooses to act on rational deliberation about his over-all good, would he be as well off if the results of the deliberation were secured without the deliberation itself? This is the question raised in the *Meno* about the value of knowledge over right belief. Perhaps deliberative control would have to be defended as a good in itself to avoid the *Meno*'s objection; but Plato has offered none of the necessary defence. He has not shown why, if we value deliberative control at all, we should not value it for 'slavish' reasons, for its good consequences.

Glaucon's demand to be shown the benefits of justice presents Plato with a dilemma. (1) He can claim that p-justice is the minimal prudence anyone will value; but then he cannot show why this is a good *in itself*; and this account of p-justice takes it too far from justice, since it will apparently allow all kinds of c-unjust plans. (2) On the other hand, any account of p-justice which makes it look like justice will apparently also make it a less obvious good. Plato has not shown that he can find a state of the soul which is both clearly justice and clearly a good in itself for the agent.

11.4. *Rational control.* Further progress requires some clearer account of the rational part of the soul, to see whether Plato can justify his claim that control by this part somehow uniquely requires justice. His vagueness about the rational part has left three questions unanswered:

1. Why is knowledge necessary for virtue?
2. Why should a p-just man benefit other people?
3. Why is justice psychic health and a good in itself?

So far, Plato fairly clearly intends the rational part to have more than a purely technical role. It does not merely consider the consequences of particular actions or find means to previously desired ends. This function of rational deliberation was enough for Socrates, since he believed all desire is rational, seeking some determinate final good, so that no deliberation about ends is needed. Plato has to reject this view both because he believes that not all desires are rational and because he believes the final good is not a determinate end; deliberation is required both to pursue a rational conception of the good against the desires of emotion and appetite, and to decide what this conception of the good should be. But if this is Plato's view, he still has further choices to make.

11.5. *Dependent rational desires.* The rational part's deliberation 'about the good of the whole soul' might be only its deliberation about the orderly and coherent satisfaction of the goals of the other two parts; deliberation would produce a rational desire for a certain combination of the ends of emotion and appetite, but no desire for any different goal. Someone who deliberated this way would not be the slave of particular emotions or appetites, and would not be guided by them unself-consciously, as a musically educated man would be. If rational desires depend entirely on the desires of other parts anyone who deliberates and chooses this way will apparently be p-just, on Plato's conditions.

This account of p-justice does not help Plato with his answer to our questions. If a man's rational desires simply aim at orderly satisfaction of non-rational desires, why would he not be as well off with right belief about his non-rational aims and the best ways to satisfy them? Nor is it obvious why a rational planner needs to plan for other people's interests as well as his own; for he surely might sometimes promote his rational plans to satisfy non-rational desires by apparent justice with secret injustice. And we have seen the problem in showing that this kind of p-justice would be a good in itself.

11.6. *Independent rational desires.* Alternatively, Plato might argue that the rational part of the soul has desires which depend on no non-rational desires, and aim at their own independent ends. He would have to explain what is rational about such desires, if they do not aim at the good of the whole soul, and how they can be developed. If Plato could defend such a conception of the rational part, he might conceivably answer our questions—though the immunity of this conception to immediate attack might simply be a sign of its obscurity. If he could show that the rational part has its own desires, they might require the kind of understanding which demands knowledge, and might include concern for other people's interests. But the third question will be harder than ever; why should control by this kind of rational desire be a good in itself or preferable to control by dependent rational desires?

Independent rational desires create a further problem of their own. A dependent rational part can seek the good of the whole soul since, unlike the appetitive and emotional parts, it has no independent desires of its own; it can be an impartial arbiter because it has no special interests to advocate. But if it has independent rational desires, why will it not demand their satisfaction? But then control by the rational part will apparently seek, not the good of the whole soul, but the fulfilment of one part's desires, which does not imply the satisfaction of all three parts. If independent rational desires solve some problems in IV, they also raise new questions.[37]

11.7. *Limitations of Book IV*. Though Plato speaks as though the argument of Books II–IV were complete in itself, it is no more than a first sketch of the possible outlines of an answer. To find a fuller answer he must choose between the options available to defend his claims about p-justice; and each option has its own drawbacks. To decide whether IV sketches a defensible view or not, we must decide which of these options support the argument in IV without raising intolerable problems.

Book IV is one expression of an aim Plato shares with Socrates. Each wants to show that morality is rational and rationally defensible; to do this, each tries to explain moral reasoning through the fairly well-understood methods of prudential reasoning. Socrates uses the CA to identify moral and prudential reasoning. In the *Republic*, and less clearly in the *Gorgias*, Plato challenges Socrates' account of morality by challenging his account of prudence; prudence requires more than knowledge, since it must eliminate conflict between incommensurable desires which do not all respond to rational prudential judgements. But we might accept this revised account of prudence, and still deny that it captures morality; Plato has not shown that a prudent man has reason to be just.

Now we should remember that Plato does not identify virtue with every condition of soul in which the rational part is supreme, but only with the *right* condition, in which each of the parts really does its own work, and which really achieves the agent's happiness; since virtue is not mere self-control, the failure of mere self-control to support justice does not refute Plato's account. But his account is still vague, and apparently unpromising; for if self-control is not what he wants, what does he want? He needs to show that if we understand real prudence—the condition of soul which advances someone's real interests, not just the mistaken conceptions of their interests which most people pursue—that will include justice. If he rejects a natural interpretation of his talk about the supremacy of reason, he owes us another interpretation, to connect p-justice and justice.

Plato faces another delicate problem here. In one way, it would have been welcome if Book IV had shown that self-control requires justice, so that someone with Thrasymachus' aims in life, who needs self-control to execute them, also needs justice. It would have been welcome because it would have removed the appearance of circularity and triviality from elenctic argument. An argument to show that justice is part of a (conventionally) virtuous man's view of happiness loses its force against someone like Thrasymachus, who rejects conventional virtue; but if Plato could show that justice is part of everyone's conception of happiness, or the indispensable means to it, he would have found an objective vindication of justice, showing it is rationally acceptable to everyone. That was what Socrates tried to do in *Republic* I. But Plato finds no proof. And if he had found one, he would have contradicted other basic principles he accepts against Socrates. If justice were proved to be a recognized good in itself, parallel to health, then the final good would apparently be to that extent a determinate end, contrary to Plato's views about the non-reducibility of moral properties; if it were proved to be an instrumental means to anyone's ends, he would be offering only slavish reasons for valuing it, contrary to Glaucon's initial demand. Plato's views about the indeterminate character of the final good and about the virtuous man's motives seem to restrict his appeals to the non-virtuous man until it is hard to see how he can convincingly defend justice to him at all. None the less Plato presents a second defence in Books VIII–IX.

12. *Knowledge and belief*

12.1. *The relevance of Books V–VII.* Books V–VII introduce the epistemology and moral psychology of the middle dialogues to deal with some of these problems arising from Book IV, and to justify some earlier assumptions. We have already seen that Books II–IV show the influence of the middle dialogues in departures from the Socratic position:

(1) Justice is to be proved good for its own sake.
(2) KNV is accepted, but not because of the consequences of knowledge—(1) rules that out.
(3) The definitions of the virtues do not eliminate moral terms, and are only hypotheses.
(4) The CA is never invoked.

The influence of the middle dialogues does not begin in V.

But the early books do not mention the doctrines which justify these anti-Socratic claims.

  (a) Separated Forms are absent, though they explain (3) and (4).
  (b) The *Symposium*'s theory of desire is absent, though it is needed for the defence of (1) and (2).

In V–VII Plato mentions some of the relevant epistemology; his account of desire is much less satisfactory; but we will find the *Symposium*'s theories relevant in a discussion of the problems in VIII–IX. It is worth while, then, to see how he introduces and explains the metaphysics and epistemology of the separated Forms, and how it affects the ethical arguments.[38]

12.2. *Education and recollection.* In IV Plato accepted KNV without explaining what moral knowledge is, or what kind of education will produce it. To fill this gap he appeals to the *Meno*'s conception of learning as recollection. The right kind of education is not a process which the pupil simply undergoes without contributing any of his own beliefs and reasoning, as though sight were being implanted in his blind eyes (518b6–c2); rather, he uses his own resources, properly guided to reach fuller understanding, like an eye with sight being turned to the light (518c4–d7). This was the *Meno*'s and *Phaedo*'s picture of recollection.[39] It will not apply to all learning; the pupil's beliefs do not contribute to his learning the names of the world's capital cities; and Plato recognizes that they do not contribute to the moral education discussed earlier in the *Republic*, which relies on habituation and practice (518d9–e2). He defends the elenctic method, relying on the interlocutor's beliefs and on what he accepts as a good reason; and he advocates this as the only way to moral knowledge.

12.3. *The sight-lovers.* Plato is challenged by opponents who see no need for recollection, because they think moral properties can be readily understood by reference to observable properties; if this is true, the elenchos is an inefficient method of moral training, to be replaced by knowledge of the relevant observable properties.[40] To defend recollection, Plato argues that the sight-lovers cannot know moral properties, because moral Forms are separated. An example of a sight-lover's account would be Meno's account of the many virtues. Plato's refutation is not meant to presuppose the Theory of Forms, but to convince the sight-lover on grounds that he will accept that his concentration on the observable properties of the many beautifuls precludes knowledge of the beautiful (476d8–e2). As in the *Meno*, an explanation is required for knowledge, and the sight-lover offers one; but Plato argues that, like those rejected in the *Phaedo*, it is inadequate.

12.4. *The argument.* If severe exegetical problems are ignored, the main points of the argument can be set out briefly.

(a) Knowledge is over what is true, ignorance over what is not true (476e6–477a10, 478a6–7, c3–4), belief over what is and is not true (478c6–e5).

The sight-lover should easily accept these descriptions of the contents of different cognitive states.

(b) The many *F*s both are and are not *F* (479a5–b10).

Plato relies on his normal refutation of accounts confined to observable properties, that they allow counter-examples. Now he must connect (a) and (b). If a sight-lover is asked to say what the just is, or what makes just things just, and replies that justice between persons in contracts is debt-paying, one of the 'many justs', his answer will not be wholly false, displaying complete ignorance of justice, since debt-paying will sometimes be just and will partly explain why an action is just. But this will not always work; a reference to debt-paying will not always identify justice, even within the sight-lover's chosen area. And so Plato takes the next steps:

(c) The views of the many about the beautiful, just, and so on, are between being (true) and not being (true) (479d3–5), neither wholly true not wholly false.

(d) These views are not knowledge, but belief (479d7–e8).

If a sight-lover had knowledge of justice, his view that justice is debt-paying would be always true; since it is not, he has only belief.[41]

12.5. *Plato's conclusion.* The refutation of the sight-lover shows that knowledge of a moral property must refer to a separated Form; a true account cannot eliminate moral terms. Plato does not appeal to the doctrines about separation we have criticized, or to any partisan metaphysics, in his refutation of the sight-lover. His conclusion, that moral knowledge requires explanations irreducible to observational terms, has important results of its own. If the sight-lover's account had worked, there would have been some hope for the CA; since it does not work, Plato should not accept the CA. He does not suggest that the philosopher knows only about instrumental means to some determinate end shared with other people; on the contrary, the many and their sophist admirers, unaware of the moral Forms, reject the philosopher's moral position (493e2–494a6)—they have never seen a real philosopher or been educated by him (498e3–499a9). This kind of conflict was never emphasized in the *Gorgias*—Plato assumed without proof that the many and the philosopher agreed about ultimate ends. He does not say here that they disagree about ultimate ends; but his remarks about the depth of disagreement would be unwarranted if they did not.[42]

The attack on the sight-lovers also affects those who have true moral beliefs from musical education. Plato attacks all musical education for leaving the soul confined to what becomes and perishes, the many beautifuls, justs, and so on, never helping it to progress towards being, to what is really beautiful and just (522e3–523b1). A virtuous man should have knowledge, so that he does not simply act on true beliefs, but acts on them for the right reason, because he chooses the right virtues for their own sake. A musically educated man regards virtue as a source of honour and pleasure in itself, but cannot explain what it is in virtue which would justify his choice of those actions; and so he does not choose virtue for its own sake, for what it is in itself. To choose it for the right reasons, someone must have reached that understanding of virtue which results only from the elenchos, since it cannot be reduced to the procedure of a craft. Plato's demand for knowledge leads him to restrictive conditions which he thinks can be satisfied only by philosophers. But they begin from his prior demand that a virtuous man should choose virtue for its own sake.

13. The Sun, Line, and Cave

13.1. *The role of the images.* The three related images of Sun, Line, and Cave develop the contrast drawn in V; they describe the conditions of belief and knowledge more fully, and divide each of them into two further conditions; they associate knowledge with the Form of the Good; they support the account of education as a turning of the soul from becoming to being. They deserve close study, then, despite their numerous exegetical problems, if we want to understand Plato's moral epistemology.

The images explore the basic contrast between the Form of *F* grasped by thought and the many *F*s grasped by sight (507a7–b10). First the Sun-image compares this contrast with seeing in the dark against seeing in the sunlight:

s1. Sight in the dark without sunlight looks at visible things, the many *F*s.

s2. Sight in sunlight looks at visible things (508c4–d2).

S1. The soul in the dark, without the Form of the Good, looks at the many *F*s, and has only belief (508d6–9).

S2. The soul in the light, aware of the Good, looks at the Forms and achieves knowledge (508d4–6, 508e1–509a5).[43]

Next the Line divides each of the two states mentioned in S1 and S2 into two, and identifies four cognitive states:

L1 (imagination) and L2 (confidence) divide S1.
L3 (thought) and L4 (intelligence) divide S2.

The Cave presents these four states allegorically; its four stages divide s1 and s2, illustrating different conditions of moral beliefs (517d4–e2) at different stages of moral education (514a1–2, 518b6–8). The three images, then, correspond as follows:

c1 + c2 = s1 illustrates S1 = L1 + L2.
c3 + c4 = s2 illustrates S2 = L3 + L4.

13.2. *Imagination.* The prisoners in the cave are 'like us' (515a5), and like most people in all cities, including the Platonic city (517d4–e2, 520c1–d1). They take shadows to be realities (515b4–c2, 516c8–d2), and cannot distinguish what seems to be *F* but really is not from what really is *F*. Similarly, most people, including sophists, accept their moral opinions unreflectively, never examining what seems to be just to see if it is really just (493a6–c8; cf. 515b4–c2). As usual, Plato's main complaint against ordinary moral beliefs and sophists' theories like Protagoras' is not that they are largely false or subversive, but that they are uncritical; that is why they need elenctic criticism.

13.3. *Confidence.* The next cognitive state is reached through elenchos. A released prisoner forced to look at the dummies and the fire cannot say what they are and is confused (515c4–e4), like anyone who begins to question what appears to the senses (524a6–10). The confusion is familiar in the Socratic elenchos; and the elenchos is meant to produce the more justifiably confident belief of c2 and L2, when someone can distinguish what seems just but is not from what is really just. Even if a Socratic inquiry reaches no definition, the interlocutor distinguishes those beliefs which survive the elenchos from those which do not, and can rely more confidently, as Socrates does, on the survivors. An elenchos forces someone to confront his beliefs about virtue with his beliefs about the good, or, in the allegory, to look at the light in the cave (515e1–4); he should be able to remove conflicts between these two sets of beliefs. This process leading to justified confidence begins with Socratic examination; it is therefore denied to anyone with only musical education, which leads a man no distance from becoming to being (522a3–b1).

Plato wants to criticize the moral beliefs of the many, for being unreasoned and unreflective, but still assumes that they will see enough of the truth to alter their beliefs in the right direction under examination. A released prisoner agrees that horse-dummies (though he does not realize that is what they are) are more real horses than horse-shadows because he has been taught that, for instance, horses are solid and enduring. Similarly, a Socratic elenchos relies on principles about virtue and the good to test other moral beliefs. As usual, the method of elenchos and recollection uses someone's own beliefs to derive previously unrecognized consequences.

13.4. *Thought*. The progress of elenctic inquiry reaches definitions which, like those offered by mathematicians, are hypotheses, assumptions defended by their consequences, not from further first principles (510b4–d3), and by the use of sensible images (510d5–511a11). The definitions of the virtues in *Republic* IV are hypotheses, not resting on a full account of the good, but assuming some beliefs about it and drawing conclusions about the virtues—that is why they are only sketches, not complete definitions (504d6–8). They can be defended, as the *Phaedo* said, by showing that their consequences are consistent with ordinary beliefs. Images are useful in this defence; to show that justice is a virtue and beneficial to the soul, Plato compares it with justice in a state and with physical health; instead of showing by a full account of the good that justice is a good, he shows that it is like two other previously admitted goods. A mathematician's use of diagrams is analogous; instead of showing that his assumed account of, say, a triangle is right by appeal to further principles, he shows that it works, by using it to prove conclusions about visible triangles. Both the mathematician and the moralist appeal to sensible images to defend their hypotheses when they lack a more systematic defence.

We have seen why Plato recognizes the importance and value of hypotheses more readily than Socrates could; and the *Republic* itself displays their importance. Though they do not provide complete knowledge, they allow someone to answer the Socratic question, and to know enough about a virtue to choose it for itself. Even a hypothetical account of justice identifies it and allows us to choose it for the essential character we correctly ascribe to it; the *Republic* takes Plato this far, even though, he insists, it does not reach complete knowledge.

13.5. *Intelligence*. Dialectic reaches L4 from L3 by examining the hypotheses, to explain them by reference to a first principle (510c6–d1, 511c8–d2, 531e4–5). The hypotheses are removed, because they lose their hypothetical character (533b6–d4) when they are justified by an unhypothetical first principle which will be the foundation for proofs of subordinate principles (533c7–d1). The method is the ordinary Socratic elenchos (538c6–539a3), practised on definitions expressed in hypotheses, not on the ordinary beliefs of imagination or confidence (534c1–2). The conditions of adequacy for a dialectical account will be the same as usual; it must explain, and, as far as possible, justify, the beliefs under examination, by reference to some general teleological principles. These were the normal conditions for success in moral inquiries.

In the *Republic* Plato extends his demand beyond ethics; intelligence should find the kind of teleological account of all reality which was his first preference in the *Phaedo*. Such an account (which we need not discuss in detail) would be analogous to the relation of the virtues to the good, because our account of each aspect of reality would be tested by showing how it contributes to some systematic theory presenting all reality as a whole, a single, coherent teleological system. The general theory will be the first principle justifying hypotheses, showing how they fit in the teleological account, and at the same time itself justified as the best synoptic account (531c6–e5, 537b8–c7) of the hypotheses. This form of justification, normal for any dialectical account, is circular, but not clearly vicious; no other form is recognized in the *Republic*.

Intelligence completes Plato's account of the growth of knowledge by the Socratic method of recollection. The Sun, Line, and Cave together describe in more detail the method first sketched in the *Meno*. They insist on a central feature of the Theory of Recollection; moral knowledge is reached by learning that uses the learner's own resources, relying on his own beliefs and reasoning (518b6–d1). Now what would someone have learnt about ethics if he could complete the programme Plato describes?[44]

14. The Good

14.1. *The role of the Form of the Good*. Plato's description of the terminus of dialectic is, as he admits, brief and impressionistic (506c2–e5). But its importance for his ethical theory justifies an attempt, unavoidably speculative, to explain his views; he means it to answer the question raised by Socrates in appeals to the final good. Plato still maintains that the Good is something greater than the virtues, and a complete account of them must relate them to it (504c8–d8); to know how other things are beneficial, we must know how they contribute to the Good (505a1–4). Like Socrates, he demands an account of virtue to show how it is beneficial (367d2–4), and demands a reference to the final good to fulfil the first demand.

However, Plato rejects other Socratic doctrines. Socrates believed that every desire and every intentional action aimed at some final good pursued by the agent. Plato assumes only that everyone pursues it and guesses that it is something (505d11–e1), not implying that everyone will pursue it in all his actions.[45] An appeal to the final good is not necessary for every desire, but in an agent's desires as a whole; and Plato assumes that the agent will prefer his aims to be ordered so that they pursue a final good; he modifies Socrates' account of desire and the final good to allow incontinence, recognized in Book IV.

Though Plato thinks a complete account of the virtues requires knowledge of the final good, he allows a sketch of them to precede knowledge of the good (504d6–8), and believes we grasp them better than we grasp the good (505e1–3, 506d2–8). Unlike Socrates, Plato values hypothetical accounts of the virtues as preconditions of a correct account of the good. Socrates thought the content of the good could be agreed without agreement on what is virtuous; to secure this agreement he appealed to hedonism in the *Protagoras*. Plato rejects this search for agreement independent of agreement about the virtues.

14.2. *Rejected candidates*. Plato denies that the final good is adequately defined as pleasure (as the *Protagoras* supposed), or as knowledge (as the *Euthydemus* and *Phaedo* suggested in different ways). Pleasure is rejected with an argument from the *Gorgias*; there are good and bad pleasures, and so the hedonist must allow that the same things are good and bad—that is, as in Book V, some are good and some are bad (505c10–11). The hedonist, then, must change the definition to 'good pleasure'—and he still owes us an account of 'good'. If he could identify good pleasures in observational terms, he could answer Plato's objection; Plato must assume, as he assumed in the middle dialogues, that such an attempt to reduce the good to un-disputed non-moral properties will fail. Similarly, the defender of knowledge is expected to agree that any knowledge which might achieve the final good would have to include knowledge of the final good; and then the reference to the final good cannot be replaced by observational terms, as Plato normally assumes.[46]

Neither of these arguments shows that the final good could not include knowledge or pleasure. Both arguments rest on the claims about non-reducibility previously asserted in Book V; these attempted definitions of the good will suffer counter-examples, just as the sight-lovers' accounts of beauty or justice would. Plato rejects an account of the final good as a determinate end, definable in agreed terms apart from someone's moral beliefs.

14.3. *Plato's reaction.* Both the rejected candidates were unitary ends, finding the final good in some single condition or activity. Plato might infer from their failure that some less obvious unitary end is needed, or he might reject any unitary end and treat the final good as a compound end. He does not explicitly decide; but he suggests the se-cond answer, when he comments obscurely that the Good is responsi-ble for the being of the things known, the Forms, though it is not itself a being, but beyond being and superior to it (509b2–10).[47] The Good is the formal and final cause of the Forms' being what they are; they are rightly defined when they are shown to contribute to the Good which is superior to them. However, the Good is not some further being besides the Forms; when we have correctly defined them, con-nected in a teleological system, we have specified the Good, which just is the system. If this conception is applied to ethics, it will make the Good an ordered compound of what we accept after examination as goods in themselves.

This account of the Good not only fits the remarks in Book VI, but also explains the claim that justice is both a good in itself, sufficient to make the just man happier than anyone else, and benefits the just man by its contribution to the final good. If justice and the other virtues are components of the final good, Plato's claims about the virtues and the Good are consistent parts of a single theory. The final good is greater than the virtues because it is realized by their systematic co-ordination; but the virtues are not merely instrumental means to the Good, as Socrates supposed, relying on TV and LG.

14.4. *Consequences of Plato's view.* Plato's account of the Good, such as it is, reflects the influence of his arguments for separation of the Forms, and especially of NR.[48] The Good cannot be explained, as Socrates would have liked, without disputed predicates, and therefore cannot provide an external standard of correctness to test accounts of virtues without appeal to moral beliefs; that is why a hypothetical account of the virtues must precede an account of the Good. Plato rejects the Socratic view of virtue and the good, dominated by the CA. If an account of the good depends on an account of virtue, virtue is no craft with an agreed product. Moral inquiry, even at its highest level in L4, can offer nothing more than dialectic, reaching and testing hypotheses, because beliefs about virtue and the good do not provide the materials for a craft. Knowledge of the good depends on a previous understanding of the virtues as goods in themselves.

15. *The Divided Soul in* Republic *VIII–IX*

15.1. *New problems.* In V–VII Plato has identified the just man with the philosopher, since only the philosopher knows what virtue is, and chooses it as a good in itself. In VIII–IX he resumes the task interrupted at the end of IV (445c1–449a5), of comparing the just man's soul with the souls of 'deviant' men with structures analogous to the structures of deviant states. Now if the discussion is really continuous with IV, the conception of the just man's soul in IV should show what is wrong with the deviant men in VIII–IX. We found, though, that this conception was neither clear nor unambiguous; and one apparently plausible reading of IV seems to raise difficulties for the claims in VIII–IX.

The later books appear to conflict with some of IV's central doctrines.

1. In IV the three parts of the soul are invoked to analyse the process of choice, as a result of agreement or disagreement between different kinds of desires, and to explain the different kinds of choice reflecting the predominant causal influence of one or another kind of desire. This analysis is not absurd or circular; a choice is the result of interaction between parts of the soul, not the result of a choice between the three parts by the agent's 'self'. If some shadowy self is required to explain a choice, then either (a) we have no explanation, since we simply 'explain' our observable choice by some unobservable one; or (b) we face a vicious regress, if the unobservable self's choice is explained by the choice of a second unobservable self between three further parts of a second soul ... and so on. Plato avoids this classic

blunder in IV; and yet he seems to commit it repeatedly in VIII when he analyses the deviant men's choices.

2. IV distinguished the parts of the soul by their different methods and procedures; the rational part is moved by deliberation about overall good, the emotional part by a non-rational conception of some good, the appetitive part by good-independent desires.[49] But in VIII–IX the emotional and appetitive parts seem to be distinguished by their objects, honour and wealth, not by their methods. It is not clear that they are the same parts of the soul as the parts with the same names in IV.

3. On one plausible view of IV, a p-just man controlled by the rational part would be guided by his rational deliberation about what is best for him, by his rational plan for his life. But all the deviant men seem to be p-just on this test; apparently Plato has no right to accuse them of p-injustice. An examination of the deviant men will show how these problems arise.

15.2. *The timocratic man.* A man becomes timocratic when his appetitive and emotional parts urge him one way, his rational part another, and he decides to deliver power within him to the emotional part; this decision by the man, as well as the struggle of the parts, is needed to make him timocratic (550a4–b7). He is liable to this change because his rational part lacks the right training—reason mixed with musical education (548b8–c2, 549b3–7). Without the philosopher's understanding of virtue and his reasons for acting virtuously, he cannot stick to his moral beliefs when his emotional part, guided by other people's views, turns against them (549c2–550a4). He decides to seek honour above all, and overcomes any previous scruples about commonly recognized sources of honour; he will turn to money-making if it brings honour (549a9–b4).

But do these objections to the timocratic man show that he lacks p-justice? He has a rational plan for his life, to gain honour, and pursues it steadfastly, even when his appetites or emotions conflict with it. Unlike the 'emotional' man described in IV, he will not give way to his desire to revenge an insult if his rational plan urges self-control; he will do what Odysseus did (cf. 441b).[50] Plato's account of p-justice apparently fails to show how the timocratic man is not just.

15.3. *The oligarchic man.* A timocratic man who sees the dangers in the pursuit of honour and the hazards of poverty resulting from disgrace (553a9–b5) decides to avoid the timocratic man's pursuits and prefers to concentrate on wealth; he sets up the appetitive part as ruler within him, and enslaves the rational and emotional parts, forcing them to concentrate on money-making (553b5–d7). He has become attracted to wealth as a source of honour, and now, when honour seems too hazardous a goal, continues to pursue wealth for its own sake. His single-minded organization is criticized on two counts.

1. He will act virtuously only when he promotes his dominant end of money-making (554c11–d3). The timocratic man could not stick to his moral scruples when they threatened his honour; but he would still respect them and feel ashamed at overriding them in other conditions. But the oligarchic man is more ruthless; his orderly and correct behaviour wins praise from the many (554a11), but he takes his chances of advantageous and unpunished injustice (554c4–9). Like the false supporters of justice in Book II, or the slavish man in the *Phaedo*, or the man with 'mortal' temperance in the *Phaedrus*, he chooses virtue only for its contribution to other ends.

2. He will subject all his appetites to his dominant ends. Someone's 'necessary' appetites must be satisfied for survival or to fulfil his overall aims (558d11–e3); 'unnecessary' appetites, such as the desire for gourmet food or expensive holidays, need not be fulfilled for either purpose. They might be removed by education (559a3–6), but the oligarchic man shows his lack of education by repressing them, not restraining them by persuasion (554c11–d3, 558d4–6). He is wrong, Plato implies, to be so obsessed by his dominant end that he completely rejects unnecessary appetites.

But do these failures imply p-injustice? The oligarchic man appears all too clearly to be controlled by his rational part; for he pursues his rational plan for making money at the expense of any emotion or appetite. Apart from insistent but repressible unnecessary desires, he need not even suffer conflict; for his emotions and appetites are directed, as far as possible, to the overall end chosen by his rational plan. Since he does not pursue the food, drink, or sex treated as goals of appetite in IV, and does not pursue good-independent desires against his conception of over-all good, why is he dominated by appetite at all?

15.4. *The democratic man.* When a young oligarchic man cannot retain control of his unnecessary appetites, they take over his soul and influence him with false and bombastic arguments, because he has no reasoned conception of worthwhile goods to resist them (559d7–561a4); if they are strong enough, his fixation on money-making cannot restrain them. But when he gets older, he receives back some of the exiled true arguments, and decides to make his life more orderly; instead of allowing unlimited scope to unnecessary desires, he insists on fair treatment for all desires (561a6–b5), deciding on a compromise between a miserly and a lawbreaking life (572c6–d3). He is not simply swept away by his desires, but himself decides on the best policy for satisfying them; he rejects the oligarchic man's dominant end, and prefers fair shares. Though he escapes Plato's objections to the oligarchic man, he is still attacked for his undiscriminating attitude to his desires; he will not agree that some pleasures result from good and admirable desires and should be valued more than pleasures resulting from inferior desires (561b7–c3). He rejects order and compulsion in his life (561d5–6) because he is unwilling to order his desires hierarchically, or to criticize various goals and prefer the better over the worse.

But is he a slave to appetite? He follows a clear and quite attractive rational plan; he does not follow his good-independent desires in particular cases. As Plato admits, he has a rational plan for a law-governed life (572c6–d3, 574d8–e2), which requires the restraint of some desires. If he likes drinking, athletics, or chess, and heavy drinking prevents his other two pursuits, he will avoid it. Especially he will avoid a subset of unnecessary desires, those law-breaking (*paranomoi*) desires which cannot be satisfied at all without damage to his rational plan. He seems to fulfil Plato's conditions for p-justice quite easily.

15.5. *The tyrannical man.* It is less clear that a man becomes tyrannical by his own decision. The lawbreaking appetites create some dominant passion (*erōs*) in him, which demands satisfaction for them (572e4–573b4). A struggle between various desires is not enough; the young man's acceptance of law-breaking desires requires the growth of a dominant passion. Though Plato does not say whether the man himself decides to follow the dominant passion, someone might easily defend such a decision; he might reject the democratic man's bad reasons for restraining desires, prefer to develop demanding desires, and seek the resources to satisfy them. The residual moral scruples abandoned by the tyrannical man are simply the result of cowardice (*G.* 492a3–b1), and the really brave man will stick to his purpose and fulfil his dominant passion despite fears or scruples or prudent worries (*G.* 491b2–4; *R.* 560d3); because of his unrestrained passion, he will be the only free man (*G.* 491e5–6; *R.* 572d8–e2).

Plato argues that the tyrannical man least of all does what he wants to, because his soul is full of confusion and reversal (572e1–3). This argument, unlike the argument in the *Gorgias*, does not rely on the Socratic paradox, or suggest that the tyrannical man needs only knowledge to set him right. But he is not simply incontinent, or liable to act against his rational plan. The rational plan itself supports Plato's description; if it aims at the satisfaction of the dominant desire at any time without thought for prudential worries, constant observance of the plan will deprive him of the material for its satisfaction.[51]

But the self-frustration involved in the tyrannical man's plan does not show it is not a rationally chosen plan, or that he is not controlled by reason, and therefore p-just. Both Callicles and Socrates mistakenly identified the tyrannical life (*G.* 491e5–492b1, 492c3–8) with complete freedom from restraint, producing psychic chaos; and Socrates supposed that the psychic order required for steady rational choice rules out a tyrannical life. But the tyrannical man's choices are not simply chaotic; they express his rational decision to prefer satisfaction of his dominant passion over all else, and he will follow this decision despite any conflicting emotions or appetites, thereby displaying his courage. Though the plan will cause him reversals and regrets, he may not regret having followed it. For he may think it worth while to have developed and satisfied his desires, even with the future costs they involve. That would be Callicles' answer; and though someone might reject the tyrannical life for its dangers and inconveniences, he might agree that with a suitably modified Gyges' ring to remove the dangers and replenish resources, it would be the ideal way of life. At least, if it is not a p-just life, Book IV's conception of p-justice does not seem to have shown why not.

16. *The purpose of the division*

16.1. *The rationality of the deviant men.* Plato's detailed description of the four deviant men allows us to see why the parts of the soul work differently here and in Book IV, without supposing that he has simply blundered. In Book IV the parts are used to analyse the decision to do this or that action. In Books VIII–IX they are not used to analyse decision at all. Books VIII–IX are addressed to a different question—'What options does a man choose between when he decides?'; and the three parts mark the different options. And they decide not primarily what to do, but what to want, what kinds of goals to pursue, a second-order choice. Plato does not say that someone's choice to be an oligarchic man, say, is an appetitive choice, caused by the overwhelming influence of the appetitive desires; for it is a rational choice, made by the rational part. Someone who acts on an appetite or emotional desire against reason is incontinent, and the deviant men are not; instead, they choose rationally in favour of the goals of a non-rational part, the kinds of ends which appeal to it. Plato's use of the divided soul in Books VIII–IX is not the same as his use in Book IV; and the two uses are equally legitimate.

16.2. *The character of the parts.* But now Plato must show that the different goals and ways of life rationally chosen by the deviant men really belong to the different parts described in Book IV. He must show that though each deviant man rationally decides on the ends he pursues, some ends are ends for him because they appeal to some non-rational desire. The timocratic man chooses honour, not because he rationally approves of it as the best over-all goal to seek, but because he is attached to it as one good he has been taught to cherish, and his rational part has no firm rational conviction about the wrongness of its immoderate pursuit. He decides rationally to adopt honour as his goal; but it is his goal because it appeals to his emotional part. The rational decision is a second-order decision to prefer one of his first-order goals above others; and the first-order goals he prefers are those chosen by the emotional part.[52] Similarly, the oligarchic man chooses wealth as his goal by a rational decision, not because of some rational conviction about the value of wealth but because he thinks it best to satisfy his appetitive part and his appetitive part pursues wealth.

The goals of the timocratic and oligarchic men satisfy the emotional and appetitive parts described in IV. The timocratic man prefers ends which appeal to his non-rational good-dependent desires, and the oligarchic man selects goods which appeal to good-independent desires. Honour and wealth, then, should not be the only possible objects for lives dominated by the emotional and appetitive parts. The honour-loving Spartan life is an example of a life satisfying the emotional part; but someone might equally satisfy it with a life devoted to charitable works or public service or some other end prescribed by a non-rational conception of the good. Plato recognizes this point more clearly for appetite. Three different types of men, oligarchic, democratic, and tyrannical, pursuing quite different ends, are all dominated by appetite; for they all pursue ends which appeal to them not on rational grounds, but because they satisfy some good-independent desires. A man might pursue wealth to satisfy his emotional part, if his pursuit depended on some conviction about its goodness and value (549l9–b4); and he might pursue honour on appetitive grounds if he simply enjoyed being honoured and did not care about its goodness. The oligarchic man attaches the emotional part to his dominant end (553d4–7), but he differs from the timocratic man who pursues wealth; whereas the timocratic man's pursuit of wealth depends on a conviction of its goodness, the oligarchic man's goes not, and would continue even without that conviction. Plato does not distinguish the parts of the soul in VIII primarily by the objects pursued, but, as in IV, by their methods.[53]

16.3. *Conditions for psychic justice.* Though each of the deviant men follows his rational plan, and is not distracted by emotion or appetite, Plato denies psychic justice to any of them. The oligarchic man subordinates his rational part to the appetitive; though he still deliberates about ways to fulfil his rational plan, and acts on the deliberation, he is not controlled by the rational part (553d1–4). Similar criticisms apply to the other deviant men, who employ the rational part in similar tasks. Plato even claims that the tyrannical man is not master of himself (579c7–8), because he is not controlled by his rational part. Though each deviant man uses the rational part for fulfilling his over-all aim, the over-all aim does not belong to the rational part.

To clarify Plato's criticism, three roles for the rational part must be distinguished:

1. The rational part prescribes means to achieve particular ends. In this sense all the deviant men follow the rational part; but we saw in Book IV that this was not all Plato expected of the rational part, which also deliberates about the good of the whole soul.
2. The rational part makes the second-order decision on the first-order ends to be pursued. All the deviant men are guided by the rational part, since they all follow this decision.
3. The rational part makes a second-order decision in favour of 'its own' first-order ends—the ends accepted on rational, not emotional or appetitive, grounds. There the deviant men are not guided by the rational part.

The deviant men are not p-just; for though their rational part decides which of their first-order ends to pursue, it is not allowed to determine what the first-order ends will be; they acquire first-order ends, not by deliberation about over-all good, but by emotion or appetite.

16.4. *Problems for the rational part.* Plato's criticism demands a decision on an unsettled question about the rational part in Book IV. If the rational part has only dependent rational desires, as in the second account above, and is concerned only with coherent satisfaction of non-rational desires, then it is not clear why the deviant men are not controlled by reason, and p-just. For each of them has a rational plan for the satisfaction of his desires; and Plato has not shown what makes one plan better than another. To reject the deviant men's claim to p-justice, he must accept the third account of the rational part, and show that it has independent rational desires; and then he must show why a decision in favour of independent rational desires is preferable to any of the deviant men's decisions. It is not at all obvious that the rational part has good grounds for making its second-order decision in favour of the first-order ends of reason, especially until Plato shows us what these ends are. The account of p-justice in the *Gorgias* allows the deviant men to be p-just; and Plato needs to show that the *Republic*'s account will expose their failure. And when he has shown this, he must face the other awkward problem in Book IV—to show that the p-just man will choose justice for itself and act justly. The deviant men clearly fail Glaucon's test; but Plato has not shown that the p-just man will pass it.

Unfortunately and inexcusably, Plato has no direct or detailed answer to these questions. He suggests that the just man of IV and the philosopher of V–VII will be the 'kingly man' who avoids the faults of the deviant men (445d3–449a2, 541b2–4, 543c9–544a1, 544e7–9, 545a5–b1); but he does not show how these faults are avoided. We have seen that IV does not prove that p-justice excludes the faults of the deviant men, or requires the choice of justice for its own sake. We must turn to V–VII to see if Plato could extract a better answer. We have already seen what kind of knowledge is required for virtue; we must now consider whether the philosopher with this knowledge also has the rational desires which make him superior to the deviant men.

17. *Rational desires*

17.1. *Recollection and desire.* The account of the deviant men raises questions already raised by Plato's epistemology. For Socrates, there was no problem about the choice of components of the final good; his theory assumed that everyone wants the same determinate end; since no deliberation is needed to reach this desire, it is a non-rational desire. We have seen in the middle dialogues and in *Republic* V–VII how Plato rejects this view. He argues that moral properties are not reducible to non-moral properties; therefore the final good is not a determinate end agreed by the virtuous and the non-virtuous; this doctrine is applied to the Good in Book VI, to show that Socrates' view must have been wrong. Plato can reply by agreeing with Socrates that there is no rational deliberation about ends; he will then disagree with Socrates in believing that people pursue different ultimate ends acquired by some non-rational affective training. Alternatively, he can claim that desires for ultimate ends can be rational, and result from deliberation. *Republic* VIII–IX suggests that Plato accepts the second view. For the deviant men do not adopt their ends unreflectively; nor are they simply compelled by powerful desires. We have seen how each of them could argue that he has rationally chosen the components of the final good he pursues.

Plato needs to show that though the deviant men have chosen rationally, they have chosen wrongly, because they have deliberated wrongly in their choice of first-order ends. To prove this, he needs to find the right way to deliberate about ultimate ends. We found that the theory of desire and ascent in the *Symposium* was meant to answer this question, and that the *Phaedrus* treated this theory as part of the general Theory of Recollection.[54] Now the *Republic* has used the cognitive aspects of the Theory of Recollection; we must see whether Plato also develops the theory of rational desire which will answer the questions raised in Books VIII–IX. His remarks are brief and unsystematic; to make sense of them, and see how they might answer the questions, we must retrace our steps and try to fill out the *Republic*'s comments from the *Symposium* and *Phaedrus*.

17.2. *The ascent of desire.* The philosopher is a lover of learning and wisdom who seeks to know the reality which 'always is' and does not wander about because of becoming and perishing (485a10–b3). The many beautifuls and justs suffer becoming and perishing, since their beauty and justice comes to be and passes away; someone who realizes their inadequacy will not be content till he finds what always is just or beautiful and does not suffer these changes.[55] To have realized their inadequacy, he must have completed the initial stages of the *Symposium*'s ascent, where someone realizes that his present objects of love are inadequate to his aspirations; then he withdraws some of his desires from these objects, and concentrates them on what is really beautiful (485d3–e1). The philosopher will not be satisfied until he has found and had intercourse with what is really beautiful, and brings forth intelligence and reality (490a8–b7). The erotic image recalls the soul's desire for the Forms in the *Phaedo* (66d7–e6), and the *Symposium*'s reference to 'birth in beauty' after the ascent (211e3–212a7). The *Republic* refers only to the last stage of the same process, part of the soul's turning from becoming to being described in the Cave. The process requires the recognition of inadequacies in previous views of (e.g.) the large, the just, or the beautiful, to reach true conceptions of what is large (fairly easy) or just or beautiful (much harder). We have considered the cognitive aspect of the theory; but it also applies to desires.

17.3. *The point of the theory.* The use of Plato's theory of ascent can best be illustrated from a problem of choice which could not be solved by Socratic deliberation.[56] If *A* wants a worthwhile job, he may pursue it as an end in itself, because it expresses some vague ideal or aspiration for a 'satisfying life'; and he may find that some job does not fulfil his ideal, since he finds something lacking when he tries it. The problem is not that the job fails to contribute instrumentally to some determinate end, that, for instance, it produces too small a quantity of some internal glow or feeling of satisfaction, but that, he finds on reflection, it does not satisfy the vague ideal it was supposed to embody. Since the ideal was vague, he may discover what it requires only when he finds that his present job does not match it; he may not have realized that he values peace and quiet, or challenging work, until he tries a job without them. Each new proposed end-in-itself reveals its inadequacies measured against the demands of his ideal, though he could not have expressed these demands until he tried this activity; each new activity reveals new capacities and demands in him which then require some further choice.

This area of vague ideals is Plato's concern in the theory of ascent—and not only because it is a vague theory. Someone looks for an adequate object of love or end in itself for his pursuit; and as he tries and rejects various candidates, he alters his conception of the end. Comparison with elenctic method is apt; just as in the elenchos, someone proposes candidates for ultimate end, and, when he reflects on them, expresses demands which he could not have expressed previously, and realizes their deficiencies. This is the process Plato advocates both for gaining knowledge and for rational deliberation to guide the choice of ultimate ends. The elenctic process described in the Cave, and the ascent described in the *Symposium* and mentioned in the *Republic*, are the same process, using the same methods.

17.4. *Rational desire and choice of ends.* If this is a rough idea of the method Plato advocates, why should someone who follows it not choose one of the deviant men's ways of life? Someone who tries various conceptions of an ultimate end and finds them inadequate will find that some of his capacities and needs are frustrated; when he considers his life as a whole he will want them realized more fully. Now if he chose to be dominated by the ends of appetite or emotion, he would be rejecting this way of deciding what to do; his first-order goals would no longer aim at a final good covering his whole life and all his capacities and aims, but he would choose to be restricted to some subset of these aims. For someone choosing his goals by the method of the ascent, this procedure would be unreasonable; for it would be a rational second-order choice, considering his whole life, to reject first-order plans considering his whole life. This decision would not be self-contradictory. We might sometimes decide by reasoning not to decide some cases by reasoning; we might deliberate about the best way to pick winners in horse-races, and find it is best not to deliberate about the merits of the horses at all, but to stick a pin in the card. But someone who decides to pursue first-order ends of the non-rational parts is still unreasonable, because he knows he will be denying consideration to some of the capacities and aims which his second-order deliberation tries to satisfy.

The method of ascent prescribes the pursuit of first-order ends chosen by the rational part of the soul. The rational part, on this view, will have independent rational desires; they will not be confined to concern for the existing ends of the non-rational parts, but will consider a man's capacities and needs as a whole, whether or not he already has a non-rational desire to satisfy them. Plato's views are still not free of obscurity. But at least he could argue plausibly that someone who follows the method of ascent, trying to find the right plan for his life as a whole, will reject the solutions of the deviant men, which concentrate on one narrow aspect of a man's aims and capacities.

17.5. *Results of the ascent.* The philosopher who completes the ascent brings forth 'intelligence and reality'; but what does that imply? Plato mentions two results.

1. The contemplative view. Some of the rational part's desires will be desires to use reason, especially in philosophical knowledge and contemplation. Plato sometimes suggests in the *Republic*,

as in the *Phaedo*, that contemplation of the Forms will be pre-eminently worth while for the philosopher.[57]

2. The practical view. The philosopher will want to express his knowledge of Justice, Beauty, and the other moral Forms in actions which embody them.

These two views need not be inconsistent. A philosopher who aims at what is best for him in his life will, Plato thinks, recognize the supreme value of philosophical thought; and therefore he will have a rational desire to engage in it. But this desire will not be rational because it is a desire *for* theoretical reasoning, but because it is a desire arising *from* practical reasoning; the philosopher can rationally defend his conviction of the supreme value of philosophical thought. But supreme value does not imply all-inclusive value; he will also have reason to value other activities expressing his view of the best activities for all his life, and they will include more than philosophical thought. The two views are inconsistent only if contemplation is taken to be the whole of the philosopher's rational aim.

The *Symposium* suggested the practical view, when it explained the work of teachers and legislators by the desire to propagate virtue. And the *Republic* agrees; though the philosopher's knowledge of the Forms separates him from the aims and pursuits of the many (493e2–494a7), they would not be so hostile if they saw him conformed to virtue as far as possible, ruling a Platonic state (498e3–4). The philosopher brings forth real virtue because he knows what is really just, good, and admirable (*Symp.* 211e3–212a7; *R.* 520c3–6); his admiration for the moral Forms stimulates him to make other people virtuous and undertake legislation (500b8–e4, 501b1–7). His view of the Forms, and especially of the Form of the Good (540a8–b1), will create a pattern in his soul (484c8–9) and a single unified goal for his life (519c2–4), to guide his actions and prescriptions. Throughout Plato assumes that the philosopher's knowledge of the Forms will create the desire to express his knowledge in his actions.

17.6. *Rational desire and the divided soul.* Plato's account of rational desire for the good, developed by ascent and recollection, affects his view of the rational part of the soul, which desires the good, and of control by the rational part. He insists that his division, and the account of the virtues which relies on it, is only a sketch reached by a short way, and that the longer way requires reference to the Forms and the Good (439c9–d5, 504a4–d3), for we will understand the rational part and its difference from other parts only when we understand rational desire. If the rational part chooses its goals by the method of recollection and ascent, not everyone who abides by his rational plan for his life is really controlled by rational desire; to meet Plato's conditions, someone must choose the constituents of the good life sought in his rational plan by the method of recollection. Now the deviant men do not choose their goals this way; they decide to satisfy ends pursued for their attraction to the emotional or appetitive parts, and do not pursue ends chosen by rational reflection and recollection. The kinds of choices which might have seemed to display the rational part's control if we had concentrated on IV will not meet the more stringent conditions implied in V–VII.

17.7. *The divided soul in the* Phaedrus. These consequences of the Theory of Recollection for the division of the soul are noticed in the *Phaedrus* more clearly than in the *Republic*. The defence of the non-lover's 'mortal temperance' and the defence of the Platonic lover rest on two different divisions of the soul. The first division defends the non-lover's claim to be self-controlled (233c1–2), and therefore temperate (237e2–3); the soul includes innate appetites for pleasure, and an acquired belief directed at what is best (237d6–9); control by good-directed belief makes a man temperate, while control by appetite fills him with insolent excess (237d9–238a2). A temperate man will avoid passionate desire (*erōs*), because it is a non-rational appetite causing violent excess (238b7–c4; *R*. 439d 4–8).

This division looks Platonic; and it allows p-justice to someone who systematically pursues his ends, whatever they are. The non-lover with slavish virtue can claim to be p-just and temperate because he restrains his desires for immediate satisfaction to ensure future satisfaction of his desires; the deviant men could claim to be p-just for the same reason. However, the division is not quite the same as in *Republic* IV. No desires are ascribed to the rational part, but all belong in the non-rational part; appetitive and emotional parts are not distinguished, since all desires belong equally to the non-rational part; the rational part is allowed only belief, not knowledge. The rational part is concerned only with the orderly pursuit of non-rational ends, not with the choice of ends—that is why it has no desires of its own. The *Phaedrus*'s division yields an account of p-justice with the faults of the account in the *Gorgias*. Plato must show that the differences in *Republic* IV are important, and that its division of the soul justifies his criticism of the deviant men.[58]

17.8. *Rational desire in the* Phaedrus. Plato tries to justify his attack on the slavish virtue ('mortal temperance') of the non-lover by replacing the first division of the soul. He reasserts the *Republic*'s tripartition; the emotional part pursues honour and feels shame at what is shameful, with the good-dependent but non-rational desires of *Republic* IV and VIII (253d6, 254a1–2). The rational part is not confined to right belief, but seeks knowledge by recollection. In recollection it develops its own desires, for reasons we have tried to suggest, though Plato does not explain them. Recollection involves deliberation about ultimate ends, not confined to previous non-rational desire. The rational part tries to reach a satisfactory view of what is worth while in itself—in the *Phaedrus*'s terms, it is excited by beauty (253e3–254a7), and seeks a better conception of it to express in action (252e2–253a3). It does not simply seek to satisfy appetites and emotional desires, but acquires new desires of its own by recollection.

This revised account of the rational part destroys the claim of the non-lover, and of the deviant men in the *Republic*, to be controlled by rational desires; for their desires are not developed by recollection. Plato must invoke recollection in his account of rational desire if his account in IV is to deny virtue and p-justice to the deviant men. The *Republic* does not face the problem; but the *Phaedrus* shows how Plato might answer it.

18. *Rational desire and justice*

18.1. *Knowledge, desire, and virtue.* The *Phaedrus*'s account of rational desire explains why knowledge is necessary for virtue, reinforcing the epistemological arguments of *Republic* V–VII. A virtuous man must choose virtue for its own sake; for this he must admire virtue for itself; for this he must know what real virtue is and admire what he knows; the way to this knowledge and admiration is the method of recollection and ascent. Someone who has only right belief about virtue lacks the understanding which will show him that it is worth while in itself.

Recollection also explains why a virtuous man will want to act virtuously. Socrates tends to explain virtuous action on acquisitive grounds, because it is necessary to achieve the final good; and he finds it hard to explain how someone will love anything else when he has reached the final good and lacks nothing (*Lys.* 214e3–215e2). Plato's theory of love and desire recognizes not only acquisitive, but also expressive motives; someone may choose virtuous action not only because it contributes to the good he pursues, but because it expresses his conception of the good he has achieved and understood. Plato stresses this kind of motive in his reference to the propagation of virtue which expresses someone's conception of beauty and of the virtues.

18.2. *The virtuous man's motives.* This account of reasons for acting virtuously does not mean that a virtuous man's actions are not guided by his conception of happiness. He will still decide which actions are worth while by deciding which contribute to what he regards as the best life for him. But he will not necessarily be moved by a desire for happiness in each of his actions. He may decide that it is worth while to do certain actions for themselves, without considering whether they contribute to his happiness. The desire for happiness is a second-order motive, deciding what first-order motives to act on; and it need not imply that the only first-order motive will be the desire for happiness. Plato's virtuous man will decide that actions which express his conception of virtue are worth while for their own sake, that the best life will include actions done for this reason; and then he will do these actions for their own sake without concern for his happiness.

This attitude explains the virtuous man's apparent madness, remarked in the *Phaedrus*. There Plato insisted that the virtuous man's passionate desire (*erōs*) for the beautiful would make him act in ways most people would regard as mad, because of his indifference to prudential considerations about his future good. To this extent, surprising as it may seem, he is like the tyrannical man; each of them is dominated by a passionate desire which makes him indifferent to ordinary kinds of prudence. In the *Gorgias* Socrates uses a defence that might equally well appeal to a tyrannical man; it is living well which matters, however bad the consequences for the future welfare may be (*G.* 512d6–e5). Aristotle argues similarly that the virtuous man who acts for the sake of what is admirable will prefer to do a single admirable action, even with disastrous consequences to himself, than to live on without having done it (*EN* 1169a22–5). Self-sacrifice is an extreme case of the virtuous man's normal attitude to virtuous action; he regards it as worth while because it expresses his conception of what is good and admirable, and the best life demands that kind of activity, with no further questions about its contribution to his happiness.

Both the really p-just man and the slavishly prudent man act prudently from rational self-love. Self-love requires a man to be concerned for his own future condition; and so he will tend to display the kinds of humdrum thrift normally associated with prudence. But he is concerned not only with his *future* self, but also with his future *self*, with acting in the way that expresses his ideal of himself. The p-just man will be concerned with himself in both ways; he will plan a life which does not sacrifice more important future interests to present satisfaction, but he will not prefer his future on any terms over present actions which express his ideal of himself. His decisions will sometimes need courage, to override future-directed desires and to what he thinks best; and this kind of courage will distinguish the really p-just man from the merely thrifty slavish or oligarchic man.[59]

18.3. *Other people's interests.* We have found that the p-just man will be prepared for actions which express his ideal of a good life, without exclusive concern for his own future interests. But why should these actions include just actions benefiting other people? Plato must appeal to the view of other-directed actions, including love of other persons, derivable from his account of recollection and the ascent of desire. Someone who has explored different conceptions of the final good elenctically, in the way we have discussed, and tries to find a satisfactory conception for his life as a whole, will learn to value for itself the p-just condition of his soul; for control by rational desire will be central in any satisfactory conception of the good. Now Plato assumes that whatever someone comes to value in the ascent he will also want to propagate; the *Symposium* explains this desire as a desire to do the second best to ensuring our own immortality in possession of what we value, if we can ensure its possession by others; the *Republic* does not mention this explanation. Anyhow, the p-just man will want to embody in the world what he admires; he wants to create as well as possess.

Now the p-just man values for itself his own p-justice; and so he will want to produce p-justice in other people's lives too. As *Republic* IV said, he will regard as just those actions which produce p-justice; but Plato's theory of desire supplies what Book IV did not supply, a reason for a p-just man to aim at other people's p-justice, as well as his own. He acts on the same motives as the Platonic lover, whose ascent to Beauty and desire to give birth in beauty moves him to create justice and temperance in his beloved or in households and states (*Symp.* 208e5–209a8). Someone who is pregnant in soul seeks someone else to make virtuous (*Symp.* 209b4–c5), and treats him as a statue in which the lover embodies the virtues he most admires (*Phdr.* 252d5–253b1). The same kind of creative desire explains the attitudes of the lover to his beloved, the just man's concern for other men's p-justice, and the legislator's desire to encourage virtue by legislation. Plato must rely on this account of other-directed creative desire to show how the p-just man can care about other men's p-justice.[60]

So far the p-just man can be expected, on Plato's theory, to care about other people's p-justice. But common beliefs about justice require the just man to care about other people's interests. To find the connection Plato must rely on his argument in IV that p-justice more than anything else is in the just man's interest. Once this is granted, the p-just man satisfies the common beliefs about justice—though his concern for other people's p-justice may well require drastic revision in beliefs about how their interest is to be promoted. Plato can now at last justify the assumption which underlay his early argument to show that the just man will benefit other people (335b2–d12); for he can show why the just man will pursue both his own interest and other people's, and why he will benefit someone else by making him more just. If the previous steps are accepted—and they are certainly controversial—Plato has shown that his account of p-justice in IV is an account of real justice, when 'control by the rational part' is rightly understood.

18.4. *The philosopher and other people's interests.* Plato's theory of the virtuous man's motives is tested in VII when he tries to explain why the philosopher who knows the Forms can fairly be expected to return to the cave and take part in ruling. But he does not make the best of his theory, because he is influenced by the contemplative view of the philosopher, and describes him in terms excluded by the practical view. He mistakenly suggests that the philosopher will want to stay contemplating the Forms and will not voluntarily undertake public service (519c4–6). Plato is right only if the philosopher thinks the final good consists entirely in contemplation of the Forms; but why should he think this? He may well decide that contemplation is an important, perhaps the single most important, constituent of the good; but if he is a virtuous man, he must also want to embody the virtues in his own and other people's lives for its own sake. If he wants to do this, he must accept public service; he may still regard the tasks of government as necessary evils for fulfilling his ends, but he should recognize them as the best means available in an imperfect world—necessary, rather than admirable in themselves (520e1–3, 540b4–5). If he is a virtuous man, he should regard public service in other people's interests as a part of the life that realizes his own happiness; though the state is not designed for his happiness (420b3–8, 519e1–520a4), he should find that his role in the state realizes his happiness (cf. 465e4–466c3).

Plato's argument requires him to accept the practical view of the philosopher as a virtuous man who values virtuous action for itself. He needs the virtuous man's knowledge of the moral Forms, so that his rule will be rule by a waking man, not a man in a dream (520c1–d1). Above all, Plato's appeal to them assumes they will care about justice for itself. He invites them to show their gratitude to the state which has supported them and needs their help, and to return what is due (520a6–c1). The demand for grateful service in return for previous support was one of Socrates' reasons in the *Crito* for obeying the law (*Cri.* 50d1–e4); returning what is due was the very first conception of recognized justice considered in the *Republic* (331e3–4), and Glaucon agrees it is a just demand on just men (520e1). Gratitude for benefits received gives the Platonic lover reason to return benefits (*Phdr.* 253a5–b1); and a p-just man will have reason to return benefits to the state. He will value the society in which he acquires and expresses his conception of the good, the relations with the state and with other citizens from which these demands arise; and he will want to express his conception of p-justice in the state. The practical conception of the philosopher justifies Plato's appeal to gratitude; but a pure contemplative has no reason to be moved by such an appeal. Plato cannot consistently claim both that the philosopher will be a pure contemplative who will not rule voluntarily, and that he has good reason to accept the state's demand for just action. The second view is much more likely to answer the questions about justice in the *Republic*.[61]

The influence of the contemplative view should neither be underestimated nor be allowed to obscure Plato's answers to the questions raised about Book IV. The account of rational desire and of the virtuous man's motives in V–VII, understood with the help of the *Symposium* and *Phaedrus*, does try to explain why the p-just man will be really just; it shows how the p-just man will differ from the deviant men, and why he chooses just action and cares about other people's interest for its own sake, to embody his conception of justice. Various parts of Plato's answer deserve criticism; but he does not simply ignore or evade the problems.

19. *Justice and the just man's interest*

19.1. *The final analogy.* Plato set himself the awkward task of showing that p-justice is both the source of just actions and a good in itself for the just man; the task is awkward because a conception of p-justice which satisfies one condition seems likely to fail the other. At the end of Book IX he restates the defence of justice in Book IV with an analogy, representing the three parts of the soul as man, a lion, and a multiform beast, all within a man (588b10–e1). Control by the rational part causes just actions producing p-justice; it is control by the man, not by the non-human desires of the other two parts (588e3–589b6). This analogy powerfully expresses Plato's claim that p-justice both produces just actions and benefits the whole soul. Now we saw that Book IV left obscure the connection between p-justice and just action; if the later account has clarified that connection, can Plato still show that the control of the rational part benefits the whole soul?[62]

19.2. *The functions of the rational part.* The rational part should benefit the whole soul, because it secures friendship between the parts (589a6–b6), as Book IV demanded, and aims at harmonious satisfaction for them all (591a10–b7). It was easy to see how the rational part could do this if it had no independent rational desires, but simply desired the coherent and organized satisfaction of the desires of the other two parts. But if it needs independent rational desires to choose just actions, what becomes of its role as impartial arbitrator?[63] It must apparently arbitrate between its own demands and the demands of the other two parts; and why will its decision here be reliable?

19.3. *Virtue and the good of the soul.* Plato must appeal to his account of the ascent of desire. Someone who tries to develop his conception of the final good elenctically develops his view of what would be best for his whole life; and he considers all his capacities, aims, and interests in this deliberation. If he values the results of this kind of deliberation, he must value for itself the condition of soul in which this kind of deliberation decides a man's choices and actions. The rational part's independent rational desires do not depend on previous desires of the other parts; but they are not indifferent to those desires either; someone with p-justice can be expected to do justice to all parts of his soul.

Plato says much less on the question we are apt to think more important, whether this p-justice is also justice. We have considered his argument about the p-just man's desire to propagate and create p-justice in other people; and we may well doubt whether this creative desire is adequately explained or justified by Plato, and whether it will really produce justice. These doubts must be examined more carefully. But at least the pattern of argument in the *Republic* is fairly clear. Plato has argued that someone who rationally reflects on the kind of life which best suits his whole soul, all his interests, desires, and capacities, will find that he has reason to include just action in his life; and nothing has shown that his defence is hopeless.

19.4. *The just man and the deviant man.* The p-just man's desires result from deliberation about the best life for the whole of a man's soul; he has reached his plan of life by rational reflection on all his desires and interests, and by efforts to integrate them. The deviant men have done something that sounds quite similar; as we saw, they have made a rational second-order decision on which first-order desires they will satisfy. But perhaps it is now clearer where they differ from the p-just man. His rational second-order decision prefers the ends chosen by first-order desires acquired by deliberation about the good of the whole soul. The deviant men allowed no rational reflection to influence their acquisition of first-order goals, but simply endorsed some appetitive or emotional goal they already pursued.

The p-just man's way of life will reject the errors of the deviant men. Unlike the timocratic or oligarchic man, he will not organize his life for the single-minded pursuit of a single goal of a non-rational part; nor will he follow his non-rational desire which at any time happens to be dominant, like the tyrannical man. Unlike the democratic man, he will not simply accept his various desires and allow them equal value; his plan for the best life will require preference for some over others. However, he will not repress all the unnecessary desires which are not law-breaking. To secure friendship between the parts of his soul, he must persuade the appetitive part that its interests are considered (cf. 554d1–3); less anthropomorphically, he must consider himself not only as a rational planner, but also as a possessor of unnecessary appetites, and provide for their satisfaction. His plan for the good of the whole soul will include desires which do not destroy the plan, and yet do not contribute to its realization.[64]

19.5. *Just and unjust action.* Plato repeats the arguments in IV that just actions are beneficial because they promote p-justice, control by the rational part, and unjust actions are harmful because they promote the growth and domination of emotion or appetite (588e3–589a6, 589b8–590c6). The agent's p-justice is promoted or harmed—that is why unpunished injustice is bad for the agent and punishment is good for him (591a10–b7). Plato defends with firmer argument his inadequately supported claim in the *Gorgias* that unpunished unjust action is the most harmful of all to the agent's soul; the firmer arguments rest on the tripartite soul, and the claim that unjust action disrupts its best order.[65] But is the claim any more convincing than in IV?

The trouble in IV was that a rational part concerned with a plan for fulfilling a man's goals in life had no obvious reason to avoid unjust actions, and no obvious tendency to be weakened by them. Even if Plato adds that the plan must seek the good of the whole soul, it does not clearly exclude unjust action against other people's interests. He must show, what he claims in accounts of the ascent of desire, that rational reflection on the good of the whole soul will require the choice of justice for itself and concern for other people's p-justice. If this claim is accepted, Plato has a better defence here than in IV. Unjust actions will tend to undermine the soul's acceptance of reason's goals which include the pursuit of justice, and to strengthen the other two parts. The result will not be chaos in the soul, as IV might have suggested, but the order in the deviant men's souls; it will reject the goals prescribed by the rational part and prefer others. Since just actions promote the rational part's control, they benefit the just man. Plato does not imply that concern for this benefit will be the just man's only motive for just action; if he is just he will pursue it for its own sake, apart from concern for its benefit to him. But the benefits of just action which assure him that he benefits from choosing justice for its own sake, justify his choice and the motive for the choice.

19.6. *Plato's conclusions*. It is easy to be unsatisfied with the results of the *Republic*, to feel that all the complex and sometimes shadowy metaphysical, epistemological, and psychological apparatus has concealed from Plato and an uncritical reader the failure to face Thrasymachus' question. We think we know what is at issue when Thrasymachus and Glaucon ask their questions, whether or not we think Plato should have tried to answer them as he does. Real justice—the other-regarding virtue—seems to be disregarded, except in Plato's complacent assurance that p-just men will avoid some c-unjust actions, and in his very dubious claim that the philosopher will do what justice demands of him in the state. The division of the soul, elaborated in Books VIII–IX and explained (I have suggested) from the Theory of Recollection, supports Plato's account of prudence, rational desire, and rational life-planning; we may think it illuminates the questions; but it seems to tell us very little about justice.

It is regrettable that Plato leaves us gaps to fill here, because of his interest in contemplative rather than practical wisdom; and he would not find them easy to fill. I have tried to show how his views might be developed to include justice. Anyhow, it is important to see why the emphasis on self-regarding rationality is relevant to his views on justice. We readily suppose that if someone thinks he has no reason to be just because it is not in his interest, he needs to be convinced that he has reason to do some things which are not in his interest, but in other people's. Plato thinks that the sceptic has a mistaken conception of what justice requires, or of his own interest, or of both. Thrasymachus and Glaucon assume that a rational man has reason to pursue power, wealth and private pleasure to an extent which conflicts with other people's interests. Plato replies that they have not reached this view by rational reflection and deliberation about their life as a whole, but simply by accepting some desires which happen to be strong and demanding; their case cannot be accepted until they present an account of the best life which justifies the assumptions. This negative reply to Thrasymachus, and to several versions of Thrasymachus' position, is not to be dismissed. It shows that a clear proof of a conflict between justice and self-interest requires an account of self-interest and of a man's own good; and by showing how someone should deliberate about his own interests, Plato suggests that Thrasymachus' results follow from bad deliberation.

Plato's positive reply is harder to defend; he must not only undermine Thrasymachus' claim to pronounce on a man's good, but must also present the account Thrasymachus fails to present, of a man's own good and its relation to the recognized virtues, including justice. Here Plato rejects the Socratic approach. Socrates relied on agreement about the ultimate end, and offered to prove that the recognized virtues are necessary instrumental means to this determinate end. Plato rejects the determinate end; he makes his task both easier, since he need not prove that justice is necessary for recognized goods, and harder, since he has to show how there can be a right rational choice of components of the final good. Definitions of the virtues and the good cannot eliminate disputed moral terms, and Plato's conception of the good will not coincide with a non-virtuous man's. None the less, Plato does not believe he has nothing to say to the non-virtuous man. Though they do not agree on components of the good, Plato seeks agreement on a procedure for finding them, the method of recollection and ascent. A rational man will accept that way of discovering the right ultimate end; and when he accepts it, he will find he values p-justice for itself; and when he sees that, he has reason to make other people p-just and thereby benefit them. This is Plato's argument to show that a true view of someone's own good requires justice; he rejects the Socratic view that virtue is a craft prescribing instrumental means to a determinate end of happiness, but defends the underlying Socratic claim, that virtue benefits the virtuous man.

We should not attack Plato, then, for failing to answer his question about justice; for his theories allow us to see how he can answer it. He does not stress the parts of the problem we might like him to stress; but that is because his view of the problem and of the right kind of answer is not the view of some more recent moralists. I have tried not to conceal the weak or controversial parts of his argument; but his over-all position has not been shown to be worthless. The issues he raises deserve further examination.

VIII. CRITICISMS OF PLATO

1. *Morality and rationality*

1.1. *Introduction.* In the previous chapters I have tried to expound Plato's views fairly, and to find the best sense that can be made of them, rather than to mention or assess the various criticisms that might be aimed at them. In this last chapter I want first of all to summarize Plato's main aims in moral philosophy, and to suggest the point of the development we have watched in progress, and then to discuss criticisms of his views. If we have understood him correctly, some criticisms will appear to be misguided, or at least far from conclusive; but other grounds of criticisms, familiar and less familiar, will appear. My comments on large issues will be hasty and superficial; but my primary aim is not to decide firmly for or against Plato, but to show what questions we must face to decide for or against him. If his general theory is not undermined by clear and easy arguments, but requires decisions on difficult and important issues in moral philosophy, its study will be worth while.

1.2. *The scope of morality.* First it will be useful to recall Socrates' and Plato's approach to what we call moral questions, and then to survey the different ways they follow this approach. A modern moralist might want to know what morality is, what moral principles or virtues are; supposing we can roughly distinguish morality from other things, he will try to explain this distinction, and give an account of the principles underlying moral judgements. Some might answer this question by saying that moral principles are the prescriptive, universalizable, and overriding principles by which a man guides his life, or that they are the principles that rational self-interested agents would choose under certain assumptions about their knowledge, or that they are the principles which produce the greatest happiness of the greatest number. Plato offers no answer to compare with these, because he is not asking the same question.

Socrates and Plato ask 'how a man should live' (*G.* 492d3–5, 500c1–4; *R.* 352d5–6; cf. *La.* 187e6–188a3; *G.* 472c6–d1); and when they want to find the virtues, they want the states which a rational man will choose when he answers this question correctly. The virtues a rational man would choose may include those we regard as moral, which are normally taken to benefit other people; but nothing in the question assumes that these will be real virtues for the rational man. We can also say that this is a moral question. For we normally believe about moral principles both (1) that they benefit other people; and (2) that anyone has reason to pursue them as his overriding principles. It is not important to decide whether (1) or (2) is part of the meaning of 'moral principle', or whether that is a sensible question; rejection of either (1) or (2) will undermine some of our central beliefs about morality. We may doubt whether the Platonic question is answerable, or has one answer of the kind Plato seeks; but it should not be confused with a narrower question which interests some modern moralists.[1]

1.3. *Morality and happiness.* Socrates and Plato explain their question about how a man should live by asking what benefits him or what contributes to his happiness. They accept a teleological principle:

T. What has a rationally justifiable claim on an agent must contribute to his happiness.

This principle controls all the dialogues we have examined. It is by no means an obvious way to answer the first question. A deontological moralist might accept Socrates' challenge to show that morality has a rationally justifiable claim on us, and deny T, if he accepts another principle:

D. If morality is rationally justifiable, an agent has sufficient reason to accept it, apart from any concern with his own happiness.[2]

He will object to Plato for the unreasonable demand on recognized morality which follows from T, and reply that T denies the rationality and supremacy of the recognized virtues. A teleologist might agree, and follow Hume, who does not believe moral sentiments are or ought to be the supreme guide to action; he is satisfied if they are strong enough to maintain morality in the areas where it is worth while.[3]

1.4. *Plato's questions.* Socrates and Plato surprisingly reject this treatment of morality, which would imply that the recognized moral virtues are not unqualified virtues, as they both assume, but conditions which sometimes harm the agent. They try to show that courage, temperance, and justice are unqualified virtues, so that it is always worthwhile to do what they require; like Aristotle, they deny that real virtue can be practised to excess (*EN* 1107a22–3), and believe these are real virtues. They do not mean it is always worth while to do what most people think is just; for most people may have a wrong view of justice. But they must agree that most people refer to a real virtue when they speak of justice; and a proof of this claim requires some connection between Platonic and ordinary judgements.[4]

Plato might be taken to say that morality is what promotes the agent's happiness; and this seems to be an absurd account of morality. We are inclined to say that moral principles apply to everyone, and it is morally intolerable to prescribe that everyone is to promote my happiness. Plato seems to be no less wrong if he means that each man ought, from the moral point of view, to pursue his own interest; for the moral point of view is concerned with anyone's interest, and Plato has not shown that the interests of individuals following his advice will be coordinated in a morally satisfactory way.[5]

These questions about ethical egosim are not about Plato's concerns. He is not trying to describe morality, as we tend to understand it, or to defend egoism from what we call the moral point of view. He wants to know what in general it is rational for someone to do; and this question remains to be asked when we understand what the moral point of view is and what it requires—if we identify morality by its concern for other people's, or everyone's, interest. Plato is not offering an absurd way to understand morality, but asking the apparently sensible question whether it is worth while to do what morality is normally supposed to require.[6]

2. Plato's rejection of Socratic ethics

2.1. *Strategies.* Even if we agree on the question Plato asks, his principle T is highly disputable. But before we consider some legitimate areas of dispute, we should recall Socrates' and Plato's different ways of applying the principle. Some criticisms which would be relevant to the Socratic answers are clearly disarmed by Plato; and we will consider the Platonic answers.

To prove that the virtues are worth while, T demands a proof that they promote the agent's happiness. But this demand does not show whether happiness or the final good is treated as a determinate or as an indeterminate end. If it is a determinate end, then T requires virtue to contribute to some fixed conception of happiness accepted by the

virtuous and the non-virtuous. We have found reason to believe that
Socrates treats the final good as a determinate end, and that the CA
expresses the resulting view of virtue. When Plato denies that the virtues and the good can be defined purely by reference to agreed properties, he denies the determinacy of the final good, and undermines the
CA. The eudaimonistic assumption will clearly not imply what it implies for Socrates. Indeed, we may wonder whether it implies anything
interesting or useful at all. We noticed earlier the problem Plato raised
by rejecting Socrates' version of eudaimonism; and his success or
failure in solving these problems deserves to be briefly reviewed, with
an eye especially on the *Republic*.[7]

2.2. *Definitions*. When Plato rejects accounts of the virtues and the
good in agreed terms, the accounts he allows may appear to be
uselessly circular; one unknown is defined by a second unknown
defined through the first unknown. This problem is especially acute in
the *Republic*, when justice and happiness are equally unknown, and
each is to be mentioned in the definition of the other. To show that his
procedure is not pointless, and that T is still informative, Plato must
appeal to a distinction which is always vital for the elenchos. We may
not be able to define either virtue or the final good adequately until we
can define both; but we can still have beliefs about each and recognize
examples of what satisfies them, without an account of either. Plato's
procedure will prove something if it can combine these beliefs about
virtue and the good to show that virtue contributes to the good; the
content of virtue or the good is not fully understood without a definition, but it is no blank cheque to be filled in with what suits the theory.
If beliefs about justice and the good restrict the admissible definitions,
Plato's task is not doomed to self-defeating success—the two sets of
beliefs might be unrelated or conflicting, and it will be worth while to
find they are not.

Plato tries to connect justice and the final good through his account
of p-justice and control by reason. He argues that (1) we agree that
justice is expected to benefit other people; (2) happiness requires direction of someone's life by the desires concerned with his capacities,
aims and interests as a whole, not by desires concerned only with particular satisfactions; (3) someone controlled by these kinds of desires
will have reason to benefit other people. If Plato can justify these
claims, he can explain justice and the final good without defining either
independently of the other. A full account of justice will depend on our
view of the final good chosen by someone controlled by rational

desires; and a full account of the final good will include reference to benefiting other people as justice requires. Plato offers a full account of neither in the *Republic*; but someone who accepts these three claims will have learnt something important and controversial about justice and the final good if they are true.

A Platonic definition rests on common beliefs about justice and about the good—not only about the kinds of actions which are just or beneficial, but also on the kinds of general assumptions noticed here. Plato may fairly revise some common beliefs about particular cases of justice; but the resulting account should justify common beliefs as a whole, especially the most important ones, if it is an account of the virtue people refer to as justice. Now the *Republic* is careless; it does not adequately show that p-justice really requires just action, or that other components of the final good besides p-justice require or allow justice. But we have found that common beliefs are not ignored, and that Plato could defend his claims more persuasively. His general method is not clearly wrong, even if particular arguments are rejected.

2.3. *Motivation.* Plato's rejection of Socrates' conditions for definition deprives him also of Socrates' account of moral motivation, of how a man can be expected to want to be virtuous. For Socrates this was easy: we already want the determinate end happiness, and when we find that virtue contributes to it instrumentally, we will want to be virtuous, because of KSV. When Plato rejects this answer, and insists that a virtuous man changes his views on the components of happiness, he implies, on Socrates' view of rational desire, that the virtuous man's desires for ends cannot be rational, since for Socrates a rational desire chooses instrumental means to a previously determinate final good.

However, Plato tries to show that the virtuous man's desire for ends is rational, by a non-Socratic account of rational desire, in the theory of ascent. A rational deliberator, on this theory, does not simply deliberate about instrumental means to a determinate end he already pursues; he alters his conception of the final good by steps which seem reasonable to him, so that he accepts the results of the whole process. The rationality of the ascent does not depend on a fixed determinate end pursued throughout, but on the rationality of each step. However vague this process sounds in Plato's description, it is a worthwhile effort to show against Socrates that someone's rational choices need not be confined to instrumental means, so that the desire to be virtuous can still be a rational desire.

2.4. *Justification*. Socrates' conditions on justification showed how someone could claim objectivity for moral judgements; they required someone with knowledge of virtue to show anyone that virtue contributes to the determinate end anyone already seeks, so that anyone has reason to acquire virtue. When Plato rejects a determinate final good, he loses this defence. While he might find that his beliefs about the final good cohere with his beliefs about justice, how can he show that anyone else has reason to agree with him? He cannot appeal to shared beliefs about components of the good; for the virtuous man's knowledge will alter his view of the good, and show him that some things are worth while which he would not previously have valued.

Plato relies on an approach first tried in the *Gorgias*, trying to show that any rational man aiming at a final good will agree that its achievement requires the plan and order of choices advocated by Plato. The *Gorgias* unsuccessfully tried to show that any orderly pursuit of ends requires the psychic order which requires justice. The *Republic* argues more elaborately from its description of p-unjust men in Books VIII–IX. A non-virtuous man who is not a Platonic philosopher will not share, or perhaps even fully understand, the philosopher's choice of ends; but Plato expects him to agree that the p-just man acquires his ends the best way, and avoids the faults of the deviant men. The questioner is expected to agree that someone who seeks the final good has reason to reject the deviant men's way of choosing ends, achieving only the goals not chosen by rational reflection, and to choose the p-just man's way, following rational deliberation about his life as a whole. Plato cannot defend himself to a questioner who does not value rationally chosen ends at all; but for a questioner who does value them, the *Republic*'s method of justification is quite legitimate, whether or not it proves what Plato wants. And throughout Plato assumes that virtue must benefit the agent; though he interprets the principle much less restrictively than Socrates did, it still counts in his argument.

3. *Egoism and eudaimonism*

3.1. *Evidence of egoism*. To decide what is still controversial in Plato's view, it will be best to begin with the most obvious criticism, that both Socrates and Plato assume the truth of some unacceptable form of egoism; the final good promoted by virtue is always the good of the agent. The evidence for this assumption is abundant and widespread in the dialogues. Sometimes psychological egoism seems to be assumed; Socrates thinks each of us wants his own happiness, and this desire prevents any possibility of incontinence. Ethical implications are drawn most clearly in the *Meno*, when Plato insists that a man's virtue must be beneficial to himself, and in the *Republic*, when everyone agrees that if justice is a virtue it must contribute to the just man's happiness.[8] When Socrates and Plato advise someone to choose virtue for the good of his soul, they seem to suggest that all virtues, including the recognized other-regarding virtue of justice, are really only self-regarding.

Similar criticisms of Aristotle will rest on equally strong evidence. He claims that the final good for each man is his own happiness, and that a virtue must contribute to the virtuous man's happiness (*EN* 1106a15–24). Though the virtues include justice and friendship, and Aristotle does not follow Plato's view that they are worthwhile because they perfect the virtuous man's soul, he cannot escape the egoistic reference to the agent's happiness, if they really are virtues; for they must be chosen by the wise man who is good at deliberating about his own happiness (1140a25–8). Here as often Aristotle's theory develops Platonic assumptions into a more detailed theory.

3.2. *Types of egoism.* The Platonic and Aristotelian assumption, psychological or ethical, seems obviously false. For it seems to imply that there are no genuinely other-regarding virtues, contrary to what we and most Greeks suppose about justice; all virtue seems to be purely self-regarding because it all ultimately seeks the benefit of the agent. But this charge against eudaimonism is not so obviously correct. Two versions of egoism must be distinguished:

1. Moral solipsism; all virtue must contribute instrumentally either to some intrinsically valued condition of the agent, or to some state of affairs he values for its own sake apart from any benefit or harm to other people.
2. Moral egocentrism; all virtue must contribute to some end valued by the agent as part of his own good.

Solipsism requires concern for other people's good to be instrumental to the agent's own good; egocentrism does not require this restriction, since other people's good might be a component of the agent's own good.

If Socrates and Plato are solipsists, they must reject other-regarding virtues. But if they are egocentrists, the obvious objections to egoism do not so easily damage them; and we may wonder whether this kind of egoism really conflicts with morality at all.[9] They believe that virtue should promote the agent's happiness; but we have noticed that they can recognize 'happiness' or 'living well' as the final good without any definite view of its components; the mere appeal to happiness does not prevent altruistic ends from being components of the agent's final good.[10] To decide whether the Socratic or Platonic view of happiness is solipsistic, we must see which first-order ends are allowed as components of the second-order end, happiness.

3.3. *Evidence of solipsism.* When Socrates treats happiness as a determinate end, he allows only those components which a non-virtuous man will accept; and so happiness will be non-solipsistic only if not all these components are solipsistic. The Socratic dialogues do not decide the question. But the *Protagoras* treats the agent's pleasure as the sole component of his happiness, and so endorses a hedonist version of solipsism.

Plato rejects this hedonist view of the final good, in later dialogues. But he shows other signs of sympathy with solipsism. Like Socrates, he advocates the practice of virtue for the benefit of the soul, and unlike Socrates, treats the soul's good condition as a good in itself. In the *Republic* he even suggests that just actions are those which make the soul just, and we might suppose that only the soul's condition is valuable for itself.[11] A different source of solipsism is Plato's contemplative ideal; when he tends to think that the soul's good is reached wholly and solely by contemplative study, he accepts a solipsist final good.

3.4. *Evidence of non-solipsism.* However, Plato does not normally intend the appeal to happiness to imply a solipsist ultimate end; a virtuous man's life will be ordered by a single goal (*R.* 519c2–4), but this goal need not be unitary or solipsist. Plato implies it is not solipsist, when he criticizes the slavish men in the *Phaedo*, those with 'mortal temperance' in the *Phaedrus*, and those who choose justice for its consequences in *Republic* II. He does not always show whether he means to criticize them only for valuing the condition of soul for its consequences, or also for failing to value just actions for themselves. But the *Phaedo* and the *Phaedrus* suggest both criticisms; and if Plato valued just action only for its effect on the soul, he would be exposed to the second criticism. This argument does not by itself show that Plato is not a solipsist; but his account of the just man's motives in the *Republic* avoids the criticism. We have seen that the just man chooses just action not only for acquisitive, but also for expressive reasons, because it fulfils his desire to embody justice in his actions and in the world. The just man's 'propagative' desire, described also in the *Symposium*, prevents his ultimate end from being solipsist.[12]

3.5. *Just men and just actions*. Plato's choice of states of soul does not require solipsism; it depends on how the right state of soul is identified. We might think that being sun-tanned is a desirable condition of the body, and that taking holidays in sunny places, lying in the sun for hours, and so on, are worth while in so far as they produce a sun-tan; but someone's being sun-tanned does not necessarily encourage him to pursue these activities further—perhaps the opposite is true—and we can decide whether he is sun-tanned without deciding whether he tends to do these activities—he may be sun-tanned without effort, because he happens to work outdoors. Now if Plato thinks of the soul's good state in this way, just actions will only be necessary instrumental means to this state of inner peace or harmony; when the harmony is reached, no further just actions are required, unless perhaps as a kind of exercise to keep the soul in good condition. If we found someone who enjoyed inner peace without just action, we should agree that he is lucky enough to have a just and harmonius soul without effort. In the *Gorgias* Plato suggests that just actions are related to psychic order in this way; and though he does not allow that someone might acquire this psychic harmony without just actions, he does not explain why this should be impossible or undesirable. *Republic* IV is imprecise enough to suggest the same view as the *Gorgias* suggested.

However, this is not Plato's normal view of psychic harmony in the *Republic*, as later books show. He does not think of just actions as instrumental means to some separate state of the soul which might persist without further just action. If someone has the inner peace and estensible psychic harmony of the p-just man, but does not care about just action, Plato will simply deny that he is p-just or is really controlled by the rational part; if p-justice were simply inner harmony, it could not be denied to the deviant men. Plato expects the really just man to have the kind of psychic order which chooses just actions or, in the *Symposium*'s terms, wants to propagate virtue. Since the final good includes the expression of p-justice in just actions, Plato will not recognize as p-justice any condition of soul which does not produce just actions. If the right state of soul cannot be identified without reference to just actions, Plato's concern for the soul does not imply solipsism. He fails to reject solipsism emphatically because he is attracted by the genuinely solipsist contemplative ideal, and does not face the problems it causes for the rest of his view. But his interest in the soul's good does not conflict with the parts of his theory which reject solipsism.

3.6. *Other people's interests.* To show that a p-just man has reason to benefit other people, Plato relies on his account of ascent and propagation; and so it is regrettable that this account is so sketchy at the crucial point. Plato assumes an initial desire to create whatever we find most admirable and worth while, and supposes that the Platonic lover will find p-justice not only beneficial for himself, but worth while to promote in anyone. He assumes that the p-just man will also want the kinds of relations with other people which will make him care about their p-justice; but he does not explain why. Either he must say it is simply a fact about the Platonic lover that he has these desires which can be fulfilled by making other people p-just, or he should explain why someone has reason to acquire and fulfil such desires.

Aristotle's theory of friendship (*philia*) is more detailed than anything Plato offers; and it deserves attention, partly because it does not rely on Platonic metaphysics, and partly because it strengthens the claim that eudaimonism does not exclude, but even requires, altruism. Aristotle argues that a virtuous man will recognize concern for others and co-operation with them as a component of his happiness. Any normal man will find himself unsatisfied if he has all the other components of a good life, but lacks any association with other people or opportunity of common pursuits with them; and a virtuous man will be anxious above all to share virtuous pursuits with others (*EN* 1169b8–22). To share virtuous pursuits, he needs a virtuous friend; and since virtue contributes to the virtuous man's happiness, making someone else virtuous will contribute to his interests. This connection between being virtuous and achieving one's own happiness partly explains why Aristotle says both that a good man loves his friend for himself and that he loves him for his virtue (1156b7–12)—he will promote the friend's interest by sharing virtuous actions with him. This concern for friends will be egocentric, because it is justified by the virtuous man's own final good; but this final good is not solipsistic. Aristotle's line of argument shows how Plato could have defended his claims about propagating virtue and concern for other people within his egocentric assumptions.

Aristotle's account of self-love shows that the reference to psychic perfection as the ultimate end does not imply solipsism. Those who think self-love is incompatible with the pursuit of virtue confuse the best kind of self-love with love of the non-rational part of the soul (1168a15–23); for the virtuous man will love the rational part of his soul, and will care about its aims, which require the pursuit of virtuous and admirable action (1168b23–1169a18). For Aristotle as for Plato, concern for the good of the soul is not an alternative to the virtuous man's pursuit of virtuous action, but necessary and sufficient for that pursuit.[13] If the rational part's desires include a desire for virtuous action, then someone who chooses the best state of his soul with the rational part in control will choose virtuous action.

4. Criticisms of teleological theories

4.1. *The general problem.* If Plato is an egocentrist rather than a solipsist, his position may still be unacceptable; but an opponent cannot simply denounce his appeal to the agent's final word, when that appeal has not been shown to exclude altruistic morality. Some deontologist critics will denounce Plato simply because he accepts a teleological view of virtue, whether or not the view is also egoistic. This line of objection deserves discussion.[14] The normal deontological criticism relies on what are taken to be firm ordinary convictions about morality, and claims that since a teleological theory rejects or cannot explain these convictions, such a theory must be mistaken.[15] Now we may well doubt some of the deontologist's claims to have identified firm convictions, and doubt whether a teleologist's rejection of a firm conviction always counts against his theory. But first we should consider whether the deontologist is right in saying that the Platonic form of teleological theory cannot cope with these convictions.

4.2. *The reduction of morality.* A teleological account of the content of morality may seem to reduce it to a set of principles promoting the good; a teleologist will insist that if an action is not optimific, it is not virtuous either. The deontologist will reply that moral principles are not restricted in their content or application by any external end; principles of justice, say, are valid whether or not they promote some non-moral end apart from them, and are not reducible to technical principles for achieving some external good.

Now this criticism clearly affects Socrates; for he presents virtue as a craft designed to produce some result pursued independently of virtue.[16] But Plato is not clearly open to the same criticism. For he certainly thinks that the virtues promote some final good; but when he rejects attempts to reduce moral to non-moral properties, he denies that this final good is to be chosen independently of morality. His position does not require an account of moral principles as purely technical maxims; virtue and moral knowledge do not decide simply about instrumental means, but are also concerned with ends. The deontologist's objection to the reduction of morality, right or wrong, does not affect Plato.

4.3. *The subordination of morality*. A teleologist might agree that moral principles are not restricted in content by any independent final good, and still insist that we are justified in following them only when they promote an independent end; even if he accepts the deontological view of the content of morality, he might reject the deontological assumption that we are always justified in following moral principles with that content. This view would reject the normal belief that a moral principle prescribes something we always have reason to do; and the teleologist might be accused of subordinating morality to non-moral ends, trying to justify it by non-moral reasons. A deontologist will reply that a virtuous man will treat his moral convictions as supreme, refusing to violate them for the sake of other goals. The teleologist seems to pervert the proper role of morality, and to insist on the wrong kind of justification; for we should not agree that morality is justified only if it is justified by its promotion of some non-moral end.[17]

Both Socrates and Plato reject the compromise of being deontological about the content of morality and teleological about its justification. Both alike insist that we always have reason to do what virtue requires, and that there are unqualified virtues, including justice. Socrates cannot defend this conviction about justice within his account of moral justification; and he is certainly open to the deontologist's objection, right or wrong, that he subordinates morality to an external goal. But Plato is not open to the same objection, for the reason we have considered. For he insists that a man is justified in doing only what promotes the final good, and that virtue always promotes the final good; but if the final good is not specified apart from virtue, it need not subordinate virtue to any non-moral ends. Plato's virtuous man is expected to value justice and just action for its own sake, as part of the final good, not only when it contributes instrumentally to some further end; he does not reject the supremacy of moral principles. Certainly, Plato includes more in the virtues than deontologists would include in morality; but he does not devalue even the virtues which they recognize as moral.

4.4. *Right and good.* Teleological theories are alleged to conflict with our alleged conviction that the right action can be decided without reference to its good consequences; the deontologist relies on this conviction to claim that the right is independent of, and prior to, the good.[18] This criticism might still apply to a teleologist who was not vulnerable to the previous two objections; if he is non-reductionist, he will not reduce what is morally right to what is non-morally good; but he may still fail to distinguish the morally right from the morally good. The issue about reductionism is separate from the question about the relevance of the good to decisions about the right.

From our previous account, Plato seems to be obviously open to this objection; and indeed we might think he would not regard it as an objection at all. For if he agrees that beliefs about virtue and about the final good should be adjusted to each other, he must agree that a decision about whether an action is virtuous depends on a decision about its contribution to the final good. At the same time, Plato does not imply that a man must always be concerned about his own happiness or the future benefits of his action when he acts. We saw that a virtuous man will display a kind of madness which makes him indifferent to ordinary prudential considerations. He will want to do the kinds of actions he values for themselves, without always considering their effects on his future welfare; as Socrates said, it matters more to live well and justly than to live long (*G.* 512d8–e5). Socrates' own theory of virtue and practical reason could not easily justify this decision; but Plato's theory does better. Plato recognizes that a virtuous man will not always be concerned with future benefits and consequences of actions he thinks worth while, but will still choose the actions, as part of the life he chooses. He can follow the deontologist, and agree that he has sufficient reason to do the virtuous action apart from its consequences.

Aristotle develops this view further. He thinks happiness is the goal of virtue; but he does not say that the virtuous man's dominant motive in acting virtuously is his desire for his own happiness; the virtuous man will choose virtuous action for its own sake (1105a31–2, 1144a19–20), and also 'because it is admirable' or 'for the sake of what is admirable' (*kalon*; 1115b11–13, 20–4, 1117b6–7, 1169a6–11). He will regard certain kinds of actions as worth while in themselves, without reference to their contribution to other goods; and he will even think it worth while to sacrifice all other goods for the sake of outstanding admirable actions (1169a18–b1). The desire to do what is admirable explains the kinds of action which Plato would explain through the good man's madness, and in the same way; a virtuous man thinks virtuous action is such a major component of the final good, that he could not tolerate a life which required the sacrifice of virtuous action. The virtuous man will do what the deontologist expects of him; for he will see that this is the virtuous thing to do, and will do it without reference to his other ends, which would require him to do something else; he decides on the action because it is admirable, not because it will promote his own happiness.

4.5. *The dispute.* However, the deontologist will not be satisfied with this limited agreement; for he still must reject Plato's and Aristotle's view of the grounds of the virtuous man's judgement. Though Aristotle's virtuous man acts for the sake of what is admirable when he sacrifices himself, and may not consider the consequences at all, he does decide that this sort of action on this motive is worth while by reference to happiness. He recognizes that part of the life which secures happiness will be virtuous action for its own sake, without caring about happiness; this is a perfectly coherent plan, and, for Plato and Aristotle, the correct plan. The deontologist must insist, not only on what Plato and Aristotle will accept, that a virtuous man will do what is right whatever the consequences, but also on what they reject, that he can justify his belief that an action is right without reference to his final good. He will argue that even if he did not see how just action could be a good in itself, or even if his conception of the good excluded just action, he would know none the less that just action is right.

The previous deontological objections could be accepted without damage by Plato's teleological theory; but this last one raises the major conflict in principle. And now it is less clear that the deontologist can rely on ordinary convictions and show that the teleologist fails to account for them. The teleologist may reply that our ordinary convictions do not appeal to the good because we are not ordinarily anxious about justification, but when we need justification we need to appeal to the good. On this view, the deontologist notices that we often need no account of the good to move us to act virtuously, and wrongly infers that no account is needed to justify our action; the result is that the deontologist seems to offer no satisfactory justification at all. To explore this question, we should consider first how a Platonic theory is supposed to be better off.

5. *Defences of eudaimonism*

5.1. *Questions.* If some initially plausible (correct or incorrect) beliefs about the character of morality do not undermine a suitably qualified eudaimonism, we may suspect that it has been qualified too severely to say anything interesting. We have insisted that Plato is not a moral solipsist, and that he does not reduce or subordinate morality to principles for achieving some wholly non-moral end. But then is his eudaimonism empty? We should consider some arguments which might be used to support eudaimonism, see whether Plato endorses or requires them, and how strong a thesis they support.

5.2. *Psychological egoism.* Neither Socrates nor Plato nor Aristotle introduces eudaimonism as a controversial moral thesis, or as a piece of moral advice; Socrates seems to assume that it is some kind of psychological fact that everyone pursues happiness. But it is not clear how he would defend it; he faces the familiar problems of psychological egoism. If he presents an empirical thesis, that people often prefer their own interest and pleasure above other ends, there seem to be equally clear counter-examples. And anyhow, the prevalence of this egoistic preference would not show its rationality. We might admit that it is easier to make people virtuous if virtue and interest do not diverge too far; but this admission justifies no ambitious claim about moral rationality.

Perhaps Plato tries a further egoist move, to avoid empirical refutation, of taking an egoistic reference to be necessary for any intelligible action. An egoist theorist might say that we cannot understand why A did x unless we know what was in x for A or what A got out of x. But how is 'what was in it for A' to be understood? (a) If it just means 'A's purpose in doing x', the principle may be true, but it has no egoistic consequences. Perhaps A does each action to achieve some purpose of his, or, we might say, to satisfy his own desires; but it does not follow that each action aims at his own satisfaction, some condition of himself. And so the principle is useless to egoists. (b) If 'what was in it for A' means 'what A gained by it', the egoist conclusion follows, but the principle is question-begging, assuming the truth of egoism in its proof. Some argument resting on a confused and equivocal notion of 'what was in it for A' underlies the feeling of egoist theorists that their view represents some kind of necessary truth about actions and motives, so that they explain away apparent non-egoist actions by the agent's presumed 'underlying' but concealed desire for his own advantage. But no sound argument is available.[19]

5.3. *The demand for a final good.* Socrates or Plato may be influenced by some such fallacious argument in thinking eudaimonism more obviously true than it is; but the arguments they use or suggest are different and less clear. Plato accepts the argument in the *Lysis*, endorsed by Aristotle, that without reference to a final good desire is somehow not worth while.[20] In the *Republic* he insists on a single goal or organize a man's life (519c2–4). Like Aristotle, Plato demands this single goal to decide how far a particular activity should be pursued; without some decision-procedure the various goods pursued are liable to conflict, leaving us with no way to decide which we should prefer on which occasions. If we have arranged them in relation to a final good, we can refer to it in settling disputes, even though we may not always have an effective method of solution. One decision-procedure could be derived from a unitary end, which also avoids some questions about the components of the good; but a unitary end is not necessary for some practical guidance.

5.4. *The virtues.* This demand for a final good to provide a decision-procedure was clear in the progress of elenctic argument, and in Aristotle's doctrine of the mean, which states more formally the principles assumed by Socrates and Plato.[21] He assumes that the mean to be achieved by each virtue is what contributes to happiness. He has no other argument to show that moral rules apply only with exceptions and are unreliable guides to particular cases, which require the sensitive judgement of the wise man. Only the wise man is really competent to pronounce on particular cases, because only he knows what happiness is and how it can be achieved. Aristotle's argument suggests that it will be much harder than a deontologist might have thought to decide what is the right thing to do. For a deontologist, a moral rule prescribes an obligation without reference to the effect of the action on other aims the agent may pursue; and if the agent knows that the situation is the one prescribed by the rule, he can know he has done the right thing if he does what the rule requires. On Aristotle's view, the deontologist simply clings irrationally to the grotesquely oversimplified view which is all a general rule can incorporate; he supposes he can settle the question without knowing all that a wise man knows, and refuses to recognize the real complexity of moral decisions, or to admit the only procedure which will make sense of them.

A deontologist need not be indifferent to the consequences of actions, or suppose that someone who observes separable sets of rules and fulfils separable sets of obligations thereby displays separable virtues; only some deontologists defend themselves by appeal to particular moral rules alleged to be unbreakable whatever the consequences.[22] But Plato or Aristotle must still reject the assumption that moral rules can specify right action without reference to what is best over all. The Platonic view assumes that we understand moral rules, as we understand any other rules, when we see their point, or the point of the practice or institution they are supposed to support. Unless the rules are restricted by attention to some end they promote, we will find different rules prescribing incompatible actions, with no rational decision-procedure. The decision-procedure comes from appeal to the final good.[23]

5.5. *Virtues and conflicts.* The difference between the Platonic and the deontological view emerges clearly from parts of their theories where superficial similarities conceal deeper differences. Plato recognizes a conflict between morality and inclination; when he divides the soul and rejects KSV, he agrees that the desire to act justly or temperately can conflict with emotional and appetitive desires. However, Plato finds a conflict between particular good-independent desires and rational desire for a man's over-all good; for the deontologist, the conflict between duty and interest remains even if this conflict between desires is resolved.[24] In Plato's view, someone who has learnt to adjust his good-independent desires into harmony with his rational plan, and has the right rational plan for achieving his own good, will also do what morality prescribes. For a deontologist, moral principles are always liable to conflict with a man's rational plan for his own good; and he allows no further principles to resolve this conflict. Though both Plato and the deontologist will treat virtue as the rational control of desire, they require different kinds of control; for the deontologist, a man's correct pursuit of his own final good is not the controlling aim, but just one of the aims a virtuous man has to control.

5.6. *Advantages of eudaimonism.* The eudaimonist facing this deontological objection will reply that he faces a question which the deontologist tries to avoid and cannot convincingly answer. Someone has to answer the Platonic question—how he is to live—and the recognized virtues are among the options open to him; why should he choose them? The deontologist cannot reply that moral principles just are the supreme ones; for the appeal to that belief about morality simply raises the question what moral virtues are. He cannot appeal to the (alleged) meaning of 'moral' to infer that there are principles prescribing the recognized virtues which a man has overriding reason to accept; it still remains to be seen whether there are any moral principles, in this sense of 'moral'.

Now apparently the deontologist does not face this question or does not offer what the eudaimonist thinks is a tolerable answer; for he simply asserts that moral principles must be supreme, refusing to justify them as any of Glaucon's three kinds of goods.

The eudaimonist thinks that a tolerable answer must refer to the agent's own good. Here he will claim an advantage over other teleological theorists; for someone who argues, say, that moral principles are those which contribute to the general happiness still needs to show why each man should care about that; and then, Plato will argue, he must also be a eudaimonist if he is to answer the question correctly. We have seen that Platonic eudaimonism does not require solipsism; but it requires examination of solipsist and non-solipsist ends together in rational deliberation about the best kind of life a man can choose for himself. The deontologist may object that it is illegitimate to extend the pattern of prudential justification to morality, and to suppose that morality must either be prudentially justifiable or be unjustifiable. But he is begging the question by assuming that eudaimonistic deliberation is *merely* prudential; it is concerned with what a man will rationally choose for his life as a whole. For a eudaimonist, the sharp distinction between self-interested and moral deliberation rests on a mistakenly narrow view of self-interest. If it is worth while to ask the general question how a man ought to live, and there is some rational procedure to show that morality and other things are good in themselves, then the eudaimonist's procedure deserves consideration; the deontologist offers no clear alternative, and does not show that the question is illegitimate.[25]

This kind of appeal to the final good shows why Plato's and Aristotle's egoism is neither merely a statement of psychological fact nor merely a moral or procedural recommendation. Socrates' account of desire assumes that every desire aims at the final good; but Plato rejects that when he rejects KSV. He makes one empirical assumption—not that everyone pursues happiness, but that elenctic examination will convince the ordinary interlocutor that he will be better off with his choices and desires organized to pursue happiness, with a plan for the best life in which the virtues are goods in themselves. The appeal to a final good is Plato's procedure for asking a question a rational man is right to ask, and for answering it; when the procedure is rightly understood, it is clearer that he does not seek to show that morality promotes a solipsist end, but that it is worth while in itself for someone who correctly decides the kind of life he has best reason to choose.

6. Eudaimonism and altruism

6.1. *More serious objections.* It is easy to agree with many critics of Plato that his eudaimonism conflicts with obvious and basic truths we all accept about the other-regarding character of morality. I have argued so far that these criticisms are unjustified, and that Plato's eudaimonism is not theoretically incapable of recognizing the truth of these convictions. I do not mean that Plato has justified other-regarding virtues, or that no objection is eudaimonism is sound, but only that eudaimonism is in principle compatible with other-regarding virtue and with our more obvious moral convictions. More positively, I have sketched a prima-facie defence of the eudaimonist approach to morality, to show why it might seem the only reasonable answer to a question which every reflective moral agent needs to decide. Further progress with this dispute requires a more detailed scrutiny of the results of eudamonism. I shall consider the Platonic and Aristotelian account of altruism; even if their theory allows the virtuous man to be concerned with other people's interests, it may not justify the right kind of concern.

6.2. *Rational choice and altruism.* We have seen how Plato's account of the altruism displayed in justice and in the philosopher's legislation depends on his theory of love.[26] The philosopher who loves justice and the other moral Forms wants to express them in his own character and actions and to reproduce them in other people's characters and actions. This desire will express itself in different situations in different kinds of action:

1. The Platonic lover will want to improve his beloved, and mould him in the likeness of the Forms.
2. The just man will want his actions to make other people just; and so he will treat them justly, since it is in their interest to be just, and just treatment considers their interest.
3. The Platonic legislator will want to embody the virtues in other people, and so will legislate to make them virtuous.

The same creative desire, expressed in different ways, explains the various other-directed actions, and the vital assumption that a man's virtue is in his own interest explains why the Platonic lover's activities will satisfy the normal requirements of justice. The first activity really contains the other two, though directed to different people; and appropriately enough, a Platonic state requires philosophers bound by love to their fellow-citizens (*R.* 462a9–e2) to display their justice in legislating for them.

Though Aristotle's views on love and friendship differ in important ways from Plato's, they are equally vital for his explanation of why a virtuous man should be just. He recognizes more clearly than Plato that justice requires concern for other people's good, and is therefore the most exacting test of a man's virtue (1129b31–1130a5). But he cannot escape Glaucon's demand to show why justice is a good in itself for the just man; and his answer must rely on his theory of friendship. Friendship creates different kinds of association or community (*koinōnia*); each community needs some kind of justice to achieve the common interest of its members (1159b25–32); political justice achieves this result for the political community (1160a8–14, 1129b17–19). Someone has a reason to be just only in so far as he takes an interest in the community supported by justice; the virtuous man will take an interest in a community and in the good of other members for their own sake, and therefore will choose justice for its own sake. Justice, as in Plato, is worth while only for someone who chooses to display the kind of friendship which requires concern for other people's good for their own sake.

6.3. *Platonic love.* What sort of treatment could be expected from someone with Plato's reasons for altruism? He will love persons as he loves other non-Forms, laws, institutions, theories and so on, in so far as they already exemplify the admirable Forms to some extent, and can be moulded so that they embody them better. The lover will be expected to educate his beloved, and to make him more virtuous. If we agree that a man's virtue is in his own interest, Plato's theory of love allows him to satisfy one of Aristotle's conditions for friendship or love, that it should aim at the beloved's interest for his own sake (*Rhet.* 1380b35–1381a1; *EN* 1166a2–5). Certainly Plato does not state this condition, or show that his account of love will meet it; but there is no reason why it should not. Love of persons is a means of knowledge of the Forms, but it is not only that; since it also expresses the lover's desire to embody the Forms in other people, it does not lose its interest when someone has come to know the Forms. We need not suppose that a person will be exploited, or discarded when he has helped the philosopher to knowledge of the Forms, or that his interests (as seen by the philosopher) will not be reliably promoted; on these points objections to the results of Platonic love are not clearly justified.

6.4. *Reciprocity*. But Plato is open to objection for his view of the beloved's role in the process; the metaphor of the lover as sculptor and the beloved as statue reveals the serious fault (*Phdr.* 252d5–253b1), as though the beloved were simply the passive material which the lover moulds to his own design. Though the beloved responds to the treatment (*Phdr.* 255d3–e2), and some co-operative activity follows (*Symp.* 209c2–7), the initiative and the direction always come from the lover; Plato never recognizes or allows for the relevance of the beloved's own aims and desires, or shows how the lover should take account of them. Admittedly, he speaks only of love between un-equals, where the lover's superior insight might be expected to form the beloved's aims; but the selection of this paradigm for Platonic lovers' ethical aspirations is significant in itself, and Plato offers no ethical account of love between equals.

Some of the faults in Plato's view are repaired by Aristotle, who recognizes co-operative activity, relying on joint initiatives, as the central and best kind of friendship—indeed it is so central that Aristotle finds it hard to explain friendship between unequals. He recognizes the importance of reciprocal esteem and partnership in virtuous activities; real friendship includes consensus (*homonoia*), which results, not simply because people happen to take the same view, but because they have reached it in common by their own deliberation (1167a22–8, b4–9). The direction and initiative does not depend entirely, as it does for Plato, on the superior knowledge of the dominant partner. A Platonic lover would have no reason to care about the aims of his un-enlightened beloved, which should be overridden for his own improvement. Aristotle's insistence on co-operation between equals shows more clearly that the lover will respct his beloved's aims equally with his own, when they decide on their co-operative projects (1167a22–8).

6.5. *Persons and their interests*. But this difference between Plato and Aristotle does not conceal their agreement on a still more basic issue, what it is about the beloved which should be valued, and what the lover should do for the beloved. Plato insists that what the lover loves is the beloved's various admirable qualities, the ways he participates in the Forms; the lover tries to make the beloved exemplify these Forms more fully (*Phdr.* 252d5–e1). The beloved is treated as though he were a bundle of admirable qualities mixed with less admirable ones; and his interest is to have the admirable qualities developed and the less admirable removed—for we still have not questioned the assumption that virtue is in the agent's interests.

Aristotle agrees with this view of the beloved. The virtuous man alone will love his beloved truly for himself and not for any advantage or pleasure to be gained from him (*EN* 1156b7–12). Loving him for himself implies loving him for his own sake, since he is not subjected to any further end of the lover's (1156b9–12); the lover is concerned about him just for what he is, and not for any instrumental benefits. But at the same time Aristotle insists that the virtuous man loves someone else for his virtue (1165b13–22); and this condition explains the first condition, of loving a person for himself. For the 'self' which the virtuous man loves in his beloved is his character; and a virtuous man will love another virtuous character, since only the good deserves his love (1156b7–9, 10–12, 1165b14–17). The virtuous man loves himself by loving what is admirable and virtuous in him (1168b20–1169a6); since a friend is another self whom the lover treats as he treats himself (1170b5–7), he will love his friend for his virtue too. The self to be loved and benefited is a set of admirable qualities, and that self's interest demands their development.

6.6. *Persons and their sakes.* Here we may want to retract our rather hasty agreement that Plato and Aristotle advocate love of persons for their own sakes. If Plato identifies the lover's attitude to his beloved with the sculptor's attitude to promising raw materials for a statue, must he not overlook Aristotle's comment that while a person has a sake, and can be loved for his own sake, an inanimate thing has no sake (1155b27–31), that we care about the interests of a person in quite a different way from the way we care about the good condition of a bottle of wine? Plato's initial conflation of improving and benefiting (*R.* 335a–e) seems to overlook exactly this distinction. While a Platonic lover may value this activity of improving another person for *its* own sake, because the activity is worth while in itself, surely he does not value it for *his*—the beloved's—own sake? Loving a person 'for his own sake' needs more explanation.

When we insist that someone should be loved for his own sake, we sometimes intend to reject purely instrumental concern, not for his own interests in themselves, but only for the sake of something else; concern for someone for his own sake is contrasted with purely exploitative concern. Now we might say that *A* is an exploitative lover if he cares only about moulding *B* closer to *A*'s ideal; *A* will then care about the ideal impersonally, not for *B*'s sake. But this objection to Plato overlooks the original reason for believing that justice is a virtue, that it benefits the agent; that was why justice was explained as control by the rational part, which was found to benefit us. And so if *A* tries to make *B* more just, then, on Plato's view, he is not exploiting *B* for some ideal irrelevant to *B*'s interests; but he is promoting *B*'s overriding interest. We may dispute *A*'s view of what is in *B*'s interest; but we cannot deny that *A* is concerned with *B* for *B*'s own sake, with *B*'s own interests as *A* sees them, and not exploiting *B* for some other end of *A*'s. Plato does not mark Aristotle's distinction between animate things with sakes of their own and inanimate things without them; but his theory does not require neglect of the distinction. Persons, like other animate things, have interests, and a Platonic lover will be non-exploitatively concerned with the beloved's interests.

6.7. *Persons and their value.* However, 'loving someone for his own sake' or 'for himself' may be understood differently, not only as non-exploitative concern, but also as concern for someone for what he is, concern for persons as persons. This important but elusive requirement on altruistic love needs further explanation; what are the relevant features of persons, and does Plato or Aristotle neglect them? Plato could defend himself from his conception of the relevant features of persons; persons have tripartite souls, and have interests including above all the supremacy of reason in the soul; and a Platonic lover who makes his beloved virtuous will be essentially concerned with him as a person. The same defence is explicit in Aristotle; the person or self whom a virtuous man loves and benefits, his own or someone else's, is the character which benefits from being virtuous. On this view, concern for persons' overriding interests and concern for persons as persons must be exactly the same.

One central criticism of this view relies on a broadly Kantian account of the relevant features of persons; a person has desires, aims and projects which are his own, not only because they belong to him, but because they reflect his own initiative, his choice of his own ends.[27] If we value a person's autonomy and initiative in choosing his own ends and affecting his own aims and goals by his own choices, then we shall expect love of persons as persons to respect and develop this aspect of persons. That is one important aspect of Kant's demand to treat rational beings as ends in themselves. If his demand means only 'Be concerned for the interests of rational beings non-exploitatively, apart from any other benefit that may result', Plato and Aristotle are beyond reproach. But if it means 'Treat rational beings as autonomous end-choosers above all else', then a Kantian has reason to complain of Plato and Aristotle.

If A is concerned with B as an autonomous individual, he will respect B and try to develop B's capacity to determine his actions and aims by his own choices. A can also reasonably want B to have the right aims, and to choose what is in B's own interest; but respect for B's autonomy will sometimes exclude coercion of B against his own choice in his own interest. If A loves B for himself, he has reason both to promote B's interest and to reject restrictions of B's freedom even in B's interests. The two demands imply that if A loves B in the right Kantian way, he will face conflicts. It is important not to over-simplify. Respect for B's autonomy does not require total refusal to impede B's freedom to do what he wants; to develop B's capacity for being autonomous, or to prevent him from destroying it, A may have to coerce B against his wants—'forcing him to be free' cannot be avoided. But none the less a Kantian will require A to respect B's freedom to act against B's own interests in cases where a Platonist will see no reason not to coerce B.

The Kantian demand explains part of what might be criticized in Plato's and Aristotle's view that the object of love is the admirable qualities of the beloved. A Platonic lover is primarily concerned with altering someone else to make him more virtuous, so that he achieves his own interests; naturally, then, he values those aspects of someone, and tries to develop them. A Kantian is not exclusively concerned with making someone virtuous, and does not value someone purely for his actual or potential virtue, but also as an autonomous agent. If we suppose that Plato cannot justify love of persons for their own sakes or for themselves because he is not a Kantian, we are wrong; for the Kantian ground is not the only ground for non-exploitative concern for persons' interests. But we are right to suppose that Plato fails to meet a Kantian requirement on love of persons. We have not shown that the requirement is correct or plausible; but if it is, we have found a legitimate objection to Plato's theory.[28]

7. *Altruism and justice*

7.1. *Platonic love and justice.* The basic assumptions of Plato's theory of love explain the just man's just treatment of other people; since justice is in their interest, his efforts to embody justice in them will be in their interest. Admittedly Plato's conception of justice will license actions normally thought flagrantly unjust; if a Platonic ruler decides I will be better off without my income or property, he will think it just to confiscate them and make me more just. This conflict with ordinary views is partly explained by Plato's conception of a man's interests. If this is our only objection to Plato's view of justice, then if we come to agree with him that being just is most of all in a man's interest, we should accept his account of justice.

7.2. *Interests and rights.* However, agreement with Plato about a man's real interests should not remove all our objections to his view of justice. We would be inclined to protest that justice is not concerned only with promoting interests, but also with protecting rights, and that respect for someone's rights may require us to leave him free to harm himself. For present purposes, these are the relevant features of rights:

1. If A has a right to x, then x is due to A, A is morally entitled to x, whatever else we might think it morally best to do to A or do with x; his justified claim to x does not require a proof that his having x will be morally best over all.
2. In particular, some of A's rights give him freedom to claim or not to claim x, as he prefers, and to have his claim granted or his failure to claim respected, whether or not the over-all moral results are best.[29]

The effect of having rights is that A can depend on other people's actions or abstentions apart from the over-all moral results. We might think rights are a good thing to secure people's interests, if we are sceptical about some decisions about their interests. We might say that people will on the whole be better off if they are guaranteed liberty, property and so on, and we do not try to decide in a particular case whether this man will be better off with his property. And we might justify the second kind of right by saying that a man is a better judge of his own interests than other people. This defence of rights would be implausible for cases where we can be justifiably confident that someone will be better off if his right is violated; and in any case we would not be disagreeing with Plato's view that *if* a man's interests are better served by coercing him we should coerce him—we would only be denying that the antecedent of the conditional is fulfilled.

A better defence of rights, apart from implausible agnosticism about other people's interests, can be found in the Kantian demands we have considered. If someone can rely on certain treatment by other people, secured by the first kind of rights, and apart from their views of what would be best over all, he can plan his actions without fear that they will treat him differently for his own or someone else's good; and if he has the second kind of right, he knows that his decisions will in these areas determine other people's treatment of him. Now if we value rational beings as autonomous agents and want their choices of ends and actions to be effective, we have reason to accord rights to them; the same Kantian principles which demand love for persons that respects their autonomy demand just treatment by other people which respects their rights, even sometimes against their interests.

7.3. *Objections to Plato*. If we recognize this value in rights, then justice raises the problems raised by love of persons; we face a conflict between promoting someone's interests and respecting his rights. To explain the objections to Plato we need not insist that rights always have priority, that we would never be morally justified in violating a man's rights for his own good; we need only agree that this conflict can arise, that respect for rights cannot easily be recognized in principles of justice which are simply concerned with people's interests. Plato's moral theory, like Aristotle's, accords rights to no one; no one has a valid moral claim to treatment which does not produce the morally best results. Plato assumes that justice will always benefit the recipient; but he recognizes no duties of justice which protect a man's rights even against his own interests.

Plato's view of justice ignores rights for the same reason that his view of love ignores Kantian respect for persons as persons. He is concerned with persons as bearers of interests; morality requires the development of those admirable features which better promote someone's interests. Since Plato sees no special value attached to a person as an autonomous agent choosing for himself, he has no reason to respect the freedom of persons when it conflicts with their interests. He advocates the same attitude to persons in love and in justice; and the same Kantian objections apply each time.

7.4. *Freedom*. Some central rights protect a man's freedom from coercion by other people, even in his own interest; and we might think that Plato's major error is his under-valuing of freedom. If he recognized that freedom is in a man's interest, could he not have met the Kantian objections without recognizing a separate category of rights? Now Plato's political theory in the *Republic* under-values freedom; the *Laws* recognizes it, and Aristotle's *Politics* is still nearer a fair estimate. But this improvement in Plato's view of a man's interest would not by itself remove the Kantian objection. For if freedom is one good among others, why could it not sometimes be overriden by some other good? If its moral claim is only its benefits to the agent, then the agent suffers no moral loss if his freedom is overridden for his benefit. But if someone has a right to freedom, he does suffer a moral loss when his freedom is violated in his own interest. Even if we sometimes think it is justifiable on the whole to violate someone's rights in his own interest, we still recognize a conflict of moral considerations, not simply a weighing of interest; a Platonic view of justice removes any such conflict. We cannot explain why justice should protect rights against a man's interests if rights are valid only when their exercise is in the right-holder's interests; and so we cannot explain the value we attach to justice if we agree with Plato that only the interests of persons are relevant to their moral treatment.

7.5. *Reasons for Plato's view.* We have considered three aspects of Plato's theory; (1) his teleological eudaimonism; (2) his view that persons are valuable for their admirable qualities; (3) his view that love and justice should promote people's interests. We began the inquiry to see if his defence of altruism is open to criticism. Now to see whether or not it is open to justifiable criticism, we must decide whether he can avoid our criticisms of (2) and (3); must he accept (2) and (3) or something even less defensible? Plato's description of 'propagating virtue' is vague enough; but neither he nor Aristotle can easily escape (2) and (3). For their teleological conception requires the virtuous man to find some coherent overall plan for a good life in which altruistic activities must fit. The Platonic and the Aristotelian account of love fit it into this plan; for the virtuous man will see why concern for other people's good is part of his own good. Plato emphasizes that altruistic activities will fulfil the just man's creative desire to embody justice in the world; Aristotle emphasizes that co-operative concern for other people will be a part of any life which fully satisfies a man's rational capacities. We can readily agree that they need to justify concern for other people's interests; but if concern for rights is also needed, and it sometimes conflicts with concern for interests, then a morally satisfactory theory has to include an area of conflict. This area is exactly what Plato and Aristotle hope to avoid with their teleological theory; but if an adequate theory must include views of love and justice which allow conflict, their teleological demands prevent them from finding an adequate theory. It is no accident, then, that their theory accepts (2) and (3), and allows no concern for rights apart from interests; it is to that extent a consistently teleological theory. We have not shown that the demands which cause trouble for a teleological theory are legitimate—that would require much longer inquiry; but if they are at all plausible, our worries about Plato's account of altruism reflect a basic difficulty in his theory which deserves to be further explored.

8. Eudaimonism and moral decision

8.1. *General principles*. This problem about altruism suggests a more general problem about the capacity of a eudaimonist theory to justify central moral requirements. We have defended Plato against the charge of solipsism, or indifference to other people's interests. At the same time we have found that the appeal to a final good is not innocuous; it implies demands on moral principles which the deontologist rejects. We have suggested ways the eudaimonist might make his position initially plausible against deontological objections. But now some more difficult questions arise; the previous objections to the eudaimonist view of altruism suggest that Plato's views may conflict not only with some deontologist convictions, but with more basic features of recognized morality.

Plato's eudaimonism requires all virtuous action, including altruistic action, to be justified by reference to the final good; if it is not instrumental to some other good, it must be good in itself, and part of the final good. Plato should not listen to a defence of altruism which presents it as a psychological necessity; even if someone has strong altruistic sentiments, perhaps he ought to restrain them as far as possible for his own good, and Plato expects a vindication of altruistic virtue to refute this objection.[30] Now admittedly it is not clear how we show that something is a component of the final good; but as far as Plato tries to show this, we have considered how altruistic actions might meet his conditions.

8.2. *The problem*. Even if Plato shows that some altruistic actions promote the final good, how often will altruistic action be justified? If altruistic virtue is just one component of the final good, then apparently it should be pursued so as to avoid conflict with the other components. Any alleged requirement of justice which conflicts with other components of the good and the virtues which secure them will not be a genuine requirement of justice; for Plato and Aristotle agree that real virtues do not conflict (cf. *MM* 1199b36–1200a11). And even if an alleged moral requirement does not conflict with the final good, there would be no reason to do it, on Plato's view, unless it positively contributed to the final good; otherwise it is not a real moral requirement.

If the previous remarks on justice and rights were correct, Plato's requirement will exclude some of the central right-protecting actions. A Platonist can defend concern for other people's interests; but he cannot defend concern for a man's rights against his own or other people's interests. A deontologist will see a moral obligation which can be overridden only by a more stringent moral obligation; a Platonist cannot be expected to find any obligation. If we have found the right connection between justice and rights, then Plato's demand for a coherent, mutually supporting final good underlying moral choice cannot justify the right moral principles.

8.3. *Plato's defence.* Plato and Aristotle might appeal to the virtuous man's 'madness', or his determination to pursue what is admirable, despite the cost to his other ends. But how far will this reply help? Aristotle does not normally suggest that the requirement of admirable action prescribe by a particular virtue will conflict with the requirements of other components of the final good. But when he recognizes a conflict, in cases of self-sacrifice, he suggests that a virtuous man will regard admirable action as such a vital component of the final good that life without it would not be worth while for him (1169a18–29). This kind of argument might explain the heroic virtue displayed in self-sacrifice; someone might argue that this admirable action compensates for all the other goods it requires him to forgo. But will it cope so plausibly with less spectacular cases of virtue? A generous man, for instance, may sometimes have to choose between generous action and securing the resources he needs for other goods he pursues, including his future generosity (cf. 1120a23–9, b2–11, 14–20, 1169a26–9); how does he decide? Does he argue that his future life would not be worth while if he failed to do this generous action now? That would be a strange argument; how could Aristotle show that someone concerned with the final good has reason to do trivial acts of generosity, at whatever cost to his other ends, just because they are admirable? Where a deontologist might recognize an obligation to generous action, knowing full well that a failure would not deprive his life of a major good, an Aristotelian must apparently treat any admirable and virtuous action as a major good justifying the sacrifice of all others; and it is hard to see what coherent or useful account of the good can be constructed to accommodate this view of virtuous action.

Plato and Aristotle face a dilemma about the relation of virtuous action and the final good:

1. They can design their theory to accommodate the deontologist's view that moral obligations should be observed despite their irrelevance to, or conflict with, the final good; then they must appeal to action for the sake of what is admirable. But then the original purpose of their appeal to the good is in danger of frustration. For we no longer have a clear rational plan to determine priority-rules and delimit the right scope for each virtue. The appeal to the final good was attractive because it seemed to promise a clear rational account of morality which would avoid the deontologist's picture of a mere inexplicable heap of obligations liable to conflict with each other, and with the rational choice of goods. But if the value of admirable action is interpreted to suit the deontologist, we apparently reintroduce the heap of conflicting values in our account of the good.[31] It will include a series of virtuous actions, each of which is admirable enough to be pursued at any cost, and we have not been shown why these actions are good by reference to their contribution to some orderly, systematic final good.

2. Alternatively, they may insist on the regulative, organizing role of the final good, and maintain that though virtuous action is one of the various goods worth pursuing, it must stick to its place; other goods have their claims too, and the virtues must not absorb undue attention which would frustrate the over-all good. If they allow the final good to determine the scope of the virtues this way, they cannot accept the deontologist's assumption about the stringency of moral obligations. An action will be worthwhile because of its contribution to the final good, and no type of action can claim to be worthwhile despite its cost to prospects for achieving the final good.

8.4. *The problem in eudaimonism.* The second horn of the dilemma will leave the rest of Plato's theory intact and retain all the theoretical benefits of eudaimonism. But it will mean that suspicion of Plato's egocentrism is not altogether mistaken, even though the more obvious objections failed. For we cannot now count on the eudaimonist to pursue other people's interests, let alone other people's rights, irrespective of his other rational aims. He will not be indifferent to other people, or care about them only for his own solipsistic ends. But his concern for their interests will reflect only one of his rational aims; while it will no doubt be a prominent aim, we have no reason to expect it will always be his dominant aim, at whatever cost. If we count on a virtuous man to respect other people's rights and promote their interests, whether or not he will achieve the good he pursues, we will not be satisfied with

Plato's view on moral obligation. The appeal to rational choice and a final good limited the concern a Platonist could allow for other people to concern for their interests, not their rights; and we have found that the same appeal limits the stringency of his rational concern for their interests. I have not defended the moral position which involves the principles rejected by Plato's theory; but if they are at least apparently attractive, they raise important objections to Plato.

8.5. *Further questions.* However, we should not let the question rest there; for here as earlier we may excusably suspect that the deontologist avoids a legitimate question which the eudaimonist is raising. Even if we agree that the grounds of moral obligations cannot be explained by appeal to an agent's final good, questions about their justification can easily seem to involve this appeal. First of all, suppose the deontologist is right in saying that the obligatory character of actions does not depend on an account of the agent's good showing these actions to be worth while; can he argue that we always have reason to observe a trivial obligation at the cost of some major good? Perhaps we have reason from what he regards as the moral point of view; but it still remains to be seen whether we have reason over all to do what we have reason to do from the moral point of view. And here Plato can insist that what we have reason to do over all is what contributes to the best life over all, when moral and non-moral goods are included. Whether the deontologist denies or affirms that we always have reason to observe moral obligations, he can fairly be asked for some defence. And unless he says the answer is intuitively obvious or rationally undecidable, Plato's procedure for finding a defence seems to be plausible enough. It is not so clear that the eudaimonist's failure to justify the pursuit of deontological morality in all conditions, whatever the cost, shows a fault in his theory; we might agree that morality should not be supreme in all conditions; and to find the right conditions, we seem to face Plato's question about when it is worth while for a man to be just.

If we are reluctant to decide firmly for either Plato or his critics, we are perhaps influenced by a deeper issue in morality. We are inclined to believe that (1) the requirements of morality do not depend on the agent's good; (2) we are normally justified in observing moral requirements above others. Someone who demands a justification which makes morality instrumental to a solipsistic final good can fairly be criticized; but Plato is immune to this criticism. When Plato's demand to be shown how morality contributes to the best life for the agent is rightly understood, it is hard to reject; but if we accept it, it seems to raise questions about our initial view of the requirements of morality. Now perhaps one of these two assumptions is false, or they can be understood so as to avoid a conflict. But if we are attracted to both of them, and do not see a clear resolution of the conflict, we have reason to sympathize both with Plato's demand and with his critics. A decision does not emerge from any easily found and obviously correct moral or practical principles, but requires further inquiry into still more complex issues. I have tried only to discuss the question far enough to show what is wrong with the easy objections to Plato, and to show what the difficult issues are.

9. *Virtues as states of persons*

9.1. *Virtue and the soul.* One puzzling and clearly controversial aspect of Plato's moral theory is its eudaimonism. We have previously mentioned another equally puzzling, though less discussed claim, that virtue is a good state of the soul to be valued for itself apart from its results in action. He goes beyond Socrates' claim that the virtuous action can be defined only by reference to virtues in an agent, and insists on the value of virtue apart from action; that is why both the *Phaedo* and the *Republic* stress the value of virtue in the soul, and say much less than we would expect from some modern moralists about the importance of virtuous action. Plato does not argue for his emphasis. He is influenced by his psychophysical dualism and his contemplative ideal to believe that the soul is more important than the body, and its inner life more important than actions which require interaction with the sensible world. But still his view rests on principles of more general ethical interest, which themselves partly explain his attraction to the contemplative ideal.[32]

9.2. *Grounds for Plato's demands.* If Plato is right to value virtue as a state of the soul, we must agree that virtuous motives, and not only virtuous actions, deserve to be valued for themselves. We might try to explain a high estimate of a virtuous man with the right motives by his reliability; someone who acts generously because he is generous and chooses generous action for itself (this does not imply that he must always reflect that this is the generous thing to do) can be relied on to decide on the generous action even when other inducements are removed. But reliability will not fully explain the high estimate of virtuous men for their motives; if the other inducements were always readily available, and the 'slavish' man did the right thing as often as the virtuous man, we would still tend to agree with Plato that the virtuous man's motives are preferable, and that he deserves higher praise for them.

To explain our attitude to virtuous men and their motives, we must, as Plato argues, abandon the view encouraged by some more recent ethical theory, that we are interested in people's being virtuous because we are interested in the actions we can expect from them, or that our moral estimate of persons depends on their capacities as sources of good actions. This restriction of interest in virtue sounds implausible as soon as it is clearly stated. Association with other persons as moral agents involves more than concern with their actions; we can also reasonably care about their attitude to other people. Since other people are sources of deliberation, feelings, attitudes, as well as actions, these aspects of a person can be morally valued, apart from their results.

9.3. *The self-sufficiency of virtue.* But if this line of argument roughly suggests why other people might value a man's virtuous state of soul, why should he value it himself? Socrates' and Plato's eudaimonism again influences their answer. A man who rationally chooses virtue should convince himself that being virtuous is best for him in all conditions. In good conditions it will produce good results for him; he will express his own ideals in the world. But this is not enough to make someone reliably virtuous; if these are his only reasons, he will not want to be virtuous when conditions are bad and his virtuous action fails to produce the intended results. Plato argues that if virtue is worth while even in these conditions, a man should know that he has chosen the condition of soul best for himself whatever happens.

Socrates accepts this view of the value of virtue when he suggests that the good man cannot be harmed, and that he is always worse off if he becomes less virtuous. One of his central concerns is to show that the achievement of happiness depends on the agent himself and his voluntary choices, not on advantages like good birth, wealth, or power, beyond the agent's control. He advises people to care for their souls; anyone can do this, and will see he did what was best for himself whatever happens. But Socrates cannot justify his claim within his own theory of virtue. For he treats virtue as a craft, valuable for its results; and if the right materials are not available, or the production always goes awry from no fault of the producer, why is it still worth while to possess the craft? Socrates assumes in the *Crito* and *Gorgias*

that it is always worth while to be just, even if his justice has some disastrous results for him; but the CA cannot explain why; and Plato
rightly insists in *Republic* II that Socrates has not answered the
hardest question.[33]

Plato argues in the *Republic* that it is worth while for someone to be
p-just, to have his soul ordered the p-just way, even if the results are
disastrous. Even if we could secure other goods with unjust souls, we
would be wrong to prefer them over a just soul. For Plato argues that
those other goods will be really good only for someone who has his
soul rightly ordered; wealth or power or honour uncontrolled by p-
justice will simply satisfy someone's appetitive or emotional desires,
and will not belong to a way of life which satisfies and fulfils his
capacities and aims harmoniously. The p-just soul is the best guide to
action; but even if it fails in action, there is no other psychic order
which a rational man will prefer; and so p-justice is best in success or
failure. The best someone can do is to arrange his decisions and aims
the p-just way; and so he has no reason to reproach himself if his
plans fail through no fault of his.

9.4. *Plato's defence.* Many deontological moralists will agree with
Plato and Aristotle (*EN* 1100b7–11, 22–35) that it is always worth
while to be virtuous. Even if they think moral requirements prescribe
what benefits people in general, not the agent in particular, they do not
argue that a virtuous man should reproach himself, or regret his
choice, if his efforts fail, or that he thereby becomes less virtuous.
Plato's insistence on the value of being just can easily sound like
Kant's insistence on the value of having a good will, neither increased
by success nor reduced by failure.[34] The difference is equally clear; for
a deontologist will reject Plato's effort to prove that being just is good
for the agent, as he rejects any other efforts to connect virtue with the
agent's happiness by Plato's line of argument.

Here again our sympathies may reasonably be divided. We may
think that Plato's defence of justice simply tries to force morality into
an alien pattern of justification; and the more he tries to describe the
p-justice which benefits the soul, the harder it is to connect with the
justice which benefits other people. But if we agree with the deontologist that someone still has reason to be virtuous and value his virtue even in failure, we should offer some defence. And here again Plato
can argue that his line of defence is the best—the virtuous soul is in a
condition we would choose for itself as part of a good life whatever the
results. We may then decide to reject the deontologist's view, and ad-

mit that someone has no reason to be virtuous if the world regularly frustrates his efforts at virtuous action. But in so far as we are inclined to believe that a man can choose a way of life which he has reason to maintain and welcome whatever the consequences, Plato's demand retains some force.

We are inclined to think of moral virtue as a way of acting on the world to achieve morally desirable results; and our tendency to look at the moral agent from other people's point of view strengthens this inclination. Plato considers the question from the agent's point of view; how should he choose to be, whether the world is favourable or adverse to his actions? We may doubt if there is a general answer to this question; but Plato can fairly argue that it is worth while to see if an answer can be found, so that someone can control his own happiness apart from his good or bad fortune in actions. The deontologist also thinks that someone can choose a condition which will always be supremely worth while for him; but as long as he does not show that a Platonist's demand for a good life for himself is illegitimate, Plato's claim that a virtuous soul is always good for the agent has not been refuted.

9.5. *Knowledge and virtue.* One part of the virtue which Plato values for itself deserves special attention. He always accepts KNV, and part of the value of virtue is the value of knowledge; but a defence of the value of knowledge raises other problems for him. The virtuous man must know what his virtue is, and offer some account of it. He must choose virtue for itself; but has has good reason to choose it as a good in itself only if he knows what it is and explains why it is a good in itself. If he can give an account of its goodness, he does not depend purely on habit or custom for his desire to pursue virtue for itself, but relies on what he accepts as good reasons. Socrates' inquiries stimulate rejection of habitual, unreflective morality; though we did not find that Socrates valued moral rationality as a good in itself, apart from its results, Plato does value it for itself. The attitude we might have thought appropriate for Socrates is more clearly developed in the middle dialogues.

Plato's view that knowledge is necessary for virtue is the reason for his restriction of virtue to philosophers; but despite this bizarre result, the condition itself should not be dismissed. Whether or not we would agree with Plato in thinking it a necessary condition for virtue, his claim that a moral estimate of someone should be guided by the way he holds his moral beliefs is perfectly defensible; we will not think it irrelevant that *A* has reached his beliefs by rational reflection and by efforts to justify his beliefs, while *B* holds the same beliefs because he has been taught them and has never bothered to criticize them, even if both *A* and *B* do the same actions. Plato rightly insists that it is worth while in itself, and can fairly be expected of a virtuous man, to try to defend and justify moral beliefs rationally. His mistake is to think that this kind of justification requires the capacities and training of the philosopher in the *Republic*; what they learn may be important, but he is wrong to suggest that it is worth while to try a rational justification of moral beliefs only for those who can achieve the complete success expected of philosophers. Self-conscious critical reflection, efforts to reconcile and justify moral beliefs and judgements about the good—this is the procedure for seeking moral understanding, for Plato as for Socrates; we should be less inclined to challenge the demand than the arguments or assumptions which imply that only philosophers satisfy it. We might claim that someone who seeks to examine, understand, and justify his beliefs as far as he can is thereby better off, without claiming that everyone has to reach the same kind of understanding; to claim that someone who has done that is more virtuous than someone who has not done it is not to condemn the other man, but only to say that the virtuous man has some state of character which is good for him. Plato's basic demand is not at all obviously indefensible.

9.6. *Problems for Plato*. However, the most plausible defence of this demand raises awkward questions about the rest of Plato's theory. A demand for knowledge and justification insists on first-hand rational beliefs; the really virtuous man must choose virtue for himself, for his own reasons, not on some second-hand support—custom, authority, training, and the rest. To value this pattern of choice, we must think it worth while in itself that a man should exercise his own independent rational capacities in adopting his beliefs; that is, we must value one part of what Kant includes in autonomy.[35] We must argue that Plato's demand includes part of what a self-directed rational agent should try to do. But it is this value attached to autonomy and to first-hand decisions which would justify the kind of respect for persons which prohibits violation of their freedom and rights. Now we have seen that this kind of respect is quite foreign to Plato's views on concern for other people. He assumes the legitimacy of his demand for knowledge as part of virtue, and values for itself the rational, self-conscious, self-justifying moral beliefs sought by Socrates. But to explain why this is desirable for itself, he must appeal to principles with moral consequences he does not notice.

Platos avoids the awkward consequences by restricting the scope of his demand. If we think it worth while to encourage an individual's efforts to find a rational justification for his own beliefs, we must face the possibility that sometimes he will find the wrong answers, and will have the wrong moral beliefs, which will not (in Plato's view) be in his interest. We must choose, then, either to encourage autonomy, or to secure correct beliefs, or to aim at some compromise. Plato avoids the need for these awkward choices by restricting rational assessment of beliefs to those who can be relied on, because of their intellectual capacities and their strenuous moral and intellectual training, to get the right answer—the carefully selected and carefully taught philosopher class in the *Republic*. He will not take the risk that other people may reach views against their interests, and does not admit a right that might conflict with their interests.

The demand for moral rationality and autonomy is not allowed to conflict with the rest of Plato's eudaimonism, or with his concern for the interests of other people against their rights. But someone who doubts that it is worth while only for someone who will get the right answers to ask moral questions will find that the view of persons justifying his doubts will also justify doubts about the rest of Plato's eudaimonist theory; for as soon as a moral theory must recognize autonomous persons bearing rights, the Platonic pattern is seriously disrupted. The danger of disruption can be found already in the demand, not fully understood or explained, for someone to give an account of his moral beliefs, which leads Socrates and Plato into moral philosophy.

9.7. *Conclusion.* I have tried to suggest how some of Plato's major doctrines might be attacked and defended; my survey has been incomplete, and has included hasty and superficial treatment of ethical questions which deserve close examination. I have not tried to reach a definite decision for or against Plato, but only to show what questions might usefully be raised about the doctrines we have discussed in previous chapters. We noticed early in this book that Plato offers us no systematic treatise on ethics. But his theories are not of merely historical or anthropological interest; though his questions are not immediately familiar to us, they can be defended as legitimate moral questions; and some of his answers at least deserve our serious efforts at refutation. I have suggested that our efforts will not always succeed at once; and though I have not examined all plausible objections to Plato, I have tried to show how his position can be defended at least against some criticisms. His questions and answers retain their interest for anyone who cares about moral theory.

NOTES

1. On these 'cardinal' virtues see Bluck (601), on *M.* 74a3, Adam (701), on *R.* 427e. They are discussed further by Cornford (719), 247–58. Definite pre-Platonic evidence is harder to find; but see North (212), 25, 41, 72, 124, who refers to Pindar, *Is.* 8.24–8, Aesch. *Sep.* 610, Eur. fr. 282 (which adds eloquence to the list), Xen. *Mem.* 4.1.16 (cf. also 3.9.1–5).

2. On the 'unity of virtue' see III.14.1, IV, n. 3, V, n. 18.

3. For the functional view of *aretē* and *agathon* see *M.* 72a 1–5, Xen. *Mem.* 3.8.2–3. *HMi.* 373c6 shows the problem raised by the extension of the functional view from *aretē* in a particular role to the *aretē* of a man in general; but unless the extension seemed natural, Socrates' arguments would lack the prima-facie plausibility they are clearly supposed to have.

4. On this argument see VII.2.2.

5. These remarks on Homer are an over-simplified summary, agreeing entirely neither with Adkins (207), 31–46, nor with Long (211). (Adkins replies in (208).) Adkins's views, especially on 'competitive' and 'cooperative' virtues, are well discussed by Creed (209), 214 f.

6. 'Law-conception' is borrowed from Anscombe (802), 191 f (who, however, mistakenly thinks it is not a Greek, but only a Hebraic and post-Reformation view of morality). 'Law' is not wholly suitable for '*nomos*', which includes all kinds of *nomoi* saying what is 'expected' or 'recognized' (*nomizesthai*) or 'the rule'—conventions, habits, customs, positive law, and also what is right or 'lawful' (*nomimon*). There is no reason to suppose any difference in the sense of '*nomos*' is recognized in these different contexts. The denial or recognition of differences in the importance, stringency, grounds and justifiability of these different kinds of *nomoi* is an important area of controversy among Socrates' contemporaries; see below 3.6, 4.4, 4.6. But 'law' is not too bad as a rough equivalent, in so far as many Greeks regard moral and legal (as we would say) *nomoi* as parts of a single set of norms for regulating communal life, with or without a divine or human legislator. But to avoid distortion, it would be as accurate to say they have an ethical view of law, since the laws are not sharply distinguished from other *nomoi*.

7. I have tried to express roughly the general difference between 'earlier' and 'later' views. Adkins (207), 67, 153, and elsewhere, recognizes the different demands, but maintains that 'the Greeks in general were too hard-headed to be just if it were not visibly advantageous to do so', so that he denies the difference in predominant motives I have suggested (see also Snell (206), ch. 8). But I see no evidence of widespread hard-headedness in the Greeks more than in anyone else; for counter-evidence see O'Brien (124), 26–39. Lloyd-Jones (205), 35 f, is sceptical about any radical change in expectations or in motives.

8. Adkins (207), 228 f, argues that Meno thinks that if justice is required for virtue it must be a means of success in private and public life, and only derivatively desirable. Nothing like this is said or implied. Adkins must explain it this way to support his thesis that the ordinary man thinks justice and so on are only a means to success measured by Homeric standards. This thesis itself is highly dubious; see Creed (209), 218–31. Meno's readiness to admit both Homeric qualities and justice as virtues without being sure which is prior to which corresponds well with the fifth-century evidence.

9. Cf. Thuc. 2.35.1, and other evidence cited by Creed (209), 219, n.6.

10. On the extension of Laches' view of courage see III, n. 7. Cf. Isoc. *Panath.* 31 f, Democritus, B214.

11. Cf. Homer, *Od.,* 23.13, 30, 4.158–60, *Il.* 21.462–4, discussed by North (212), 3–6. We should reject, however, her suggestion that when *sōphrosunē* refers to good sense in one's own interest, this is a 'non-moral' use of the term—this is a misleading assumption about any of the Greek authors considered here.

12. The fused concepts covering both (what we should call) cognitive and affective conditions are discussed by O'Brien (124), 39–54, who effectively rebuts the view of, e.g., Dodds (202), 17, that the Socratic paradoxes represent a traditional Greek tendency to explain action by reference to cognitive conditions alone.

13. The association of *sōphronein* and *eu phronein* in *Pr.* 333d5 is exploited by Socrates for argumentative purposes, but it represents one belief about *sōphrosunē.* Cf. Hdt. 3.71.3, and other evidence cited by Adkins (207), 247 f, and North (212), 77.

14. *Hēsuchia;* Santas (345), 107 n. *Apragmosunē;* North (212), 156.

15. Justice and temperance combined are treated as the whole virtue of a good man or good citizen, at *M.* 73b2–3 (see VI, n. 5), *Phd.* 82b, *Symp.* 209a, *Pr.* 325a; and this is taken to be a standard view in all those passages. The rejection of temperance; *V.* 3.3; cf. Aristoph. *Nub.* 1071–4. It is hard to find anyone else who explicitly denounces what he calls *sōphrosunē;* its association with good sense and *aretē* make people less inclined to say '*Sophrosune* is bad'. The other examples of 'opposition to *sōphrosunē*' quoted by North (213), 4–14, all seem to be examples of unusual beliefs (even Thuc. 3.82.4), rather than of explicit opposition to *sōphrosunē* itself. Aristophanes and Plato's Callicles, for their different purposes, seem to be emphasizing what they take to be an awkward consequence of ordinary views on *sōphrosunē,* not simply reporting widespread explicit opposition.

16. Justice and piety; III, n. 57, *Eu.* 4b7–c7 reflects an old, though not universal, opposition to a purely ritualistic view of piety, such as that presented in *R.* II; see Hesiod, *Op.* 225–47, Solon, 1.7–32, and, still more clearly, Aesch. *Supp.* 381–6, *Ag.* 67–71. Euthyphro's claim that his action is pious is not wild or fanatical, but a scrupulous defence of the primacy of justice in piety. The fear of pollution from unjust killing is genuine; see Antiphon, *Tetr.* 1.1.10, Soph. *Ant.* 372, Harrison (222), I.169 f. Contrast Grote (105), I.315 f, Allen (344), 20–2.

17. Justice as the whole of virtue; Theog. 147 ff, Adkins (207), 78 ff. Helping friends and harming enemies; Hom. *Od.* 6.184 f, Theog. 337–50, and often (Adam (701), on *R.* 331e, Adkins, 279, n. 6). Usually this is treated as virtue in general (cf. *M.* 71e) rather than as justice specifically (except Xen. *Cyr.* 1.6.31); it is associated with justice because justice can also be taken as virtue in general, as in *R.* 332a. Justice as law-observance; Xen. *Mem.* 4.4.13–18, Anon. Iamb. 3.6, Ps.–Dem. 25–15, Guthrie (203), III.75f. The same view is presented less sympathetically in Critias, B25.5–8, Antiphon, B44A, col. 2.31–col. 3.25 (pp. 348 f). It is wittily attacked in *Mem.* 1.2.41–6, and more elaborately in the *Minos;* III. 6.3, n. 23. The broad range of *nomos* and *nomimon* explains the attraction, and also the weakness, of this view of justice as *nomos*-observance; see above, n. 6. Protagoras' account of human virtue; IV, n. 2.

18. '*Sophos*' and '*sophia*' are commonly applied to practical shrewdness in life, the kind of 'wisdom' recommended by the 'Seven Sages' (Theog. 1074 f, Hdt. 1.20.2) as well as to skill in crafts (Hom. *Il.* 15.412, Pind. *Ol.* 7.53), and to less exalted kinds of adroitness (Hdt. 1.60.3). '*Phronimos*' is used similarly. Eur. fr. 52.9, Aristoph. *Lys.* 42, 507. '*Phronēsis*' seems to be rare in this sense before Socrates; but cf. Democritus, B119, 193. On the importance of *phronēsis* see Adkins (207), 244–6, and on the moral ambiguity of wisdom see O'Brien (124), 30–9.

19. The importance of craft-knowledge; O'Brien (124), ch. 2, Guthrie (203), III, ch. 10. Plato follows normal usage in regularly allowing the inference from '*A epistatai x*'

to '*A* has the *technē* of *x*', and vice versa; see Lyons (132), 159–63. This easy inference makes it hard, but also important, for Plato to claim in the middle dialogues against Socrates that moral knowledge is *epistēmē*, but not *technē*; see VI. 5.2.
20. On Euripides see Walsh (129), 16–22. It is not clear how far this talk of psychic conflict is crystallized in a division of the soul anticipating Plato's later theory; see V, n. 17, VII. 6.3. Burnet (201), 296n., and Stocks (731), 168–71, claim a Pythagorean origin for tripartition, but it is hard to find good evidence of a division within one soul, as opposed to a division between different souls with different kinds of lives (as in *R*. IX; see VII, n. 62).
  The connection between virtue and craft is not at all intuitive to Greeks; cf. Anon. Iamb. 2.7, O'Brien (124), 77. Nor does everyone agree in associating teaching with a craft; *M*. 92e3–6, 95d3–e1. Socrates and the sophists are on the same side here.
21. The connection between the *Pr.* and the *Tht.*; see Vlastos (401), xvii f. (on *Pr.* 356d3–4; see IV. 3.2), xxiii f, Kerferd (218). I have tried to combine, as I think Protagoras does, the 'subjectivist' and 'utilitarian' aspects of his doctrine, which Cole (215) tries to separate (unconvincingly, I think).
22. I assume, following *M*. 95c, that Gorgias is a sophist. See Guthrie (203), III, 39n., Harrison (217). Contrast Dodds (501), 7.
23. The position of Callicles closely resembles that of the 'young oligarchs' addressed by Athenagoras, Thuc. 6.38.5. There is no inconsistency between his holding oligarchic views and being a politician in a democracy, for his personal advancement, as Alcibiades elegantly explains in Thuc. 6.89.4. It is suitable that Callicles should be a friend of Andron, one of the Four Hundred (*G*. 487c3; see Dodds (501), ad loc.).
24. I have assumed that Thrasymachus defines justice as 'the interest of the stronger' in 338c (contrast Hourani (708), refuted by Kerferd (709)), and that this definition is consistent with his remark in 343c that justice is another's good; contrast Kerferd (710), supported by Nicholson (711), who believes that 'another's good' is Thrasymachus' real definition of justice. Briefly, Thrasymachus' position is consistent as long as justice and injustice are ascribed only to subjects of some superior (*kreittōn*). The unjust man of 343 ff, is not a *kreittōn* within the meaning of Thrasymachus' definition; he is an office-holder (343e1–2) in a democracy, where the people are the collective *kreittōn* (338e7–339a4). Someone acts unjustly if he rebels against the regime, but when his unjust acts are completed (*ēdikēkota*, 344c2) and he has become tyrant, Thrasymachus no longer says he is unjust. A ruler is neither just nor unjust in pursuing his own interests, and there is no conflict with the original definition. Not only individuals but also states can be regarded as a collective *kreittōn* for the purposes of the definition; and in 358b1–3 a state is only said to be unjust when it undertakes (*epicheirein*) to enslave other states, not when it *is* their ruler (cf. Thuc. 2.63.2; it was unjust to acquire (*labein*) the empire).
  Thrasymachus' and Glaucon's views on justice may be compared with the view of Thuc. 5.89, that justice depends on equal compulsion. In a normal state a superior compels people equally, and they act justly, as in the agreement imagined by Glaucon; but wars and other disturbances remove the equal compulsion, and give people reason to be unjust, 3.82.2, and the absence of stable compulsion to be just gives reason to each state to increase its own power and security without concern for justice, 5.105.2, 1.76.2. These speakers in Thucydides agree with Thrasymachus and Glaucon that justice depends on compulsion by a stronger party, individual or collective.
25. On the sense of '*eudaimonia*' see III. 4.4. Some common views are suggested by *Eud*. 279a ff, which does not distinguish components of happiness and instrumental means to it (cf. III. 13.2). Cf. *M*. 78c, *G*. 451e. Adkins (207), 252–4, wrongly suggests that Socrates accepts such common conceptions of *eudaimonia* at face value and tries to show that the recognized virtues contribute to *eudaimonia*, so understood. We shall find Socrates' view rather more complicated; see III. 13.7.

26. My remarks on Democritus generally follow Vlastos (214). Guthrie (203), II. 489–97, is more sceptical about the authenticity of the relevant fragments of Democritus. But it is unsafe to assume that all the remarks which sound Socratic, especially on the importance of a good condition of the soul, must be attributed to Socratic influence.

27. Cornford (719), 252 ff, cites Isoc. 9.22, Stob. *Flor.* 74–61, as evidence of the division of *aretai* by age and sex; they say that some virtues are appropriate especially (not, as Cornford suggests, solely) for particular ages, sexes, and roles. Among the various *agatha* proposed at *Eud.* 279a4–c8 the title of '*aretē*' is not conventionally restricted to the virtues mentioned in 279b4 ff. The 'class' use of '*aretē*' for aristocratic qualities shows that birth and inherited advantages might be thought part of *aretē*; see Ps.–Xen. *Ath. Pol.* 1.7, and for a similar class-use of '*kalos kagathos*' Aristoph. *Eq.* 185, 733–40, Xen. *Oec.* 6.12–7.3, De Ste Croix (221), 371–6. Socrates uses '*kalos kagathos*' only with great care, denying its class-use by extending it to women and tying it to justice, *G.* 470e9; contrast the more standard use of the term by Callicles, 484d1–2. See Dodds (501), on 470e9, V, n. 25.

28. Socrates suggests that Charmides ought to have a good soul when he comes from such an illustrious family, *Ch.* 154e1–155a7, 157d9–158b4. Hereditary claims to *aretē*, though, do not really impress him; cf. *La.* 179c2–6, *Pr.* 319d7–320b3, *M.* 93–4. Plato may also be thinking of Socrates' problems with the Thirty, including Charmides and Critias; see Xen. *Mem.* 1.29–38. See further Santas (345), 105, O'Brien (124), 125 f, Crombie (101) I. 214, Tuckey (346), 15–17. See III. 15.3.

29. On these disputed terms which concern Socrates see *Cra.* 411a3, Dodds (501), on *G.* 459d, III, n. 41. They cover the general area of our term 'moral', and this is the sense in which I use 'moral' in discussing Socrates and Plato, without the implication (which might be thought to belong to our term 'moral'; see VIII. 1.2) that morality is necessarily concerned with other people's interests. The nearest Greek term to 'morality' in this more restricted sense is '*dikaiosunē*'; but the claim that all *aretē* is *dikaiosunē*, though defensible (see above, 3.6), is not tautologous.

I normally render '*kalon*' by 'admirable' (though sometimes' beautiful' is needed; cf. VI. 12.2); this term (or perhaps 'fine') perhaps comes nearest to '*kalon*' in its generality, while 'admirable' may suggest the distinction between the sense of '*kalon*' and of '*agathon*', though something will often be *kalon* by being *agathon*, and vice versa. We may distinguish (with LSJ, s.v.) three relevant uses of '*kalon*'; (a) Aesthetic, for various kinds of beauty; (b) Functional, where something is *kalon* for a task or purpose; Hom. *Od.* 6.623, Thuc. 5.60, Xen. *Anab.* 4.8.26. (c) Moral, referring to people and actions. These are three general areas in which the term is used; it would be a great mistake to find three 'senses' of the term here, or to suppose that a Greek speaker would be aware of any ambiguity. A general account in terms of (b) is offered in Xen. *Mem.* 3.8.4–7, and *HMa.* 295c.

In Homer '*kalon*' is used for what is suitable or appropriate; *Od.* 3.169, 8.549, and also with '*agathon*', *Il.* 24.52, and associated with the standard Homeric values of fame, *Od.* 18.255, and honour, *Od.* 4.614. These passages count against Adkins's view (207), 41f, that '*kalon*' is not the true contrary of '*aischron*' in Homer; see also Creed (209), 214, n. 1. In the fifth century '*kalon*' is applied to whatever actions are admired—to success of various kinds (Eur. *Supp.* 528–30, Thuc. 5.9.9), but also to just and other virtuous actions (Pindar, *Py.* 1.85, Thuc. 5.105.4). Contrast Adkins 156 ff, 185, and see Creed, 216. In general it seems fair to say that for Socrates' contemporaries '*kalon*' is neither an unequivocally moral term, nor yet a term with a clear 'moral sense', but still applies easily and without surprise to justice and other recognized virtuous actions—Socrates is no innovator here.

On *kalon* and *agathon* see III. 3.3, V. 2.3, VI. 12.3–5. Thuc. 5.105.4 shows that many people would accept a connection between *to dikaion*, *aretē*, and *to kalon*, and expect someone to do these kinds of actions, without any guarantee that they would be beneficial to the agent (*sumpheron*); see Andrewes (220), ad loc.

30. Socrates sometimes acknowledges a debt to Prodicus, *M.* 96d5–7, *La.* 197d1–5. Elsewhere he refers to Prodicus politely, but distinguishes Prodicus' interest in names from his own interest in knowing about the referents of the names; *Cra.* 384b3–6, *M.* 75e1–5, *Tht.* 151b2–6, *Pr.* 340e8–341a2, 358a5–b2, d5–e1, *HMa.* 282c1–6, *Eud.* 277e3–278b2, *Ch.* 163d1–7. On the difference between Socrates' 'What is it?' question and questions about the meanings of terms see III. 7.4.

31. On the *Dissoi Logoi* see Guthrie (203), III. 316—19. Its three chapters on the problems of distinguishing the *agathon* from the *kakon*, the *kalon* from the *aischron*, and the *dikaion* from the *adikon*, are concerned with the three moral properties which concern Socrates (see n. 29 above); and the relevance of the chapter on whether virtue can be taught is no less clear. The tendency of Socratic dialectic to induce scepticism about the claims of 'King Nomos' is well emphasized by Grote (105), I. 248–64 (though I do not think his view is the whole truth about the elenchos; see III, n. 1).

32. On the debate about Socrates, Plato, and the sophists see Popper (125), I. 185–97, Guthrie (203), III. 10–13. I am not primarily concerned with Socrates' and Plato's political views in this book. But I hope it will be clear that Plato does not 'betray' either Socratic methods of inquiry or Socratic ethical principles; on the main issues, the praise or blame belongs to both alike.

My general view of the sophists mostly follows Sidgwick (219), 351–71, who defends a modified and improved version of Grote's thesis in (216), ch. 67. Sidgwick rightly insists that Plato's own account exonerates the sophists of any collective 'immoralist' doctrines; '. . . Socrates attacked their doctrines not as novel or dangerous, but as superficial and commonplace' (360). Callicles has had an ordinary Athenian education; he would be regarded as *pepaideumenos*, G. 487b6–7; he deplores *philosophia* in a grown man, 484c–485d, and despises the sophists who promise to teach virtue, 520a1–2. Thrasymachus ostentatiously demands payment for his services, as either a sophist or a rhetorician might, *R.* 337d6–10; but Plato does not take the opportunity to represent him as one of a number of sophists who hold his moral views; he is never called a sophist in *R.* I.

33. *The order of the dialogues.* Throughout this book I assume a chronology of the dialogues which is widely, though not universally, accepted in its general outlines. Though I have not discussed questions of chronology, and try to make my arguments as far as possible independent of particular chronological hypotheses, I have to take some position, which I simply summarize, without all the detailed arguments needed for its defence:

1. I divide the dialogues I shall discuss into (a) Socratic dialogues: *Ap., Eu., Cri., Ch., La., Lys., HMi., Eud., Ion*; (b) transitional dialogues: *Pr., G., Cra., HMa.*; (c) middle dialogues: *M., Phd., Symp., R., Phdr.* Ross (134), 2, summarizes the results of some stylistic investigations, and (though the details of them are unreliable) they agree broadly with this order, except for the *Cra.* (See also Dodds (501), 18 ff.)

2. Apart from stylistic evidence, I rely on the following arguments for separating Group (a) from the rest:

(1) I accept Aristotle's testimony that (a) Socrates did not 'separate the universals', and that the theory of separated Forms is Platonic; see VI. 7.1; (b) he was concerned with definitions and with ethics, *Met.* 1078b18 ff; (c) he disclaimed knowledge, *SE* 183b3 ff. All these conditions are satisfied by the first group of dialogues. The separated Forms first appear in the *Phd.*; but the way is prepared by the Theory of Recollection in the *M.*, which deserves to be placed near to the *Phd.* The subject matter of the first group of dialogues is ethical or clearly related to ethics (the *Ion* and the *Eud.*), as Aristotle suggests; but the greater diversity of content in the *Cra.* and the *M.* links them to the third group.

(2) The first group of dialogues generally proceed by question and answer rather than by direct exposition of positive doctrine (the *Ap.* and *Cri.* are obvious special

cases). There is more continuous exposition in the *Pr.* and later dialogues, except for the *HMa.*

(3) The *Phd.* argues for the separation of the Forms and the immortality of the soul; interest in immortality, without the supporting arguments, is displayed in the *G.* and *M.*, but not in earlier dialogues.

None of these tests is at all conclusive; but together they point in roughly the same direction, and reinforce each other. I have tried not to rely on ethical doctrine alone for the dating of a dialogue.

3. A few notes on dialogues which cause special problems:

(1) Some date the *Pr.* very early; see von Arnim (112), 34–7, Moreau (107), 27; contrast Taylor (111), 235, who places it in the third group because of its artistic maturity. I do not think the argument for an early date based on an alleged correction of *Pr.* 349d ff. in *La.* 192b ff. is at all sound, since the *La.* does not contest the *Pr.*'s position. Nor is the artistic character sufficient to justify a late date; but it suggests that the dialogue is probably not one of the earliest. Otherwise there are no arguments except those based on content for placing it later than the Socratic group. I try to show in Ch. IV how it deals with problems raised in the first group. On the *Pr.* and *La.* see III, n. 11.

(2) I accept an early date for the *Lys.*, and reject attempts to find references there to the separated Forms; see Vlastos (648), 35–7, against Levin (349).

(3) I follow Dodds (501), 16–21, and Rudberg (502), and place the *G.* after the first group and the *Pr.*, for these reasons; (a) Socrates is more positive and dogmatic in tone than in the early dialogues and the *Pr.*; it is no longer a question, as it is in the *Pr.*, whether virtue is a craft and is teachable, and he is ready to give an account of knowledge and belief, 454d, 465a, 501a, and of the virtues, 507ac. He assumes a fairly elaborate method of classification by genus and differentia, 463e–465e. (b) The interest in psychophysical dualism and immortality, and the closing myth, have parallels in the third group, not in the first. (c) On the other hand, the epistemological doctrine is less worked out than in the *M.*, with no Theory of Recollection, and the separated Forms are absent, suggesting a date before the third group. Again each point by itself is not decisive; but they point in the same direction, with no good counter-evidence; see V, n. 15.

(4) I assume an early date for the *Cra.*, following Luce (309).

(5) I also assume an early date for the *Eud.* It shares some interests with much later dialogues, the *Soph.* and *Pol.*; see Crombie (101), I. 223. But these questions could well have interested Socrates earlier.

(6) I see no grounds for suspecting the authenticity of the *HMa.*; and some of its interests are closely connected with the origins of the separation of Forms; see VI. 7.4, Malcolm (623).

(7) Some believe that *R.* I is a Socratic dialogue, later incorporated into the rest of the *R.*, and refer to it as the *Thrasymachus*; see, e.g., Friedländer (102), III. 63. I think there is insufficient reason for this hypothesis. I shall try to explain (a) why it is not surprising that the Socratic dialogues do not examine justice in detail (III. 6–3); and (b) why it is appropriate for the *R.* to begin with a Socratic dialogue, especially one which treats the Socratic craft-analogy seriously; see VII. 2.1, 3.6.

(8) I follow Hackforth (643), 3–5, in placing the *Phdr.* later than the *R.* I have referred to its views on love and on the divided soul because they explain and combine some of the less clear suggestions of the *Symp.* and the *R.*—though we cannot assume that Plato had the *Phdr.*'s views clearly in mind in writing the earlier dialogues, they are the best guide for making a coherent position out of them. It is harder, but also less important, to decide the relative dates of the *Phd.* and the *Symp.*, and of the *Symp.* and the *R.*; I am inclined to date them in that order (on the first two see Hackforth (621), 10, Cornford (641), 119).

4. I have sometimes cited passages from dialogues whose authenticity has been

doubted. (i) The authenticity of the *Clt.* is persuasively defended by Grube (307), though I think it is probably earlier than *R.* I. (ii) Like Grote (105), I. 426–9, I see no good reason for pronouncing the *Minos* spurious; *II. Alc.* and *Amatores* are too slight to allow confidence. But I have cited them only when they illustrate a position also adopted in admitted genuine dialogue. (iii) I am more doubtful about the genuineness of the *Alc.*, a rather dull handbook to Platonic ethics; but dullness does not prove inauthenticity, and its subject matter is suitable. See III, n. 69.

5. In later chapters I shall try to trace the development of Socrates' and Plato's views through these three groups of dialogues. The case against efforts to find development in Plato's ethics has been presented most forcibly by Shorey (127), 11–18 (110), 67–73, and by O'Brien in (124), summarized in (123). The crux of Shorey's and O'Brien's case is their interpretation of the relation of the *Ch.*, *La.*, and *Pr.* to *R.* IV. They both argue that the earlier dialogues are not meant to present as Socrates' own the view that each of the virtues is simply knowledge; rather they explore the arguments for and against the claims of knowledge and of non-cognitive states (endurance, self-control) and find neither satisfactory by itself; this is how they prepare for the *R.*'s solution, which strikes the right balance between cognitive and non-cognitive states. On this view, we should not suppose that the different statements in the Socratic dialogues and the *R.* mark different doctrines; the early dialogues are silent for dramatic effect, but present the pieces which are fitted together in the *R.*

I argue in later chapters that Plato's ethical theory does change from its Socratic origins, and that this method of making the dialogues consistent fails; above all I argue that Socrates denies incontinence and claims that knowledge is sufficient for virtue in the early dialogues, and Plato rejects both these positions in *R.* IV. The issue depends especially on our interpretation of the Socratic denial of incontinence and claims about the power of knowledge. My arguments relevant to Shorey's and O'Brien's case have to be developed gradually in later chapters; but the main points are in III, n. 59, IV, n. 7, 14, V, n. 15, VII, n. 21.

NOTES TO CHAPTER III

1. *Socrates' ignorance.*

1. The profession of ignorance is taken seriously by Grote (105), I.240 ff. I think he goes too far in denying any connection between the doctrine of different dialogues (276 f). Robinson (329), 22, argues from the *ad hominem* character of the elenchos that Socrates may perfectly well use arguments he knows to be fallacious (against this see Vlastos (407), 223 n.), so that the conclusions cannot be taken as evidence of his positive views. But I think the recurrent pattern of argument in the dialogues and the convergence of their conclusions show that the conclusions are to be taken seriously.

2. Vlastos (401), xxx, takes the disclaimer of knowledge seriously, and suggests that the elenchos can reach no positive conclusions, but simply displays the logical relations between propositions. This is all the elenchos's formal structure allows; but see 1.7.

3. Gulley (308), 62 ff, doubts the sincerity of Socrates' disclaimer because the elenchos is purposefully managed in a way that shows he has positive convictions, which must therefore be derived from outside the elenchos (64–7). This argument would be sound only if any positive conviction required a claim to knowledge, and if the elenchos itself could not support positive convictions. Neither assumption is sound.

2. I mean that no acceptable *definition* is found in the Socratic dialogues, not that no true description is even found; on the account of courage at *La.* 194e11, endorsed at *Pr.* 360d4–5, see 14.4.

3. Not all counter-examples are accepted; on *La.* 197a and 199e6 see notes 27 and 62 below.

4. Geach (344), 34 (cf. Grote (105), I. 496) believes that Socrates thinks we cannot recognize an example of *x*, or use the word '*x*' correctly, unless we can define '*x*'. Beversluis (318) shows the disastrous consequences of Geach's principle for Socratic method. But does Socrates accept the principle?

1. *La.* 190b7–c5 requires us to know what *x* is if we are to be advisers on how to acquire *x*.

2. *M.* 71b3–7, 100b4–6, *HMa.* 286c8–d2, 304d8–e2, *R.* 354c1–3, *Pr.* 361c2–6, all say that I must know what *x* is to *know* anything about *x*, not 'to have any true *beliefs* about *x*'.

3. *Lys.* 212a4–7, 223b4–8, suggests that we cannot be friends unless we know how one person becomes a friend to another or know what a friend is. Socrates takes friendship to be a virtue, and requires knowledge for virtue; see below, 15.2.

4. *Tht.* 147a7–b2 says that someone does not understand (*suniēsi*) the name '*x*' unless he knows what *x* is, not that knowing what *x* is is necessary for correct use of '*x*'.

5. At *Ch.* 158c7–159a10 Socrates says that if temperance is present to Charmides, he will have some perception (*aisthēsis*) of it and belief (*doxa*) about it, which he can express, since he can speak Greek. Some presence of temperance does not imply that Charmides is temperate (which requires knowledge; see below 15.2, n. 64); cf. *Lys.* 217c3–e1. And only belief, not knowledge, is ascribed to him as an ordinary speaker.

We might suppose, especially in *M.* 71b, that Socrates has confused 'know *x*' or 'know what *x* is' meaning (a) 'can recognize *x*' or 'have a concept of *x*', with (b) 'being able to give a Socratic definition of *x*'; while (a) might be a plausible precondition for recognizing *x*s, (b) would not be. But there is no reason to attribute this confusion to Socrates. He requires (b), but only as a condition for knowing about examples, not for having true belief about them. Santas (331), 140 f, offers a solution quite near to mine, except that he unconvincingly denies that Socrates means to deny knowledge about examples to someone without a definition; he uses loose, and I think un-Socratic, conditions of knowledge. Similar issues arise with Meno's Paradox; see VI. 4.1.

The distinction between knowledge and belief I have used is not explicit in the Socratic dialogues; but there is nothing to prevent Socrates from observing it. (Contrast Beversluis, 333 f. See below, 7.2.) Vlastos (311), 12, thinks Socrates must claim some kind of knowledge because he accepts KNV and is encouraged by the belief that no evil can happen to a good man, *Ap.* 41c8–d2. But since he thinks that his non-virtuous audience should also be encouraged by this thought, 41c8, Socrates need not claim to be virtuous himself; if a virtuous man is so well off, someone who is near to being virtuous can also be hopeful. At *Ap.* 37b3–4 Socrates claims only to be convinced (*pepeismenos*), not to know, that he does injustice to no one.

5. Some critics think the interlocutor misses the point of the question; see Allen (301), 320, Taylor (111), 149. Socrates is criticized for neglecting examples by Wittgenstein (333), 20, followed by Geach (344), and McDowell (324), 115. Robinson (133), 51, states Socrates' view more fairly. On the problem of projecting rules see II. 6.2.

6. On *Ch.* 159b7 ff, see Burnyeat (303), 215 f, Santas (345), 113–17, and on the fallacy at 159d10–11, Lutoslawski (131), 203, Tuckey (346), 19. Socrates argues: (1) Temperance is admirable. (2) Often, in physical and psychic actions doing something quickly is more admirable than doing it slowly. (3) Speed is more temperate than slowness. To derive (3) from (2) he needs to assume that all admirable action is temperate, relying on UV, see *Pr.* 332a6–7, IV, n. 6. He has no right to UV at this stage of the argument. But (3) is not essential. What he needs is (4) Slowness is not admirable. Why should slowness not be *something* admirable in an action even though speed would sometimes be more admirable? Socrates must take 'admirable' to imply 'always the best thing to do'—just as he uses 'good' and 'beneficial' with the 'always' and the superlative understood (see 3.5).

7. Vlastos (401), xlvii–xlix, commenting on *La.* 191de, rightly praises Socrates' efforts to point to important similarities in states thought to display different virtues. Santas

(348), 187, suggests that Socrates over-widens the concept of courage to include recognized modest, self-controlled, or temperate actions. But this is *over*-widening only if the common distinctions must be preserved at all costs. This question is relevant to UV; see n. 62 below. Cf. II. 3.2.

8. In *R.* I a behavioural account is several times refuted, amended, and again refuted. (1) 331d1–de; Cephalus' first account faces counter-examples. (2) Polemarchus suggests that justice gives each man what is owed, 331e3–4, and is invited to explain 'what is owed'; on one reading, it is open to the objection against Cephalus, 332a1–8. (3) 332a9–10; 'justice gives what is due, good and harm, to friends and enemies'. Socrates refutes 'what is fitting', 332b10–333e2 (see n. 46 below), 'friends and enemies', 334b7–e4, and 'good and harm', 334e5–335e5 (see VII. 2.2, n. 3). Each qualification of the attempted behavioural account exposes it to refutation. The inadequacy of behavioural accounts of virtue is noticed by Joseph (703), 7, von Wright (834), 141 f, Burnyeat (303), 230–2.

9. Socrates' argument from adverb to abstract noun to a single referent (cf. *Pr.* 332c1–2, 360c1–2, *M.* 73b1–2; see VI, n. 5) is well criticized by Burnyeat (303), 225–8; see also Penner (404), 51 f, 56–8. The A-powers, which Penner and I call 'tendencies', are called 'dispositions' by Ryle (330), 43 f; but that term is also used for B-powers, e.g. by Quine (327), 123. The new standards of similarity associated with newly discovered B-powers are noticed by Quine (328), 128 f.

10. Socrates' initial question about the pious in every pious action, *Eu.* 5d1–2, 6e3–6, leads into a discussion of actions, 8e6–8, 9a8–b2, 14b3–7. But he also thinks of person-piety, when he thinks of piety as a science, 14c3–6. The terms '*hosiotēs*' and '*to hosion*' are used equivalently at 5d4, 14c5 (contrast Crombie (101), I. 209 f), and the argument, including 12c10–d3, applies both to act- and to person-piety (contrast Vlastos [407], 231 n. 25); what is common to all pious *actions* is some reference to *person*-piety. On the whole argument see Burnyeat (303), 223 f.

11. This account of the argument (see also Santas (348), 189–95) undermines von Arnim's suggestion (112), 34 (see also Moreau (107), 86, Gulley (308), 18–21), that any correction of *Pr.* 349e1–350c5 is intended here. Nor does Socrates suggest any distinction between knowledge of facts and knowledge of values (Taylor (111), 63, Santas, 192 f), or between craft-knowledge and moral virtue (Hirschberger (122), 55); nothing prevents moral knowledge from being a particular craft knowing particular facts. But the argument raises other problems inadequately treated in the *La.*; see below, 14.1, VII. 7.3.

12. On this argument see Cohen (343).

13. To make *Ch.* 160e11 intelligible in context I follow Goldbacher (see Burnet's apparatus), and read: *ar'oun an eiē agathon ho mē agathous, kai mē agathon ho agathous apergazetai*. Cf. *M.* 87d8–e4.

14. Socrates moves confidently from *kalon* to *agathon* or *ōphelimon* at *Pr.* 351b7–c3, 359e4–7, *Cri.* 48b8–9. The Socratic dialogues offer no clear general statement. (1) *Ch.* 167e1–8 distinguishes *erōs* for *to kalon* from *boulēsis* for *to agathon* and *epithumia* for *to hēdu*. (Socrates himself does not endorse these distinctions, which are only examples.) But this still allows all *kala* and *hēdea* to be *agatha*. (2) *Lys.* 216d2 suggests that to *agathon* is *kalon*, and thereafter *agathon* replaces *kalon* in the argument. See II, n. 29, V. 2.3, VI. 12.3–5.

15. The fallacy in the *Lys.* is ascribed to Aristotle by Anscombe (801), 34. Aristotle is defended by Hardie (817), 16 f, among others. The remark, 'for that way our choosing goes on to infinity, so that desire is empty and vain' at *EN* 1094a20–1 need not indicate an *absurd*, but only an undesirable, consequence of refusal to admit a single ultimate end; desire might be empty and pointless, but still possible, though, as *EE* 1214b11 says, 'a sign of much folly'.

16. *Eud.* 281b4 ff, does not allow that someone could be brave or temperate without wisdom (contrast Penner (404), 42 n.), but only that *if* he could be, he would go wrong

more than a coward, 281c6–7. *M.* 88b3–c1 notes that *if* courage is not wisdom but mere confidence, it harms a man; and Socrates infers from this and 87e1–3 that courage is wisdom, 88d2–3—he allows no real virtue without wisdom (contrast O'Brien (124), 95 n.).

17. On the worthwhileness of virtue see II. 6.2. Socrates needs to maintain both (a) if *A* has good reason to do *x*, *x* benefits *A*, and (b) if *A* believes that he has good reason to *x*, *A* believes that *x* benefits *A*. The desire for the final good is taken to be implicit in everyone's deliberation; see below, 13.5.

18. Socrates leaves open at least five possible conceptions of happiness. It might be (a) the properly limited use of some one of the recognized goods; (b) a compound of the recognized goods, properly used; (c) some single good apart from the recognized goods; (d) some compound of non-recognized goods to which the recognized goods contribute; (e) a compound of recognized and non-recognized goods.

19. On Aristotle's concept of *eudaimonia* I generally follow Austin (803), 273–83, Mabbott (716), 62 f, against Prichard's hedonist account (829), 218 f.

20. On egoism see VII. 5.2–4, VIII. 3.2.

21. On the *Lys.* see Vlastos (648), 6–11. He points out (7) that 210cd alone does not imply that *A phistei B* iff *B* is useful *to A*. But this is strongly suggested by the examples at 209d–210a, where, e.g., the Persian king *philei* us if we are useful *to him*; and, as Vlastos says, this is implied at 213e ff.

221e–222d raise a problem about the previous account of *philia*. If we love what is *oikeios* to us, and if the good is *oikeion* to good men and the bad to bad men, then bad men will be *philoi* as much as good men, which we had previously denied; 221c3–d5. But if only the good is *oikeion*, only good men can be *philoi*, which we also denied; 222d5–8. This dilemma can be avoided by recognizing that the good is *oikeion* to everyone—which is just the Socratic doctrine that all men pursue what they take to be the good; good men differ in so far as they pursue what is really good. This Socratic doctrine saves the *Lys.*'s claim that all *philia* is for the *oikeion* and the good.

22. On *R.* I see VII. 3.4.

23. *HMa.* 284d1–e9, *Min.* 317b2–d1, show that Socrates takes *nomos* and *nomimos* to mean (a) 'what is lawful, i.e. right and legitimate', and not (b) 'what is lawful, i.e. permitted by positive law' (see II, notes 6 and 17).

24. In *Cri.* 47d6–7 *to dikaion* and *to adikon* may be just and unjust states of soul; but 49b4–6 makes the stronger claim that unjust action, *to adikein*, is bad and dishonourable for the agent.

25. On the just man's attitude to enemies see Vlastos (314), VII. 2.2.

26. Grote (105), I. 303, believes that the *Cri.* maintains a doctrine of 'absolute obedience' and is inconsistent with the *Ap.*, because it is a piece of democratic rhetoric conflicting with Socrates' more critical reflections. Grote ignores Socrates' claim that he relies on arguments secured by arguments, surely referring to the elenchos. Woozley (316), 305–8, and Vlastos (312), reject Grote's view, and Vlastos well stresses the limits of Socrates' explicit commitment to obedience (it is another question whether Socrates clearly sees the logical limits of his argument).

27. Laches mentions animals and men universally agreed to be brave without wisdom, 197a3, c6; and no one denies the universal agreement.

28. *Ap.* 22de should mean that craftsmen can give some kind of explanation of what they do—not necessarily that they are good at defining an awl or a shoe, but that they can explain each step and its function. Socrates can hardly be testing them only for practical competence; for he does not allege that poets are incompetent at composing odes and dramas, but that they cannot explain themselves when they are asked *ti legoien*, 22b4. Craftsmen, then, should be able to explain what they do.

This demand for expressible knowledge undermines Gould's view (120), 31, that the knowledge Socrates seeks is not theoretical or necessarily expressible in words, but a technique or competence. (His view is well refuted by Vlastos (313), 204–10; see also Rist (126), 115–42.) However, Gould's view points to an important problem—why Socrates should demand more than practical competence; see 15.6–7.

29. On *M.* 98a see VI. 4.3, notes 15 and 23.

30. For the 'conceptual' view see Hare (322), 35 f, Guthrie (203), III. 431 f, Gulley (308), 12, Taylor (111), 28; it is rejected by Gordon (320), Penner (404), and Gosling (104), 180 f.

The relevant 'linguistic' intuitions would express someone's sense of what follows from the meaning of '*F*', or what is logically absurd and self-contradictory to say about *F*s, as opposed to mere factual truths and falsehoods about *F*s. See Grice and Strawson (321), 150 f. The existence of such purely linguistic intuitions is not uncontroversial; but a defender of the 'conceptual' view of Socratic definition must believe in their existence.

31. The example of 'healthy' is borrowed from Ar. *Met.* 1003a34–6. Aristotle's implied criticism of Socrates and Plato for neglecting this possibility (cf. *EE* 1236a23–30) is justified; see VII. 10.3. (Contrast Allen (341), 118–20.) On the problem about single B-powers see VI. 2–3.

32. This objection is borrowed from Bennett's similar objection to an account of initial learning which appeals to abstract ideas (317), 11–17. On the claim that Plato uses the Forms as quasi-ostensive samples for learning see VI, n. 39. Since Socrates' definitions and standards are not meant to explain the learning or correct use of words, they are not open to the Wittgensteinian objection of Theopompus, that we can speak significantly and communicate without definitions as standards; see Epictetus 2.17.4–10, quoted by Grote (105), I. 324.

33. Here I skate over several problems about the *Cra.* But at least the account of how a name preserves the *tupos* of its referent, 432d11 ff, is independent of the special theory, examined but not endorsed at 391b9 ff, which makes correctness of names depend on their etymology, and ultimately on resemblances between their letters and syllables and features of the world. Truths about the referent can as well be conveyed by descriptions associated with the name by convention; and this answer would suit Socrates' recognition of convention at 435b ff.

34. On Prodicus see II, n. 30.

35. Socratic *ousiai* share their explanatory character with Locke's 'real essences'; cf. *Eu.* 11a with (323), III. 3.13—though Locke has different views about the character of the explanation. The problem of revising ordinary beliefs in 'real definitions' is treated inadequately by Nakhnikian (325), 145–7, and better by Putnam (326).

36. I refer to the 'fallacy' in the *R.* alleged by Sachs (717) (see VII, n. 33); the general relevance of the question to Socratic definitions is noticed by Penner (404), 48 n. An analogous problem arises about alleged 'meaning-change' between scientific theories; see Feyerabend (319), 20–4. Scheffler's suggestion (332), 61, that conflicting theories are commensurable if their terms have the same reference, also raises a problem for Socratic definition, since Socrates' accounts will involve some change in beliefs about the reference of virtue-terms; the *Cratylus*'s 'outline' theory comes closest to answering this question for Plato.

37. Protagoras' teaching: II. 4.4.

38. Rawls (830), 46–9, accepts a 'Socratic' account of moral theory, in so far as he thinks it requires the articulation of principles and their adjustment to considered judgements, by revision of both judgements and principles. He differs from Socrates (rightly or wrongly) in offering no general account of the direction of revision; his view does not imply that revision will make our beliefs more consistent, still less that it will make them converge on a final good. The final good is Socrates' device for ensuring that revision all goes in the same direction.

39. Many critics think Socrates sees limitations in the CA, and does not think it an adequate account of virtue; see, e.g., Shorey (127), 9, O'Brien (124), 17 (though he also recognizes, 18, that the CA is defensible when combined with Socrates' views on

motivation), Gulley (308), 82, Moreau (107), 36, 108, 113, 178, Hirschberger (122), 30–2, Gould (120), 42–5. Robinson (329), 19, and Penner (339), take the CA seriously. On *technē* see II. 4.1.

40. Grote (105), I. 388, noticing the oddity in the *Cri.*'s appeal to an expert, suggests that Socrates assumes the expert's role, inconsistently with his normal disclaimer of knowledge. But if Socrates' appeals to the elenchos and previous agreements are noticed (see 1.2), his positive advice need not mean he claims expert status.

41. On *Eu.* 7b6 ff. see II, n. 29, Strang (629), 195 f, Geach (344), 35–7, Allen (341), 32 f, Burnet (342), ad loc. Socrates does not deny the existence of undisputed examples of just etc. things (see VI, n. 39) or distinguish facts from values (see above, n. 11). He says only that these 'moral' properties (as I shall call them) sometimes cause disputes not decidable by measurement. He does not say that (as Allen, Burnet, and Taylor (111), 150 n., assume) these disputes should be soluble by measurement; though the 'measuring craft' of *Pr.* 357a5–c1 offers one answer to the problems, it is not necessarily the answer intended in the *Eu.* See IV. 3.4, VI, n. 41.

42. See Murphy (704), 6 f.

43. On the *Pr.* see II. 4.2. The comments at 312b3–5, 313e, *G.* 485a4, do not show that Socrates recognizes that moral education should be *paideia* as opposed to *technē*; he does not endorse this common-sense distinction. Contrast Moreau (107), 35.

Socrates might believe (a) that real virtue cannot be taught entirely by Protagorean methods; (b) that Protagorean methods are entirely useless for teaching virtue, though no doubt useful as means of social control. He never clearly decides between (a) and (b); but he never says a good word for (a). At *Lys.* 210a9–c4 he suggests, not that Lysis needs his choices and affections trained by Protagorean means, but that his problem is lack of knowledge, and when this is remedied, he will need no control from his parents. Since it would often be relevant for Socrates to mention (a) if he believed it, his silence supports (b) fairly strongly.

44. *Ch.* 166a3–b6 raises an important issue. 'What a science is of' might refer to its subject matter, or its product, or both. An artefactual craft like shoemaking is 'of' working leather into shoes, and a non-artefactual craft like flute-playing is 'of' making finger movements on flutes to produce tuneful sounds. We might think that 166a5–b3 recognizes that *logistikē* can be *tou artiou kai tou perittou* with no product, and that non-productive *epistēmē* is allowed. But the next phrase, *plēthous hopōs echei pros hauta kai pros allēla* suggests the product—the right answer is a result of the calculation distinct from the steps of the calculations themselves. Socrates does not, then, recognize Aristotle's distinction between *poiēsis* and *praxis*, despite Moreau (107), 57 n. 116, Gould (120), 38 f, Taylor (111), 53; though this is no doubt Aristotle's source, Socrates does not show that he draws his conclusion.

45. A few remarks to connect the *Ch.*'s problematic discussion of self-knowledge and 'knowledge of knowledge' with the rest of the dialogue:

1. Plato intends a connection. Critias' suggestion that temperance is 'knowing (*gignōskein*) oneself', 166d4, is a standard view, though loosely connected with Socrates' claim that a temperate man must know he is temperate. When Socrates expands and alters Critias' suggestion into 'knowing the things one knows (*oiden*) and the things one doesn't know, that one knows them and that one doesn't know them', 167b2, he refers to his own attitude (*Ap.* 21d2–8, *Ch.* 165b5–c2).

2. The transition from 'knowing (*gignōskein*) oneself', 165b4, and 'knowledge (*epistēmē*) of oneself', 165e1, to 'knowledge (*epistēmē*) of knowledge', 166c3 (see Tuckey (346), 33–7), is fallacious unless 164c5–6 is invoked. They agree that a temperate man must (a) know he is temperate; (b) know himself. Socrates asks what (b) means, what temperance knows about the temperate man, 165c4–e2. Critias replies that (c) it is knowledge of itself and of other kinds of knowledge, 166b4–c3. He wants to say, as Socrates sees, 167a1–7, that a man's temperance is his knowledge about his own knowledge and ignorance; but now, by (a), he must also know this

knowledge of his own knowledge and ignorance; and so he must have knowledge of knowledge—which Socrates examines next. Socrates assumes (as Santas (345), 119, notices without explanation) that (b) is satisfied by (c)—that self-knowledge requires no knowledge of non-cognitive states; here as usual he assumes KSV.

3. 166e4–171c9 concludes reasonably that the expert in knowledge can state general conditions for knowledge, but cannot decide that someone has knowledge of medicine without being a medical expert; the general conditions for knowledge are only necessary conditions for knowledge of *medicine*. It is harder to see the point of 167c4–169a2. Socrates shows that if knowledge and its object are taken to be related as senses are related to their objects, or greater and lesser to their relata, paradox results. He does not infer that therefore the proposed account of temperance fails, 169a1–8; and perhaps his point is exactly that a *mathēma* is not the same sort of object for knowledge as colour is for sight, some separate entity to which the mind is related. Anyhow, he treats 'knowledge of knowledge' as a feasible notion, with its rules and limitations, 170b11–d3; he is not misled by the ambiguity of, e.g., 'I know what the doctor knows' into the conclusion that knowledge of knowledge must be encyclopaedic.

4. Socrates is right to raise questions about the benefits of science of science; if it is used inopportunely without knowledge of the good, it will not always benefit us, and therefore cannot be the kind of knowledge which is temperance. But the argument from 174e3 is dubious. Socrates argues: (1) Each craft is the producer only of what it is the craft of, its proper product. (2) Temperance is not the science of benefit. (3) Temperance is not the producer of benefit, 175a3–4. (4) Therefore, temperance is not beneficial, 175a6–7. He illegitimately assumes that a craft can produce *x* only if it is the craft of *x* and the producer of *x*. But Socrates would be right to say that if temperance is not *the* science of benefit, but only a subordinate science like medicine, which may or may not benefit us, it is not an unconditional benefit, as a virtue should be. Only the knowledge of good is an unconditional benefit; for if knowledge of knowledge controls everything and is not controlled by knowledge of good, it may be used inopportunely.

46. *R.* 333d10–e3 says that if justice 'gives what is fitting' and is merely co-ordinate with other crafts which give what is fitting, its competence will be absurdly limited. (This argument need not by itself indicate doubts about the CA, as Joseph (703), 7–9, Moreau (107), 109 f, and Gould (120), 45, believe; it shows only that justice must be a superordinate craft. However, see VII. 2.1.) The problem is not avoided if the virtuous man is an all-round amateur less competent in each area than the specialized expert; II *Alc.* 147a5–b4, *Am.* 136d9–e3.

47. Before *Eud.* 292b1 Socrates has argued that only knowledge will reliably secure goods for us, and is therefore the only invariably reliable *instrumental* good. It does not follow that (as the argument now assumes) it is the only *intrinsic* good (see von Arnim (112), 135). Perhaps the confusion represents a genuine ambivalence in Socrates about the status of knowledge, so that he holds the view criticized at *R.* 505b8–10 (see VII. 14.2). But the fallacy is not necessary to raise the problem about the product of the royal craft, when '*eudaimonia*' is too vague an answer (see von Arnim, 133). Von Arnim, 132–7, Hirschberger (122), 113–15, suppose that the argument is meant to suggest some absolute good as the object of the royal craft. Moreau (107), 187–9, Sprague (310), 22, Taylor (111), 94, 99, think Socrates means that the royal craft has no product, or that, like Kantian morality, it can determine its object only formally and not materially. I see no sign of these views in the Socratic dialogues.

48. Moreau (107), 107 f, Gould (120), 42 f, Hirschberger (122), 100–9, Taylor (111), 38, believe that the *HMi.* is meant to discredit the CA. But while rejection of the CA would be *one* way to avoid the paradox, it is not the only way; the doctrine that everyone pursues the good, and that virtue contributes to the good, solves the paradox too—and this is the solution Socrates adopts. See Penner (339), 140 f, O'Brien (124), 100 n.

49. The Socratic dialogues' views on incontinence are implicit, they are defended only in later dialogues, the *Pr.*, *M.*, and *G.*, and I omit the *Pr.* here because of its hedonism (see IV. 2.6). These arguments, then, may be Platonic rather than strictly Socratic; but something like them is required to defend the Socratic position, and this is the most suitable place to discuss them. On the *G.*, see V. 2.2.

50. On 'good-dependent' desires see V. 2.2, VII. 6.2. A quasi-Socratic principle for attributing desires is endorsed by Dennett (336), 93–5, Davidson (335), 97 (without endorsing the Socratic position on incontinence).

51. The *M.* argument is analysed by Santas (340) and Nakhnikian (338). Meno claims that two kinds of people might choose what they know to be evil; (a) some think the known evils will benefit them; (b) some know that the evils will harm them, but still want them, 77b6–d4. Now (a) requires us to say:

1. *A* knows *x* is bad on the whole.
2. *A* believes *x* benefits him on the whole.
3. *A* wants *x*.

Now Socrates thinks (1) rules out (2), because of an assumption: S1. *A* believes *x* is good or bad (to acquire) on the whole if and only if he believes *x* benefits or harms him on the whole. This principle rules out the conjunction of (1) and (2), if 'good' in (1) means 'good to acquire', as Socrates and Meno agree (at 77c7–d1) it does. For a similar 'egoistic' account of 'good' see V, n. 8.

4. If *A* chooses *x* knowing *x* to be bad and harmful for him, he believes he will be wretched in so far as he is harmed, 77e5–78a2.
5. *A* believes that if he is wretched he will be unhappy, 78a3.
6. *A* does not want to be wretched and unhappy, 78e4–5.
7. Therefore *A* does not want what he knows to be bad, 78a6–7.

For says Socrates, being wretched is desiring actual evils and acquiring them; and no one wants to be in that condition, 78a7–8. To rule out the reply that *A* does *x* *although* (not *because*) he knows it is bad, Socrates needs: S2. *A* wants *x* if and only if he believes *x* contributes to his own happiness. The argument does not prove, but relies on S1 and S2.

52. I have taken a 'traditional' view, derived from Aristotle, of the Socratic paradox about incontinence. (1) I assume it is as paradoxical to Socrates' original audience as to us; see II, notes 12, 20. (2) I take Socrates to argue that propositional knowledge—information about what benefits the agent—is sufficient for action. (Contrast Allen (334), 257 f) Socrates does not suggest a redefinition of 'knowledge' which would make action a criterion of knowledge; however plausible or implausible this view may be, it does not appear in his arguments, and if it did, it would remove the paradox which he and his audience take to be there. (3) I take Socrates to deny that incontinence really occurs (contrast Santas (340), 164) because alleged incontinence is really ignorance; and so he is open to Aristotle's criticism that he assumes people always desire what they think best for them *EN* 1145b26–7.

53. Instrumental and component means are distinguished by Greenwood (306), 46–8, and exploited by Cooper (304), and Wiggins (315), in interpreting Aristotle on *ta pros to telos*. The distinction might be drawn as follows:

1. If *x* is an instrumental means to *y*, then (a) *x* causally contributes to the achievement of *y*; (b) if *z* would causally contribute to *y* more efficiently than *x* would, then, to that extent, we should have reason to choose *z*; (c) *x* is not identical with *y*, and need be no part of *y*.
2. If *x* is a constituent of *y*, then (a) *x* is identical with *y*, or with a part of *y*; (b) if *z* causally contributes to other ends more efficiently than *x* would contribute, it does not follow that we have reason to choose *z* rather than *x*; (c) if *w* is a component of *y* preferable to *x*, it does not follow that we have no reason to choose *x*.

The point of the distinction is that an instrumental means depends on its causal properties for its value, and the end it contributes to is entirely distinct from it; neither of these conditions holds for a component.

54. Perhaps the doctor here only changes my view of instrumental means, by showing me that this condition of the bodily elements contributes to the same healthy activities I have wanted all the time. But this explanation will not always work; e.g., if I want to do karate, the expert tells me that karate consists in these movements.

55. There are two further possibilities: (a) Happiness is a determinate end, and virtue prescribes its components. (b) Happiness is an indeterminate end, and virtue prescribes only instrumental means and components already chosen under another description. (a) leaves virtue with nothing to do; if we already know the components of the end, we do not need virtue to discover them. (b) would require something besides virtue to discover the components of the end—and Socrates offers nothing. Neither (a) nor (b) is plausibly ascribed to him.

The distinction between TV and NTV is meant to suggest possible differences between virtue and craft not discussed by Gibbs in his defence of the CA (337), 25, 41. The actions prescribed by a craft sometimes have no further end (e.g. dancing). But even here the craftsman does not prescribe the end; he relies on someone else's view of what good dancing is—and, significantly, we would be more inclined to call someone who prescribed this a connoisseur than a craftsman, a man of taste rather than skill. Socrates rightly concentrates on craftsmen concerned with the rational, systematic, explicable, teachable crafts which deal with means, rather than on connoisseurs, where the features that appeal to him in crafts are much less evident. I do not mean that connoisseurship is irrational, or that it is necessarily a good analogy for virtue, but only that Socrates has good reason to ignore it, given his interest in crafts.

56. See IV. 3.3.

57. The *Eud.* and *M.* suggest the basic argument for UV:

1. The only thing which always benefits us is wisdom, *Eud.* 281e2–5, *M.* 87d4–8, 88c6–d1.

2. Virtue always benefits us, *M.* 87e3.

3. Therefore virtue is wisdom, *M.* 88c4–d3.

In (1) 'benefits' must mean 'benefits on the whole', not 'benefits to some extent—otherwise there would be no argument for (3) (on a similar claim in the *Ch.* see n. 6 above). The argument relies on KSV. *M.* 87d6 says: (a) 'If there is no good which knowledge does not include (i.e. if every good is a kind of knowledge), (b) then in suspecting that it is some knowledge (*epistēmēn an tin' auto*) we are suspecting rightly'. (b) is the natural conclusion from (a). 89a1–3 argues similarly; (c) Wisdom is what is beneficial (*to ōphelimon*); virtue is beneficial; 'then we say virtue is wisdom, either the whole (of wisdom) or a part (of wisdom)'. (See Bluck (601), ad loc.) 89a1–3 repeats the argument. O'Brien (124), 95 n., wants to read *ti autou* for *tin' auto* in (b) (with Bluck), and to understand 'of virtue' instead of 'of wisdom' in (c), making wisdom only a part of virtue. But that is less than Socrates claims in (a) and (c), and in 89a1–3. On 88b4–5, c6 see n. 16 above.

At *Eu.* 11e4–12d10 Socrates suggests that piety is a part of justice; but Euthyphro's efforts to find the subset of just actions and people loved by the gods (cf. 15b1–9) fail. One possible conclusion is that piety is indistinguishable from justice; and this conclusion is drawn at *Pr.* 331b. Euthyphro had suggested that the gods were concerned with justice in general, 8b7–9, and though Socrates diverts attention from justice at 9c1–d5, this is the answer endorsed in the *Pr.*, explaining Euthyphro's failure in the last part of the dialogue. Socrates does not endorse the view that piety is only a part of justice (contrast Vlastos (407), 228); he says only that Euthyphro seems to have spoken well (*phainē(i)*) with the infinitive, 12e9, the non-veridical use; see VI, n. 29). Nor can the *Eu.*'s argument be confined to act-piety, and the *Pr.*'s to person-piety (as suggested by Vlastos, 231 n.); see above, n. 10. The *Eu.* removes one, though only one, obstacle to UV.

58. 'Doing one's own work' is treated much less fully and sympathetically in the *Ch.*

than in *R*. IV, where it is part of the account of justice; see VII, n. 30. But KSV, assumed in the *Ch*., leaves no room for the explanation of 'one's own' at *R*. 443c9–d3; and other explanations (e.g. 'doing what is the best thing for us to do') are redundant.

59. Here as elsewhere the *La*. develops and defends positions assumed in the *Ch*.: e.g. (1) the *La*. develops the *Ch*.'s claim that concern for virtue must refer to a state of the soul; *Ch*. 157a–c, *La*. 185b–d; (2) the *La*. explains what the *Ch*. assumes, the kind of Socratic definition which is preferable to a list of behavioural examples; (3) the *La*. presses further the *Ch*.'s suggestion that a virtue may be indistinguishable from knowledge of good and evil.

Shorey (127), 12 f, O'Brien (124), 113 f, von Arnim (112), 26 (against Pohlenz (108), 28, with which I agree), Santas (348), 194 f, believe that the *La*. is meant to suggest that the right account of courage should include reference to endurance. But while we might advise Socrates to solve his problem this way, he does not agree. (1) 194c7–d2 says that the definition which omits reference to endurance is Socratic; and the omission of endurance is never blamed for their troubles. (2) KSV is assumed in this definition, is assumed in this definition, and makes endurance superfluous. (3) If endurance is omitted, it is hard to distinguish courage from the other virtues; but that will worry Socrates only if he rejects UV.

60. Socrates means to claim, as 199b6–7, *kai mellontōn kai pantōs echontōn*, shows, that others besides temporal restrictions are irrelevant to the scope of a science; e.g. a science of goods should not apply just to people in Athens or to people under six feet tall. His point is that a science should rely on general principles resisting any arbitrary limits (not easy to describe in general terms) on its scope; cf. Socrates' criticism of Ion's arbitrarily limited pseudo-science, *Ion*. 531d12–532c9, and see Gosling (104), 59 ff.

61. Vlastos (407), 267 f, denies that (c) (in my numbering) follows from (1) and (2); he accepts only 'Courage *requires* the science of all goods and evils'. But it requires nothing else, if KSV is accepted. Nor can we insist that courage is only one *aspect* of the science of goods, or is the science qua science of future goods. As Penner (404), 52 f, argues, Socrates seeks the state which causes brave actions, and legitimately (given KSV) finds that this state is identical with the science of goods.

62. Socrates does not explicitly endorse UV. He points out, 198e8–11, that they cannot consistently agree that (1) courage is only a part of virtue; (2) Nicias' definition was correct; (3) UV follows from Nicias' definition. Possible answers are:

    (a) accept (2) and (3), rejecting (1);
    (b) accept (1) and (2), rejecting (3);
    (c) accept (1) and (3), rejecting (2).

(c) is implausible; for Nicias' definition is admitted to be Socratic, and is endorsed at *Pr*. 360d4–5. (b) is ruled out, if the previous note was right. (a) is the best answer for Socrates, as Pohlenz suggests (108), 28 f. (See, on the other side, von Arnim (112), 26). (1) is quite weakly supported. At 190c8–d3 Socrates says that most people think the part of virtue to which learning to fight in armour is relevant is courage; they are wrong in thinking that fighting in armour, rather than knowledge of the good, is especially relevant to courage, and they may equally be wrong to think courage is a separate part of virtue.

Does UV rule out all distinctions between the virtues? (a) Socrates will hardly agree that they are distinct branches of a science, as arithmetic and geometry are branches of mathematics, since they do not have their own subject-matter and principles. A brave man will act from wise confidence, because he owes it to his fellow-citizens, and because he rejects any intemperate desire for safety; the knowledge he needs could equally well be called courage, temperance or justice. (b) UV still allows Socrates to identify temperance and bravery, but distinguish temperate and brave actions by their circumstances (e.g., brave actions in battle, etc.). But 191de suggests that he finds this kind of distinction (later accepted by Aristotle) misleading.

On the interpretation of UV see further IV, n. 3.

63. *La.* 193e1, 'for our actions (*erga*) do not harmonize with our speech (*logos*)', alludes to a standard allegation of hypocrisy—the speeches are all right, but the actions are not (e.g. Thuc. 2.65.9)—but reverses it; someone might say they partook in courage in action but not in speech, 192e2. Socrates implies that a brave man must be able to say the right things, not just act rightly; see O'Brien (124), 114–17.

64. KNV also explains why the interlocutor's ignorance is thought to be disgraceful; *La.* 200a4–c6, *Alc.* 117d4–118c2, *Sph.* 229c1–9, 230b4–d3. KNV is suggested by the criticism at *Eu.* 15d4–8—Euthyphro would surely not have done what he did, claiming to be pious, unless he knew what the pious is—and by the doubt at *Ch.* 176a about whether Charmides is temperate if he cannot say what temperance is.

65. The most pointed comment on Nicias is the distinction between knowledge of what is fearful and the diviner's knowledge, 195e1–196a2; Nicias is invited to agree that the general must control the diviner, 198e2–199a8. Nicias' career suggests that he did not always heed this advice, especially when he failed to save the Syracusan expedition because of diviners' warnings; Thuc. 7.50.4, 86.5. See Vlastos (407), 268 f, O'Brien (124), 114–16, (347), 145. Charmides and Critias: II, n. 28.

66. This conclusion does not cope with the more radical criticism of Callicles or Thrasymachus, not faced in the Socratic dialogues; see II. 4.6–7, V. 3.2.

67. Santas (340), 159, 161 f, thinks we can know what is virtuous, or that this action is virtuous, without knowing it is beneficial. But Socrates' conception of virtue and conditions for knowledge make it unreasonable for him to agree; he ought to test a claim to know (not just believe) that an action is virtuous by asking whether it can be shown to be beneficial and to conform to the definition of the virtue, which will show how the virtue is beneficial. These conditions on knowledge are strongly suggested by *M.* 71b, *La.* 190b7 ff. See above, 1.6.

68. On Socrates' more ambiguous attitude to psychic health in the *G.*, see V. 5.4.

69. Many have thought that Socrates takes the good state of the soul to be the final good, or at least a good in itself; see Burnet (302), 244 f, Gulley (308), 191 f, Jaeger (204), II. 39–41, Guthrie (203), III. 467.

1. Some think (including those cited above) that the soul's value is derived from its metaphysical status, because it is immortal and immaterial. But in the Socratic dialogues, though Socrates accepts the immortality of the soul at *Cri.* 54b2–8, he does not argue from it for the soul's value. The only metaphysical argument is *Alc.* 127e9–130e9, where Socrates'. advice to a man to care for himself and his soul is associated (by a fallacious argument) with a claim that the soul is separate from the body. But this dualism is not necessary for the advice to care for our souls; nor is it normal Socratic doctrine. Contrast Burnet, 139, Guthrie, 472.

2. This point does not depend on a decision about the *Alc.*'s autheticity; see II, n. 33. Even if it is genuine and early (both of these claims are doubtful), its metaphysical doctrine is unparalleled in the earlier dialogues; and there is no reason why the metaphysics should be the basis of Socrates' moral advice, rather than the other way round.

3. Some who reject the metaphysical reasons for valuing the soul still think Socrates takes its perfection to be valuable in itself; see Vlastos (412), 74, (311), 5. Burnyeat (303), 210, defends this view by taking *chrēmata* in *Ap.* 30b1–2 to be 'valuables', not only money, and supposes, citing 41d, that Socrates thinks the mere possession of virtue provides someone with all the valuables he needs. This would be a legitimate interpretation if we had other evidence that Socrates thinks virtue intrinsically valuable; but such evidence cannot be found.

70. See VII. 4.1.

71. Burnyeat (303), 211, 232, mentions the priority of being virtuous over acting virtuously in Socratic ethics. He seems to ascribe to Socrates two theses: (a) the priority considered in 2.4–5 above, requiring definitions of virtues in non-behavioural terms;

(b) .he intrinsic value of a virtuous state of soul. Now (b) does not obviously follow from (a); Socrates might easily believe that we cannot define in purely behavioural terms the state which achieves the best results (except emptily, as 'the state which achieves the best results'), and might still value the state only for the results. Zeller (113), 153–8, notices Socrates' instrumental view of virtue, though he thinks Socrates supposes it to be intrinsically valuable too. He sees that Plato rejects the instrumental view in *Phd.* 68d, *R.* 362e. See VI. 11.4, VII. 4.5.

NOTES TO CHAPTER IV

1. Socrates' demand for an account which makes virtue teachable; II. 4.1, III. 10.2. Protagoras' views on moral education; II. 4.4, III. 10.2.

2. UV in the *Ch.* and *La.*; III. 14.2–3. Protagoras describes his subject matter as good deliberation about one's own affairs and the state's, 318e5–319a2, as *hē politikē technē*, 319a3–7 (he accepts Socrates' description), 322b5, b7–8, *aidos kai dikē*, 322a2, c4, c7, d5; *politike arete,* 322e2, 324d1, *dikaiosunē kai hē allē politikē aretē,* 323b2; *dikaiosunē kai sōphrosunē kai to hosion einai, kai sulēbdēn auto prosagereuō einai andros aretēn,* 325a1–2; *dikaiosunē kai aretē,* 327b2; and often he calls it simply *aretē.* Cf. II. 4.4.

3. UV; III. 14.4. On the main issues about the interpretation of Socrates' views I mostly agree with Penner (404), who ascribes UV to Socrates, against Vlastos (407), who defends RV. First, Vlastos offers some general arguments about the Socratic dialogues.

1. He rightly rejects a further thesis: that all the names of the virtues are synonymous. Socrates has no reason to believe, and never tries to prove, that, e.g., 'bravery' and 'temperance' are synonymous. But they may have different senses and the same reference, as in the standard example of 'Morning Star' and 'Evening Star'.

2. Certainly Plato does not *mention* this distinction; but he could still have *observed* it. There is no presumption (as Vlastos suggests, 227, n. 12) that talk of 'names for the same thing' should naturally refer to synonymy rather than to co-reference; the concept of synonymy is no less technical than the concept of co-reference. We can only decide which is more appropriate for Plato's views by examining the views themselves.

3. There is reason to believe Plato observes the sense-reference distinction. (a) *Pr.* 357b7, *Phil.* 60a10 imply that (for a hedonist view) '*hedu*' and '*agathon*' are two names of the same thing. The onus of proof is on someone who thinks Plato means this as a claim of synonymy rather than co-reference; the claim would be implausible and unnecessary. The question whether the virtue-names are five names for the same thing should equally be taken to concern co-reference rather than synonymy. (b) *Cra.* 391d4–393b4 allows two proper names, 'Astyanax' and 'Scamandrius', for the same thing, the son of Hector. (c) Plato's epigram on Aster (*Astēr, prin men elampes eni zōoisin Eōos, num de thanōn lampeis Hesperos en phthimenois,* Diehl (138), fr. 4) plays on the co-reference of '*Eōos*' and '*Hesperos*'. This does not require him to formulate the sense-reference distinction, but it suggests that the distinction would not be alien to his practice (cf. *Epin.* 987b).

4. Further general arguments against ascription of UV to Socrates: (a) Vlastos finds it absurd to suggest, as UV would, that a definition of courage could show (as a definition of piety should) how an action is pious. But if courage is knowledge of the good, then (on Socrates' theory) its definition will equally show how an action expresses all the virtues. This will seem absurd to us only if we have already decided that UV is absurd; it is not an extra argument against acceptance of UV. (b) Common sense is outraged if 'courage' is used beyond its common meaning, to refer to all of virtue (Vlastos, 267). But *La.* 191cd (and Vlastos's comments; see above, III, n. 7) show that Socrates will outrage common sense for the sake of a better theory. (c) *M.* 78d–79c does not (as Vlastos thinks) show that Socrates recognizes parts of virtue; he

simply allows Meno this view, to refute him (the refutation would have been easier if UV had been assumed; Socrates makes the maximum concession to Meno). (d) Aristotle says that Socrates thought all the virtues were *logoi* or *phronēseis*. If the plurals mean 'branches of knowledge', Aristotle may not ascribe UV to Socrates (Vlastos, 238, n. 28), but may identify Socrates' position with his own, RV. But he may just mean 'instances (not kinds) of the same knowledge'.

These are Vlastos's general arguments against UV. Two passages in the *Pr.* make Socrates' position clearer:

1. First he offers a series of three choices between alternatives, until he finds exactly what Protagoras wants to maintain. First he asks whether virtue has parts.

(1) Virtue is one thing and the virtues are parts of it.

(2) Virtue is one thing, and the names of the virtues are all names of that one thing. (329c6–d1.)

When Protagoras chooses (1), Socrates offers him two versions of it:

(1a) The parts of virtue are like parts of a face.

(1b) The parts of virtue are like the parts of gold, differing only in size. (329d4–8.)

The difference is that (1a) implies, and (1b) denies, that each of the parts has its own particular capacity (*dunamis*, 330a4–b1). Protagoras accepts (1a), and Socrates offers two versions of it:

(1aa) Some men possess one of these parts, others another.

(1ab) It is necessary that anyone who has one of them has them all. (329d2–4.)

Protagoras accepts (1aa), and Socrates sets out to refute it.

Vlastos argues, 225, that (a) Socrates does not endorse (2); (b) he thinks (1b) and (1ab) are equivalent, and (1ab) is all that he defends against Protagoras. But, as Vlastos admits, 230 (1b), unlike (1ab), seems to make the virtues qualitatively indistinguishable. We need not follow Vlastos in rejecting this implication because it would be 'absurd and self-defeating', since we have found that (2) is perfectly sensible. (1b) seems to mean that the virtues are like lumps of the same stuff (cf. the atomists' analogy, Ar. *DC* 275b31–276a2); people can be more or less virtuous, but not by displaying different virtues in isolation. (The qualitative uniformity of virtue excludes an allusion to the genus–species relation, suggested by Vlastos.)

2. When the argument resumes, Socrates states the question at issue; whether the five names of the virtues are in fact names of one thing, or each is the name of its own separate reality (*ousia*) with its own capacity (349a8–b6). Protagoras, says Socrates, had rejected (2) and (1b) (349b6–c5); it is clear that he is also taken to have rejected (1aa), since he denies it at once (349d5–8). The Socratic thesis which he has been denying is clearly identified as (2), stronger than any version of (1). When Socrates later summarizes his position, by saying he has argued that justice, temperance and courage are all knowledge, he shows that he has been defending (2). But (2) is just the UV thesis defended (by implication) in the *La.*, that all the virtues are really not distinct, but are exactly the same knowledge.

Vlastos denies that Socrates endorses (2) here; he distinguishes the claim that five names are *of* one thing, 329d1, from the later claim that they are 'over' (*epi*) one thing, 349b2–3, and thinks the second claim, unlike the first, does not make them all proper names of one thing; they might be predicates (as in *Phd.* 104a5–7; Vlastos, 239). But there are objections. (1) Vlastos does not show any difference in use between 'name *epi*' and 'name of' (they seem to be equivalent at *Sph.* 244c1, d6); and 'name of' clearly refers to a proper name, not just a predicate, at *Phd.* 104a5. (2) Whatever we decide about this, Socrates' claim that the virtue-names all apply to just one and the same thing, with no separate reality underlying each, conflicts with Vlastos's view, which requires a separate reality for each name. (3) It is odd on Vlastos's view if Socrates has earlier rejected (2) and now recalls the previous discussion only to endorse a slight variant of (2), instead of (1ab). Contrary to what we would expect on

Vlastos's view, Socrates does not even mention (1ab) as his view in the later discussion (it is alluded to, 349d5–8). It is simpler to suppose he accepts (2) throughout, when we have found nothing nonsensical about UV to stop us from ascribing it to Socrates.

4. See III. 14.2–3.

5. The account of the hedonism as purely *ad hominem* is widely accepted; see, e.g., Taylor (111), 200, Moreau (107), 64–6, Sullivan (409), 28, Vlastos (412), 75 f. The hedonism is taken to be Socrates' own view by Grote (105), II. 87–9, Hackforth (408), Dodds (501), 21 f, and Vlastos (401), x1. On the *G*. and *Phd*. see V. 3.5, VI. 14.4.

6. I have not discussed the first series of arguments for UV because I do not think they are necessary for the main argument of the *Pr*.; though Socrates uses the hedonism only to argue for the unity of courage and wisdom, assuming that the previous arguments have proved the unity of the other virtues, in fact the same line of argument can be applied to all the virtues, independently of the first arguments. The acceptance of hedonism and KSV allows Socrates to prove what he initially argues for unsuccessfully. I offer here a few comments only, on the general tendency of the arguments. (For full discussion see Gallop (402), Savan (405) and (406), and Vlastos (407).)

1. The first argument relies on the assumption that justice and piety are both just and pious. I see no need to follow Vlastos, 252 ff, in translating these claims into 'Pauline' predications, saying that necessarily men are pious if they are just. Vlastos argues for this reading on the ground that Socrates thinks of 'justice' as the name of a universal, an abstract entity which would be an implausible bearer of moral properties. I do not see that Socrates thinks 'justice' names a universal rather than a condition of a person which is the source of a person's just actions, and can then fairly readily be called 'just'. Socrates' justice, we might say, is what is really just about Socrates, what is just in Socrates. (Cf. 'the largeness in us', *Phd*. 102d7, which is also large. See VI, n. 25.) The same account of justice will explain why it can also be pious.

To show that justice is pious and piety just, Socrates resorts to a fallacious slide from 'non-just' to unjust' (331a7–b1). But the claim might be supported by an argument of this form:

(1) A state of the soul is just if it produces just actions.
(2) An action is just if it is right and beneficial.
(3) Piety produces right and beneficial actions.
(4) Therefore piety is just.

The controversial assumption here would be (2) which seems to extend the use of 'just' beyond normal bounds. However, Socrates endorses the analogue to (2) in (7) below. The trouble is that no one would agree with (2) unless he accepted UV, so that it is useless for Socrates' present purposes.

2. The second argument, 332a2 ff, proceeds as follows:

(6) Each thing has only one opposite.
(7) If men act rightly and beneficially, they act temperately (332a6–8).
(8) If men act temperately, they act rightly and beneficially.
(9) An action done temperately is done by temperance (332a8–b1).
(10) An action done by folly is done in the opposite way to an action done by temperance (332b3–4).
(11) An action done not-rightly is done by folly (332b1–2).
(12) An action done by folly is done not-rightly.
(13) Temperance and folly produce opposite actions (from 7, 8, 11, 12).
(14) Temperance and folly are opposites.

The crucial steps here are (7) and (11), which Socrates offers no reason to believe (Vlastos, 244 ff). Of course someone who accepts UV will accept these two steps, but that is no help to Socrates.

3. The third argument begins at 332d, and clearly aims to find a link between an

action's being just, good, and beneficial, which will prove the identity of justice, temperance, and wisdom. But again the link needs some controversial steps in its proof.

These arguments rely on premises which require some previous defence of UV, and are unnecessary when Socrates introduces his later defence of the thesis.

7. The curious feature of this argument is that whereas Socrates has argued only that *wise* confidence is sufficient for courage, 350 c1–5, Protagoras replies as though Socrates had argued that confidence alone is sufficient, since that is what Protagoras now rejects. But however exactly his objection is to be understood, his main point is a fair reply to Socrates; knowledge is only sufficient for confidence; for real courage, nature and good training are required, and the training may or may not produce knowledge, as long as it produces confidence and the desire to use it rightly. Confidence is one part of courage, and knowledge is one source of confidence, but neither necessary nor sufficient for courage. Other views on this passage; Vlastos (401), xxxii ff, O'Brien (124), 183 f, (403). O'Brien (124), 141–3, argues that Plato means Protagoras' account of moral training to be accepted, because it is accepted in the *R*. But the rest of the *Pr*. does not suggest acceptance, and agreement with the *R*. is a hazardous criterion; see VII, n. 21.

8. Protagoras' agreement, 352c8–d3, on the importance of *paideia*, is taken to involve KSV—illegitimately (contrast Moreau (107), 63 f), though the later argument does not depend on his agreement here. The *paideia* advocated by Protagoras in the Great Speech is not purely cognitive.

9. Vlastos (412), 79 n. denies that Socrates endorses hedonism in 351b6 ff, supposing that the formula 'pleasant things qua pleasant are good', 351c4–6, allows other things to be goods too, and that Protagoras is wrong in 351e3–7 to ascribe hedonism to Socrates. But Socrates has persuaded Protagoras to agree (a) that pleasure is necessary for living well, 351b4–5; (b) living pleasantly is sufficient for living well, b6–7. In b6–c1 Socrates endorses hedonism, and Protagoras' comment at e3–7 is fair.

10. 'Pleasant' and 'good' are not taken to be synonymous. Socrates'. argument is concerned with what people actually consider in their choices, as opposed to what they find it intelligible or absurd to say (the normal evidence of an argument about meaning; cf. III, n. 30); it is not a good argument for a claim of synonymy. He suggests that 'pleasant' and 'good' are two names for the same thing (353b3–c1; cf. *Phil*. 60a7–b4); but the 'same thing' (*pragma*) or 'reality' (*ousia*) need not be the same meaning.

11. Like Socrates, I move between 'pleasant' and 'pleasure'. He explains his use of *hēdu*, both for instances of pleasure or enjoyment and for what causes pleasure, at 351d7–e1, and no fallacy is involved in his moves.

12. *The argument against incontinence.*

1. Socrates' views on desire and the good; III. 12.2, V. 2.2. Here I offer only a few comments to support the outline of the argument in the text.

2. The Socratic assumption (3) is needed to justify the transformation of (1) into (2). Socrates construes 'overcome by the pleasures of *x*' as 'because he desires the pleasures of *x*'. To justify the substitution of 'goods' for 'pleasures' it is not enough to prove only that *A* believes all pleasures are goods; for he might know this, and still not choose *x* because he wants its goods—if *A* chooses *x* because it is sweet, and believes that all sweet things contain many calories, it does not follow that he chooses *x* for its many calories. Either the substitution in (2) is fallacious, or Socrates can show that *A* chooses pleasures only because of their goods. (3) will justify this claim; but (3) depends on HP.

3. My view of the argument depends on taking 'being overcome by pleasure' to mean 'because he believes *x* to be pleasanter', so that 'being overcome' refers to the agent's beliefs, not to what is in fact the case. When 'being overcome by goods' is

taken similarly, the many's view is ridiculous; and this result, on my view, is reached at once in 355d1–3. This view of the argument is nearest to Vlastos (401). At (412), 81 f, he rejects it; he objects that if (1) A prefers x to y for x's goods, it does not follow that (2) A prefers x because he thinks x is better on the whole. This objection is fair, and shows either that Socrates' argument is invalid, or that my account of it is wrong, unless HP is taken into account. From HP it does follow that (1a) A prefers x because he believes x pleasanter on the whole; and, substituting 'good' for 'pleasant', (2) follows from (1a). There is no objection, then, to finding the 'ridiculous' result of the many's argument where it is said to be, in 355d1–3.

4. The next steps of the argument are:

5. When A chooses x over y, 'overcome by' the goods in x, these goods are not worthy to overcome the evils in x, 355d3–6.

6. Goods and evils are worthy to overcome each other if and only if they are (actually) greater or more numerous, 355d6–e2.

7. Therefore 'being overcome' is simply choosing (actually) greater evils in return for (actually) smaller goods, 355e2–3.

These steps reduce 'being overcome' to some phenomenon Socrates accepts, described in (7). Vlastos and Santas (411), 275–82, find the 'ridiculous' result in (7). But (7) is not said to be absurd at all; the principles which Vlastos and Santas rely on show that 355d1–3 was already absurd, as argued above.

13. *The role of hedonism.* Vlastos (412), 83 f, maintains that the argument of 355a–e relies only on the claim that everything pleasant is good, which does not imply hedonism. In any case, he thinks, the absurdity of the many's case can be proved from certain Socratic principles: (S1) If one knows that x is better than y, one will want x more than y. (S2) If one wants x more than y, one will choose x rather than y. And these in turn follow from two other Socratic principles: (S3) All men desire welfare (i.e. *eudaimonia*). (S4) Anything else they desire only as a means to welfare. Vlastos remarks, 87 f, that these four principles by themselves would allow an even stronger attack on the many than is provided by Socrates' explicit argument. Santas offers similar principles (411), 286, to allow Socrates to accommodate the other cases of incontinence mentioned by the many at 351b besides being overcome by pleasure.

There are some objections to these efforts to eliminate hedonism from Socrates' argument.

1. I have explained in n. 12 why I think more than 'everything pleasant is good' is required for the substitutions in 355ae—unless choosing something for its pleasure just is choosing it for its good, Socrates' argument will be fallacious. Either hedonism or S3–S4 is needed to license the substitutions. But if S3–4 is allowed, the absurdity arises at once in 355d1.

2. I agree that S1–4 will provide an argument against incontinence (it will in fact be the argument in *M.* 77–8; see III. 12.3). But should the many accept S3–4? These two steps simply deny the many's claim at 351b; and if Socrates' argument relied on them, it would grossly beg the question, and completely fail to deal with the many's purported counter-examples. Now since the many's position is found to be inconsistent, they must somewhere have agreed to something inconsistent with their other beliefs. But hedonism makes a difference, in that it seriously attempts to explain away their counter-examples, and *argues* them into accepting step (3) of the argument—Vlastos's S4—because they have accepted HP. The refutation relying on HP differs from Vlastos's refutation in being an argument from the many's position, rather than a simple question-begging denial of it. If we want to leave Socrates with an *argument* for step (3), we cannot do without the hedonism.

Others suggest (e.g. Taylor (111), 260, Sullivan (409), 25) that Socrates argues from hedonist premisses he knows to be false, to show that *even* on these false premisses accepted by the many KSV can be proved. There are problems with this view too.

1. It is curious that Socrates does *not* represent hedonism as the position which the many advocate; he has to *convince* them that in their own choices they accept it. Cf. Hackforth (408), 41, Dodds (501), 21 n.

2. If Socrates thinks his argument proves anything important, he should be able to defend KSV, not only from the false-hedonist premisses of the many, but also on the true theory he accepts; otherwise he has no right to draw the conclusions he draws for *himself* (not only on behalf of the many) about the truth of KSV and UV. But it is not clear what other premisses he can fairly invoke to justify him. For these reasons it is not so easy to suppose that Socrates can admit the falsity of hedonism and still maintain his argument.

This second argument is not decisive; for even if we see that Socrates' step (3) is question-begging without the support of HP, Socrates may not have thought so; for in the *M.* and *G.* he apparently accepts KSV because of (3), with no hedonist premisses. Perhaps Plato realizes in later dialogues that the principles M and H are no substitute for P; it does not follow that he sees their limited use when he writes the *Pr.* But anyhow it is significant that Plato does not try to refute claims of incontinence in later dialogues; he offers no substitute for HP, and so, at least implicitly, recognizes its importance. (Santas (411), 281, sees the importance of HP.)

14. At 357a5–6 Socrates leaves open the question about what kind of science is required. I do not think that this question, or the sceptical conclusion of the dialogue, suggests that he is dubious about his proof that a science for measuring pleasures and pains will guarantee living well; it just shows that he has not explained how exactly this science will proceed, how exactly the measurement will be done. We should not follow O'Brien (124), 136, who infers from the end of the dialogue that the identification of virtue and knowledge is not the unambiguous conclusion of the *Pr.* Socrates betrays no doubts about the soundness of the principles and the argument leading to this conclusion, either here or in the Socratic dialogues; cf. VII, n. 21.

15. On 356d3–4 see II, n. 21.

16. TV; III. 13.3. The instrumental status of virtue; III. 16.1.

17. ED; II, n. 29; III. 9.5, 17.5.

18. See III. 17.7.

19. The only sign of qualitative distinctions among pleasures is Prodicus' distinction between *euphrainesthai* and *hēdesthai*, 357c1–4. But Socrates seems to reject any such distinction, 358a5–b2, as though it were, if not illusory, at least irrelevant to his argument, and he says nothing more about the scope of *hēdonē*; there is no sign of a distinction among *hēdonai* until the *G.* appears to accept exactly the division rejected by Socrates at 351b3 ff. See V. 3.5.

20. See III. 7.7.

21. See VII. 4. 4–5. On Protagoras see II. 4.4.

22. On the craft-principles see III. 17.1.

NOTES TO CHAPTER V

1. On the relative date of the *G.* see II, n. 33. Some connections between the *Cri.* and the *G.* are particularly plain. In both dialogues Socrates insists that living well matters more than mere length of life, *Cri.* 48b3–6, *G.* 513e; that it is better to suffer than to do injustice, *Cri.* 49c; and that care of the soul is supremely important, *Cri.* 47e, *G.* 479b. Polus, like Crito, tries to scare him with a bogey, 'what the many think', 474d3, *Cri.* 46c4, and wants the question put to a vote, 473e6–474b1, *Cri.* 46c8–d4. As before, Socrates believes that he can make any sincere interlocutor with some ordinary moral beliefs agree with him, 495a7–8, 482b2–6; he wants to abide by the agreements reached in discussion, 480b2–5, *Cri.* 49a4–b6; he is confident of reaching the truth, 487a1–7, *Cri.* 48b3–6, but does not claim unrevisability, 508e6–509b1, *Cri.* 48d8–e1.

2. The radical critics; II. 4.6–7.

3. Hedonism in the *Pr.*; IV, n. 5.

4. Socrates treats Gorgias unfairly to make his position look incoherent. When Socrates presses him, Gorgias agrees that he will tell his pupil what is just, good, and admirable if the pupil does not previously know. This does not imply that he teaches another craft, or that he regards himself as an expert in it—he will 'teach' only in the sense in which all citizens can teach virtue; cf. *Pr.* 323b3–c2.

5. The *HMi.* paradox; III. 11.3. Socrates assumes as usual that someone who knows that an action is just will also know that it benefits him; III, n. 67.

6. The rejection of good-independent desires; III. 12.3. 'Good' and 'good for the agent'; III, n. 51. I do not think any special sense of '*boulēsis*', making it refer only to the desire for ends (O'Brien (124), 88 ff), is needed—that would make Socrates' claim that we have a *boulēsis* only for the good trivial, which it is not meant to be. *M.* 77c5–78b2 treats *boulesthai* and *epithumein* as equivalents in a similar argument (but on *epithumia* later in the *G.* see below, n. 17). *Ch.* 167e1–8 associates *boulēsis* with the good, *epithumia* with the pleasant, and *erōs* with the admirable; but if Socrates believes we desire the pleasant only in so far as it is good (which does not commit him to hedonism), the distinction will be unimportant for him.

Nor does the use of *boulesthai* here imply reference to a 'real will' not displayed in the agent's choices, suggested by Dodds (501), on 467c5 ff, Gould (120), 50 f. Socrates means only that if *A* chooses *x* for the sake of *y* and fails to achieve *y* through *x*, *A* does not get what he wants from *x*. He is not entitled to the further claim that *A* has no power or capacity at all, 466d7–467a10; he need only insist that *A* lacks the power to get what he wants.

7. *Kalon, agathon*, and *ōphelimon*; see *Alc.* 115a1–116d3, II. 6.2, III. 3.3, VI. 12.3–5.

8. The slide from 'pleasant to the beholder' in 474d8 to 'pleasant to the agent' in 475b8–c4 (I use 'agent' for the subject of *adikein* or *adikeisthai*) is pointed out by Vlastos (503), 457 f. The analogous slide from 'good for the community' to 'good for the agent' is necessary for Socrates' conclusion in 475e3–6 that no one would think unjust action good *for him* and for the conclusion that just punishment must be good for the man punished, in 476d5–477a4. This slide is noticed by Dodds (501), 249. Vlastos rightly protests against the view of Dodds and others that Plato's argument, on which he rests important conclusions, is consciously fallacious; but I do not think it is a simple mistake in logic; rather it is an argument which (like some in the *Pr.*; see IV, n. 6) rests on assumptions accepted by Socrates which cannot uncontroversially be accepted in the context. The limitation of goods to possible objects of choice has already been assumed in the argument about desire and the good; see III, n. 51.

9. The account of *to kalon* here does not tell for or against the acceptance of hedonism in the *G. To kalon* is so called with reference to either *hedone* or *ophelia*. The *hedea* mentioned in 474e seem to be examples of things which cause pleasure by themselves, so that the *ophelima* might be things which cause pleasure through their results. A hedonist account is neither required nor excluded.

10. Callicles' position is made a little unclear by his use of *adikein* and *adikeisthai* to refer to doing and suffering conventional injustice, 483a7–b5. But in 483c1–d2 he shows that t.ie use of *adikein* for *pleon echein* is the many's use, not his—he does not think *pleon echein* is really or naturally *adikein*. He does not commit himself, then, to the view that real *adikein* is less *aischron* than real *adikeisthai*. (Though he would no doubt say this; for to *adikein* someone would presumably be to prevent him from exercizing his superiority, and someone would be *adikoumenos* if he suffered this kind of treatment.) This failure to align his use of *adikein* and *adikeisthai* with his use of *dikaion* and *adikon* does not betray any deep confusion in Callicles' position.

11. Justice; II. 3.5, III. 6.3, VII. 2.3; Socrates' standard assumptions; III. 1.7.

12. For this conception of courage see II. 3.2, VII. 15.5.

13. The argument at 495e1–497d8 proceeds as follows:

(1) Doing well and doing badly are opposites, 495e2–4.

(2) Opposites (e.g., being healthy and being unhealthy) cannot both be present to the same person or to the same part of him at the same time, 495e6–496c5.

(3) Pleasure and pain can both be present to the same man at the same time, 496e6–8.

(4) The presence of pleasure is not identical with doing well, nor the presence of pain with doing badly, 497a3–4.

(5) The pleasant is not identical with the good, 497a4–5.

The steps (1)–(3) are acceptable; there is nothing wrong with Socrates' example of the simultaneous pleasure of drinking and pain of thirst. And from all this (4) follows; not just any pleasure is sufficient for someone to be well off. But Socrates could as easily prove that not just any good is sufficient for living well; a part of my body might be in good condition while I am badly off on the whole, because 'well off' and 'badly off' represent the result of an overall judgement. But now if pleasure in some respect is not the same as being well off over all, it clearly does not follow that having pleasure over all is not the same as being well off over all, or that the pleasant and the good are not identical. The argument collapses at the move from (4) to (5). For this diagnosis see Crombie (101), I. 247. For a different objection, see Adkins (207), 280 n.

14. The argument at 497e1 ff, is as follows:

(1) A man is good in so far as goods are present to him, and bad in so far as evils are present to him, 497e1–3.

(2) A brave and wise man is good, and a cowardly and foolish man is bad, 497e3–5.

(3) Anything is a good iff it is a pleasure.

(4) Cowardly and foolish men have pleasures equal to, or greater than, the pleasures of wise and brave men, 497e6–498c1.

(5) Cowardly and foolish men have goods present to them equal to, or greater than, the goods present to brave and wise men.

(6) Cowardly and foolish men are as good as, or better than, brave and wise men.

(7) Bad men are as good as, or better than, good men, 499a7–b3.

The argument Socrates presents is ruined by (1), which Callicles has no reason to accept. Socrates simply moves unjustifiably from 'x is *kalon* by the presence of *kallos*' (for this talk of 'presence' cf. *Lys.* 217d1–e4) to 'x is *agathon* by the presence of *agatha* (or *to agathon*; cf. 506d1–2). But he has no right to assume that the presence of *any* kind of *agatha* is enough to make a man *agathos* or to produce *aretē*. The relevant kind of *agathon* would be a capacity to acquire pleasure (a *dunamis*; cf. 466b6, *M.* 78c4–5). Then the question Socrates should ask is not whether the coward on some occasion gains as much pleasure as the brave man, but whether he has an equal capacity for gaining pleasure. But his argument still has some force if it is modified this way—and I have discussed the modified version.

15. This account of the argument adds something to what the text says. But we must add something to explain the relation to the *Pr.* Either (a) Plato still accepts the *Pr.*'s answer, or (b) he has some reason for rejecting it, or (c) he rejects it for no reason. If (a) is right, why does he not simply say that Callicles is just wrong about what is pleasantest, and that hedonism requires an orderly life? That would be easy to say; but instead Plato creates the misleading (on this view) impression that he has tried to refute hedonism.

The impression is not misleading at all if we accept (b); and though the defence of (b) is not explicit, its materials are readily available in the rest of the *G.*, especially in the denial of a science of pleasure.

It is hard to exclude decisively the view that the *G.* is an early attack on hedonism and the *Pr.* a later correction when Plato sees more in hedonism. But (1) on this view we still have to explain the anti-hedonism of the *Phd.* (VI. 11.4); and the *G.* is an intelligible intermediate stage between hedonism and the *Phd.*'s position. (2) The argument of the *Pr.* would be rather weak if Plato ignored the objections to hedonism and the measuring science he had already raised. (3) There are other reasons, apart from the issue about hedonism, to place the *G.* between the *Pr.* and the middle dialogues; see II, n. 33. (4) Even if these arguments are not decisive, they do not affect the logical relations between the arguments in the two dialogues; it remains true that the *G.* contains objections to the epistemological hedonism of the *Pr.* It is possible Plato did not realize their force until after he had written the *G.* and the *Pr.*, in that order; but in the absence of strong counter-arguments, it is simplest to assume that the statement of the doctrine precedes the criticism.

16. The objection to pursuit of pleasure in general is the best I can make of Socrates' criticism of the orator. He had earlier argued that rhetoric can give no *logos* or *aitia* of what it does, 465a. But he could not plausibly claim that no 'Ars Rhetorica' could be produced to provide general principles for different kinds of speeches and their likely effects—Polus had written just such a work, 462b11, which, Socrates implies, was not enough to make a craft out of rhetoric. Its failure must rest on the inherent failings of pleasure as a goal. Socrates implies (if we have read his anti-hedonist arguments rightly) that what gives someone pleasure depends on his other goals, so that the orator always depends on his audience's preferences, and has no objectively valid procedure of his own.

17. It is not clear exactly what view of the soul is implied in 493b; but it seems to be more than the 'popular distinction between reason and impulse' mentioned by Dodds (501), ad loc., citing Aesch. *Pers.* 767, Theog. 731. A possibly similar division is recognized in the *Phdr.*; VII. 17.7. The division here may not rest on a particular Platonic theory, certainly not on the developed theory of the *R.* (though the pre-Platonic evidence for a division of the soul is scarce and weak; II. n. 20). Anyhow, the scope of *epithumiai* in 493b1 is narrower than the scope of *epithumein* in *M.* 77b4 ff (see above, n. 6); not all desires could be described as belonging to an 'insatiable and intemperate' part of the soul. *Epithumiai* are now more like the *epithumiai* in the *R.*, though without the theory to justify the division. (On the scope of *epithumiai* in the *R.* see VII, n. 20.)

18. Dodds (501), 333, and Adkins (207), 274, object to the move in 507e1 from *kosmia* to *sōphrōn*. I do not think this is indefensible—for Socrates' argument against Callicles has shown that the *kosmos* required will include the control of desires which might be held to make someone *sōphrōn*. The trouble is in the move from *sōphrosunē*, so understood, to *dikaiosunē*, if that is taken to include concern for other people's interests.

The attitude of the passage to UV is interesting. Socrates claims that a single *taxis* of the soul will be necessary and sufficient for all the virtues—it assumes the role filled by knowledge in earlier dialogues. But the *G.* shows how to distinguish the virtues; *sōphrosunē* is linked to *kosmos* (507a1; cf. *Ch.* 159b3), and courage to endurance (507b8; cf. *La.* 192b9). It is striking that these distinguishing features are exactly the non-cognitive components of the virtues which were eliminated from the discussion in the *La.* and *Ch.* and were ignored in the *Pr.*—for the good reason that they were irrelevant if KSV was true (see III. 14.1). The reappearance of these non-cognitive components in the *G.* is associated with the treatment of virtue as a *taxis* of the soul—dubiously compatible with KSV. The view hinted at here is fully developed in the *R.*, where Plato has the account of the soul he needs to justify and explain this talk of psychic order; see VII. 7.1.

19. Problems with the reference of 'justice'; III. 18.6, VII. 10.1. Socrates cannot accuse Callicles of arbitrarily misusing the 'ordinary concept' of justice. Callicles appealed to the connection of justice with *nomos* 483e2, to show he was talking about justice; see II. 3.6. He departs no more radically than Socrates departs from the common concept.

20. On other people's interests see VII. 2.4.

21. The *M.*'s argument against anyone wanting what he knows to be bad is equally ill equipped to deal with the counter-examples offered by the many; see III. 12.5, IV, n. 13.

22. 505b may also assume the existence of non-rational desires, if the control mentioned here can be exercised by a man over his own desires; but the context is primarily concerned with control imposed by others; cf. 504d5–e4.

23. The *La.* and *Ch.*; III. 14.2.3; The *Pr.* on 'being overcome'; IV.2.5 The *R.* on self-mastery; VII. 7.5.

24. Perhaps Socrates might (though he does not) defend the compatibility of non-rational desires and KSV, by arguing that non-rational desires will be controlled as soon as someone sees that they are bad for him. But this unargued assertion would be open to easy empirical refutation; or else it would require a sense of 'knowledge', making action necessary for knowledge, which would deprive Socrates' thesis of interest; cf. III, n. 52.

25. The CA and TV; III. 13.3, IV. 3.3. Socrates answers yes to Polus' question, 470d8, 'Is all of happiness in this (i.e. in justice and culture [*paideia*])?' If 'in' means only 'dependent on', Socrates may mean only that justice is necessary for happiness. He replies, 'I say that the admirable and good man and woman is happy and the unjust and depraved is wretched'. Being admirable and good is sufficient for being but Socrates does not say whether being just is sufficient, or only necessary, for being admirable and good—the last clause implies only that justice is necessary for happiness. The position here is obscure; the *R.*'s position is clearer—VII, n. 11.

26. Virtue and happiness; III. 16.1.

27. The problem about experts in the *Cri.*; III. 9.3. Elenchos and craft; III. 17.1.

NOTES TO CHAPTER VI

1. On the 'middle dialogues', and their chronology see II, n. 33. Grote (105), I. 271, and Mill (106), 285, 290, deny a connection between Plato's elenctic inquiries and his constructive doctrine (though Grote recognizes, II. 18, the connection between dialectical inquiry and the Theory of Recollection). I am arguing that, on the contrary, some of Plato's constructive doctrines are meant as solutions to Socratic problems. Not all his doctrines need be explained the same way; and they may not be good solutions; I am only trying to show a reasonable connection for *part* of Plato's metaphysics and epistemology.

2. Here and elsewhere I use an initial capital letter in 'Forms' and in the names of particular Forms, when separation (to be explained in 9.1–3) from sensibles is implied, and small initial letters when it is not.

3. On the priority of definition see III. 1.6, 7.3.

4. On the *G.* see V. 1.1, 5.5.

5. On Socrates' earlier defence of UA, and on A- and B-powers see III. 2.4. His argument against Meno is as follows:

(1) A man's virtue is to govern a city well, a woman's to govern a household well. 73a6–7.

(2) Anyone who governs well governs temperately and justly, 73a7–9.

(3) Anyone who governs temperately and justly governs by temperance and justice, 73b1–2.

(4) Therefore a good (i.e. virtuous) man or woman needs the same things, temperance and justice, 73b2–5.

(5) If a child or old man is intemperate and unjust, he never becomes good, 73b5–7.

(6) If he is temperate and just, he becomes good, 73b7–c1. (*alla sōphrones kai dikaioi ontes* [sc. *agathoi en eien*]; unless justice and temperance are sufficient for being good, (7) will not follow.)

(7) Therefore all men become good by acquiring the same things, temperance and

justice, 73c2–3.

(8) Therefore all men become good in the same way, 73c1–2.

(9) But if they are all good in the same way, they all have the same virtue, 73c3–5.

(10) Therefore all men have the same virtue, 73c6.

Robinson (133), 57, and Bluck (601), ad loc., think this argument prematurely ends Socrates' search for a definition; but 'justice and temperance' is not a sufficient account of virtue for Socrates.

The argument moves dubiously from adverbs to underlying states in (3), and from 'the same thing' and 'the same way' in (7)–(8) to 'the same virtue' in (9). Socrates needs more argument to identify a single B-power. On the account of virtue relative to function see II. 1.3, Gosling (104), 34. On justice and temperance as complete virtue see II, n. 15.

6. On ED see III. 9.5, 17.5.

7. Socrates would be satisfied—*agapō(i)ēn an*, 75c1, if Meno could give him a formula coextensive with 'virtue', as Socrates has given a formula coextensive with 'shape'. *Agapō(i)ēn* suggests that this result would be less than ideal; it does not show that Socrates will accept a coextensive formula as a complete answer to his search for a definition; contrast Robinson (133), 54, followed by Bluck (601), 7, criticized by Allen (341), 76–8. For *Agapān* cf. *R.* 330b6, *Tht.* 207a3–7. This formula would be open to the criticism at *Eu.* 11a6–b1.

8. Socrates rejects an Empedoclean definition of colour, because it demands specialized knowledge unavailable to an ordinary interlocutor, 76c–e. It is *tragikē*, 76e3, i.e. to a non-specialist it is just a riddle, like the definition of dust as 'mud's thirsty sister'; cf. Aesch. *Ag.* 435, *Sep.* 494, and *R.* 413b4, 545e1. Cf. Bluck (601), ad loc., Nakhnikian (325), 135, Taylor (111), 135 n. This requirement on definitions should not be confused with the DR; for moral terms are not a complete puzzle to us like specialized scientific terms (cf. *Alc.* 110b1–c5), but accounts which include them fail the DR.

9. 4c. If the DR required a definition of x as y, a definition of y as z, then a definition of z, and so on, it would require an infinite regress or a simultaneous definition of everything, or else Socrates would have to allow some claims to knowledge unsupported by a definition. But the DR requires only the definition of y, not the further definition of z; on another occasion it might be fair to require a definition of z too; but it is not needed to support a claim to know x by defining it as y. And so the DR avoids both a regress and simultaneous definition of everything.

10. First Meno suggests that virtue is 'desiring *kala* and having the power to acquire them', 77b4–5. On Socrates' argument to show that the reference to desire is superfluous see III. 12.3. Socrates then substitutes *agatha* for *kala*. This is a standard move, but especially dubious here (cf. III. 3.3); even if all *kala* are *agatha*, virtue might still be the desire for the subset of *agatha* which are also *kala*. To justify himself, Socrates must show that all *agatha* are *kala*, a harder task. See V. 2.4, and VI. 12.2–5.

Bluck (601), ad loc., and Penner (339), 149 f, think Meno is wrong only in restricting his list of goods to recognized goods; they hardly do justice to Socrates' objections. For his earlier views on the soul see III. 16.2, V. 5.4.

78e2–5 shows that we can still be virtuous even if we do not succeed in acquiring goods; Socrates over-confidently claims that a *dunamis tou porizesthai agatha* is irrelevant to virtue—but it might still be relevant even if it need not always be successful. Socrates is confused by, or equivocates on, *aporia*, meaning (1) (what he is entitled to) 'failure to provide', and (2) (what he is not entitled to) 'inability to provide'—failure to provide on some occasion does not imply general complete inability.

11. On UV see IV, n. 3.

12. At 80e Socrates fairly restates Meno's objection as an eristic argument (i.e. not in

the spirit of constructive dialectic, 75c8–d4) against the possibility of inquiry; if we know *x*, we can't inquire into *x*, for no further inquiry is necessary or possible; and if we don't know *x*, we can't inquire into it, for we don't know what we are inquiring into.

I have used 'inquire into' to translate *zētein*, to represent Socrates' and Meno's use, parallel to the uses of *eidenai*, with (a) a direct object alone; (b) a noun-clause, e.g. *ho ti pot'estin*; and (c) both the direct object and the clause. *Zētein* covers both looking for a person or thing (e.g. Meno) and looking for the answer to a question; and this wide scope helps Meno's objection. He asks first (1) 'How can I look for *x* unless I know what *x* is?', which may seem reasonable enough applied to persons and things; and then (2) 'How can I look for the answer unless I know it?', which is a genuine paradox. But his main point works in any case if we allow the exclusive and exhaustive disjunction of knowing *x* or being wholly ignorant about *x*. (Contrast White (610), 290–4, who thinks that Plato treats looking for the answer as a case of looking for an object.) For while 'I can't inquire into *x* unless I know *x*' is plausible, if 'know' means only 'can recognise', it is absurdly strong if 'know' means 'can give a Socratic account'. The shift from the first sense to the second which creates the paradox is licensed by the disjunction assumed by Meno; and the disjunction is more plausible if we think knowledge is purely a matter of acquaintance—either we grip something or we are out of touch with it. A similar disjunction, made plausible by a similar assumption, underlies the argument at *Tht.* 188ac; see McDowell (324), ad loc., who, however (without reference to Meno's paradox) ascribes the mistaken assumption to Plato. The argument against the paradox suggests that here at least Plato rejects the disjunction and the assumption about acquaintance.

The paradox does not raise puzzles about how I learn that's a horse if I am confronted with one and told 'That's a horse' (see Phillips (607), 87). But it is not confined to *a priori*, as opposed to empirical, truths—it arises in any kind of inquiry which involves some previous identification of the subject of inquiry, whereas my being told that this is a horse requires no previous inquiry by me.

13. There is more to the Theory of Recollection than the account of Socratic elenchos, and it is an understatement to say, as I do, that Socrates *compares* the slave's learning to recollection; he thinks it *is* recollection of pre-natal knowledge, and that the pre-existence of the soul explains how the slave's learning is possible. There is no regress in the explanation; the discarnate soul's learning was not the result of inquiry, and so is not exposed to Meno's objections. But the claim about pre-existence is not required for the answer to the paradox, as the progress of the argument shows: (1) 81a5–e2; Socrates tells the priests' and priestesses' story about pre-existence. (2) 81e3–82a6; Meno asks Socrates to explain his claim about recollection. (3) 82a7–85b7; Socrates agrees and examines the slave. (4) 85b8–d5; Socrates remarks that the slave drew his answers from within him—let us say they displayed quasi-recollection (QR). (5) 85d6–86b4; Socrates argued that the slave could manage QR only if he really recollected, and knew the answers before his birth, so that the story abour pre-existence must be true.

The argument demands that we recognize the 'evidence' for the full theory before we accept the theory (cf. Vlastos (609), 143, 158 f); i.e. we must accept (4), that the slave performs QR, before we accept (1) or (5). If we accept (4), we accept that QR is possible, and then (5) tells us how it is possible. Now the answer to Meno's paradox in 85e6–7 comes in (4), requiring no appeal to (5); to show where Meno was wrong, we must agree that QR is possible, but we are free to reject the explanation in (5). I think it is fair, then, to treat the Theory of Recollection as an account of knowledge relying on QR, which is independent of (1) and (5)—this part of the theory is important in its own right.

The steps in the interrogation of the slave follow the standard pattern of the elenchos:

(1) He states a general rule, 82e4–6, that a square A with a side double the length of the side of a square B will have double the area of B. Laches and Euthyphro too are confident they know general rules to answer Socrates' questions, and so is Meno himself; *La.* 190e4, *Eu.* 4b9–5e2, *M.* 71e1. They, like the slave, will answer 'freely, and to many people, and often', 84b11–c2.

(2) The counter-example of the figure in front of him refutes his general claim and shakes his confidence, 82e14–84a2. Like other interlocutors (see III. 1.3) he must answer sincerely, not trying to fit the case to his general rule, 83d1–2. Vlastos, 145–8, argues that the diagrams are irrelevant to recollection, because the same results could be achieved by pure logical reasoning. I agree that (a) the diagrams are dispensable here; but reject two further claims, that (b) they are irrelevant (see against this Bluck (601), 14), and that (c) any use of the senses or of particular examples is always irrelevant to recollection. The slave's realization that this case refutes his general rule makes him change his mind; particular examples have the same role in the Socratic dialogues; see III. 1.3. Similarly, in *Phd.* 73a10–b2, 74b4–6, d4–7, 75a5–7, sensible examples stimulate someone to a better conception of the equal.

(3) 84a3–b8; the slave is reduced from confident belief to numb confusion, like Meno, 79e7–80b4, and other interlocutors; *Eu.* 11b6–8, *La.* 193d11–e6, *R.* 334b7–9. The confusion benefits him by making him aware of his ignorance and anxious to learn, 84c4–6; cf. *Sph.* 230c3–d4, III. 1.2.

(4) Socrates improves the slave's beliefs, asking questions which yield a true answer. He does not teach (84c10–d2; cf. *Ap.* 19d8–e1), but acts like a midwife to make beliefs explicit and tests them for soundness; cf. *Tht.* 150a8–b4, c7–d8, 151b6–c5, Bluck on *M.* 84d1, Cornford (604), 27 f.

(5) In the *Meno* Socrates knows the answers to his questions, and the inquiry reaches a positive conclusion. The absence of these features in the Socratic dialogues, though, does not show a decisive difference; for Socrates has positive beliefs, and reaches positive conclusions, though neither of these constitute knowledge.

14. The emphatic pleonasm, at 85c6–7 (*to(i) ouk eidoti ara peri hōn an mē eidē(i) eneisin alētheis doxai peri toutōn hōn ouk oiden*) refers to the initial statement of Meno's Paradox, and shows Plato's answer. Thompson (608), 115, notices the importance of *doxa* here; contrast White (610), 304 n., who does not mention this passage, or the anticipation of 98a in 85c9–d1.

15. On knowledge in the Socratic dialogues see III. 7.2. In 99a3, as often, *aitia* includes much more than we normally call a 'cause', and 'explanation' has roughly equal scope. Sometimes, e.g. in mathematical cases, the *aitia* will be a demonstrative proof; but I think Vlastos (609), 154 f, is wrong to restrict *aitias logismos*, and recollection as a whole, to reasoning relying on logical necessity; *logismos* (as Vlastos agrees) is often used for 'reasoning' more broadly, and the *Meno* suggests no restriction to logical necessity—which would not establish the conclusions Socrates wants about the virtues (see III. 7.4.).

Bluck (601), 7, 32 f, wrongly generalizes from the Larisa example at 97a9–b7, and thinks recollection is meant to produce some 'view', with a feeling of inner conviction (see also Gulley (605), 76). None of this is said or implied in the *Meno*.

16. On problems of reference see III. 7.7, and cf. White (610), 297–302.

17. The scope of recollection is left vague; at 81c6 it includes (a) 'all things', and then (b) 'virtue and other things', and then at 81d4–5 (c) all *zētein kai manthanein*. If (c) is taken to exclude knowledge which demands no inquiry, we might be allowed to know the road to Larisa without recollection, since it requires perception, but not inquiry; facts about the world can hardly be recollected, unless the discarnate soul was fed an encyclopedia. It is best to suppose that (c) restricts (a) to the kinds of things a soul could know and use in different incarnations. This need not confine recollection to *a priori* truths (as Moravcsik (606), 65 f, suggests); some empirical contribution (like the perception of equals in the *Phaedo*) may still begin the recollection and influence

the conclusion.

18. See VII. 12.2.
19. See III. 17.7.
20. See IV. 3.3 and V. 5.3.
21. See Taylor (111), 144 f, Gould (120), 140 f, Vlastos (412), 73 n. See also VII, n. 26.
22. The argument is as follows:
   (1) Virtue is knowledge if and only if it is teachable, 87c1–9.
   (2) Virtue is always beneficial, 87e3. ('Beneficial' here must mean 'beneficial in action', as the examples in 88b3–c3 suggest; without this restriction step (12) below does not refute KNV, since it does not show that right belief is as beneficial as knowledge, except in action.)
   (3) If only knowledge is always beneficial, virtue is knowledge, 87d6–8.
   (4) If anything else is always beneficial, perhaps (tach'an) virtue is not knowledge, 87d4–6. (On this argument see III, n. 57.)
   (5) Only knowledge is always beneficial, 88c1–d1.
   (6) Therefore virtue is knowledge, 88d2–3.
   (7) Therefore virtue is teachable, 89c2–4.
   (8) If anything is teachable, there are teachers of it, 89d6–8.
   (9) There are no teachers of virtue, 96b6–8.
   (10) Therefore virtue is not teachable, 96b10.
   (11) Therefore virtue is not knowledge, 98e7–8 (implied, 96d).
   (12) Right belief is always as beneficial in action as knowledge, 96c1–3.
   (13) Recognized virtuous men have only true belief, 99b11–c5.
   (14) According to this argument virtue comes by divine fate, 100b2–4.
   (15) But we shall know the clear truth when we consider what virtue is before we consider how it is acquired, 100b2–8.
   There are three separate arguments here:
      A. 2, 3, 5, 6. The Socratic argument for KNV.
      B. 1, 8–11. A refutation of KNV.
But Plato can hardly mean (8) seriously (see Cornford (603), 60; contrast Bluck (601), 22); for it would assume that if virtue could be taught, the Athenians would know this, and would have it taught, whereas Plato insists strongly that they do not know that it can be taught.
      C. 1–4, 12–15. A more serious attack on KNV.
But C is still not valid. (14) depends on one of two further premisses not explicit in the argument:
      2a. If a state of the soul is always beneficial in action, it is virtue;
or
      13a. Recognized virtuous men are really virtuous.
Either (2a) or (13a) will justify:
      13b Right belief is sufficient for virtue;
and (13b) and (1) imply that virtuous men do not aquire virtue by teaching. But Plato never endorses either (2a) or (13a).
   There is evidence that Plato accepts (13a) only if his compliments to eminent Athenians can be taken at face value, a strange contrast with both G. 516e9–517a6 and the R. (cf. Bluck, 368). At 93a5–b1 Socrates is quite non-committal, and the comparison with the inspired ignorance of diviners is recognized as unflattering to statesmen, 99b11–e2; finally Socrates says that someone with knowledge would be the only one with real virtue, 100a6–7. Plato does not commit himself, then, to rejection of KNV.
23. Right beliefs bound by an explanation are altered in two ways: (a) 'first of all they become pieces of knowledge (epistemai), (b) and then stable; (c) and because of this knowledge is more honourable than right belief', 98a5–7. Here (a) and (b) are two dis-

tinct results of the binding, and two distinct grounds for (c); even if right beliefs could be as stable as knowledge (cf. *R.* 429e7–430b5; VII, n. 26), knowledge would still be more honourable.

24. Some think forms are inaccessible to the senses because they are universals, and Plato appeals to a type-distinction between universals and particulars (see Ross (123), 17, et. attacked by Bluck (613), 175–7.) But (1) if universals are abstract entities, Socrates does not clearly think of forms as universals. 'The just' or 'justice' which is 'present' in particulars (*Ch.* 158e7, *Lys.* 217d6–e1; cf. *Phd.* 100d5) need not be an abstract entity, any more than a virus or a neural condition is an abstract entity; it may be a 'dispersed particular' (see Quine (327), 95–100), with parts in different people. (2) The type-distinction would not suit Plato here; for even if the universal Red is unobservable, because abstract, we might still find out by observation what it is, whereas Plato denies this of the forms which interest him. He may have overlooked this point; but it should make us hesitate to ascribe the type distinction to him in this passage.

25. I do not discuss the self-predicative character of the Forms (see Vlastos (633), 248–51); but I think it is clearly assumed. Its use for Socratic forms, implied at *HMa.* 291d1–3, *R.* 524a7–10, is instructive. It is easy to assume that 'the just in Socrates' (cf. *Phd.* 102d7, Vlastos (632), 84 f) is just, what is just about Socrates (*Pr.* 330c3–e3 can be explained this way); and Plato takes over this self-predication for separated Forms.

On *phainetai, HMa.* 291d1–3, see n. 29 below.

26. Two views are possible on *R.* 523e3–524c13; (1) The senses report that some particular (e.g. a finger) is both large and small (see Adam (701), ad loc., Vlastos (630), 67 n. 40, Kirwan (622), 121–3. (2) The senses report that the property they take to be largeness is also smallness.

(1) and (2) are compatible; but (2) is Plato's major interest. 523e3 asks whether sight adequately sees the *megethos* and *smikrotēs* of the fingers; after other examples Socrates asks whether the senses do not deficiently (*endeōs*—cf. *Phd.* 74d6) reveal 'such things' (*ta toiauta*, d7)—i.e. the largeness, smallness, etc. In fact 'the sense assigned to the hard (*to sklēron*) is forced to be assigned to the soft (*to malakon*) also', 524a1–2; here *to sklēron* and *to malakon* are the *sklērotēs* and *malakotēs* of 523e6—they are 'the hard (soft) in the finger' (cf. *Phd.* 102d7). The next clause, 'and it announces to the soul that it perceives that the same thing is hard and soft (*hōs tauton sklēron kai malakon aisthanomenē*)', should also refer to the hard in the finger, saying that it is also soft; and the neuter articles with adjectives in 524a6–10 should mean the same. Plato, then, means (2). If he meant only (1), he could not show that the senses present opposite properties confused together, 524c3–4; we might see that a cone, e.g., is round and not-round, and distinguish its roundness from its non-roundness with no confusion. But with (2) the argument is powerful.

27. See Heracleitus B59–61, 91, Guthrie (203), I. 439–46. The Heracleitean theory at *Tht.* 152d2–31 treats not only S-change but also A-change as a clear case of flux.

28. Some think the Heracleiteanism of the *Tht.* is Plato's own view of the sensible world in the middle dialogues; see e.g. Cherniss (617), 9, Bluck (613), 178 f, Brentlinger (615), 132–8. Their view depends on passages about change discussed below, 8.6–7, and on *Cra.* 439c6 ff. I do not think this passage is relevant. (1) There is no argument for separated Forms; the existence of forms is assumed, not argued for, at 439c7–d1, and they need not be separated Forms. (2) Flux in sensibles is not affirmed. 439d3–4 says, 'Let us then consider that very thing, not whether some face is beautiful or any of such things, and these all seem to be in flux', where the last clause is within the 'whether . . .' clause (contrast Brentlinger, 134). (3) Plato argues only that if particulars change their characters, the characters themselves cannot change their characters; he does not argue for separation.

29. *The argument of Phd. 74bc.*

1. The contrast between *idontes* and *enenoēsamen*, 74b4–6, recalls *R.* 523–4, and

shows that the same process is discussed here.

2. I follow most critics in taking *tō(i) men* . . . *tō(i) d'ou*, 74b8, as masculines, not neuters (contrast Murphy (704), 111, n. 1, Owen (628), 306, n. 2; see Mills (624), 129–33); cf. *HMa.* 291d1–3, *Symp.* 211e2–5, for masculine in similar contexts.

3. *Auta ta isa* in 74c1 are the same thing as *hē isotēs*, and the same as what Plato asserts to be a separated Form in step (3)—though we cannot assume it is already separated in (2), where it must be only 'what makes sticks and stones equal'. I agree with Heindorf (quoted by Archer-Hind (611), ad loc.), Geach (619), 269, Mills, I. 142–5, that the plural indicates self-predication, that the Form of Equal is a pair of equals. (Contrast Owen (626), 114 f; but if Plato simply, as Owen thinks, isolates the predicate in the grammatical form it happens to have in the context, it is odd that he only does this with plurals where they might suggest self-predication, and never with e.g. 'just'.)

4. *Ephanē*, 74c1, might mean (a) 'seemed to be' (with no implication that they were, with *einai* understood), or (b) 'evidently were' (with *onta* understood); see LSJ s.v. B. II. 1, for examples of the omission of infinitive or participle). With (a), (2) is satisfied by illusions or mistakes, and the move from (2) to (3) rests on a fallacious application of Leibniz's Law, as if we argued, 'I never thought Jekyll was not Jekyll; I sometimes thought Jekyll was not Hyde; therefore Jekyll is not Hyde.' But with (b) the argument is fair. The same problem arises at *R.* 479a5–b7, *HMa.* 289a8–b7; Plato assumes that what *phainetai* is also true, *R.* 479b6–7, *HMa.* 289b5–7. (At *R.* 476a7 what *phainetai* is not true.) (b) is better supported, both by the parallels, and by the demands of the argument. Contrast Kirwan (622), 116 f.

30. On examples and definitions see III. 2.1.

31. *Phd.* 75c1–d3 refers to the elenchos; cf. *Cri.* 50cd, *Cra.* 390c, *R.* 534d. Since Socrates does not inquire into bees and shuttles (though he admits forms for them), the passage does not require Forms for more than (B) and (C).

32. Vlastos's view of the puzzles, that Plato objects only to the confusion of physical causation and logical implication (632), 95–101, does not explain the emphasis on the contradictory results of the rejected explanations, or the parallel between this passage and *Phd.* 74 f, *R.* 479. See Murphy (704), 111.

I agree with Vlastos, 91 f, that 'The F' is a place-holder for a definition, following Plato's normal demand for a *logos*. Contrast Strang (629), 198.

33. On *R.* V see also VII. 12.3–4. I mention 'forms', not 'Forms', in 476cd because no separation is implied; the sight-lover's fault is that he does not accept UA, which does not commit him, without further argument, to separation. The argument for separation is mentioned only at 479ab.

34. '*The many Fs.*'

1. '*ta polla kala*' and similar phrases can refer to types or properties; see Murphy (704), 110, Owen (628), 305, notes 3, 4, Gosling (620), Crombie (101), II. 79, 293–5; contrast Vlastos (630), 67 n. (a) Plato and the sight-lover disagree about whether the *kala* are many, 479a3; while a disagreement about whether one property or many properties will answer the Socratic question would be sensible, why should Plato deny that there are many beautiful objects? (b) The argument in 479ab will not work for all the predicates involved unless it is applied to types, and not tokens. Plato never argues that a particular, brave action like Leonidas' last stand is both brave and not-brave; but he can easily show how standing firm is sometimes brave (e.g. when done by Leonidas on that occasion), sometimes not brave. The compresence of opposites applies to types, not tokens, at *HMa.* 293b5–c5, *R.* 505c10–11 (see VII. 14.2).

2. Admittedly, for relative predicates like 'large' or 'equal' *F* tokens as well as *F* types will be *F* and not-*F*; since these are favourite examples of predicates needing Forms, Plato may not have realized that the parallel move for 'just' or 'brave' would be illicit. But his arguments rely on no illicit move.

3. I speak of both 'types' and 'properties'. The two ways of speaking are

equivalent, if Plato is careful; if bright colour is now beautiful, now ugly, then bright-coloured things *qua* bright-coloured are both beautiful and ugly. But Plato is not careful; see 9.2.

4. It is not clear whether Plato means that each of the many *F*s will (a) make some things *F*, and make others not-*F*; or (b) make some things *F* but fail to make other things *F*. The *Phd.*'s rejected explanations suggest (a). But 'debt-paying is just and unjust' suggests only (b). Plato's examples do not suggest clarity; but (b) is all his arguments need.

35. Alex. *in Met.* 83.9 says, *kineitai gar to poson en tois aisthētois kai metaballei sunechōs kai ouk estin aphŏrismenon.* If this remark refers to S-change, it will apply to equals no more than to men (against the express aim of the argument; see Owen (628), 309); but it makes good sense if it refers to A-change. This passage suggests strongly that Aristotle should refer to A-change in the very similar phrases in the *Met.* passages on flux.

36. *Phd.* 78e2–3, *oute auta hautois oute allēlois hōs epos eipein oudamōs kata ta auta,* implies only that the many *F*s always change in some respect, and this change need not be more than A-change; they need not undergo constant and total S-change. 78d10–e4 mentions men, horses, etc., all plurals; the claim explicitly applies to types or classes, and extension to tokens is neither excluded nor implied.

37. It is interesting that Plato comes nearest to formulating IE clearly at *Parm.* 130a1–5, exactly when he begins to raise difficulties for his theory; other evidence cited by Ross (134), 226–31, is ambiguous. *Symp.* 211a8–b5 says that the Form is *auto kath' hauto meth' hautou monoeides aiei on,* apart from the many beautifuls; Plato may just mean that it does not require mention of them in its definition, but he may not distinguish that from IE. If the word *chŏris* is evidence of IE, the *Parm.* makes the Form of *F* exist independently of 'the *F* which we have'. But the contrast in *Phd.* 102d6–7, 103b5, between 'The *F* Itself' or 'The *F* in nature' and 'the *F* in us' does not imply IE for the Form; the contrast would apply if The *F* Itself in nature simply consisted of all the *F*s in particular things which are parts of nature—it would still be a 'dispersed particular' (see above, n. 24). Plato may mean more than this; but he needs, and says, no more.

38. I claim that Plato's arguments in the *Phd.* and *R.* aim only to find separated Forms for (B) and (C), not that these are the only Forms he recognizes.

39. Owen (628), 305–7, and Strang (629), think Plato separates Forms because of problems about relative predicates; we cannot learn such a predicate or decide what satisfies it by reference to any example in this world, and so we must refer to some quasi-ostensive sample in some other world (cf. Owen (627), 346).

1. Strang, 195–7, distinguishes S- ('straightforward') things, our (A), and D- ('disputed') things, our (B) and (C). He wrongly assimilates (B) to (C) as sources of dispute; Plato never says that (B) arouse the kinds of disputes aroused by (C). Strang oddly does not mention that *Eu.* 7b–d suggests that 'large' (one of Strang's D-predicates) does not arouse disputes—and Strang says that these predicates which do not arouse disputes are S-predicates (195).

2. Strang thinks D-predicates arouse disputes because there are no undisputed examples of things satisfying them. But Plato never says this. (1) *Eu.* 7b–d says only that disputes sometimes break out about C-properties. (2) *Phdr.* 263a6–7 says we all think the same thing for (A), but not for (C). *Alc.* 111b1 says (3) most people agree *poion esti lithos ē xulon,* and (4) aim at the same thing when they want to get one. (4) refers to agreement on examples, but (3) and (2) refer to agreement in conceptions of what a stick or stone is like. If we lack this agreement with (C), we may still agree on examples; disagreement about some difficult examples does not imply complete absence of any accepted samples.

3. Strang thinks the S/D distinction 'with some minor exceptions which need not concern us' (197) coincides with the non-relative/relative distinction. I have argued

that 'just' and 'brave' are not treated as relative or 'incomplete' predicates (Owen's term). Any particular large mouse is also a small animal; but my just action need not also be unjust in some respects (though the same *kind* of action may be unjust in other conditions). The 'many larges' are also small, and 'the many justs' unjust, but for different reasons; Plato does not suggest that all C-predicates are relatives.

4. If this is right, no reason has been given to show that (a) Plato wants Forms primarily to solve disputes about examples, or that (b) he wants them to be quasi-ostensive samples, because of his views on meaning and language-learning. Plato does not think awareness of Forms is necessary for learning or competent use of meaningful terms, but for giving an account of the properties that some terms refer to (see III. 7.5). (For accounts of 'incomplete predicates' and the Forms, without the reference to ostensive samples see Brentlinger (614), Nehamas (625); I do not think they show that the problems are confined to these predicates.)

My account of Plato's rejection of observational similarities as the basis for definitions of moral properties is indebted to Kovesi (637), 1–32, Anscombe (635) which show how one problem underlying Moore's 'open question' argument against the 'naturalistic fallacy' (see (639), 15f; cf. Nakhnikian (325), 150f) applies more generally. Plato, unlike Moore, does not think there is a problem with 'good' as opposed to 'just', 'brave', etc.; and he does not infer that good is simple or unanalysable.

41. On Socrates' hedonism see IV. 3.4. Plato might reasonably reject Socrates' demand for an ED-account if he believes that disputes about the components of the final good, and not only about instrumental means, affect beliefs about virtue. His analysis of B-properties, which Socrates took to be unproblematic, shows one reason why Socrates might have been over-optimistic. Measurement and observations settle disputes about whether a mouse is large only if disputes about the relevant standard of comparison are settled—measurement will not settle these disputes. Similarly, Plato might argue from the *Gorgias*, a measuring technique might decide whether (e.g.) one physical pleasure is greater than another, but the decision between physical and other pleasures depends on other principles not reducible to a measuring technique. If Socrates could find an observational account of the final good, he could perhaps show that some kind of measurement settles moral disputes, since the relevant standards of comparison will then be agreed; but since he cannot find such an account, he must allow that moral disputes concern the relevant standards of comparison themselves, and therefore cannot be solved by a measuring technique which depends on agreement about these standards.

42. *Phd.* 99c6–e6; Plato abandons the direct search for a teleological explanation, and tries the second-best method, hoping that definitions of various Forms will show how they contribute to some final good. Plato does not exclude, though he does not explicitly demand, an eventual teleological explanation; see VII. 13.5, n. 44.

At 101d4–5 Plato says he examines *ta ap'ekeinēs* (the hypothesis) *hormēthenta*, to see if they are consistent or inconsistent (*allēlois sumphōnei ē diaphōnei*). This is the normal elenctic method, if *ta hormēthenta* are 'the consequences for our beliefs of adopting the hypothesis', i.e. all our beliefs, including, but not confined to, what is deducible from the hypothesis alone (see Cross and Woozley (702), 230). See further Robinson (133), 126–36.

43. On *R*. IV. see VII. 7.2.

44. On Socrates' principles see III. 13.3–4, 17.5.

45. On the use of 'moral' here see III, n. 41, II, n. 29.

46. On elenchos and craft see III. 17.5.

47. Cherniss (617), 2, 4, Stenzel (135), 19–41, and others suppose that Plato wants 'absolute standards'. They rely on the view, shared by Bluck (612), that Forms are known by some kind of direct acquaintance issuing in greater certainty about morals than an elenctic definition could provide. There is no reason to ascribe such a view to Plato (cf. Gosling (104), ch. 9). See VII, n. 44. Nor is it clear what is meant by saying

that the standards should be 'absolute'. Plato certainly wants to show that they are objective, not merely a matter of opinion. But he agrees with Socrates that moral rules are not absolute and exceptionless, but depend on judgements about the good—otherwise the arguments against the sight-lovers (which show that, e.g. debt-paying is not always just) would fail. The rejection of Socrates' external test for an account of the good makes it harder, not easier, to find an 'absolute' standard; and such a standard is not one of Plato's obvious aims.

48. On the *G*. see V. 5.2–3. In the *Phd*. it is not clear if soul and body have rival conceptions of the good, or the body has good-independent desires (see Gosling (104), 28, 75); Plato has not yet drawn the distinctions of *R*. IV. (See VII. 6.1.)

49. On *Phd*. 69a–c see Burnet (616), ad loc., Verdenius (640), 205 f, Bluck (613), 154–6, Hackforth (621), 192 f, Luce (638), 60.

1. *Pros aretēn* a6–7, means 'from the point of view of virtue'; cf. *M*. 100a7, Burnet, Verdenius. From virtue's point of view the balancing of pleasures and pains like sums of money, to find the greater balance of pleasures (a7–9) is not the right form of exchange—though it was prescribed by the measuring science of *Pr*. 356a.

2. *Phronēsis* is the right standard of value, *nomisma orthon*, for which all the hedonistic calculation should be abandoned, a9–10. But Plato need not mean that pleasures and pains themselves should be abandoned—he rejects calculation of consequences (hedonistic or others) as the sole method of decision, but need not demand indifference to pains and pleasures. Similarly virtue is not a *katharsis of or from* pains or pleasures, c1–3, but from hedonistic calculation without wisdom, described in b5.

3. 69b1–2, *kai toutou men panta kai meta toutou ōnoumena kai pipraskomena*, means 'buying and selling everything for this and with this'; i.e. all transactions should aim at wisdom or be guided by wisdom (see Hackforth). In b1–3 *kai . . . pipraskomena* is the subject of *ē(i)* and *kai . . . aretē* is the complement; *chorizomena . . . allēlōn*, b5–7, is the subject of *ē(i)* in b7 (see Bluck, Verdenius). Plato means 'carrying on transactions with wisdom is virtue; carrying them on without it is a mere illusion of virtue'.

4. The passage is recognized as an attack on the *Pr*. by Hirschberger (122), 58 f, Tenkku (128), 69, 100, Crombie (101), I. 249, Pohlenz (108), 143 f. Contrast Shorey (127), 27 f . (110), 527, Moreau (107), 87, von Arnim (112), 15 f.

50. In Plato's attack on all non-philosophers as slavish notice the phrases 'suits only these [the philosophers]', 68c10; 'all the rest', d6; 'the orderly among them [the non-philosophers]', e2; 'all except the philosophers', d12–13. Those with popular or citizen virtue, who do what is prescribed by the recognized virtues from habit and practice without philosophy, 82a10–b3, are among these non-philosophers. Though in the *R*. Plato does not think all non-philosophers are slavish (see Vlastos (732), 137 n., against Archer-Hind (611), 149–55), he is not so generous in the *Phd*., partly because he has not developed the *R*.'s theory of education; see VII, n. 26.

51. On the CA and the value of virtue see III. 16.1.

52. Socrates' views on the soul's value; see III. 16.2, V. 5.4.

53. See III. 13.3–4 on TV and LG.

54. I use both 'admirable' and 'beautiful' for *kalon*.

55. The *Symp*. neither implies nor denies that *erōs* aiming at the good includes all desire; it is neutral between the Socratic view (ascribed to it by Robin (647), lxxxiii, Markus (645), 137 f, O'Brien (124), 224 f) and the *R*.'s division of the soul. See Moravcsik (646), 290, 293 (I am indebted to his account of the ascent). The restriction of the ascent to those who are pregnant in soul—cf. 210a7–8, 209a8–c2—suggests that Plato does not think that every desire is equally a desire for the good and suitable for the ascent. Animals are said (a) to have *erōs*, 207a6–b6, and (b) to achieve immortality by propagation, 208b2–4, but not (c) to desire immortality; they need not desire the immortality which is the result of their acting on *erōs*. Not all desire, then, need be the kind of desire which interests Diotima. But in any case the

rejection of KSV in the *Symp.* does not require the acceptance of incontinence. Even if Plato believes, as in the *M.*, that all desire is for the good, it does not follow that knowledge of instrumental means is sufficient to make this rational desire virtuous.

56. If *to agathon* in *HMa.* 297a2–d1 includes all particular good things, then the conclusion, *oude ara to kalon agathon estin, oude to agathon kalon*, c3, confuses predication and identity, if it means that the class of *agatha* and the class of *kala* do not intersect. Sometimes Plato uses this type of phrase for a simple denial of identity (cf. *Eu.* 10d12–13, 11a6–b1, where he agrees that *to hosion* is *theophiles*), but mere nonidentity of *kalon* and *agathon* might not seem to be the absurdity Plato finds in the *HMa.* But if *to agathon* is 'what is really good' a description restricted in the *Lys.*, to the final good, the argument proves that the final good cannot be *kalon*—a paradoxical result for Socrates, in view of *Lys.* 216d2. For Socrates' views on *kalon* and *agathon* see III. 3.3, V. 2.3–4.

57. On 'becoming and perishing', 211a1, see 8.7, n. 37.

58. An 'exclusive' interpretation of the ascent (with the higher objects replacing the lower) is defended by Vlastos (648), 33–5, and Moravcsik (646), 293, on these grounds: (1) 210b5–c6; at the higher stages someone will *kataphronein* and *smikron hēgeisthai* the lower objects. But this does not imply he will think nothing of them and abandon them. (2) 211d5–e3; anyone would be enthralled by a view of the Form free of human flesh, colours and such other mortal rubbish. But this does not imply the rejection of mortal or human objects of love; Plato may infer that someone who has seen the Form will love them better, because he sees what is worth loving in them. These arguments fail to prove the exclusive interpretation, and the issue must be resolved less directly.

59. See VII. 18.1, VIII. 9.2.

60. On the *Phdr.* see further VII. 17.7–8.

61. The non-lover does not ask the boy to do anything commonly thought *aischron*; cf. *Symp.* 184b7–8. That is why people praise him for his virtue, *Phdr.* 256e5, just as they praise the oligarchic man, *R.* 554a11; see VII. 15.3.

62. The *Phdr.* does not repeat the *Symp.*'s account of the whole ascent. But the two accounts fit together. (1) Beauty has immediately-appealing sensible likenesses, 250d4–6, unlike the likenesses of other Forms, 250b1–5; but it is not understood all at once—the lover must search for a full understanding, 250a1–4, 251a1–7. (2) The *Phdr.* mentions sudden possession by *eros*, the *Symp.* gradual ascent; but the *Phdr.* does not deny ascent, and the *Symp.* allows it to be punctuated by episodes of possession; cf. *Symp.* 207a5–c1. (3) The *Phdr.* mentions a person as the object of love, and does not suggest that the lover will later abandon love of persons—but I have argued that the *Symp.* does not mean this either; see n. 58 above (contrast Gould (642), 120). (4) The reference to *aporia*, 251d8, 255d3, recalls the procedure of the elenchos (cf. *M.* 84a7–b1, *R.* 505e1), which we found was the procedure of the *Symp.* (5) The philosophical lover will try to make his beloved philosophical, 252e1–5, and will himself be changed in the process, 252e7–253b1—the *Symp.*'s account is quite suitable here.

63. On craft-principles and elenchos-principles see III. 17.1–6. I have spoken as though Plato were consciously criticizing Socrates' conscious views; while I think this is quite likely, it goes beyond what the text absolutely demands—I may have exaggerated Socrates' conscious acceptance of these views, and Plato's conscious selection of Socrates as a target. But whether Plato thinks the CA is Socrates' view, or a perversion of it which someone might (quite fairly, I think) derive from Socrates' favourable remarks about crafts, he rejects the general view, and his rejection opens the problems I have mentioned.

NOTES TO CHAPTER VII

1. The problem about the CA might be solved by dating *R.* I earlier than the rest of the dialogue; see II, n. 33, von Arnim (112), 75 f, who sees the conflict between the

view of justice as a craft in I and the division of the soul in IV. But this solution still leaves us with the question why Plato should have retained I., if he rejected the CA. I hope my account will explain the role of I, and so remove the temptation to accept an earlier date for it. It is especially important that the criticisms of Socrates in II. apply to I; see below, 4.2, and contrast von Arnim, 73 f.

2. See III. 2.2–3.

3. Socrates argues as follows:

(1) The just man will harm some men by his justice (i.e. he will damage their interest—'i-harm').

(2) If dogs or horses are harmed, they become worse as horses or dogs, and thereby lose the excellence (or virtue; arete) of horses or dogs (335b6–11; i.e. we damage their excellence—'e-harm').

(3) If men are harmed, they become worse as men, and lose human virtue, 335c1–2.

(4) But justice is human virtue, 335c4.

(5) Therefore, if men are harmed, they become more unjust, 335c6–7.

(4) must be an identity-statement, if (5) is to follow; but Socrates has not argued for this controversial claim. Even then (5) proves something only about e-harm, not about i-harm, which was our initial concern.

(6) Musical or equestrian experts do not make men less musical or equestrian by the musical or equestrian crafts, 335c9–12.

(7) Just men do not make men unjust by justice, nor in general do good men make men bad by virtue, 335c14–d2.

(8) It is not the work of heat or dryness to make cold or wet, but of their opposites, 335d3–6.

(9) It is not the work of good to harm, but of its opposite, 335d7.

(10) But the just man is good, 335d9.

(11) Therefore it is not the work of the just man to harm, but of his opposite.

(6)–(7) and (8)–(10) are alternative defences of (11). The examples mention craftsmen and pupils; but not all objects of crafts are pupils—e.g. sheep are not made into shepherds. (Thrasymachus later exploits this problem.) And (8)–(11) require 'good' to mean 'beneficial to others'; but if we have shown only that injustice i-harms its possessor, and therefore justice benefits him (as (1)–(5) assumed, though they did not prove it), we have not shown what is needed for (11), that justice benefits other people. On this argument see Allan (707), 25, Cross and Woozley (702), 21, Vlastos (314). On the relation between virtue and the agent's and other people's expectations see II. 1.4–5.

4. On justice see II. 3.6, III. 6.3–9, V. 3.2. On Thrasymachus see II. 4.7.

5. Socrates argues as follows:

(1) A craft considers the interest of the craftsman qua craftsman, 341d1–8.

(2) A craft, or a craftsman qua craftsman, has no interest except the craft's perfection, 341d10–11.

(3) A craft need not be especially concerned for its own interest, 341e2–342b2.

(4) A craft considers the interest of its object, 343b3–c6.

(5) A craft rules over its object, 342c9–10.

(6) A craft considers the interest of what it rules over, 342c11–d1.

(7) A ruler is a craftsman ruling over his subjects.

(8) A ruler considers the interest of his subjects, 342c6–11.

Socrates moves first from the interest of the craftsman to his interests qua craftsman in (2), to the interests of the craft, and in (3) and (4) to the interests of the object. But (4) is unjustified; the craft may be concerned about the perfection of the object, but that need not be in the object's interest, unless Socrates is allowed the converse of his earlier equivocation on 'harm'. Thrasymachus rightly objects to (4); the perfection of sheep for market does not benefit them, 343b1–4.

Socrates replies that Thrasymachus has confused the specialized crafts with the money-making craft, 345b9–346b11, and continues:

(9) Each craft produces a benefit peculiar to itself, 346c2–3.

(10) If all crafts produce a common benefit, it is produced by a single common craft, 346c5–7.

(11) Money is a common benefit produced by all the crafts, using the money-making craft, 346c9–11.

(12) Ruling is a specialized craft.

(13) Neither ruling nor any other craft produces money, or considers its own benefit, but the benefit of what it rules, 346d1–e7. (12) is unstated and disputable. For criticisms of the argument see Gibbs (337), 36 f, and for the 'druler' objection see Nozick (712), 234 n.

6. Cf. *Lys.* 214b8–d3; see III. 6.6, V. 5.4.

7. The 'function' (*ergon*) argument is this:

(1) The soul's work (*ergon*) is overseeing, ruling, deliberating, etc., and also living, 353d3–9.

(2) When something has its proper virtue (*aretē*) it does its work well, 353c5–7.

(3) Justice is the virtue of the soul, 353e7–8.

(4) The just soul will live well, 353e10–11.

The soul's work includes instrumental functions—overseeing and so on—and the activity controlled by them, living. Socrates argues that since justice performs the instrumental functions well, it will ensure good performance of the activity they control. (3) depends on the previous argument about the benefits of justice. On virtue and function see II. 1.3.

8. *Views of R. II.* The *Lys.* on goods; see III. 13.4. Some critics think that Glaucon (for convenience I sometimes use 'Glaucon' to include Adeimantus as well) really wants to divide c-goods into (c1) goods valuable for their natural consequences, and (c2) goods valuable only for their artificial consequences. See Foster (713), Sachs (717), 38–43, Cross and Woozley (702), 66–9, Contrast Mabbott (716), Kirwan (715). The 'consequentialist' view has been defended as follows:

(1) 358a4–6 demands that justice should not be praised for its rewards; but this rejection of c2 still allows c1.

(2) The demand to know what *dunamis* justice has, 358b5–6, 366e5–6, 367b3–5, e3, or how it benefits its possesser, 367d3, 392c3–4, 457b4–5, is taken to refer to natural consequences.

(3) From 360e Glaucon attacks those who praise justice for its artificial consequences, with no objection to natural consequences.

These arguments are not decisive:

(1) The consequentialist view conflicts with the initial threefold division of goods, which makes justice a b-good, not a c-good. Two replies have been offered: (a) Foster accepts the conflict, and claims that Plato ignores the threefold division later (as the consequentialist view requires), so that he is simply inconsistent. But Plato relies on the initial division later also, at 359a7–b1, 361a2–4; cf. 357c8, 358a4 (see Kirwan, 167). Foster's view requires a more thorough confusion in Plato than he realizes; while Plato might well be as confused as Foster's view implies, strong evidence will be needed to show it. (b) Sachs argues that b-goods are not meant to exclude c-goods from being goods in themselves, if their consequence is happiness or pleasure. He takes the *hēdonai* in 357b7 to be causes of pleasure rather than episodes of pleasure themselves, because Plato says *mēden dia toutōn gignetai allo ē chairein echonta.* But this *mēden*-clause also applies to *to chairein* in b7; and this must refer to episodes of pleasure, so that *dia toutōn* cannot refer to the causal consequences of *to chairein*. The *dia*, then, should be logical, not causal; cf. Mabbott, 60 f. If Sachs were right, Plato would find it hard to distinguish a-goods and b-goods from c-goods, and would lose the grounds for criticizing the slavish men in the *Phd.* (cf. Moreau (107), 87).

(2) The demands to know what *dunamis* justice has and what it does, do not necessarily refer to consequences of justice. We say what a *dunamis* is by saying what it is set over and what it does, 477c9–d5. To say what justice is is to say what power of the soul it is; that is why the question about its *dunamis* is coupled with the demand to know what it is, 358b4–6. Nor do the references to benefits indicate consequences of justice; justice benefits by contributing to happiness, and it contributes as a component, not only as an instrumental means—see Kirwan, 170–3. 'What justice does in itself' refers to logical, not causal, consequences of its being what it is; they are the 'effects' which explain the other effects, and constitute what it is in itself.

(3) I have suggested why artificial consequences appear later in the argument, when Glaucon's first argument rules out natural consequences. The consequentialist interpretation must be rejected as an account of Plato's argument, though some might wish it had been his argument.

9. See Hume's defence of justice (821), *T*. III. 3.2, 497 f, and Gauthier (815), 168.

10. See VI. 11.3–4.

11. Plato does not claim that justice is sufficient for happiness (though 392a10–c5 by itself might suggest it). 444e–445b, 580a9–c4, 587b claim only that the just man is always happier than the unjust. 612a3–d3 promises *eu prattein* as a consequence of justice, but only when the consequences of justice have been re-admitted at 612a8–613b1; they guarantee happiness after death. *G*. 470e9–11, 507b8–c5 (cf. *R*. 354a1–4) accepted the extreme view attacked by Aristotle at *EN* 1095b32–1096a2, 1100a5–9, 1153b19–21; but the *R*.'s view is nearer the view accepted by Aristotle at 1100b32–1101a8. Cf. V, n. 25.

12. Other views of Plato's question have been taken. (1) Prichard takes it to mean 'Show us that what we recognize as justice contributes to what we recognize as happiness', and interprets 'happiness' in hedonist terms; see (829), 101, Sidgwick (832), 60–2. This requires misinterpretation of *eudaimonia*; see III. 4.4–5. Though Plato believes, and in *R*. IX. argues, that the pleasures of being just will seem to the just man to outweigh any pleasures gained from injustice, it is not implied in II. (2) Sachs (717), 146–50, thinks Plato begins with a fixed conception of justice, though not of happiness; this view does not explain why Glaucon should emphasize so strongly that they still do not know what justice is.

13. See VI. 10.1–2.

14. The demand for good natural consequences of justice is accepted by Grote (105), III. 143–5, Foot (812), 96–9 (though contrast (811), 307 f), and in the system described by Gauthier (see above n. 9). On teleological and deontological theories see VIII, n. 2.

15. See Prichard (829), 119, 222. Contrast Morris (738), 131–4.

16. See III. 14.1, IV. 2.5, V. 5.2, VI. 11.2.

17. Plato's reply to Glaucon proceeds in four stages: (1) the description of the ideal state and the rulers' education in II–III; (2) the virtues of the state and the expected analogues in an individual; (3) the division of the soul; (4) the virtues of the individual fulfilling the expectations of (2) because of (3). I have not followed Plato's order, because I do not think it represents his ethical argument best. He thinks (2) can be decided without (3) or (4), simply by inspection of the structure of the state; but it depends on (3), as 430e ff, makes clearest. Plato distinguishes the different parts contributing to the state's temperance by appeal to a division of the soul which is justified only if (3) is correct. He is wrong, then, to suggest at 435b9–436b3 that the division of the state does not depend on (3). The difficulties are serious for his political theory; but I think the ethical argument is independent of them. See further Joseph (703), 82–9.

18. *The argument for dividing the soul*. On Socrates see III. 12.3. Plato's argument, in over-simplified outline, is as follows:

(1) The same thing cannot have opposite tendencies, i.e. cannot act or be affected

in opposite ways, at the same time, in the same aspect, and in relation to the same thing (436b5–437a9; the 'Principle of Opposites').

(2) Acceptance and rejection of the same object are opposite tendencies, 437b1–5.

(3) A desire for x is an acceptance of x, and a refusal to pursue x is a rejection of x, 437b7–c10.

(4) Desire for x, *qua* desire for x, is desire just for x, and not for x as a good, 437d2–439b2.

(5) Sometimes a man at the same time both desires x and refuses to pursue x because it is bad, 439c2–4.

(6) Therefore he must desire and refuse in different aspects of himself, 439c5–7.

1. Robinson (729), 39, emphasizes that step (1) is not the Principle of Non-Contradiction, since it does not mention contradictories. The claim (a) 'Not (A desires x and not [a desires x])' would be true, but Plato's claim (b) 'Not (A desires x and A rejects x)' is more controversial. Perhaps Plato confuses (a) and (b); but nothing in the argument suggests that (a) is in play at all.

2. Plato is most unclear about steps (2) and (3). I have skated over the difficulties in speaking of 'acceptance' and 'rejection'. In 437b1–3 *epineuein* and *ananeuein* suggest this is what he means, that not just any tendencies towards and from objects will require parts of the soul. But some restriction on the scope of (1) is needed to exclude the unwanted cases; and this problem shows how little use (1) is to the argument—Plato would have done better to introduce his argument about desires at once.

3. This problem is important for deciding how Plato's principle of division works. If a desire for x and simultaneous aversion from x prove two parts of the soul, a thirst for, and aversion from, this gin will prove two parts. But Plato recognizes conflicting appetites, 558d4–6, and so does not require a division of the soul for every conflict (see Crombie (101), I. 351 n.; contrast Joseph (703), 53 n., Penner (728), 115 f). If we require rejection of the object, this objection fails. If my ambivalent appetites produce a simultaneous desire for x and aversion from x, my aversion need not include any attitude to the appetitive pursuit of x—if, e.g., I both like and detest the taste of gin. Plato needs to explain 'rejection' as 'rejection of the desire for the object', and to restate (2) corresopondingly.

4. 438a1–3 contrasts 'desire for drink' with 'desire for good drink'; but *pantes ara ton agathon epithumousin* suggests that Plato means 'desire for drink as a good—this is the sense relevant to the Socratic position stated in this phrase. (A bad drink may be desired as a good by a man dying of thirst. See Murphy (704), 45 f) In (4) the talk of 'desire *qua* desire' by itself proves nothing about the kinds of desires there are, any more than 'the doctor *qua* doctor is no money-maker' proved anything about the doctors there are (see above, n. 15, Robinson, 40). Plato needs to show that there really are some desires which are not desires for the good—and so (5) is the crucial example.

5. The Principle of Opposites, especially the clause 'in the same respect' (*kata ta auta*) allows Plato to protect the general principle by finding a different aspect for any two opposed desires (Robinson, 48). To avoid this trivialization of his thesis, Plato must show when he will and will not recognize two interesting distinct 'aspects' of the soul. These cases of the archer standing still with his arms moving and the top with moving circumference and stationary axis, 436c8–e6, are different enough to leave us puzzled about the parallel for the soul. But Plato recognizes different tendencies in the soul, and thinks it is still a further question whether they belong to different parts, 436a8–b3; there will be different 'kinds' (*eide,* 435c1, *gene,* 441a1 or 'parts' (*mere,* 442b11) or 'things' (neuter adjectives and pronouns, 436b9 and often) in the soul if Socrates is wrong in thinking all desire is for the good. For the purposes of Book IV, then, Plato's general claims about 'kinds', 'parts', and 'things' amount to the claim that there are desires differing in kind in a way unrecognized by Socrates. I have assumed that the archer and the top, with different parts or aspects in different con-

ditions, are meant to be parallel to the soul, which is also one thing with different parts or aspects; see the parallel language at 436a8–b3, 436c5–6, 436d4–e6, 439b10–11, 439d4–5, Penner, 105 f; contrast Crombie, 365–8.

6. Penner, 106, takes 438a to say that thirst is always desire for drink described as 'drink', never for an object under a description (e.g. 'the stuff in the glass') which requires some inference to show the object is a drink. He identifies the division between rational desires and appetites with the division between 'thought-dependent' and 'thought-independent' desires. (See Hampshire (722), 37, 46–9. Kraut (737), 208, follows Penner.) But (a) Penner's evidence is drawn from *R*. 602–3. Even if his view of that passage is right, he does not show that IV makes the same point. (b) Penner's view allows only primitive biological urges to count as appetites; but Plato recognizes non-primitive appetites in VIII–IX and at 436a1–3—and the primitive character of Leontius' corpse-gazing desire, 439e–440a is not clear. (c) To deal with apparent clashes of appetites Penner must make one of them a desire for the good (113–15, 117 f). But Plato does not always agree that any deliberation about satisfying an appetite makes a desire rational; cf. 580e11–581a1. Here he agrees with Aristotle, *EN*. 1111b13–14, 1142b18–20.

19. Cornford (719), 262–4, Hardie (723), 142 f, Penner (728), 111–13, reject the *thumos* as a third part of the soul; Joseph (703), 63–9, and Cross and Woozley (702), 120–3, rightly defend it. Plato is wrong to concentrate so heavily on anger and to ignore other operations of *thumos*; but his choice of *epithumiai* is equally narrow. If he divides desires by their relation to reasoning about the good and not just any kind of reasoning (as Hardie and Penner think), he leaves room for a third part. Hardie and Penner are wrong to allot rational anger to the *logistikon* and non-rational anger to the *epithumētikon*. Anger which is not sanctioned by reason is still not a good-independent appetite—it requires some conception of a harm done; and even if it is sanctioned by reason, it may not be wholly responsive to reason, like Aristotle's over-hasty servant.

20. Appetite is restricted by what comes *ek logismou*, rather than by *logismos* itself, suggesting that *to logistikon* consists of rational desires, and not just of reasoning. The question is harder because Plato has no generic term for all desire (like Aristotle's *orexis* except for *epithumia* (cf. *M*. 77b6, 78b3, V, n. 6, 17) which in IV is normally restricted to appetitive desires. Joseph (703), 51, 167, quotes examples of the generic use of *epithumia*, and other terms ascribing desires to the rational part, from later in the *R*.; 474c9, 475b2, 485b1, d4, 6, 490a9–b7, 501d2, 505d11, 572a2, 480d3, 581a10, b6, 582c4–5, 586d7, 611e2, 613a3. 431c5–d2 is evidence of the same view in IV. One kind of *epithumiai* are 'simple and moderate, which are led by reasoning with intelligence and right belief', c5–6; this description of the desires of the rational part suggests that the division of the soul is a division of desires.

21. I assume that the division of the soul conflicts with Socrates' denial of incontinence (see III, n. 52). Moreau (726) believes that Plato allows appetite and emotion to prevent someone from deciding that something is good, but not to prevent him from acting on his decision. But this account will not work for Leontius, who must have decided it is bad to look at corpses. 412e10–413c4 suggests ways that true belief, once formed, is lost because of appetite and emotion, among other things. This need not be Plato's only way of dealing with apparent incontinence (as O'Brien (124), 153, thinks), and the case of Leontius shows it is not; but even if it were, it will still show a disagreement with Socrates, who recognized none of these problems for his view.

Against Shorey (127), 15–18, O'Brien, 149, 155, 164 f, I do not think that *R*. IV is consistent with the Socratic dialogues, that it makes explicit qualifications that they hinted at. I have suggested that we can claim to find these qualifications in the KSV thesis defended in the early dialogues only if we already assume that those dialogues must be consistent with the *R*.; and if we assume that, we are at a loss to explain Socrates' perfectly serious defence of KSV and UV in the *Pr*. Arbitrary interpretation is needed to explain away the acceptance of KSV in earlier dialogues and its rejection in *R*. IV, and to justify the supposed 'deliberate' silence in earlier dialogues; Plato in *R*. IV certainly does not suggest that he is accepting the Socratic thesis, as Socrates really intended it, and simply making explicit qualifications Socrates always accepted—none of the language of KSV appears in the *R*. O'Brien notices, 141–3, the parallel between *Pr*. 351b2 and *R*. 430a4–5 on the importance of nature and good training as well as knowledge in moral education. But the difference is that Plato agrees with Protagoras (to this extent) in the *R*., and disagrees in the *Pr*. See III, n. 59, IV, n. 7.

22. Elenchos and craft; III. 17.1. Elimination of moral terms; III. 17.5, VI. 5.3, 10.1. Hypotheses; VI. 10.3, and below, 13.4.

23. See III. 14.1.

24. Self-knowledge; III. 14.2. Self-mastery; III. 14.1, IV. 2.5, V. 5.2. Falk (808), 359–61, offers an account of courage and temperance quite close to Plato's. The connection between virtue and the possibility of conflicting desires is stressed by von Wright (834), 147–9; cf. Antiphon B59, II. 4.1.

25. On the different criteria for temperance see Hackforth (721), 269, Williams (733), 202 f. On the anthropomorphic talk of friendship between the parts of the soul see below, 19.4.

26. *Knowledge and virtue.* See VI. 6.3, 11.4. The evidence on KNV in the *R*. is quite difficult.

1. 429b8 says that the state will be brave because a part of it has tenacious true belief about what should be feared, and 430b2–5 says that this true belief belongs to the military class; only the state's courage has been defined here. Plato says it is courage, *politikēn ge*, 430e2, which is ambiguous between (a) 'courage in the city' (as opposed to the individual), and (b) 'citizen-courage' (as opposed to top-grade courage), like the *dēmotikē kai plitikē aretē* of *Phd*. 82b (see VI, n. 50). Adam (701), ad loc., thinks (a) is the primary sense, but also recognizes (b), accepted by Shorey (706), ad loc. If (a) is right, 430b2–5 need not define the individual's courage. 442b5–d1 ascribes courage and temperance to a soul with wisdom, c5, without suggesting that right belief might suffice for these virtues. Contrast Vlastos (732), 136–8.

2. In a temperate state (a) the same belief about who should rule *enestin* in rulers and ruled, 431a9; (b) this concord about who should rule is temperance, 432a4; (c) the state's temperance, unlike its wisdom and courage is not *en merei tini* of the state, 431e10, but is spread through the whole city, 432a2. These uses of *en* might mislead us into thinking all the individuals are temperate (see Skemp (730), 36). But Plato says only that all the classes in the state contribute to the state's temperance, which implies nothing about the temperance of individuals.

3. Two other passages in the *R*. seem to allow virtue without knowledge: (a) In 500d8 *dēmotikē aretē* may be the *dēmotikē aretē* of *Phd*. 82b, or it may be the virtue of the people (as opposed to individuals; cf. *idia[i] kai demosia[i]*, 500d5). (b) 619c7 mentions the citizen of a well-ordered state, *ethei aneu philosophias aretēs meteilēphota*. The term '*dēmotikē aretē*' is not used here, and *meteilēphota* does not imply that he is virtuous. Plato naturally agrees that there are better and worse non-philosophers, but allows real virtue to none of them.

4. We might think that someone who contributes to the state's temperance or courage must have virtue, because he must be controlled by his rational part. But Plato's conception of the rational part does not imply this; someone can have an orderly, law-abiding life without deliberating at all about what is good for his whole soul. In 590c2–591e3 Plato argues that the lower classes' own rational parts are too weak to control them, and they must be controlled by the rational parts of the philosophers. (Kraut (737), 216–18, 221 f, takes Plato to mean only that the lower classes *would* be non-rationally controlled without the philosophers' help, but with the philosphers' help they are controlled by their own rational part. But in 590e2–591a3

Plato makes it clear that someone who is controlled by the rational part, like a fully educated child, is free of tutelage (cf. *Lys.* 210a9–c4); since the lower classes are not free of tutelage, they are not controlled by the rational part.) The lower classes may enjoy their place, if they are suitably rewarded; but they do not accept it because they are virtuous.

Overall, then, Plato rejects KNV nowhere in the *R.*; some passages might be taken to concede virtue to someone with right belief if we had unequivocal evidence elsewhere that Plato concedes it, but there is no such evidence in the *R.* His comments are obscure, and perhaps indicate some ambivalence; he never clearly says what the lower classes have if they have no virtue, since he is not interested in the lower classes in the *R.* On his reasons for accepting KNV see below, 12.5, VIII. 9.5.

27. See III. 13.5.

28. Some of Plato's comments about virtue and reason are puzzling.

1. 374e4 ff, mentions two natural tendencies, the 'philosophical' and the emotional, trained by moral education. These two tendencies are identified with the rational and emotional parts in IV, 441e8–442a3; cf. 474d4–475b9. The philosophical part, like the rational, is associated with learning, 376b8, 435e7, 581b9. Someone's philosophical part alters its attachments as it learns, so that he is not confined to his primitive emotional desire to attack all supposed offenders; 375a11–b11, 411c4–e2; it will be attached to what is admirable, 403c4–7, but it must not be allowed to make him soft, 411a5–c2.

2. But still, the philosophical part does not do what the rational part does in IV. It does not deliberate about the good of the whole soul; the musically educated man (including the soldiers in IV) is still controlled by his emotional part (in Book IV's terms), though (in Book II–III's terms) he has had his philosophical and emotional tendencies trained. The identification of the original philosophical and emotional tendencies with the rational and emotional parts of IV is wrong, unless it means only that the training of these tendencies is necessary (though not sufficient) for the harmony of rational and emotional parts described in IV.

3. However, Plato goes further because of carelessness or confusion; he suggests that musical education will produce the right harmony of the philosophical or rational and the emotional parts of the soul, 441e8–442a2, 376c4–5, and even that this harmony is courage and temperance, 410e10–411a1. Plato may confuse (a) harmony between the philosophical and emotional tendencies, requiring restraint of both tendencies and the rule of neither; (b) harmony of the parts ruled by reason, which needs no restraint. If the virtuous man's harmony consists only in (a), he needs only lack of conflict and right action for virtue; if it requires (b), he needs rational control. If Plato confuses (a) and (b), he might well suppose, contrary to what he ought to say in IV., that (a) suffices for virtue.

4. For perhaps similar reasons, Plato suggests that rulers have knowledge, 428a11–d7; if musical education produces virtue, and virtue includes knowledge, they must have knowledge—the first clause here confuses the two kinds of harmony again. But he also recognizes that the rulers' initial education produces only right belief, 425d7–e2, 427a2–7, 413e–414a. Later Plato admits gaps in his earlier account, 497c7–d6 (see Adam (701), ad loc.), 502d8–503b1; but he did not admit them at 413e5–414a6, 424a2.

5. But it is clear in 401e–402a that the first kind of harmony, between the philosophical and emotional tendencies, is not enough. The 'reason' which comes later cannot just be the technical reasoning which everyone learns; for that is no independent source of moral beliefs, and so could not clash with the previous desires, however ill educated someone might be. The relevant kind of reason must agree that musical education has encouraged the right desires which reason approves on independent grounds.

6. Plato does not even make it clear who receives moral education. (1) Often the

guardians alone are mentioned: 376c, 378c1–3, 383a3–5, 386a6–7, 387b4–6, 395b8–c3, 398a8–b4, 398c6, 391a1–6, 401c1, 402c2, 403e4–9, 404a9–b8, 410b5–8, e1–3, 416b5–6, 451c–452a, 456d8–10, *Tm.* 18b (see Murphy (704), 78, Hourani (724)). (2) And yet the education seems to affect the state more generally, or to inculcate attitudes which everyone should have; 378c6–d3, 386a1–4, 389d7–e2, 391e12–392a1, 397d6–398b1, 399a5–e4, 400e5–6, 405ac, 407a1–2, 410a7–b3, 414b8–c2. Plato insinuates that the training will extend beyond the guardians, but he never says so.

7. Plato's views about virtue, reason and knowledge are more complex and confused than my account in the text suggests, perhaps because (a) it is naturally tempting to suppose that the ordinary good citizen has some kind of virtue, and (b) it is easy, especially with the help of (a), to extend 'control by the rational part' to the limited use of reason which is required for being musically-educated. But I have tried to suggest the view Plato normally holds, and has to hold to be consistent with the rest of the *R.*

29. The Socratic dialogues and the *G.* on justice and the good of the soul; III. 6.5, V. 4.1–2. Two views of the political analogy might be taken: (a) macrocosm–microcosm (MM); the structure of the state is analogous to the structure of the soul; (b) whole-part (WP); the state has a virtue only because the individuals in it have that virtue. Now Plato endorses only MM, 435a5–c2, 441e4–442c8; see Murphy (704), 20–2, 68–86. But some (e.g. Vlastos (732), 123 f, Williams (733), 196–200, Mulgan (727), 84) find evidence of WP. (1) If Plato claimed that the members of the military and productive classes were brave and temperate, he would rely on WP; but see n. 26—even if his vague language sometimes suggests WP, it does not follow from the previous arguments and plays no part in the main argument of IV. (2) 435e3–436a4 says that the same *eidē* and *ēthē, to philomathes, to thumoeides* and *to philochrē-maton* (seen renamed as three parts of the soul) are found in the state and in individuals and are in the state because they are in individuals; cf. 544de. This claim about desires and aims does not commit Plato to WP; the state's virtue requires the right blending of psychic tendencies present in individuals and state; but it does not follow that the blending makes individuals virtuous too.

30. Plato's argument, simplified and expanded in places, is this:

(1) A virtue of any psychic compound (i.e. a compound of human psychic elements) is a condition promoting its happiness.

(2) The soul and the state are psychic analogues (i.e. psychic compounds composed of the same psychic elements), 435e1–3.

(3) Good order (i.e. a harmony between the different psychic elements, with the rational part in control) promotes the happiness of the state.

(4) Therefore good order is a virtue in a state, 433d7–9.

(5) Good order is justice in a state.

(6) Therefore justice in a state is a virtue in a state, 434a7–10.

(7) The same psychic conditions promote the happiness of all psychic analogues.

(8) Therefore the same conditions are virtues in all psychic analogues.

(9) Therefore good order is a virtue in the soul.

(10) 'Justice' is the name of the same condition of state and soul, 435a5–c6.

(11) Therefore justice in the soul is good order in the soul, 441d12–e2.

(12) Therefore justice in the soul is a virtue in the soul.

Steps have been added to clarify some of Plato's assumptions:

1 He needs (1) and (2) to defend his careless move to (6). He assumes both (a) the Platonic state is completely good, 427e6–8; and (b) it will be wise, brave, temperate and just, 427e10–11. These assumptions need defence. He defends (a) by appeal to his state's concern for the good of the whole state and its common happiness, 421b3–c6, as opposed to concern for some restricted class-interest, 422e7–423a5. But (a) cannot be used to prove (b) without a gross begging of the question against Thrasymachus,

who denied that justice is a virtue and will not agree without persuasion that a virtuous state is a just state. To defend himself Plato must prove (4) and (6); to show that a condition in the state makes the state good, he must prove that it promotes the common happiness of the citizens; and so he must rely on (1).

2   (2) makes clear a point obscured in Plato's exposition, that the division of the state relies on the division of the soul. The soul is divided without reference to the division of the state; and unless some connection is ensured, any analogy between the two might be purely fortuitous. (2) rules this out; the state has to deal with the same rational, emotional and appetitive tendencies as the individual, because the tendencies in states are tendencies of individuals; to identify the tendencies, we must already have distinguished correctly the tendencies in the individual soul.

3   (7)–(9) show how Plato has two separate tasks, of finding a virtue corresponding to justice in the state, and of proving that this virtue is really justice in the individual. Vlastos (732), 128 f, rightly criticizes Plato's reliance on UA for 'just'. An appeal to WP is useless here; for even if a p-just state is composed of p-just citizens, Plato has not proved (without assuming UA) that their p-justice is the virtue we call 'justice'; and even if the state's justice is p-justice, it does not follow without UA that the citizens' justice which makes the state just is also p-justice.

Some have tried to find a closer connection between p-justice and justice through Plato's use of 'doing one's own' (*ta hautou prattein*). But the connection is not there.

(1) 422e3–423a5 emphasized the contribution of each member's doing his own work and 'being one and not many', 423d2–6, to the common good of the state.

(2) 433a1–b5 suggests that 'doing one's own work or some form of it' is individual justice; but the content of 'doing one's own work' is left open, a3, b3—it is not necessarily to be identified with being a good citizen, as in (1) ('Doing one's own' applies also to non-citizens; see Vlastos (739), 125).

(3) 433b7–e2; Plato describes the state's justice; doing its own work by each class and individual supports and strengthens the other virtues; a condition which does this is justice; so this condition is justice in the state.

(4) Justice in the state is what judges try to restore; they try to restore the condition in which each does his own, avoids *pleonexia* and grasping other people's goods, and therefore has his own. This still refers to the state's justice; 434b9–c2 mentions *kakourgia* by classes in the state. 434c4–5 says that *kakourgia* is *adikia*, suggesting that the classes are unjust, and do not merely contribute to the state's injustice. This is a common notion of individual injustice; but it does not contribute to the argument.

(5) 434b4–435a3 shows that individual justice is still undefined; and so 'being a good citizen' cannot have defined it.

(6) 441c9–d3 stresses that the same structure will be virtue in state and in soul. Then Plato says (a) the just man will be just in the same way as the just state, 441d5–6; (b) the state is just when each part does its own work, d8–10; (c) therefore (i) a man is just and *does his own* when (ii) each part (sc. of his soul) does its own, d12–e2. (ii) is explained in 441e4–442d8. 'Doing his own' in (i) refers to step (2) above, where the phrase was left unexplained; it is explained in 443c4–444a2, where (2) is said to be only an 'image' of real justice, 443c4–7. (See Murphy (704), 12–16.) Vlastos (732), 130, thinks (i) refers to the justice of the good citizen, and that (c) asserts that a man will be p-just if and only if he is a good citizen. Plato does not defend this claim (as Vlastos agrees), and there is no reason to read it in here, since (3)–(5) offer no account of individual justice.) See Aronson (734), 388 f.

31. On justice and the other virtues see Murphy (704), 17–19. Socrates and the *G*. on UV; see III. 14.4, IV. 2.8, V, n. 18.

32. von Wright (834), 149, explains virtue as self-control, underestimating the difference between himself and Plato and Aristotle. See further Joseph (703), 161–77—though he is unfair to Aristotle's doctrine of the mean (see III. 5.2, VIII. 3.1).

33. On problems of Socratic definition and pre-theoretical judgements see III. 7.7. Prichard (829), 106, and Sachs (717), 46, argue that to show p-justice is justice Plato should prove a biconditional: (J) (1) If a man is p-just, he is c-just; (2) if a man is c-just, he is p-just. See above, n. 30. But Plato has no reason to accept J2; in II Glaucon emphasized the inadequacy of ordinary views of justice; and Plato's criticism of the c-just slavish men would be absurd if he accepted J2 (see above 4.5). Glaucon's question in II did not demand a proof of J. Plato does not even defend J1; 442d10–443b2 says only that the p-just man will avoid some flagrantly c-unjust actions, not that he will do nothing c-unjust. I agree with Sachs that Plato's argument would be fallacious, if he meant to prove J; but Sachs has not shown why J is a reasonable demand. At 343de Thrasymachus draws unwelcome consequences from Cephalus' original view of justice at 331d; part of Plato's answer is to suggest that there is more to justice than Cephalus thought (see Murphy (704), 2).

Some argue that Plato can prove J. Weingartner's defence of J2 (741), 251 f, neglects slavish men. Vlastos (732), 136–9, tries to exclude slavish virtue by reading 'reliably c-just' in J2. But a slavishly just man may be reliably c-just, for the consequences of justice (see above 4.4–5). Vlastos (and Kraut (737)) must also assume that there can be p-justice without knowledge; see n. 26.

34. Plato assumes without justification that a citizen who does what the state requires of him, and in that sense 'what is suited to his nature', will also do what is in his interest, 'what is suited to his nature' in a quite different and perhaps unrelated way. His sweeping claims about doing one's own, parallel to the claims about justice, are important for the political theory of the R.; VIII, n. 28.

35. See II. 3.6, III. 6.3.

36. See III. 18.6, V. 5.4.

37. Kraut (737), 208–11, distinguishes a 'non-normative' and a 'normative' sense of 'control by reason', and argues that p-justice requires normative control. His account of non-normative control assumes that any desire conflicting with an appetite is rational; see n. 18. On his 'normative' sense see below, n. 64. The prudence displayed in dependent rational desires is discussed by Mabbott (725), 113–16.

38. 472b3–c2, 484a5–b1 show that Plato realizes that he has not yet fully described the just man or how his life differs from the unjust man's.

39. See VI. 5.1–2.

40. On 'the many beautifuls' see VI, n. 34.

41. *The argument in R. V.* I am indebted to Fine's detailed analysis and interpretation in (743), 8. Here I offer only a summary of what I take to be the main line of argument. The main controversy concerns the reading of 'Knowledge is set over what is' (*epi to(i) onti*, 477a9), and corresponding remarks about belief and ignorance. We might take 'what is' existentially, predicatively or veridically. (Plato's lack of explicit distinction between these uses of 'to be' is noticed and exploited in different ways by Owen (746), 223–5, Vlastos (631), 44–7, (630), 59–63, Furth (744).) If Plato's claims are to be acceptable to the sight-lover (as 476d8–e2 requires; see Gosling (745), 120 f, Murphy (704), 105), the veridical reading (i.e. 'knowledge is set over what is true' rather than 'what exists' or 'what is really *F*') is by far the most plausible; it assumes a standard condition on knowledge (if I know *p*, *p* is true; cf. *G.* 454d6–7), while the other readings require Plato to insist on strong and implausible conditions which the sight-lover has been given no reason to accept at the outset of the argument (contrary to 476d8–e2). This veridical reading of 'to be' also allows us to understand Plato's claim correctly, and acquit him of fallacy, when he says (477b3–478b2) that knowledge and belief are different powers with different functions, and therefore set over different things. If these 'different things' are 'what is true' and 'what is true and false', Plato is saying fairly that knowledge and belief have different propositional contents. If the existential or predicative reading is accepted, Plato will be saying that knowledge and belief are correlated with different kinds of entities; he has not justified

such a claim, and his argument here from different functions to different objects will be invalid. If we accept the veridical reading, we need not ascribe this unjustified claim to Plato. See Crombie (101), II. 58, Gosling, 122–5; contrast Allen (742), 165, Cross and Woozley (702), 146 f.

The veridical reading makes good sense of the argument up to 478e5. But at 479a5–c5 the predicative use of 'to be' is needed, since the many beautifuls (etc.) are said to be and not be beautiful. By itself this claim does not show that the sight-lovers have only belief, since belief is concerned with what is and is not true. However Plato can argue for the conclusion he seeks. Since the sight-lovers offer to tell us what the beautiful is by offering us something which is and is not (beautiful), they cannot be telling us only what is true about the beautiful; therefore they have no knowledge about it. But neither are they completely astray, saying only what is altogether false about it; therefore they do not merely have ignorance (cf. 478b6–c1). And so what they say will count as belief; 'the many beliefs (*nomima*; cf. 484d2, 589e7, G. 488d9, *HMa.* 294e8) of the many about beautiful and the rest roll around between what is not (true) and what fully is (true)' (479d3–5). Plato does not make explicit the crucial connection between the nature (being and not being beautiful) of the many beautifuls and the nature (being and not being true) of the sight-lovers' claims about the beautiful based on the many beautifuls. Confusion cannot be ruled out. But no confusion is required to reach Plato's conclusion.

The argument in *R.* V, then, does not assume at the outset that knowledge and belief are correlated with separate entities. Plato assumes only the *M.*'s account of knowledge and belief, and shows that the sight-lovers do not have knowledge; what they say is not true, and it does not give the correct explanation of beliefs about the beautiful. (There are problems about the way 'true and not true' describes the content of belief. It should apply to the class of beliefs as a whole—some are true and some are false, without implying that every particular belief is both true and false. Plato may be confused on this point at 478e1–479d1. But these problems do not undermine the whole argument.) No new or non-standard definition of knowledge or belief is required for the argument. Nor does Plato claim that knowledge can only be about unchanging entities; he claims that knowledge of Forms is necessary for knowledge of anything, but he does not infer directly that there can be no knowledge about the sensible world. *Tm.* 51d3–e6 and *Phil.* 59ab claim that the sensible world is not an object of knowledge, but this claim rests on further assumptions besides the conclusions of *R.* V. Nor does Plato imply that Forms are always objects of knowledge and never of belief; he claims only belief about the Form of the Good, 506c (see Murphy (704), 116 f). *R.* V. says that someone who recognizes only the many *F*s, and not the form of *F*, has no knowledge about *F*.

42. 488a7–489a2 might be taken to show that Plato still accepts the CA. But though he compares the philosopher to a craftsman in *one* way—that he has specialized knowledge unrecognized by the many—he does not suggest, as in the Socratic dialogues and *R.* I, that the virtuous man's virtue is simply a craft and nothing more. Plato does not claim or assume that the philosopher and the many disagree only about instrumental means; 493d7–494a6 suggests disagreement about ends. Contrast Bambrough (718), 195 f, 202.

43. I use small initial letters (e.g. 's1') for states which illustrate others, and capitals (e.g. 'S1') for the states illustrated. I use 'Sun', etc., for the name of the whole image, and 'sun' for the sun mentioned in the Sun-image.

44. *The Sun, Line, and Cave.*

1. How should S1–S2 be understood? We might think that since s1 and s2 refer to the same kinds of objects, so should S1–S2. But Plato does not contrast two ways of being aware of Forms; the soul is confused and confined to belief when it looks at what becomes and perishes; when it looks at what is illuminated by reality and truth it has knowledge, 508d4–9. 'What becomes and perishes' refers to the many *F*s; cf.

490b1, 493e3, 507c2. The whole simile does not contrast two ways of being aware of Forms, but the two conditions of the sight-lover and the philosopher.

2. When 509d1–3 refers to the visible and intelligible kinds of things, and their regions, we might think the four sections of the Line are meant to match s1, s2, S1, S2. But references to the visible region could as easily refer to S1. Plato thinks some further division beyond what was offered in the Sun is offered in the Line (509d6–8); but there is no further division if the four Line-stages simply repeat the Sun. It is better to take them as subdivisions of S1 and S2, so that L1 and L2 are cognitive states in their own right, not illustrations of L3 and L4.

3. 517a8–b6 says that (a) living in the cave corresponds to the area appearing through sight; (b) the fire corresponds to the power of the sun; (c) the ascent from the cave is the soul's ascent to the region of thought. (a) and (b) correspond to s1, and like it illustrate L1 + L2. c2 allows a reference to the sun in the visible world because it illustrates L2; in ethical beliefs the sun represents some conception of the good. If both the Line and the Cave correspond to the Sun in the same way, they correspond to each other, 517b1. 532ac does not show that c2 begins mathematics, as Robinson (133), 184, Ross (134), 74 f, Murphy (704), 163, suppose. The claim that 'all this business of the crafts we have mentioned', 532c3, turns the soul to reality includes other crafts besides mathematical—they began with confusion and then confidence, i.e. at L2, 523–4, before they reached L3.

4. Imagination (eikasia). (a) The description of L1 as awareness of shadows seems hard to reconcile with the view that the prisoners at c1 are like most people; Plato seems to be denying that most people have reached L2, awareness of physical objects (see Joseph (751), 34). Two answers can be found. (i) Imagination is being 'aware of' shadows, not necessarily in the sense that someone is actually confronted only with shadows, but in the sense that he cannot distinguish shadows and reality, but thinks shadows are real, whatever he is confronted with. Different states are correlated with different objects that we distinguish (though we may not realize it; see (6) below), not with different objects confronting us. (ii) The kind of imagination shared by most people is moral imagination; see Cross and Woozley (702), 220–2, Malcolm (752), 44. The description of L1 at 510a mentions an example (drawn from images of physical objects) of the condition most people are in with their moral beliefs, just as the descriptions of L2–L4 give examples of the conditions. (b) Imagination includes the condition of those with correct moral beliefs from musical education; contrast Nettleship (705), 247, Malcolm, 43. Someone passing from imagination to confidence is turned nearer to to on and to mallon onta, and sees more correctly, 515d3–4; but music and gymnastics, the pre-philosophical education, do not turn us from gignomena to onta, 521d13–522b3. The non-philosophers in Plato's state are just as unreflective and uncritical as in every other state, though their beliefs are truer and more beneficial.

5. Confidence (pistis). Our account implies that some dialectic is used at L2; L4 employs dialectic and nothing else, but it is not the first stage where any dialectic appears. L4 examines kat' ousian, 534c2, requiring previous definition of the ousia reached by elenctic argument kata doxan at earlier stages. Plato's 'prohibition of dialectic' for people under thirty, 537d2–3, 539a9–10, prevents them from learning how to conduct an elenchos, 539b1–c3, and from learning how to use it in debate. But someone convinced, like Meno's slave, of his ignorance by an elenchos need not be an eristic debater; and so Plato can still allow some dialectic at L2.

6. Thought (dianoia). (a) On thought and images outside mathematics see Gallop (749), (748), 192–6. (b) 510d5–511a6 make it fairly clear that the hypotheses are not the diagrams (contrast Hare (750), refuted by Taylor (754)), but are defended by the use of diagrams. Plato probably thinks that the mathematicians' hypotheses, like his own accounts of the virtues, include definitions; the dialectician's examination and justification of the definitions takes him beyond the mathematician's sphere of com-

petence. (c) In 510d5–7 Plato says that the mathematicians use *logoi* about 'visible things, thinking not about them, but about the things they are like'. These other things are the Forms; but the mathematician need not explicitly recognize Forms. His claims about 'the square' and so on will be justifiable only by reference to the Forms, though he says it with his eye on diagrams, and perhaps with not the slightest interest in ontology or knowledge of the Forms. Plato's other phrases in 510d8, e3 can be taken the same way.

7. *Noēsis.* (a) On hypotheses in the *Phd.* see VI. 10.3. *Phd.* 101e1, requiring examination of the hypotheses until we reach something *hikanon*, does not say what would be *hikanon*; it leaves room for, though it does not require, the *R.*'s *anhupethetos archē* (contrast Robinson (138), 146 f, 157). (b) Shorey (753), 232–4, denies that the *R.* goes beyond the hypothetical method except metaphorically. Robinson, 172–7, Cornford (747), 93, think a leap of intuition is needed (cf. *Symp.* 210e) to reach firm conclusions. But the *Symp.* suggests only that the *insight* may be sudden, not that knowledge can dispense with the normal Platonic *logos*; see VI, n. 47. If the definition justifies the hypotheses, they in turn justify it, since it has been reached from them; the whole body of knowledge will then have its parts supporting each other. On teleology see Murphy (704), 181–6, Joseph (751), 16–21. (c) The comment that the dialectician will want to argue *kat' ousian*, not *kata doxan*, 534e2 (see Adam (701), ad loc.), suggests that accounts of other *ousiai* will be used to reach an account of the Good. This is not the ordinary Socratic elenchos, where the interlocutor's suggestions (hypotheses; cf. *Eu.* 11c5) are examined *kata doxan* without reference to any previous definition. (Contrast Cornford, 85–7.) (d) Plato tells the philosopher returning to the cave that when he is accustomed to it, he will see far better than the cave-dwellers, *kai gnōsesthe hekasta ta eidōla hatta esti kai hōn*, because he has seen the truth about admirable, just and good things, 520c3–7; he does not lapse from intelligence (L4) to confidence (L2) just because he looks at physical objects. The use of 'know' (*gnōsesthe*) shows that the objects correlated with each Line-stage are not meant to determine someone's cognitive state; Plato means that someone with that cognitive state can recognize only certain objects, whatever he may be confronted with. On this view, it is not surprising that someone can have knowledge about physical objects; see above, n. 41.

45. On Socrates see Shorey (753), and III. 4.1–2, and 12.3. The description of the Good as 'what every soul pursues and for the sake of which does everything' (*panta prattei*, 505e1) conflicts with the anti-Socratic view of Book IV if 'does everything' means 'does everything that it does'; cf. *G.* 468b1–5. But it can also mean 'go to all lengths', like the unscrupulous people mentioned in 505d5–9 and attacked in Book II. See LSJ (139), s.v. *pas*, D. III. 2; *Ap.* 39a, *M.* 89e7, *Phd.* 114c7, *Symp.* 218a1, *R.* 488c1, 504e1. Plato, then, allows the existence of incontinence.

46. Hedonism; IV. 2.3, V. 3.5. There might be two possible targets for the attack on wisdom as the final good; (1) Perhaps Plato refers to the infinite regress of wisdom producing wisdom, in the *Eud.*; see III. 11.2. That regress rested on a confusion between instrumental and intrinsic goods, which Plato may be alluding to here. (2) The *Phd.* sometimes suggests that a different kind of wisdom—contemplation of Forms—is the final good; VI. 11.6. The *R.*'s objection will show that wisdom must include knowledge of the good, and it does not follow that that knowledge is the whole of the final good. However, it is not clear that Plato intends his argument here to have that force.

47. 509b6–10 is easiest to understand if *einai* and *ousia* are taken predicatively (see Gosling (104), 67 f; contrast Joseph (751), 22–4). Plato will then claim that the virtues, e.g., are what they are because of their contribution to the Good. On *epeikeina tēs ousias* see Joseph, 23 f.

48. See VI. 10.2.

49. 435e1–436a3 is the only passage in IV to distinguish parts by their objects.

50. See Kraut (737), 212.

51. If, e.g., a tyrannical man's dominant *erōs* is to drink, or to kill his enemies, single-minded pursuit of his goal will deprive him of resources for its pursuit, if he cannot buy drink, or his enemies successfully conspire against him. See Murphy (704), 54, Joseph (703), 133. On the *G.* see V. 2.2 and 5.3.

52. On the *thumos* in IV and VIII see Gosling (104), 42–4, Williams (733), 205 f. I do not think the ideal to which a thumoeidic man is attached need be an ideal of manliness (as Gosling suggests)—though Plato does not clearly distinguish the thumoeidic type from a prominent example in the Spartan philotimic man. My remarks on a second-order desires are indebted to Frankfurt (720), 7–14.

53. These comments evade problems in Plato. He often speaks as though one part of the soul has one object; (a) He associates *thumos* with anger in IV and with *philotimia* in VIII. (b) *Epithumia* is associated with basic biological appetites in IV, and with money-making in VIII, with a feeble effort to reduce the two objects to one at 580d11–581a1. (c) The rational part is associated with *manthanein*, 435e7, and with *sophia*, 581b5–10. Though Plato's discussion of the three parts is normally better than these associations allow, if they exhaust the content of the three parts, he does not always do justice to his own discussion.

54. On Socrates see III. 13.3–4. On the *Symp.* see VI. 14.2.

55. On 'becoming and perishing' see VI. 8.7. On the philosopher's love for the Forms see Vlastos (631), 48–56. In *tois doxazomenois einai pollois hekastois*, 490b1, *einai* should be predicative ('is beautiful' etc.), since the claim depends on the argument at 479b9–10, 479c10–480a4.

56. See III. 13.2 and VI. 14.2–3.

57. On the ambivalent conception of the philosopher and wisdom in the *Phd.* see VI. 11.6.

58. On this passage see VI. 15.2.

59. See VI. 15.5. The contrast between the p-just and the 'merely thrifty' man is similar to Falk's contrast between mere prudence and the wisdom which sometimes requires courage (808), 361. Horsburgh (818), 60 f, accepts the narrow conception of prudence; Mabbott (825), 62 f, suggests a wider, more Platonic conception.

60. My account of the philospher's motives is indebted to Morris (738)—though I think he is wrong to deny (142) that the philosopher is moved by desire for his own good. On 'propagating virtue' see Kraut (644), 339–43; on the philosopher's 'impersonal' admiration for the Forms see Demos (735), 55.

1. Waterlow (740), explains the philosopher's desire to replicate his own justice by the impersonal character of the philosophical reason in a man. But will this philosophical reason be the same as the prudential *logistikon* in IV, concerned for the good of the whole soul? It is hard to see how it can be if it is impersonal; and then how could a clash between philosophical and prudential reason be avoided?

2. Kraut, 336 appeals to 462a9–d5 on the fellow-feeling in a Platonic state, to show why the philosophers will not be egoists; but it shows at most that they will not be egoists until they ask if they have good reason to do what they have learnt to do; cf. 538d6–e1. They must still be convinced they are better off with these altruistic desires; see VIII, n. 30.

3. Gosling (104), 70 f, citing *Phdr.* 246–9, *Phil.* 27–30, *Tm.* 29e–30b, suggests that the philospher will want to share in the general good ordering of the universe. This motive (not mentioned in the *R.*, except vaguely at 500b8–c7) will supplement others; but it will not show either that the philosopher's share will be action rather than contemplation, or that good order in the universe requires attention to other people's interests; these further moves depend on the theory of *erōs* in the *Symp.*

61. *The return to the cave.*

1. Plato mentions *anankē* imposed on the philosophers, at 500d4, 519e4, 520a8, e1–3, 540b4–5. In all these passages except 519e4, 520a8 he may mean only that the

philosopher will think it a disagreeable necessity, but still the best thing to do, and will not need to be forced to do it (see Kraut (644), 342 f, Murphy (704), 54 n.). But these two passages (contrasting persuasion with *ananke* and saying that others will *prosanankazein* the philosophers) seem to imply more than the minimal sense of *ananke*.

2. 519c4–6 is a problem for the view that the philosopher thinks legislation best for him in the circumstances (see Murphy, 53, n. 2); that is what Plato should say, and does say in most of his comments on this question, but not here. We might perhaps suppose that academic seclusion would make the philosopher forget the problems of the cave, so that simple ignorance, rather than moral indifference, would explain his reluctance. But Plato does not suggest this rather dubious excuse.

3. Plato does not admit either in 519d8–9 or in 419a1–421c6 that the rulers sacrifice their own happiness. The state is not designed for their exclusive happiness, but for everyone's happiness, 420b3–8, 519e1–520a4; but it does secure their happiness, 466b2, and it would be a childish mistake about happiness to want a different life, 466b4–c3. Plato's answer to the question in 519d8–9 should be no.

4. Adkins (207), 290–2, Foster (736), 301–4, Aronson (734), 393–6, believe that the philosopher sacrifices his own happiness; for they assume that his happiness is pure contemplation. While Plato is sometimes attracted to this view, it is not his only view, or his normal view in the *R*.

5. Plato offers two reasons why the philosophers will rule well: (a) They have better things to do, and will not care for the spoils of office, 520d1–521b5. (b) They have the knowledge needed to rule well, 520c4–7. (a) belongs to the contemplative picture of the philosopher (cf. 517d4–518b4, *Tht.* 174b1–6, 175b1–3); it is a poor defence for the competence of the philosopher, and needs support from (b), which is unsatisfactorily combined with (a) in the suggestion that after initial confusion the philosopher will see better than the others in the cave.

6. Plato is less concerned with these issues because he has argued at 485a4–487a6 that a philosopher's training and interest exclude the recognized vices. (See 485d6–e5, Kraut (737), 214–16.) But (a) Plato has not shown why a pure contemplative should not act c-unjustly to secure resources for his study or to avoid the distractions of public office (cf. Kraut, 215, Gosling (104), 39). (b) Mere refraining from c-injustice will not make the philosopher choose justice for itself—it will only be a means to his philosophical study. To avoid these objections Plato must appeal to the practical conception of the philosopher.

62. *The arguments about pleasure.* I have not discussed in detail the arguments at 580d–588a to show that the just man and philosopher has the pleasantest life. Plato rightly says that they are not the main proof of his claim in the *R*. (the first *apodeixis* is said to be over at 580c9). Anyhow, the arguments are quite puzzling, and often dubious. I offer a few comments.

1. The question about pleasure is relevant because Plato believes, without being a hedonist, that pleasure is a necessary or a major part (he does not make clear which he thinks it is) of the best life; the just man would have reason for some regret if he found that some other life would be pleasanter than his own—though it does not follow that he would have overriding reason to choose that other life; and Plato wants to show that no regrets are needed. He need not try, though, to prove from some neutral standpoint that the just man's life is pleasantest; if we were right about the *G*. (see V. 3.5), he thinks there is no neutral standpoint for judgements of comparative pleasure, apart from different moral beliefs; all he needs is to prove that the just man will not find another life pleasanter. When he promises to compare the pleasantness, and not only (or 'let alone'—*me hoti*, 581e7) the goodness or admirability, of lives, he does not imply that pleasantness can be judged apart from the other two features (contrast Murphy (704), 208).

2. 580d3–581c7 claims to repeat the tripartition of the soul in Book IV. But here

Plato divides the parts by their objects of desire, learning, honour, and wealth, and the corresponding pleasures, 580d7–e5 (cf. 435e3–436a3). His argument for calling the appetitive part 'gain-loving' is feeble, 580e5 (the oligarchic man's desire for wealth required restraint of his other appetites, and disproves Plato's claim here that desire for wealth aims at the satisfaction of other appetites); and he does not show that the other two objects are especially appropriate for the emotional and rational parts. To identify this division with Book IV's, he needs to show that the rational second-order decision will correctly choose philosophical contemplation as the ultimate end. This kind of argument shows a problem in the conception of the rational part which has arisen before. (a) It is contemplative, loving learning (see n. 53); and (b) it must be practical, desiring something because it is best on the whole for the whole soul. Plato does not consider someone with a craving for contemplation without reference to his over-all good; here (a) would make his desire rational, while (b) would make it appetitive. Now Plato speaks as though the philosophical part satisfied only (a); but we shall see that at crucial points the argument works only if it also satisfies (b)—and he does not show that the two criteria coincide in the philosophical part described in 580 f.

3. 581c8–583a11 argues that the philosopher will judge his life pleasantest, and that his judgement is to be accepted because of his superior 'experience, wisdom, and reason', 582a5. The appeal to experience, 582a8–d3, is dubious; even though the philosopher has had some experience of appetitive and honour-loving pleasures, he has not lived the life of the single-minded appetitive or honour-loving man. But how does 'wisdom and reason' help? If it is only the philosopher's knowledge of non-sensible reality, it does not obviously qualify him to judge about pleasures. But practical wisdom is much more promising; if the philosopher can claim against the deviant men that he has organized his life to benefit the whole soul and each part, he can claim he has the right standard to judge pleasures (as Socrates argued in the *G.*), and even though he is not a hedonist, he can claim to choose the best and greatest pleasures (contrast Murphy, 209 f), though someone with a disordered soul might disagree. For this argument to work in Plato's support, the rational part which dominates the philosopher cannot be purely contemplative.

4. The argument of 583b1–587b10, to show that the philosopher has the truest pleasures, is complicated by its combination of two claims: (a) Non-philosophers fail to realize that health is pleasant only relative to sickness, and so they expect that mere restorations to normal conditions will always be pleasant, when in fact they will only sometimes be pleasant, 583c3–584a10. These 'restorations' are deceptive because they are not always reliable sources of pleasure (see Murphy, 212). (b) Non-philosophers fail to realize that there are other pleasures besides the restorations preceded by pain, and so they do not gain the truest and most reliable pleasures, 584b1–585e5. There are further problems in Plato's claims; but both of these imply a practical conception of the rational part. The philosopher is expected to know when and how far it will be pleasant to pursue the restoration preceded by pain, and when to pursue other kinds of pleasure. Though Plato suggests that pleasure in immaterial objects is the only true pleasure, he also claims that the philosophical part's control will make the pleasures of the other two parts truer too, 586d4–587a11. The philosopher must not only concentrate on his contemplation, but also use practical wisdom in combining and organizing pleasures into a good life.

5. Plato does not face the problems by his contemplative conception of the rational part. But even here, when that conception is very prominent, it is not the only one; he also implies that the rational part's desires are formed by practical wisdom about the good of the whole soul.

63. See Murphy (704), 82 f, 55 f.

64. Unnecessary desires are those which are necessary neither for survival nor for other benefits to us, 558d1–2. While the contemplative view of the philosopher might

suggest that he ought to rid himself of unnecessary desires, Plato does not endorse this view.

(1) 559a3 says that someone could remove them by education, not that he should.

(2) Some of these desires are harmful, 559b8; but not all unnecessary desires are said to be harmful.

(3) In a philosopher's training these desires will weaken (*ekleipoien*, 485de); they will not necessarily disappear, though a purely contemplative philosopher will not need them, 581e3–4.

(4) 461b9–c7 allows the satisfaction of apparently unnecessary desires for non-procreative sexual relations to some guardians (see Murphy (704), 26). Despite Plato's ascetic tendencies, supported by the contemplative view of the philosopher, his theory does not sanction the total rejection of unnecessary desires. Though they do not aim at activities worth while for themselves or for other goals, the philosopher will persuade them that a rationally planned life, concerned for the good of the whole soul, secures the resources for their satisfaction.

Kraut (644), 343 f, thinks Plato is wrong to equate justice with control by reason (see also Joseph (703), 154). But his objection is sound only if the philosopher who avoids his duty of ruling to gain leisure for philosophy (an offence against justice supposed to be consistent with control by the rational part) is really controlled by the rational part. If Plato accepts the practical view of the rational part, he can meet this objection. Someone who rejects justice rejects (on Plato's view) the life chosen by reason, and chooses the goal of a good-independent appetitive desire for contemplation—and this desire does not cease to be appetitive (on Book IV's and VIII's criterion) just because it requires the use of reason. Plato's attachment to the contemplative view of the philosopher might well make this answer unwelcome; see notes 61, 62. But it follows from the view of the rational part required by most of his argument.

65. The *G*. on punishment; V. 2.4.

NOTES TO CHAPTER VIII

1. Scepticism about Plato's question is expressed by Warnock (835), 89–92, who thinks the choice of ultimate ends is not a question for morality. On problems about the definition of morality, and especially on the relative weight of its overriding status and its specific content, I generally follow Falk (808), 389; Frankena (813), 167–73, emphasizes content more strongly.

2. Teleological and deontological theories are distinguished by Frankena (814), 13; 'A teleological theory says that the basic or ultimate criterion or standard of what is morally right, wrong, obligatory, etc., is the non-moral value that is brought into being. The final appeal, directly or indirectly, must be to the comparative amount of good produced . . .' I use this account, but with 'non-moral' deleted. Frankena objects that this deletion makes the teleological theory circular. He is right, but he does not show that the circle is vicious. See also Rawls (830), 24 f. I also use 'deontological' in a slightly non-standard sense: someone might agree that (a) the content of morality cannot be described in teleological terms, but deny that (b) we have reason to be moral when it is not teleologically justifiable; see 4.3. But I am speaking of a deontologist, like Kant or Prichard, who accepts both (a) and (b).

3. See Hume (821), *T*., III. 3.3, 603; (820), *E*., V. 229; Warnock (835), 157–9.

4. Connections between Platonic and ordinary judgements; see III. 7.7, VII. 10.1.

5. Rawls (830), 135 f, argues, for the kinds of reasons I mention, that egoism is not a possible moral view satisfying the formal constraints of the concept of right.

6. On Plato's question see Nielsen (828), 759.

7. On the 'uninformativeness' of Plato's version of eudaimonism see VI. 16.2, VII, 5.2.

8. Incontinence; III. 12.3. Virtue and the agent's benefit; III. 4.1, Justice and happiness; VII. 5.1.

9. On the varieties of egoism see Broad (806). Sidgwick (832), 91 f, thinks hedonistic solipsism is the only interesting and controversial formulation of egoism; egocentrism, he remarks, was assumed by the whole ethical controversy of ancient Greece, and we learn nothing about Greek ethics (he implies) by knowing only this. Contrast Brandt (805), 685 f.

10. On happiness see III. 4.5. Mill gropes towards a similar conception of happiness (826), IV. 5, when he tries to show that someone can desire virtue, wealth, etc., for its own sake and for the sake of happiness, as 'ingredients' or 'parts' of happiness. Sidgwick (832), 93 n., sees that this view of happiness conflicts with Mill's normal hedonistic view, which requires us to choose virtue for the sake of its pleasure—Mill confuses this with the choice of virtue as part of happiness (see also Moore (639), 71 f). But Mill is right to think that happiness can be regarded as a compound of activities—as Plato and Aristotle regard it; see Bradley (804), 120 n. Failure to take account of this part of Plato's doctrine of happiness undermines most of Hospers's criticism (819), 174–84, which assumes that a certain state of feeling is necessary and sufficient for happiness. It is fair to object that Plato's view of happiness makes his claim much harder to test, and harder even to understand; but it is not refuted by pointing out that immoral people can feel cheerful.

11. Care of the soul; III. 16.2, V. 5.4, VI. 11.2, VII. 10.4.

12. See VII. 18.1–2.

13. My remarks on Aristotle ignore his attraction to the solipsistic end of philosophical contemplation, for reasons similar to Plato's.

14. Anti-egoistic and anti-teleological arguments are conflated by Prichard (829), 2–7, and elsewhere. His opponents sometimes say (a) that morality must benefit the agent, sometimes (b) that it must have some purpose. He seems to argue, 116, that (b) collapses into (a)—but his position is neither clear nor cogently defended. One reason for conflating (a) and (b) is that Prichard's and other people's appeals to what we are aware of in our awareness of moral obligations are equally objections to both. But I have tried to avoid this conflation in considering anti-teleological arguments.

15. Anti-teleological arguments are drawn from Prichard (829), esp. 2–11, 95–128, who draws on Kant; but I have formulated them differently.

16. Socrates' view is explained by Mill (826), IV. 5, explaining the original conditions by which virtue is made virtue; '. . . actions and dispositions are only virtuous because they promote another end than virtue'. On his attempt to reconcile this claim with the choice of virtue for itself see n. 10 above.

17. For objections to the justification of morality by appeal to non-moral ends see Bradley (804), 58–64. He concludes, 'Has the question, Why should I be moral? No sense then, and is no answer possible? No, the question has no sense at all, it is simply unmeaning, unless it is equivalent to, *Is* morality an end in itself; and, if so, how and in what way is it an end?' (He refers to the Greek moralists, 81.) A non-moral justification is rejected for different reasons by Gauthier (815), 175.

18. The Kantian belief in the priority of the right over the good (see Kant (823), 62–5) is defended by Ross (831), 16–19, Rawls (830), 446–52. I have not fully discussed the grounds of this belief, but only mentioned some intuitive convictions its defenders have tended to rely on.

19. The general psychological egoist argument is rejected by Bradley (804), 258 f; see also Feinberg (809), 503 f.

20. The *Lysis* argument; III. 4.1.

21. The doctrine of the mean; III. 5.2.

22. Not all deontological views need to operate with simple rules, easy to apply to particular situations; Kant's 'supreme principle' requires unity in the virtues as much as Aristotle's theory does. But Kant himself sometimes wants moral decisions to be easier than, on his theory, they should be, for the inexperienced and ignorant; see (824), 403.

23. Prichard (829), 114, recognizes that teleological theories seem to offer a common ground of obligations without which they will be 'an unconnected heap' (quoted from Joseph (822), 67). Prichard himself does not explain how his theory will deal with conflicts of obligations, unless he assumes that answers can always be found intuitively.
24. The analogy (at least) between rational concern for one's own good and moral concerns is explored by Falk (808), 372–4.
25. Reasons for taking Plato's question seriously are offered by Falk (808), 375–7.
26. See VII. 18.3.
27. On the Kantian 'end in itself' principle see Vlastos (833), 48 f. In associating the principle with self-determination and freedom to pursue one's own ends (a much broader notion of autonomy than Kant's own), I am going beyond what Kant explicitly says (I will not discuss the interpretation of the principle in Kant himself), though I think this line of thought is Kantian.
28. My account of Platonic love and its defects is deeply indebted to Vlastos (648), 30–3; but I do not think all his criticisms are justified. After criticizing the passivity of the beloved in Platonic love, he writes, 'Plato seems barely conscious of the fact that this "holy image" is himself a valuing subject, a centre of private experience and individual preference, whose predilections and choice of ends are no mere reflex of the lover's and might well cross him at some points even while returning his love. Transposing this from erotics to politics, we see the reason for the tragedy of the *Republic*; we see why its effort to foster civic love obliterates civil liberty. The fashioner of this utopia has evidently failed to see that what love for our fellows requires of us is, above all, imaginative sympathy and concern for what they themselves think, feel and want. He has therefore missed that dimension of love in which tolerance, trust, forgiveness, tenderness and respect have validity. Apart from these imperatives, the notion of loving persons as "ends in themselves" would make no sense' (32).

I have quoted at length because I think distinct and separable objections to Plato are unacceptably conflated. Vlastos appears to raise these objections:

(1) Plato's theory does not allow for love of persons as ends in themselves.

(2) It does not allow for the love of whole persons, but only of their admirable qualities (Vlastos, 31).

(3) It does not allow for the love of an individual as the individual he is.

(4) Plato underestimates the importance of individual freedom in love.
The quoted passage suggests that (4) is explained by Plato's other views, especially (2). I think these changes are logically independent.

(1) is unjustified, on the first view I have suggested of loving someone for his own sake. If we had accepted the 'exclusive' interpretation of the ascent in the *Symp.* (see VI, n. 58), we might have supposed that love of persons is worth while only for its help in the ascent. But we have found this account unjustified, so that Plato need not make concern for persons' interests instrumental to any other ends; a Platonic lover can be concerned both for his own happiness and for his beloved's interest for the beloved's own sake, non-exploitatively.

Vlastos's objection (2) can be justified on Kantian grounds (as he suggests, 32, 10, n. 24). But this objection should be separated from (1). For Vlastos' assimilation of the two makes it look as though only the Kantian demand will prevent the exploitation of persons which subordinates their interests to other people's; my comments on Plato and Aristotle are meant to show that this charge is false, and that the Kantian demand must be justified on other grounds.

The different issues raised in (1) and (2) become clearer in Aristotle. Vlastos, 33 n., notices that Aristotle uses 'loving a person for himself' to mean both (a) 'loving him for his own benefit, not the lover's', and (b) 'loving him for his virtue'. Vlastos comments, '(b), of course, need not be disinterested and *could* be egoistic'. He does not support the last charge. We might think of a case where *A* appreciates *B*'s being virtuous because virtuous men are useful (e.g. to be non-executive directors making a new company look respectable). But this is no counter-example to Aristotle; for it is not a case of *A*'s loving *B* for his virtue, which requires that *B*'s virtue should be sufficient by itself, and apart from its consequences, for *A* to love *B*. Aristotle's conditions (a) and (b) equally prescribe non-exploitative love for the beloved's sake; and this point about his and Plato's theory should not be obscured, as it is in Vlastos's account, by their failure to meet Kantian demands.

Objections (3) also needs to be separated. Vlastos suggests, 31, that Plato's reduction of whole persons to bundles of qualities explains why personal affection ranks low on Plato's *scala amoris*. I am not sure if he means that acceptance of the Kantian demand would require a proper valuation of personal affection; it is hard to see the connection. To value a person (understood in Kant's way) as an end in himself will require respect for his ends and purposes; but a Kantian might display this attitude impartially to any other person, and any candidate for being an end-in-himself would be a suitable object of this respect. Personal affection apparently requires some attitude to the individual characteristics of just this person, which distinguish him from those other persons who benefit from the Kantian interpretation of loving our neighbour (see Kant (824), 399). I am not sure what connection, if any, Vlastos sees between Kantian 'practical love' and personal affection; but it is perhaps worthwhile to insist that we do not meet all his criticisms of Plato's position by replacing it with Kant's. Personal affection is not easily seen to be intelligible or justifiable simply from the demand that persons should be treated as ends in themselves with their preferences respected.

Vlastos connects (4) with the other objections by claiming that Plato undervalues liberty because he values people only for their usefulness. I do not say that in the *R*. Plato explicitly *rejects* this view; but Vlastos's arguments do not prove that he holds it. Here we must distinguish two kinds of objections to Plato's political theory; (a) how we think a state constructed on Plato's principles would really work; and (b) what we think of the principles themselves. I shall concentrate on (b), and ignore (a). The central concept leading from Plato's moral to his political theory is deeply confused (see VII, n. 34). Someone's 'work' or 'function' is taken to be (1) what his nature suits him for; and (1) is explained by (2) what will best achieve his good; and (3) what he is naturally suited to do for the good of the state. Plato simply assumes that (2) and (3) will require exactly the same actions. But even if the state aims at my good as well as everyone else's, it does not follow that the work assigned to me for the common good will always be the work which would be best for me, if my interests alone were consulted. But anyhow Plato definitely insists that the state will benefit everyone. The lower classes benefit from the rule of men controlled by reason (*R*. 590cd), and the rulers achieve their own happiness—only a mistaken belief about happiness would make them reject their present life (466b4–c3).

Vlastos quotes two passages to show that Plato thinks the state's protection of my interests depends on my usefulness to the state:

(1) Plato says that judges aim at justice in the state, a condition in which each citizen and class has and does his or its own, *R*. 433e6–434a1 (see Vlastos (732), 119–21). He assumes that each man will do his own work only if he has 'his own'—what he needs to do his own work. But this assumption implies no promise to a citizen in return for services. Plato's state aims to secure the distribution of resources needed for the common good. It makes no promise to individual citizens, and certainly does not say that a man can keep, say, the wages he earns as a craftsman; if the common good would be better served by making him work without pay, the state has no reason to pay him, and he has no valid claim to pay. Plato's citizens are accorded no 'rights', except in a vacuous sense in which 'rights' refers to nothing morally distinctive, and implies no protection against coercion in the state's interest or the interests of the right-holder himself (see n. 29 below). And so I do not

agree with Vlastos (l.c.) in finding any view about rights here. But equally I find no claim that a man will receive benefits (Vlastos's interpretation of 'has his own', not required by the text) only if he benefits the state. Scarce resources may require the reallocation of useless producers for the common good; but that does not imply that usefulness by itself is always a necessary condition for receiving benefits from the state.

(2) Vlastos's prize exhibit is Plato's ruthless policy with useless invalids (407de); but it tells the other way. For Plato supposes that a man has a work which he must do to gain any benefit from living at all, 407c1–2; an invalid who cannot do his own work benefits neither himself nor the state, 407e1–2. Plato equivocates on 'work', as we noticed; but the important point is that he assumes it is sometimes not in my interest to stay alive, when I cannot fulfil the plan aimed at my own happiness; cf. *La.* 195c7–d9, *G.* 512a2–b2. We may disagree; but we cannot argue from this comment that he does not value persons for their own sakes, or values them only for their usefulness. He insists that the withdrawal of medical care counts as euthanasia in a man's own interest; considerations of usefulness are not taken to be decisive by themselves. Plato is open to serious objections; but these should not include the claim that he values persons only for their usefulness.

The denial of personal liberty in the *R.*'s regime is taken by Vlastos (648), 19, as a sign that Plato values individuals only for their usefulness; 'He could not have reached this result if he had thought of love as (a) wishing another person's good for just that person's sake, (b) looking upon the loved one's individual being as something precious in and of itself' (reference-letters added). Though Vlastos appears to identify (a) and (b), I have argued that they are separable. With his view of interests, Plato could easily argue that restrictions on liberty are required by the interests of a citizen, for paternalistic reasons (cf. *Lys.* 207e1–9, *Laws* 687de). The restrictions on freedom do not show that persons are not valued for themselves; he can argue that the condition of soul which is most in their interest requires restriction on their freedom, so that they will have the right psychic order, or come as near to it as they can, 590c–591a. Plato's restrictions can be defended from his conception of people's interests; and if we are morally concerned with interests only, we will find it hard to defend rights to freedom. Vlastos is right to argue that Plato's attitude to freedom exposes a deep flaw in his theory of love; but the flaw is not that he values persons only for their usefulness. That view is clear enough in the *Lys.* (see III. 18.5); but I can find no reason to believe Plato endorses it in the *R.*

29. My comments on rights are indebted to Vlastos (833), 36–40, and Feinberg (810). My description of rights excludes theories (like Mill's (826), V. 24) which make the possession of rights conditional on their contribution to social utility or some other over-all good. If we like to say that this exclusion is mistaken, my conditions can be taken to describe 'morally distinctive rights', i.e. the kind of rights which are morally distinctive in that their possession and exercise cannot be replaced by other people's benevolence or sense of duty to the right-holder. The claim I want to make is that Plato recognizes no morally distinctive rights in this sense. I have not explored the relations between the two conditions for rights. Perhaps the second condition is a special case of the first, and in '*x* is due to *A*' we can substitute for '*x*' 'a moral service and the freedom to demand or not to demand it'. But not all rights need include a right to freedom, since sometimes rights may protect right-holders against their own desires and interests. If *A* sells *B* into slavery, even with *B*'s consent and in *B*'s interest, we might (rightly or wrongly) insist that this option should not be open to *B* because it violates his rights. We could not claim to be protecting *B*'s interests by refusing to let him do what he wants to, but might still claim to be protecting his rights. Such a case would show that not all rights are of the second kind, requiring the right-holder's consent to initiate the action by others. Such cases suggest (though I cannot argue this point now) that we cannot make sense of our beliefs about rights by reference to the

right-holder's interests alone.

30. Some defences of altruism which will not satisfy Plato are these:

1. He will see no point in appealing to a sentiment of benevolence to justify altruistic actions (see Hume (820) *E*, V, 225 f). For even if we agree that we have a strong innate or acquired sentiment disposing us to care about other people's good, we need not agree that it is a good thing to pursue it. Even if it is psychologically necessary to indulge this sentiment sometimes, we might decide to minimize the indulgence.

2. A metaphysical argument to show that anyone with a coherent and adequate (in a way needing further explanation; see Nagel (827), 125–31) conception of himself as a person must show some concern for other people's interests will equally fail to show that this concern should be welcomed or persued beyond the unavoidable minimum.

3. Appeals to the authoritative character of conscience (see Butler (807), iii. 5) will not impress Plato. He may agree that some people are aware of authoritative guidance of this kind; but he needs to be convinced that conscientious action will contribute to a final good. If this defence cannot be found, someone who follows conscience is simply deluded.

4. These objections also show why Plato does not defend altruism himself by simply remarking that all the citizens of the Platonic state will identify themselves so strongly with each other's joys and sorrows that they will want to benefit each other, *R*. 462b4–e2; see Kraut (644), 335–8. A reflective philosopher in the Platonic state can fairly ask whether he is better off with this habitual desire than he would be without it; his strong desire for altruistic action does not by itself justify the action.

31. Intuitionism—the absence of priority-rules to decide between conflicting values—is discussed by Rawls (830), 34–40.

32. The 'priority of being over doing' in Platonic ethics is discussed by Burnyeat (303), 231–4; see III. 16.3, VI. 11.5. A similar view is suggested by Hume's comment that virtuous action is valuable as a sign of a virtuous character (821) *T*, III. 1.1, 575. Contrast a recent attempt to explain our view of one motive as morally better than another by reference to its probability of producing good actions, in Grice (816), 178 f. This view implies the implausible result that *if* conditions made self-seeking motives produce as good results as generous motives produce, they would deserve equal admiration; we will believe that only if we already believe we value people only as sources of good actions.

33. Self-sufficiency; II. 6.1, III. 18.7, V. 5.4, VII. 4.2.

34. See Kant (824), 394–6.

35. Here again (cf. above, n. 27) I am using Kant's term loosely, and not in his full technical sense, though I again hope to have captured one part of his views on autonomy.

BIBLIOGRAPHY

1. General works on Plato

(a) General Books

101. CROMBIE, I. M., *An Examination of Plato's Doctrines*, 2 vols., Routledge, London, 1962.
102. FRIEDLÄNDER, P., *Plato*, trans. H. Meyerhoff, Princeton U.P., Princeton, vol. 1, 1958; vol. 2, 1964.
103. GOMPERZ, T., *Greek Thinkers*, 4 vols., Murray, London, 1901–12.
104. GOSLING, J. C. B., *Plato*, Routledge, London, 1973.
105. GROTE, G., *Plato and the Other Companions of Socrates*, 3 vols., Murray, London, 1875.
106. MILL, J. S., 'Grote's Plato', in *Dissertations and Discussions*, vol. 4, Longmans Green, London, 1875.
107. MOREAU, J., *La Construction de l'idéalisme platonicien*, Boivin, Paris, 1939.
108. POHLENZ, M., *Aus Platos Werdezeit*, Weidmann, Berlin, 1913.
109. RAEDER, H., *Platons philosophische Entwicklung*, Teubner, Leipzig, 1905.
110. SHOREY, P., *What Plato Said*, University of Chicago Press, Chicago, 1933.
111. TAYLOR, A. E., *Plato; the Man and his Work*, 4th edn., Methuen, London, 1937.
112. VON ARNIM, H., *Platons Jugenddialoge*, Teubner, Leipzig, 1914.
113. ZELLER, E., *Socrates and the Socratic Schools*, E. T., Longmans, Green, London, 1885.
114. ——, *Plato and the Older Academy*, E. T., Longmans, Green, London, 1876.

(b) Collections of Essays on Plato

115. ALLEN, R. E., ed., *Studies in Plato's Metaphysics*, Routledge, London, 1965.
116. BAMBROUGH, J. R., ed., *New Essays on Plato and Aristotle*, Routledge, London, 1965.
117. VLASTOS, G., ed., *Plato*, vol. 1 (Metaphysics and Epistemology), and vol. 2 (Ethics, Politics), Doubleday, New York, 1971.
118. —— ed., The Philosophy of Socrates, Doubleday, New York, 1971.
119. ——, *Platonic Studies*, Princeton U.P., Princeton, 1973.

(c) Ethics

120. GOULD, J. P. A., *The Development of Plato's Ethics*, C.U.P., Cambridge, 1955.
121. HALL, R. A., *Plato and the Individual*, Nijhoff, The Hague, 1963.

122. HIRSCHBERGER, J., 'Die Phronesis in der Philosophie Platons vor dem Staates', *Philol.* Supp. 25.1 (1932).

123. O'BRIEN, M. J., 'Modern Philosophy and Platonic Ethics', *JHI* 19 (1958), 451–72.

124. ——, *The Socratic Paradoxes and the Greek Mind*, University of North Carolina Press, Chapel Hill, 1967.

125. POPPER, K. R., *The Open Society and its Enemies*, Vol. 1, 5th edn., Routledge, London, 1966.

126. RIST, J. M., *Eros and Psyche*, U. of Toronto Press, Toronto, 1964.

127. SHOREY, P., 'Plato's Ethics', in (117) II. 7–34, from *The Unity of Plato's Thought* (U. of Chicago Press, Chicago, 1903), ch. 1.

128. TENKKU, J., 'The Evaluation of Pleasure in Plato's Ethics', *Acta Philosophica Fennica*, 11 (1956).

129. WALSH, J. J., *Aristotle's Conception of Moral Weakness*, Columbia U.P., New York, 1963.

(d) *Epistemology and Metaphysics*

130. GULLEY, N., *Plato's Theory of Knowledge*, Methuen, London, 1962.

131. LUTOSLAWSKI, O., *Origins and Growth of Plato's Logic*, E.T., Clarendon Press, Oxford, 1897.

132. LYONS, J., *Structural Semantics*; *An Analysis of Part of the Vocabulary of Plato*, Blackwell, Oxford, 1963.

133. ROBINSON, R., *Plato's Earlier Dialectic*, 2nd edn., Clarendon Press, Oxford, 1953.

134. ROSS, W. D., *Plato's Theory of Ideas*, Clarendon Press, Oxford, 1951.

135. STENZEL, J., *Plato's Method of Dialectic*, trans. D. J. Allan, Clarendon Press, Oxford, 1940.

(e) *Other Works*

136. BURNET, J., ed., *Platonis Opera*, 5 vols., Clarendon Press, Oxford, 1900–7.

137. DIELS, H., and KRANZ, W., eds., *Fragmente der Vorsokratiker*, 6th edn., Weidmann, Berlin, 1951. (Cited as 'DK'.)

138. DIEHL, E., ed., *Anthologia Lyrica Graeca*, Teubner, Leipzig, 1949.

139. LIDDELL, H. G., and SCOTT, R., *Greek–English Lexicon*, 9th edn., revised by H. Stuart Jones, Clarendon Press, Oxford, 1940 (cited as 'LSJ').

140. ANTON, J. P., and KUSTAS, G. L. eds., *Essays in Ancient Greek Philosophy*, SUNY Press, Albany, 1971.

141. LEE, E. N., MOURELATOS, A. P. D., and RORTY, R. M., eds., *Exegesis and Argument*, Van Gorcum, Assen, 1973.

142. THOMSON, J. J., and DWORKIN, G., eds., *Ethics*, Harper & Row, New York, 1968.

2. Background to Plato

(a) *General Philosophical Background*

201. BURNET, J., *Early Greek Philosophy*, 4th edn., Black, London, 1930.

202. DODDS, E. R., *The Greeks and the Irrational*, U. of California Press, Berkeley and Los Angeles, 1951.

203. GUTHRIE, W. K. C., *A History of Greek Philosophy*, C.U.P., Cambridge, 1962 (vol. 1), 1965 (vol. 2), 1969 (vol. 3), 1975 (vol. 4).
204. JAEGER, W. W., *Paideia*, trans. G. Highet, 3 vols., Blackwell, Oxford, 1939–45.
205. LLOYD–JONES, P. H. J., *The Justice of Zeus*, U. of California Press, Berkeley and Los Angeles, 1971.
206. SNELL, B., *The Discovery of the Mind*, trans. T. G. Rosenmeyer, Blackwell, Oxford, 1953.

(b) *History of Ethics*

207. ADKINS, A. W. H., *Merit and Responsibility*, Clarendon Press, Oxford, 1960.
208. ——, 'Homeric Values and Homeric Society', *JHS* 91 (1971), 1–14.
209. CREED, J. L., 'Moral Values in the Age of Thucydides', *CQ* 23 (1973), 213–31.
210. DOVER, K. J., *Greek Popular Morality in the Time of Plato and Aristotle*, Blackwell, Oxford, 1974.
211. LONG, A. A., 'Morals and Values in Homer', *JHS* 90 (1970), 121–39.
212. NORTH, H., *Sophrosyne*. Cornell U.P., Ithaca, 1966.
213. ——, 'A Period of Opposition to *Sophrosyne* in Greek Thought', *TAPA* 78 (1947), 1–17.
214. VLASTOS, G., 'Ethics and Physics in Democritus', in *Studies in Presocratic Philosophy*, ed. R. E. Allen and D. J. Furley, vol. 2 (Routledge, London, 1975), 381–408, from *PR* 54 (1945), 578–92, and 55 (1946), 53–64.

(c) *The Sophists*

215. COLE. A. T., The Apology of Protagoras', *YCS* 21 (1966), 101–18.
216. GROTE, G., *A History of Greece*, (10 vols., 6th edn., Murray, London, 1888), ch. 67.
217. HARRISON, E. L., 'Was Gorgias a Sophist?', *Phoenix* 18 (1964), 183–92.
218. KERFERD, G. B., 'Protagoras' Doctrine of Justice and Virtue in the *Protagoras* of Plato', *JHS* 73 (1953), 42–5.
219. SIDGWICK, H., 'The Sophists', in *The Philosophy of Kant and Other Essays* (Macmillan, London, 1905), 323–71, from *Jl. of Philology* 4 (1872), 288–307, and 5 (1873), 66–80.

(d) *Other Works*

220. ANDREWES, A., DOVER, K. J., GOMME, A. W., *A Historical Commentary on Thucydides, V–VII*, Clarendon Press, Oxford, 1970.
221. DE STE CROIX, G. E. M., *The Origins of the Peloponnesian War*. Duckworth, London, 1972.
222. HARRISON, A. R. W., *The Law of Athens*, vol. 1, Clarendon Press, Oxford, 1968.

3. Socrates

(a) *General*

301. ALLEN, R. E., 'Plato's Earlier Theory of Forms', in (118), 319–34.

302. BURNET, J., 'The Socratic Doctrine of the Soul', in *Essays and Addresses* (Murray, London, 1929), 126–62. From *PBA* 7 (1915–16), 235–59.

303. BURNYEAT, M. F., 'Virtues in Action', in (118), 209–34.

304. COOPER, J. M., *Reason and Human Good in Aristotle*, Harvard U.P., Cambridge, Mass., 1975.

305. DEMAN, T., *Le Témoignage d'Aristote sur Socrate*, Les Belles Lettres, Paris, 1942.

306. GREENWOOD, L. H. G., *The Sixth Book of the Nicomachean Ethics*, C.U.P., Cambridge, 1909.

307. GRUBE, G. M. A., 'The *Cleitophon* of Plato', *CP* 26 (1931), 302–8.

308. GULLEY, N., *The Philosophy of Socrates*, Macmillan, London, 1968.

309. LUCE, J. V., 'The Date of the *Cratylus*', *AJP* 90 (1964), 136–54.

310. SPRAGUE, R. K., *Plato's Use of Fallacy*, Routledge, London, 1962.

311. VLASTOS, G., 'The Paradox of Socrates', in (118), 1–21.

312. ——, 'Socrates on Political Obedience and Disobedience', *Yale Review*, Summer 1974, 517–34.

313. ——, 'Socratic Knowledge and Platonic "Pessimism"', in (119), 204–17. From *PR* 66 (1957), 226–38.

314. ——, 'Socrates' Contribution to the Greek Concept of Justice' (unpublished).

315. WIGGINS, D. R. P., 'Deliberation and Practical Reason', *PAS* 76 (1975–6) 29–51.

316. WOOZLEY, A. D., 'Socrates on Disobeying the Law', in (118), 299–318.

(b) *The Elenchos*

317. BENNETT, J. F., *Locke, Berkeley, Hune*, Clarendon Press, Oxford, 1971.

318. BEVERSLUIS, J., 'Socratic Definition', *APQ* 11 (1974), 331–6.

319. FEYERABEND, P. K., 'How to be a Good Empiricist', in *Philosophy of Science*, ed. P. H. Nidditch (O.U.P., Oxford, 1968), 12–39, from *Philosophy of Science; the Delaware Seminar*, vol. 2, ed. B. Baumrin (Interscience, New York, 1963), 3–39.

320. GORDON, R. M., 'Socratic Definitions and Moral Neutrality', *JP* 61 (1964), 433–50.

321. GRICE, H. P., and STRAWSON, P. F., 'In Defence of a Dogma', PR 65 (1956), 141–58.

322. HARE, R. M., 'Philosophical Discoveries', in *Essays in Philosophical Method* (Macmillan, London, 1971), 19–37, from *M* 69 (1960), 145–62.

323. LOCKE, J., *An Essay Concerning Human Understanding.*

324. MCDOWELL, J. H., *Plato's Theaetetus* (translation and commentary), Clarendon Press, Oxford, 1973.

325. NAKHNIKIAN, G., 'Elenctic Definitions', in (118), 125–57.

326. PUTNAM, H., 'Meaning and Reference', *JP* 70 (1973), 699–711.

327. QUINE, W. V., *Word and Object*, M.I.T. Press, Cambridge, Mass., 1960.

328. ——, 'Natural Kinds', in *Ontological Relativity* (Columbia U.P., New York, 1969), 114–38.

329. ROBINSON, R., 'Plato's Consciousness of Fallacy', in *Essays in Greek Philosophy* (Clarendon Press, Oxford, 1969, 16–39, from *M* 51 (1942), 97–114.
330. RYLE, G., *The Concept of Mind*, Penguin, Harmondsworth, 1963 (originally Hutchinson, London, 1949).
331. SANTAS, G., 'The Socratic Fallacy', *JHP* 10 (1972), 127–41.
332. SCHEFFLER, I., *Science and Subjectivity*, Bobbs-Merrill, New York, 1967.
333. WITTGENSTEIN, L., *The Blue and Brown Books*, Blackwell, Oxford, 1958.

(c) *The Socratic paradox*

334. ALLEN, R. E., 'The Socratic Paradox', *JHI* 21 (1960), 256–65.
335. DAVIDSON, D., 'Mental Events', in *Experience and Theory*, eds. L. Foster and J. W. Swanson (U. Mass. Press, Amherst, 1970), 79–101.
336. DENNETT, D. C., 'Intentional Systems', *JP* 68 (1971), 87–106.
337. GIBBS, B. R., 'Virtue and Reason', *PASS* 48 (1974), 23–41.
338. NAKHNIKIAN, G., 'The First Socratic Paradox', *JHP* 11 (1973), 1–17.
339. PENNER, T. M. I., 'Socrates on Virtue and Motivation', in (141), 133–51.
340. SANTAS, G., 'The Socratic Paradox', *PR* 73 (1964), 147–64, reprinted in *Plato's Meno*, ed. A. Sesonske and N. Fleming (Wadsworth, Belmont, Calif., 1965), 49–64.

(d) *Particular dialogues*

341. ALLEN, R. E., *Plato's Euthyphro and the Earlier Theory of Forms*, Routledge, London, 1970.
342. BURNET, J., *Plato's Euthyphro, Apology and Crito* (text and commentary), Clarendon Press, Oxford, 1924.
343. COHEN, S. M., 'Socrates on the Definition of Piety', in (118), 158–76, from *JHP* 9 (1971), 1–13.
344. GEACH, P. T., 'Plato's *Euthyphro*; an Analysis and Commentary', in *Logic Matters* (Blackwell, Oxford, 1972), 31–44, from *Monist* 50 (1966), 369–82.
345. SANTAS, G., 'Socrates at Work on Virtue and Knowledge in Plato's *Charmides*', in (141), 105–32.
346. TUCKEY, T. G., *Plato's Charmides*, C.U.P., Cambridge, 1951.
347. O'BRIEN, M. J., 'The Unity of the *Laches*', *YCS* 18 (1963), 131–47.
348. SANTAS, G., 'Socrates at Work on Virtue and Knowledge in Plato's *Laches*', in (118), 177–208, from *RM* 22 (1969), 433–60.
349. LEVIN, D. N., 'Some Observations Concerning Plato's *Lysis*', in (140), 236–58.

4. The *Protagoras*

(a) *General*

401. VLASTOS, G., 'Introduction', in *Plato's Protagoras*, trans. M. Ostwald, ed. Vlastos (Bobbs-Merrill, New York, 1956), vii–lvi.

(b) *The Unity of the Virtues*

402. GALLOP, D., 'Justice and Holiness in *Protagoras* 330–1', *Phr.* 6 (1961), 86–93.

403. O'BRIEN, M. J., 'The "Fallacy" in *Protagoras* 349d–350c', *TAPA* 92 (1962), 408–17.

404. PENNER, T. M. I., 'The Unity of Virtue', *PR* 82 (1973), 35–68.

405. SAVAN, D., 'Socrates' Logic and the Unity of Wisdom and Temperance', in *Analytical Philosophy; Second Series*, ed. R. J. Butler (Blackwell, Oxford, 1965), 20–6.

406. ——, 'Self-Predication in *Protagoras* 330–1', *Phr.* 9 (1964), 130–5.

407. VLASTOS, G., 'The Unity of the Virtues in the *Protagoras*', in (119), 221–65. From *RM* 25 (1972), 415–58.

(c) *Hedonism*

408. HACKFORTH, R., 'The Hedonism in Plato's *Protagoras*', *CQ* 22 (1928), 38–42.

409. SULLIVAN, J. P., 'Hedonism in Plato's *Protagoras*', *Phr.* 6 (1961), 9–28.

(d) *Incontinence*

410. GALLOP, D., 'The Socratic Paradox in the *Protagoras*', *Phr.* 9 (1964), 117–29.

411. SANTAS, G., 'Plato's *Protagoras* and Explanations of Weakness', in (118), 177–208. From *PR* 75 (1966), 3–33.

412. VLASTOS, G., 'Socrates on Acrasia', *Phoenix* 23 (1969), 71–88.

5. The *Gorgias*

501. DODDS, E. R., *Plato's Gorgias* (text and commentary), Clarendon Press, Oxford, 1959.

502. RUDBERG, G., '*Protagoras, Gorgias, Menon*; Eine Platonische Übergangszeit', *Symbolae Osloenses* 30 (1953), 30–41.

503. VLASTOS, G., 'Was Polus Refuted?', *AJP* 88 (1967), 454–60.

6. The Middle Dialogues

(a) *The* Meno

601. BLUCK, R. S., *Plato's Meno* (text and commentary), C.U.P., Cambridge, 1961.

602. BUCHMANN, K., 'Die Stellung des *Menon* in der platonischen Philosophie', *Philol.* Supp. 29.3 (1936).

603. CORNFORD, F. M., *Principium Sapientiae*, C.U.P., Cambridge, 1952.

604. ——, *Plato's Theory of Knowledge*, Routledge, London, 1935.

605. GULLEY, N., 'Ethical Analysis in Plato's Earlier Dialogues', *CQ* N.S. 2 (1952), 74–82.

606. MORAVCSIK, J. M. E., 'Learning as Recollection', in (117) I, 53–69.

607. PHILLIPS, B., 'The Significance of Meno's Paradox', in *Plato's Meno* (see (340)), 77–83. From *Classical Weekly* 42 (1948–9), 87–91.

608. THOMPSON, E. S., *Plato's Meno* (text and commentary), Macmillan, London, 1901.

609. VLASTOS, G., '*Anamnesis* in the *Meno*', *Dialogue* 4 (1965), 143–67.

610. WHITE, N. P., 'Inquiry', *RM* 28 (1974–5), 289–310.

(b) *The Theory of Forms*

611. ARCHER-HIND, R. D., *Plato's Phaedo* (text and commentary), Macmillan, London, 1883.

612. BLUCK, R. S., '*Logos* and Forms in Plato', in (115), 33–41. From *M* 65 (1956), 523–9.

613. ——, *Plato's Phaedo* (translation and commentary), Routledge, London, 1955.

614. BRENTLINGER, J. A., 'Incomplete Predicates and the Two-World Theory of the *Phaedo*', *Phr.* 17 (1972), 61–79.

615. ——, 'Particulars in Plato's Middle Dialogues', *AGP* 54 (1972), 116–52.

616. BURNET, J., *Plato's Phaedo* (text and commentary), Clarendon Press, Oxford, 1911.

617. CHERNISS, H. F., 'The Philosophical Economy of the Theory of Ideas', in (115), 1–12, from *AJP* 57 (1936), 445–56.

618. CROSS, R. C., '*Logos* and Forms in Plato', in (115), 13–31. From *M* 63 (1954), 433–50.

619. GEACH, P. T., 'The Third Man Again', in (115), 265–77, from *PR* 65 (1956), 72–82.

620. GOSLING, J. C. B., '*Republic* V; *Ta Polla Kala* etc.', *Phr.* 5 (1960), 116–28.

621. HACKFORTH, R., *Plato's Phaedo* (translation and commentary), C.U.P., Cambridge, 1955.

622. KIRWAN, C. A., 'Plato and Relativity', *Phr.* 19 (1974), 112–29.

623. MALCOLM, J., 'On the Place of the *Hippias Major* in the Development of Plato's Thought', *AGP* 50 (1968), 189–95.

624. MILLS, K. W., *Phaedo* 74bc', *Phr.* 2 (1957), 128–47, and 3 (1958), 40–58.

625. NEHAMAS, A., 'Predication and Forms of Opposites in the *Phaedo*', *RM* 26 (1972–3), 461–94.

626. OWEN, G. E. L., 'Dialectic and Eristic in the Treatment of the Forms' in *Aristotle on Dialectic*, ed. Owen (Clarendon Press, Oxford, 1970), 103–25.

627. ——, 'Notes on Ryle's Plato', in *Ryle*, ed. G. W. Pitcher and O. P. Wood (Doubleday, New York, 1970), 341–72.

628. ——, 'A Proof in the *Peri Ideōn*', in (115), 293–312. From *JHS* 77 (1957), 103–11.

629. STRANG, C., 'Plato and the Third Man', in (117) I. 184–200. From *PASS* 37 (1963), 147–64.

630. VLASTOS, G., 'Degrees of Reality in Plato', in (119), 58–75. From (116), 1–19.

631. ——, 'A Metaphysical Paradox', in (119), 43–57, from *Proc. Amer. Philos. Assoc.*, 39 (1966), 5–19.

632. ——, 'Reasons and Causes in the *Phaedo*', in (119), 76–110, from *PR* 78 (1969), 291–325.

633. ——, 'The Third Man Argument in the *Parmenides*', in (115), 231–63, from *PR* 63 (1954), 319–49.

634. WEERTS, E., 'Platon und der Heraklitismus', *Philol.* Supp. 23 (1931).

(c) *Ethics*

635. ANSCOMBE, G. E. M., 'On Brute Facts', in (142), 71–5, from *Analysis* 18 (1958), 69–72.
636. GOOCH, P. W., 'The Relation between Wisdom and Virtue in *Phaedo* 69a–c3', *JHP* 12 (1974), 153–9.
637. KOVESI, J., *Moral Notions*, Routledge, London, 1967.
638. LUCE, J. V., 'A Discussion of *Phaedo* 69a6–c2', *CQ* 38 (1944), 60–74.
639. MOORE, G. E., *Principia Ethica*, C.U.P., Cambridge, 1903.
640. VERDENIUS, W. J., 'Notes on Plato's *Phaedo*', *Mnemosyne* IV. 11 (1958), 193–243.

(d) *Theory of Love*

641. CORNFORD, F. M., 'The Doctrine of Eros in Plato's *Symposium*', in (117) II. 119–31, from *The Unwritten Philosophy*, ed. W. K. C. Guthrie (C.U.P., Cambridge, 1950), 68–80.
642. GOULD, T., *Platonic Love*, Routledge, London, 1963.
643. HACKFORTH, R., *Plato's Phaedrus* (translation and commentary). C.U.P., Cambridge, 1952.
644. KRAUT, R., 'Egoism, Love and Political Office in Plato', *PR* 82 (1973), 330–44.
645. MARKUS, R. A., 'The Dialectic of Eros in the *Symposium*', in (117) II. 132–43, from *Downside Review* 73 (1955), 219–30.
646. Moravcsik, J. M. E., 'Reason and Eros in the Ascent-Passage of the *Symposium*', in (140), 285–302.
647. ROBIN, L., *Platon*; *Le Banquet* (text and translation), Les Belles Lettres, Paris, 1951.
648. VLASTOS, G., 'The Individual as an Object of Love in Plato', in (119), 3–42.

7. The *Republic*

(a) *General*

401. ADAM, J., *Plato's Republic* (text and commentary), 2 vols., C.U.P., Cambridge, 1902.
702. CROSS, R. C., and WOOZLEY, A. D., *Plato's Republic,* Macmillan, London, 1964.
703. JOSEPH, H. W. B., *Essays in Ancient and Modern Philosophy*, Clarendon Press, Oxford, 1935.
704. MURPHY, N. R., *The Interpretation of Plato's Republic*, Clarendon Press, Oxford, 1951.
705. NETTLESHIP, R. L., *Lectures on the Republic of Plato*, Macmillan, London, 1901.
706. SHOREY, P., *Plato's Republic* (Loeb), 2 vols., Heinemann, London, 1935.

(b) *Book I*

707. ALLAN, D. J., *Republic I* (text and commentary), Methuen, London, 1940.

708. HOURANI, G. F., 'Thrasymachus' Definition of Justice in Plato's *Republic*', *Phr.* 7 (1962), 110–20.
709. KERFERD, G. B., 'Thrasymachus and Justice; a Reply', *Phr.* 9 (1964), 12–16.
710. ——, 'The Doctrine of Thrasymachus in Plato's *Republic*', *Durham Univ. Jl.* 9 (1947), 19–27.
711. NICHOLSON, P. P., 'Unravelling Thrasymachus' Arguments in the *Republic*', *Phr.* 19 (1974), 210–32.
712. NOZICK, R., *Anarchy, State and Utopia*. Basic Books, New York, 1974.

(c) *Glaucon and Adeimantus*

713. FOSTER, M. B., 'A Mistake of Plato's in the *Republic*', *M* 46 (1937), 386–93.
714. GROTE, J., and SIDGWICK, H., 'Plato's Utilitarianism', *CR* 3 (1889), 97–102.
715. KIRWAN, C. A., 'Glaucon's Challenge', *Phr.* 10 (1965), 162–73.
716. MABBOTT, J. D., 'Is Plato's *Republic* Utilitarian?', in (117) II. 57–65. From *M* 46 (1937), 468–74.
717. SACHS, D., 'A Fallacy in Plato's *Republic*', in (117) II. 35–51. From *PR* 72 (1963), 141–58.

(d) *The Divided Soul and the Virtues*

718. BAMBROUGH, J. R., 'Plato's Political Analogies', in (117) II. 187–205, from *Philosophy, Politics and Society, First Series*, ed. P. Laslett (Blackwell, Oxford, 1956), 98–115.
719. CORNFORD, F. M., 'Psychology and Social Structure in the *Republic*', *CQ* 6 (1912), 246–65.
720. FRANKFURT, H. G., 'The Freedom of the Will and the Concept of a Person', *JP* 68 (1971), 5–20.
721. HACKFORTH, R., 'The Modification of Plan in the *Republic*', *CQ* 7 (1913), 265–72.
722. HAMPSHIRE, S. N., *The Freedom of the Individual*, Chatto & Windus, London, 1965.
723. HARDIE, W. F. R., *A Study in Plato*, Clarendon Press, Oxford, 1936.
724. HOURANI, G. F., 'The Education of the Third Class in Plato's *Republic*', *CQ* 43 (1949), 58–60.
725. MABBOTT, J. D., 'Reason and Desire', *Phil.* 28 (1953), 113–23.
726. MOREAU, J., 'Platon et la connaissance de l'âme', *Revue des études anciennes* 55 (1953), 249–57.
727. MULGAN, R. G., 'Individual and Collective Virtues in the *Republic*', *Phr.* 13 (1968), 84–5.
728. PENNER, T. M. I., 'Thought and Desire in Plato', in (117) II. 96–118.
729. ROBINSON, R., 'Plato's Separation of Reason and Desire', *Phr.* 16 (1971), 38–48.
730. SKEMP, J. B., 'Comment on Communal and Individual Justice in the *Republic*', *Phr.* 5 (1960), 35–8.
731. STOCKS, J. L., 'The Divided Soul in the *Republic*', in *The Limits of Purpose* (Benn, London, 1932), from *M* 24 (1915), 307–21.

732. VLASTOS, G., 'Justice and Happiness in the *Republic*', in (119), 111–46, from (117) II. 66–95.
733. WILLIAMS, B. A. O., 'The Analogy of City and Soul in Plato's *Republic*', in (141), 196–206.

(e) *Justice*

734. ARONSON, S. H., 'The Happy Philosopher; a Counter-Example to Plato's Proof', *JHP* 10 (1973), 383–98.
735. DEMOS, R., 'A Fallacy in Plato's *Republic*', in (117) II. 52–6, from *PR* 73 (1964), 395–8.
736. FOSTER, M. B., 'Some Implications of a Passage in Plato's *Republic*', *Phil.* 11 (1936), 301–8.
737. KRAUT, R.', 'Reason and Justice in Plato's *Republic*', in (141), 207–24.
738. MORRIS, C. R., 'Plato's Theory of the Good Man's Motives', *PAS* 34 (1933–4), 129–42.
739. VLASTOS, G., 'Does Slavery Exist in Plato's *Republic*?', in (119), 140–6, from *CP* 63 (1968), 291–5.
740. WATERLOW, S., 'The Good of Others in Plato's *Republic*', *PAS* 72 (1972–3), 19–36.
741. WEINGARTNER, R. H., 'Vulgar Justice and Platonic Justice', *Phil. and Phenomenol. Research* 25 (1964), 248–52.

(f) *Knowledge*

742. ALLEN, R. E., 'The Argument from Opposites in *Republic* V', in (140), 165–75, from *RM* 15 (1961), 325–35.
743. FINE, G. J., 'Plato's Two World's, *AGP* (forthcoming).
744. FURTH, M., 'Elements of Eleatic Ontology', *JHP* 6 (1968), 111–32.
745. GOSLING, J. C. B., '*Doxa* and *Dunamis* in Plato's *Republic*', *Phr.* 13 (1968), 19–30.
746. OWEN, G. E. L., 'Plato and Not-Being', in (117) I. 223–67.

(g) *The Sun, Line, and Cave*

747. CORNFORD, F. M., 'Mathematics and Dialectic in the *Republic*', in (115), 61–95, from *M.* 41 (1932), 37–52, 173–90.
748. GALLOP, D., 'Dreaming and Waking in Plato', in (140), 187–201.
749. ——, 'Image and Reality in Plato's *Republic*', *AGP* 47 (1965), 113–31.
750. HARE, R. M., 'Plato and the Mathematicians', in (116), 21–38.
751. JOSEPH, H. W. B., *Knowledge and the Good in Plato's Republic*. Clarendon Press, Oxford, 1948.
752. MALCOLM, J., 'The Line and the Cave', *Phr.* 7 (1962), 38–47.
753. SHOREY, P., 'The Idea of the Good in Plato's *Republic*', *University of Chicago Studies in Classical Philology* 1 (1895), 188–239.
754. TAYLOR, C. C. W., 'Plato and the Mathematicians; an Examination of Professor Hare's Views', *PQ* 17 (1967), 193–203.

8. Other Works on Ethics

801. ANSCOMBE, G. E. M., *Intention,* Blackwell, Oxford, 1957.
802. ——, 'Modern Moral Philosophy', in (142), 186–210, from *Phil.* 33 (1958), 1–19.

803. AUSTIN, J. L., 'Agathon and Eudaimonia in the Ethics of Aristotle', in Aristotle, ed. J. M. E. Moravcsik (Doubleday, New York, 1968), 261–96, also in Philosophical Papers, ed. J. O. Urmson and G. J. Warnock, 2nd edn., Clarendon Press, Oxford, 1970.

804. BRADLEY, F. H., Ethical Studies, 2nd edn., Clarendon Press, Oxford, 1927.

805. BRANDT, R. B., 'Rationality, Egoism and Morality', JP 69 (1972), 681–97.

806. BROAD, C. D., 'Egoism as a Theory of Human Motives', in Ethics and the History of Philosophy (Routledge, London, 1952), 218–31.

807. BUTLER, J., Fifteen Sermons Preached at the Rolls Chapel (cited by Sermon and paragraph numbers).

808. FALK, W. D., 'Morality, Self and Others', in (142), 349–90, from Morality and the Language of Conduct, ed. H. N. Castaneda and G. Nakhnikian (Wayne State U.P., Detroit, 1963), 25–67.

809. FEINBERG, J., 'Psychological Egoism', in Reason and Responsibility, ed. Feinberg (Dickenson, Belmont, Calif., 3rd edn., 1975), 501–12.

810. ——, 'The Nature and Value of Rights', Journal of Value Inquiry 4 (1970), 243–57.

811. FOOT, P. R., 'Morality as a System of Hypothetical Imperatives', PR 81 (1972), 305–16.

812. ——, 'Moral Beliefs', in (142), 239–60, from PAS 59 (1958–9), 83–104.

813. FRANKENA, W. K., 'The Concept of Morality', in The Definition of Morality, ed. G. Wallace and A. D. M. Walker (Methuen, London, 1970), 146–73, from Univ. of Colorado Studies, Series in Philosophy 3 (1967), 1–22.

814. ——, Ethics, Prentice-Hall, Englewood Cliffs, N J., 1968.

815. GAUTHIER, D. P., 'Morality and Advantage', in Morality and Rational Self-Interest, ed. Gauthier (Prentice-Hall, Englewood Cliffs, N.J. (1970), 166–80, from PR 76 (1967), 460–75.

816. GRICE, G. R., The Grounds of Moral Judgment, C.U.P., Cambridge, 1967.

817. HARDIE, W. F. R., Aristotle's Ethical Theory, Clarendon Press, Oxford, 1968.

818. HORSBURGH, H. J. N., 'Prudence', PASS 36 (1962), 65–76.

819. HOSPERS, J., Human Conduct, Harcourt Brace, New York, 1961.

820. HUME, D., Enquiry Concerning the Principles of Morals, ed. L. A. Selby-Bigge, Clarendon Press, Oxford, 1902.

821. ——, A Treatise of Human Nature, ed. L. A. Selby-Bigge, Clarendon Press, Oxford, 1888.

822. JOSEPH, H. W. B., Some Problems in Ethics, Clarendon Press, Oxford, 1931.

823. KANT, I., Critique of Practical Reason (cited by pages of the Akademie edition).

824. ——, Foundations of the Metaphysics of Morals (cited by Akademie pages).

825. MABBOTT, J. D., 'Prudence', PASS 36 (1962), 51–64.

826. MILL, J. S., Utilitarianism (cited by chapter and paragraph).

827. NAGEL, T., *The Possibility of Altruism*, Clarendon Press, Oxford, 1970.

828. NIELSEN, K., 'Why Should I be Moral?', in *Readings in Ethical Theory*, ed. W. S. Sellars and J. Hospers (2nd edn., Appleton Century Crofts, New York, 1970), 747–68, from *Methodos* 15 (1963), 275–306.

829. PRICHARD, H. A., *Moral Obligation* (including *Duty and Interest*), Clarendon Press, Oxford, 1968.

830. RAWLS, J., *A Theory of Justice*, Harvard U.P., Cambridge, Mass., 1971.

831. ROSS, W. D., *The Right and the Good*, Clarendon Press, Oxford, 1930.

832. SIDGWICK, H., *The Methods of Ethics*, 7th edn., Macmillan, London, 1907.

833. VLASTOS, G., 'Justice and Equality', in *Social Justice*, ed. R. B. Brandt (Prentice-Hall, Englewood Cliffs, N.J., 1962), 31–72.

834. VON WRIGHT, G. H., *The Varieties of Goodness*, Routledge, London, 1963.

835. WARNOCK, G. J., *The Object of Morality*, Methuen, London, 1971.

ADDENDA TO BIBLIOGRAPHY

Some relevant works published or forthcoming too late to be used in this book:

BARROW, R. *Plato, Utilitarianism, and Education*, Routledge, London, 1975.

COOPER, J. M., 'The psychology of justice in the *Republic*', *APQ* April 1977.

DEVEREUX, D. T., 'Courage and wisdom in the *Laches*', *JHP*, forthcoming.

GALLOP, D., *Plato's Phaedo*, Oxford, Clarendon Press, 1975.

IRWIN, T. H., 'Euripides and Socrates', forthcoming in *The Tragic Moment*, ed. R. L. Gordon, C.U.P., Cambridge, 1977.

—— 'Plato's Heracleiteanism', *PQ* January 1977.

KAHN, C. H., 'Plato on the unity of virtues', in *Patterns in Plato's Thought*, ed. W. H. Werkmeister, Van Gorcum, Assen, 1976.

KOSMAN, L. A., 'Platonic Love', in *Patterns in Plato's Thought*.

TAYLOR, C. C. W., *Plato's Protagoras*, Clarendon Press, Oxford, 1976.

VLASTOS, G., 'What did Socrates understand by his "What is X?" question?', in *Platonic Studies*, 2nd edn., Princeton U.P., forthcoming.

WHITE, N. P., *Plato on Knowledge and Reality*, Hackett, Indianapolis, 1976.

WILSON, J. R. S., 'The argument of *Republic* IV', *PQ* 26 (1976) 111–23.

WOODRUFF, P., 'Socrates on the parts of virtue', in *Canadian Journal of Philosophy supp. vol. 2* (1976).

GENERAL INDEX

Adam, J., 287, 318, 329
Adkins, A. W. H., 287, 289, 290, 311, 312, 328
Admirable (*kalon*; *see also* Beautiful), 290; Aristotle on, 261; disputed property, 72; and good, 33, 59, 117, 165 f., 294, 295, 314; and justice, 28, 58; love of, 202
Allen, R. E., 314, 334
Altruism, basis, 241; Plato's justification, 11 f., 277, 337, 345; objections to Plato's view, 269, 278; and happiness, 255, 258, 267–72; and justice, 272–6; and philosopher, 242, 337 f.; and rational choice, 267; and value of persons, 271
Anger, and emotional part, 194
Anscombe, G. E. M., 287, 321
Archer-Hind, R. D., 322
Aristotle, on activity and production, 76; on the admirable, 261; on common beliefs, 61; on conflict of virtues, 56; on continence and temperance, 200; on courage, 19, 87, 197 f.; doctrine of the mean, 55, 264, 332; egoism, 255; on emotion, 194; on final good, 52 f., 86, 264, 295 f.; on friendship and love, 258, 268–70, 342; on justice, 23, 209; on self-sacrifice, 240, 277; on Socrates and Plato, 40, 42, 145, 291; on temperance, 87; on theory of Forms, 148; on virtues, 87, 207; on virtue and craft, 77, 92
Aronson, S. H., 332, 338
Autonomy, 97, 271 f., 275, 289

Bambrough, J. R., 334
Beautiful, beauty (*kalon*; *see also* Admirable), higher and lower objects, 169; and love, 57, 164, 239; and madness, 240; and pleasure, 165; and virtuous man's motives, 239
Belief, *see* Knowledge; in Socrates' method, 40
Berversluis, J., 294

Bluck, R. S., 287, 301, 314–19, 321 f.
Bradley, F. H., 341
Brandt, R. B., 341
Brentlinger, J. A., 318, 321
Broad, C. D., 341
Burnet, J., 289, 303, 322
Burnyeat, M. F., 303, 345
Butler, J., 345

Callicles, 19, 21, 29, 31, 35, 118–24, 230; and Thrasymachus, 30, 180, 211, 289
Cave, *see* Sun; and ascent of desire, 234
Change, *see* Flux
Cherniss, H. F., 318, 321
Circularity in argument, 9, 137, 175, 189, 247, 252
Coherence, and justification, 159, 223, 225, 254
Confidence (*pistis*), 221, 335
Conflicts, moral, treatment by Plato, 275
Cornford, F. M., 287, 290, 317, 328, 336
Counter-examples, 138, 152, 156, 219, 225, 293
Courage, bravery (*andreia*), 19, 288; and action, 43–6; admirable and good, 47; and agent's good, 56, 124; Callicles on, 119; and endurance, 72, 87, 128, 198, 206, 302, 312; and ignorance, 47; and justice, 19; ordinary conception, 19, 55, 61; and pleasure, 112, 121 f.; and p-justice, 241; range of, 43, 198; in state and soul, 329; and tyrannical man, 229; and wisdom, 72, 103, 203, 295, 307
Craft (*technē*), advantages of, 73–5; and elenchos, 94–7; and explanations, 71; and knowledge, 288; misuse, 77; and objectivity, 75; and product, 84; and rationality, 73; and subject-matter, 75; superordinate, 76, 93; and teaching, 74
Craft-analogy (CA), 71–3, 93–5, 116, 127–9, 137, 142, 164, 175 f.; and care of soul, 164; and disputes, 7, 76, 96,

INDEX LOCORUM

(Titles of spurious or doubtful works are bracketed)

II. Other Authors